AF691335

BRITAIN AND COLONIAL MARITIME WAR IN THE EARLY EIGHTEENTH CENTURY

Britain and Colonial Maritime War in the Early Eighteenth Century

SILVER, SEAPOWER AND THE ATLANTIC

Shinsuke Satsuma

THE BOYDELL PRESS

© Shinsuke Satsuma 2013

All rights reserved. Except as permitted under current legislation
no part of this work may be photocopied, stored in a retrieval system,
published, performed in public, adapted, broadcast,
transmitted, recorded or reproduced in any form or by any means,
without the prior permission of the copyright owner

The right of Shinsuke Satsuma to be identified as
the author of this work has been asserted in accordance with
sections 77 and 78 of the Copyright, Designs and Patents Act 1988

First published 2013

The Boydell Press, Woodbridge

ISBN 978 1 84383 862 3

The Boydell Press is an imprint of Boydell & Brewer Ltd
PO Box 9, Woodbridge, Suffolk IP12 3DF, UK

and of Boydell & Brewer Inc.
668 Mt Hope Avenue, Rochester, NY 14620-2731, USA

website: www.boydellandbrewer.com

The publisher has no responsibility for the continued existence or accuracy of URLs for external or third-party internet websites referred to in this book, and does not guarantee that any content on such websites is, or will remain, accurate or appropriate.

A CIP catalogue record for this book is available
from the British Library

Papers used by Boydell & Brewer Ltd are natural, recyclable products
made from wood grown in sustainable forests

MIX
Paper from responsible sources
FSC® C013604

Typeset in Adobe Caslon by Avocet Typeset, Somerton, Somerset
Printed and bound in Great Britain by
CPI Group (UK) Ltd, Croydon, CR0 4YY

CONTENTS

For My Parents

ILLUSTRATIONS

Acknowledgements

During the course of my research, I have been helped and encouraged by a number of individuals and institutions. Without their assistance, I could not have accomplished this long and arduous voyage. First and foremost, I would like to thank Professor N.A.M. Rodger. In the vast ocean of naval history, he directed me in a right direction and patiently guided me throughout my research. It was an immense honour for me to have worked with him. I am also deeply indebted to Professor Shin Matsuzono, who first ushered me into the world of British political history. His generous assistance and in-depth knowledge of eighteenth-century British politics have hugely contributed in improving the quality of my work. I also wish to express my gratitude to Professor Bill Speck and Professor Harry T. Dickinson, both of whom have kindly helped me since I first met them in Japan. Their warm encouragement has been strong moral support in carrying on my research.

Many other scholars in Britain and Japan also gave me valuable comments and assistance. In particular, I would like to thank Professor Jeremy Black, Professor Alan Downie, Dr Michael Duffy, Dr Philip Woodfine, Professor Yasushi Aoki, Professor Shusaku Kanazawa, Professor Mariko Mizui and Professor Yuko Takemoto. I am also grateful to Professor Steven Pincus for kindly letting me see two manuscripts of his unpublished articles. Thanks also to the staff of the libraries and archives that I have visited, particularly those at the British Library and The National Archives. At the production stage, I have to thank Peter Sowden, my editor at Boydell & Brewer. The faults and errors that remain are entirely my own responsibility.

My research was supported by a scholarship from the University of Exeter and a travel grant from the Royal Historical Society. A large portion of Chapter 5 and Chapter 6 originally appeared in *Parliamentary History* and *Historical Research*, respectively. I am grateful to the Trustees of the Parliamentary History Yearbook Trust and the Institute of Historical Research for their permission to reproduce the materials. In addition, I would like to thank the Old Royal Naval College for generously allowing me to use the image of part of the Painted Hall for this book.

Many friends also helped me throughout my research. In particular, I would like to thank Edmund Clipson, Trever Hagen and Anette Dujisin-Muharay, Joshua Newton, Manu Sehgal and Samiksha Sehrawat, Satoshi Tsujimoto, Hideki Nakamaru and Hiraku Yabuki. Finally, I would like to take this opportunity to express my gratitude to my parents, Junkichi and Akiko Satsuma. Without their support, I would have never been able to pursue my career as a historian so far. This book is dedicated to them.

ACKNOWLEDGEMENTS

ABBREVIATIONS

Add MS	Additional Manuscript
ADM	Records of the Admiralty
AHR	*American Historical Review*
BIHR	*Bulletin of the Institute of Historical Research*
BL	British Library
Bolingbroke Correspondence	Viscount Bolingbroke, *Henry St. John, Letters and Correspondence, Public and Private, of the Right Honourable Henry St. John, Lord Visc. Bolingbroke* ... (4 vols, London, 1798)
Chandler	Richard Chandler, *The History and Proceedings of the House of Commons from the Restoration to the Present time* (14 vols, London, 1742–44)
Ch (H) MSS	Cholmondeley (Houghton) Manuscripts
C.J.	*Journals of the House of Commons*
CO	Records of the 'Colonial Office' [Colonial State Papers and records of the Old Board of Trade]
Cobbett	*Cobbett's Parliamentary History of England: From the Norman Conquest, in 1066, to the Year, 1803* (36 vols, London, 1810)
EcHR	*Economic History Review*
EHR	*English Historical Review*
FH MSS	Finch Hatton Manuscripts
HAHR	*Hispanic American Historical Review*
HJ	*Historical Journal*
HLQ	*Huntington Library Quarterly*
H.M.C. *Carlisle*	*Manuscripts of the Earl of Carlisle, Preserved at Castle Howard* (London, 1897)
H.M.C. *Egmont Diary*	*Manuscripts of the Earl of Egmont: Diary of the First Earl of Egmont (Viscount Percival)* (3 vols, London, 1923)
H.M.C. *Portland*	*Report on the Manuscripts of the Duke of Portland, preserved at Welbeck Abbey* (8 vols, London, 1891–1931)
H.M.C. *Stuart*	*Calendar of the Stuart Papers belonging to His Majesty the King, Preserved at Windsor Castle* (7 vols, London, 1902–23)
House of Commons, 1690–1715	David Hayton, Eveline Cruickshanks and Stuart Handley, *The House of Commons, 1690–1715 (History of Parliament)* (5 vols, London, 2002)

JEBH	*Journal of Economic and Business History*
JICH	*Journal of Imperial and Commonwealth History*
JMH	*Journal of Modern History*
Knatchbull Diary	Aubrey Newman, ed., *The Parliamentary Diary of Sir Edward Knatchbull, 1722–30* (London, 1963)
Letters of William III and Louis XIV	Grimblot, Paul, ed., *Letters of William III and Louis XIV and Their Ministers (1697–1700)* (2 vols, London, 1848)
L.J.	*Journals of the House of Lords*
Marlborough–Godolphin Correspondence	Henry L. Snyder, ed., *The Marlborough–Godolphin Correspondence* (3 vols, Oxford, 1975)
Marlborough–Heinsius Correspondence	B. Van 'T Hoff, ed., *The Correspondence 1701–1711 of John Churchill, First Duke of Marlborough and Anthonie Heinsius, Grand Pensionary of Holland* (The Hague, 1951)
MM	*Mariner's Mirror*
MSS Eng. Hist.	Manuscripts English History
NMM	National Maritime Museum
ODNB	*Oxford Dictionary of National Biography*
PO	Portland Papers
Review	Daniel Defoe, *Defoe's Review: Reproduced from the Original Editions, with an Introduction and Bibliographical Notes by Arthur Wellesley Secord* (New York, 1938)
SP	State Papers
Statutes at Large	*The Statutes at Large, of England and of Great Britain: From Magna Carta to the Union of the Kingdoms of Great Britain and Ireland*, ed. Thomas E. Tomlins (10 vols, London, 1811)
T	Treasury Papers
TNA	The National Archives
TRHS	*Transactions of Royal Historical Society*
Vernon–Wager MSS	Vernon–Wager Manuscripts [microfilm]
WMQ	*William and Mary Quarterly*

A Note on Dates

In this book, all dates are given in the Old style of the Julian calendar except where the New Style is indicated or both dates are used (e.g. 6/17 August). The new year is taken to have begun on 1 January, not 25 March.

INTRODUCTION

Purpose

In early modern England (after the Union with Scotland in 1707, Britain), there was an argument supporting war at sea, especially in Spanish America, as a suitable means of warfare. As N.A.M. Rodger has pointed out, this argument's origin can be traced back to a joint struggle at sea involving English and Huguenot seamen against Catholic powers in the 1560s.[1] This idea recurrently appeared in the seventeenth and eighteenth centuries, when conflicts with Spain occurred, and continued to exist until the early nineteenth century.

Several historians have dealt with the argument supporting maritime war. Richard Pares has referred to a 'maritime and American policy' as one of the major policies in the debates on British war aim and war strategy in the mid eighteenth century.[2] Also, Philip Woodfine has analysed a popular idea about the omnipotence of the British navy, especially against allegedly impotent Spain, which was strengthened by the memories of the Elizabethan and Cromwellian maritime wars. The idea of the British navy's omnipotence was current in the late 1730s and early 1740s among the public and many politicians.[3] More recently, Rodger has examined the English 'national myth' of sea power in the seventeenth and eighteenth centuries. According to him, this was composed of three tenets. First, English sea power was essentially Protestant and exercised for the defence of religious freedom. Second, exercising English sea power also could defend the liberties of Englishmen from foreign and domestic threats. Third, the exercise of this power could bring profit to the English nation, especially seamen and merchants, in the form of plunder and, later, trade.[4] Thus, several historians have pointed out the existence of an idea supporting maritime war, not least, colonial maritime war, in early modern Britain, especially in England.[5]

[1] N.A.M. Rodger, 'Queen Elizabeth and the Myth of Sea-Power in English History', *TRHS* 14 (2004), 153–4.

[2] Richard Pares, 'American versus Continental Warfare, 1739–63', *EHR* 51, no. 203 (1936), 430. It should be noted that Pares has divided the upholders of this 'maritime and American policy' into those who supported conquest in North America and those for conquests in the West Indies.

[3] Philip Woodfine, 'Ideas of Naval Power and the Conflict with Spain, 1737–1742', *The British Navy and the Use of Naval Power in the Eighteenth Century*, ed. Jeremy Black and Philip Woodfine (Leicester, 1988), pp. 71–2.

[4] Rodger, 'Queen Elizabeth and the Myth of Sea-Power', 157–8.

[5] Exertion of maritime force against the Spanish American colonies, combined with economic motives, was also seen among some other countries that arrived in the 'New

In British political and naval history, this idea is often loosely called 'blue water policy' (or 'blue water strategy'), which Daniel Baugh used in an article in 1988.[6] However, there seems to be some confusion in the usage of this term. What Baugh means by 'blue water policy' appears to be a policy that gradually developed from the mid seventeenth century and eventually became part of Britain's national defence strategy, based on the nation's navy, trade and financial system and supported by her maritime empire. Baugh explains that the basic rationale of this 'blue water policy' was 'defence of the realm against foreign invasion', and its central point was 'naval command of the English Channel and North Sea'. This policy rested upon a particular system to sustain the cost of the naval force, in which trade supplied funds and a source of government revenue and where the shipping industry provided valuables, such as shipbuilding skills and seamen. Also, this policy entailed a concept of cost-effectiveness that aimed to minimise internal taxes. According to Baugh, the 'blue water policy' was 'cost effective, practical, and mundane', and 'it installed a calculating commercialism at the heart of the most important task of government'. Thus, Baugh claims, in line with these principles, Britain's grand strategy was 'essentially defensive in Europe (and European waters) and aggressive overseas'.[7]

The 'blue water policy' described by Baugh seems to be somewhat different from what is referred to by political historians of the early eighteenth century or

World' after the Iberian powers and tried to obtain a slice of its wealth. For example, interception of the Spanish silver fleet, which was often proposed in the English pro-maritime war argument as an effective means of depriving the enemy of its sinews of war, was also attempted by the Netherlands. In 1628, a fleet of the Dutch West India Company under Piet Heyn succeeded in this. Arthur P. Newton, *The European Nations in the West Indies, 1493–1688* (London, 1933), pp. 152–4. On the other hand, interception of the silver fleet also was proposed or actually attempted by the French during the Franco-Dutch War (1672–78) and the Nine Years War (1689–97). Also, one of the main aims of the expedition against Cartagena under the command of Baron de Pointis in 1697, which will be explained in Chapter 1, was plunder of the Spanish colonies and the capture of prizes and booties. James Pritchard, *In Search of Empire: The French in the Americas* (Cambridge, 2004), pp. 290, 321–30. Thus, exertion of maritime forces in America motivated by the expectation of gaining riches was not unique to England. Nevertheless, it can be conjectured that influence of the argument was more pervasive in England than in other countries, given that the pro-maritime war argument was accepted as sort of a 'national myth', as Rodger has stated, and that the argument appeared in almost all wars in the 'long eighteenth century'. However, further research will be necessary regarding this point. Also, how this idea was accepted or not accepted in other parts of the British Isles, such as Scotland, Wales and Ireland needs further examination.

[6] Daniel Baugh, 'Great Britain's 'Blue Water' Policy, 1689–1815', *International History Review* 10, no. 1 (1988), 36.

[7] *Ibid.*, 40–1. In another article, he also describes the policy as 'a uniquely successful mode of national defence, heavily dependent on financial and naval means'; the policy developed during the period between 1650 and 1750. Daniel A. Baugh, 'Maritime Strength and Atlantic Commerce', *An Imperial State at War: Britain from 1689 to 1815*, ed. Lawrence Stone (London and New York, 1994), pp. 185–6.

historians who study the mid eighteenth century as a discourse on ideal war policy, which appeared in the press and in parliamentary debates in those periods. Various political groups sometimes used this discourse to criticise rival groups or for other political purposes, and the discourse was not always in accord with the actual policy of the government, especially in the early eighteenth century, although, as this study reveals, it had some influence on the domestic politics and naval policy. This discourse is close to what Rodger describes as an 'English national myth about sea-power'.

This is not to say that the two were irrelevant to each other. Baugh's 'blue water policy' was, to a certain extent, the realisation of a part (though not all) of the latter political discourse that had existed since the later sixteenth century. However, it is problematic to use the same term to refer to both the discourse on maritime war, often based on exaggerated ideas about the wealth of Spanish America, and the soberer strategy of national defence actually adopted by the British government, not least for the period of the early eighteenth century, when a large discrepancy still existed between them. Therefore, in this book, I use the phrase 'pro-maritime war argument' instead of 'blue water policy' to refer to the ideology in favour of war at sea, which existed since the sixteenth century.[8] It can be said that this 'pro-maritime war argument', a discourse supporting maritime war that existed since the sixteenth century, is a broader concept encompassing Baugh's 'blue water policy', the naval policy actually adopted by the British government, especially after the mid eighteenth century. What this book examines is not the latter 'blue water policy' but the former pro-maritime war argument, which was not necessarily identical to the actual policy of the government but still had a certain influence on politics and naval policy.

This pro-maritime war argument, which appeared in the political discourse in early modern England (later Britain), has been referred to mainly by political and naval historians. However, some problems exist in the approaches that these historians have taken. The first is a tendency to analyse this argument within the dichotomous conceptual framework of party politics or war strategy, especially in considering the question of its supporters. The pro-maritime war argument tends to be attributed to either of two opposing political groups such as the Tories and the Whigs, the Court and the Country in 1689–1713, and the government (the Walpole ministry) and the opposition in the 1730s. This political dichotomy is often connected with another division – between the continental strategy, which involved commitment to the land war on the continent, and maritime strategy, which favoured war at sea, especially in the American waters, by the navy and privateers.

[8] The reason I do not use the word 'naval' is because privateers were also regarded as an important, albeit not the main, player. Moreover, I use the term 'colonial maritime war' in a broad sense, and it is not strictly confined to battles between ships but also includes amphibious operations against the enemy colonies, which often entailed the use of land forces.

As far as the period of the War of the Spanish Succession is concerned, the pro-maritime war argument has been construed by political historians such as Geoffrey Holmes and naval historians, such as Sir Herbert W. Richmond, as a Country or Tory ideology, which was opposed to the continental war policy of the Marlborough–Godolphin ministry.[9] This customary view, however, is questioned by T.J. Denman, who has pointed out that there was support for maritime war also on the Whig side.[10] For the period of the Anglo-Spanish war of 1739–40 (what is called the 'War of Jenkins' Ear'), Kathleen Wilson has attributed this pro-maritime war argument to the opposition composed of the 'patriot' Whigs and the Tories, which severely criticised the Walpole ministry for its pro-Hanoverian policy and demanded colonial expansion in Spanish America, with support from overseas merchants.[11] Nevertheless, as Woodfine has revealed, in this period, there were supporters of maritime war also within the ministry.[12]

The pro-maritime war argument has also been dealt with in the dichotomous framework regarding British war strategy. Pares denies the correlation between political allegiance and support for each strategy in the mid eighteenth century, placing much importance on the division between the continental and maritime war strategy.[13] However, Richard Harding argues that even this distinction between the two strategies as well as the 'Whig–Tory' or 'Court–Country' political division was not necessarily important, at least in the actual decision-making in the 1740s, and that politicians adopted either policy in response to the changing circumstances.[14] Likewise, Baugh maintains that the role of the 'maritime' and 'continental' schools of thought should be seen as 'setting limits on what kind of diplomatic and strategic plans would be allowable'. The plans that were favoured depended on domestic political and diplomatic circumstances as well as strategic opportunities.[15]

Instead of the dichotomous view, recent studies came to stress the interrelation

9 Geoffrey S. Holmes, *British Politics in the Age of Anne* (London, 1967, repr., London and Ronceverte, 1987), pp. 73–5; Sir. Herbert W. Richmond, *The Navy as an Instrument of Policy, 1558–1727*, ed. E.A. Hughes (Cambridge, 1953), p. 283.

10 T.J. Denman, 'The Political Debate over War Strategy, 1689–1712' (unpublished Ph.D. thesis, Cambridge University, 1985), pp. 38–9.

11 Kathleen Wilson, 'Empire, Trade and Popular Politics in Mid-Hanoverian Britain: The Case of Admiral Vernon', *Past and Present* 121 (1988), 96–9.

12 Woodfine, 'Ideas of Naval Power', pp. 84–6.

13 Pares, 'American versus Continental Warfare', 429–30. It should be noted that, in terms of the British objects of war, Pares has further divided policy supporting continental commitment into a 'continental policy' and a 'Hanover policy'. While the former policy aimed to maintain European balance of power in alliance with a continental power such as Austria or Prussia, or to defend certain parts of Europe in which Britain had a vital interest (such as Portugal and the Low Countries), the latter policy had defence of Hanover as its main priority.

14 Richard Harding, *Amphibious Warfare in the Eighteenth Century: The British Expedition to the West Indies, 1740–1742* (Woodbridge, 1991), pp. 185–6, 192–3.

15 Baugh, 'Great Britain's 'Blue Water' Policy', p. 34.

between the two strategies. Harding has emphasised a close interconnection between the continental war, especially battles over Flanders and the defence of Hanover, and maritime war in America, pointing out that colonial conquests gained by the latter could be returned in peace negotiations to offset the enemy's territorial acquisition in Europe.[16] Likewise, Brendan Simms argues that many of the British statesmen recognised the close link between war on the continent and colonial maritime war in that the continental commitment helped Britain to maintain her naval superiority and to secure her colonies, while denial of overseas resources to the enemy would contribute to keeping the European balance of power.[17] Thus, the clear-cut division between political groups or two schools of war strategy has been questioned, although it cannot be denied that they had some influence on the pro-maritime war argument.

Moving beyond the political and strategic dichotomy view, Rodger has recently examined the argument in a new light. By investigating the process of how the belief in the English sea power developed, Rodger reveals how this ideology, which was often used by the opposition to criticise the government in the seventeenth century and most of the eighteenth century, came to be appropriated by the government of William Pitt the Younger. By the end of the eighteenth century, this ideology was turned into the 'national myth' of sea power in a true sense.[18] This is a more synthetic approach that transcends the existing dichotomy framework. However, some questions still remain. Why was this pro-maritime war argument endorsed by various political groups? What allowed this argument to continue to exist for more than two centuries in different political and diplomatic situations?

In order to answer these questions, we need to examine the argument from a new perspective: that is, the emphasis on the economic advantages of maritime war – a feature that was constantly present in the pro-maritime war arguments of the various periods, irrespective of the political background of their supporters. This ideological connection between maritime war and economic advantage has been pointed out by historians who have examined this argument, such as Pares, Denman, Baugh, Woodfine and Rodger.[19] However, there is still no study that delves deeply into this aspect. This book focuses on this ideological connection between maritime war and profit as the core element of the pro-maritime war

16 Richard Harding, 'British Maritime Strategy and Hanover 1714–1763', *The Hanoverian Dimension in British History, 1714–1837*, ed. Brendan Simms and Torsten Riotte (Cambridge, 2007), pp. 267, 272–3.

17 Brendan Simms, *Three Victories and a Defeat: The Rise and Fall of the First British Empire, 1714–1783* (London, 2007), pp. 672–3.

18 Rodger, 'Queen Elizabeth and the Myth of Sea-Power'.

19 Pares, 'American versus Continental Warfare', 453–4; Denman, 'Political Debate', pp. 301–5; Baugh, 'Great Britain's 'Blue Water' Policy', pp. 40–2; Philip Woodfine, *Britannia's Glories: The Walpole Ministry and the 1739 War with Spain* (Woodbridge, 1998), pp. 174–5; Rodger, 'Queen Elizabeth and the Myth of Sea-Power', 158.

argument, and it examines exactly why colonial maritime war was believed to be economically advantageous.[20]

The second problem with the preceding studies on the pro-maritime war argument is a tendency to regard the argument as a single ideology and to overlook its diversity. As mentioned, the dichotomy between Whig internationalists and Tory 'blue water' isolationists has been rejected by Denman, who points out that some of the Whigs supported maritime war and colonial expeditions as well.[21] However, he does not seem to consider fully the difference between the two pro-maritime war arguments. This book makes clear the variation within the pro-maritime war argument and examines its background and political functions. In particular, the book points out the existence of two different pro-maritime war arguments during the War of the Spanish Succession. In addition to the well-known Tory pro-maritime war argument, which became dominant in the late stage of the war, there was another pro-maritime war argument with a 'Whiggish' tone that appeared in the period just before the war.

The third problem with previous studies on this topic concerns the relationship between the pro-maritime war argument and reality. In regard to the period of the War of the Spanish Succession, the focus of political historians such as Holmes and Denman is mainly on its relationship with party politics; these political historians do not examine its impact on actual naval policy. Likewise, the influence of the pro-maritime war argument on legislation during the war has not been fully appreciated. J.A. Johnston, who has investigated how naval affairs were dealt with in Parliament in the period from 1688 to 1714, has stated that Parliament 'had little interest in or insight into the strategic functions of the navy, outside considerations of security', and this need for security 'provided the argument most frequently put forward against a Blue Sea strategy [*sic*]'.[22]

Consequently, the impact of the pro-maritime war argument during the War of the Spanish Succession tends to be downgraded by historians. Denman has claimed that 'Blue-water' ideas were simply 'a negative and isolationist reaction to England's changing European role'. According to Denman, the Tory maritime strategy was 'merely an external reflection of their domestic obsession with low taxation, abhorrence of placemen and government bureaucrats, and for rectitude in

20 As already mentioned, Rodger also points out two other elements in the 'national myth' of sea power that were associated with maritime war: 'Protestantism' and 'political freedom'. These two elements were also often, though not always, present in the pro-maritime war argument and were often interconnected with one another. In particular, in the sixteenth and seventeenth centuries, the defence of Protestantism was closely associated with colonial maritime war. Although this study does not deny the affinity of the pro-maritime war argument in England with Protestantism and political freedom, it focuses on the emphasis on the economic advantages of maritime war. This is done in order to shed light on ideological as well as actual connections between early modern warfare and profit, which will be explained later.

21 Denman, 'Political Debate', pp. 38–9.

22 J.A. Johnston, 'Parliament and the Navy, 1688–1714' (unpublished Ph.D. thesis, University of Sheffield, 1968), pp. 25–6.

government finance', which had been the agenda of the Country politicians – an agenda that was taken over by the Tories after 1688.[23] Likewise, Johnston has asserted that, 'There was only spasmodic and minority interest in the merits or demerits of a Blue Sea strategy in parliament' in the reign of William III and in the early years of Anne's reign.[24]

It is probable that this negative evaluation of the effects of the pro-maritime war argument on actual policy in our period partly results from the fact that there were few colonial maritime expeditions actually carried out during the war in contrast to the wars in the mid eighteenth century, which saw several successful expeditions. It might also be due to the fact that by the late 1730s, the argument had mainly become the opposition's tool to criticise the government's policy of continental commitment. However, these facts do not necessarily mean that the argument had no influence on the leading politicians in the ministry and on the government's policy during the War of the Spanish Succession. The effects of the argument on reality, especially its influence on government policy, should be re-examined.

This book investigates how much influence the pro-maritime war argument had on actual naval policy and legislation during the War of the Spanish Succession. As for the impact on naval policy, it examines how seriously the government was committed to maritime war in Spanish America during the war years. It also analyses why the attempted colonial maritime expeditions, one of the main measures of colonial maritime war, were unsuccessful, and why the support for the expeditions survived despite the repeated failures. As to its impact on legislation, the book focuses on the process of the enactment of the American Act of 1708, which is a culmination of the attempts to support maritime war by legislation during the war.

Moreover, through the analysis of the impact of the pro-maritime war argument on the naval policy and legislation, this book also reveals what kind of political groups and vested interests were behind the promotions of colonial maritime war. In particular, the relations between the pro-maritime war argument and British commercial interests have not been fully examined. It is true that the issue of trade protection, one of the components of the pro-maritime war argument that directly concerned mercantile community, has been referred to by some historians. For example, Denman has mentioned the attempts of the opponents of the continental strategy to exploit the merchants' anger over trade protection, especially during the Nine Years War.[25] This concern over trade protection was certainly an important aspect of maritime war in the War of the Spanish Succession as well as in the other wars in the eighteenth century.[26] Still, the relation between overseas

[23] Denman, 'Political Debate', p. 302.

[24] Johnston, 'Parliament and the Navy', pp. 22–3.

[25] Denman, 'Political Debate', pp. 78–9.

[26] For the problem of attacks on British sea-borne trade by French privateers in the eighteenth century, the British merchants' concern about them and the navy's effort to protect the trade by the convoy system, see Patrick Crowhurst, *The Defence of British Trade 1689–1815* (Folkestone, 1977), Chapters 1 and 2.

merchants and a more aggressive aspect of maritime war, especially colonial expeditions, remains unclear. Therefore, this study investigates the attitudes of the British mercantile and colonial interests – not least, those engaged in the Spanish-American trade – towards colonial expeditions, as well as the conflict that existed between them. In particular, the study casts light on the clash of interests among the West Indian merchants who traded with Spanish America via the British West Indian colonies, privateers based in Jamaica, and the South Sea Company.

The fourth problem with preceding studies concerns the continuity and changes in the pro-maritime war argument in the period between 1714 and 1729. As already stated, the pro-maritime war argument during the War of the Spanish Succession has been mentioned by political historians such as Holmes and Denman, whereas the argument in the mid eighteenth century, especially the Anglo-Spanish War of 1739–40, has been dealt with by Pares and Woodfine.[27] By contrast, the argument in the interim period has attracted far less attention. The reason is probably because this was a relatively peaceful period, which only saw the two short conflicts with Spain: the War of the Quadruple Alliance of 1718–20 and the Anglo-Spanish War of 1726–29. Nevertheless, this period was important in understanding the characteristics of the pro-maritime war argument, which revived in the years before the War of Jenkins' Ear. This book also deals with this interim period and investigates how the pro-maritime war argument changed or did not change during the period. In particular, it examines how Britain's acquisition of legal access to the Spanish-American market through the Asiento Treaty of 1713, one of the main prizes of the war for Britain, affected the pro-maritime war argument and also the British naval policy towards the Spanish American colonies.

In short, the aim of this book is, first, to analyse the pro-maritime war argument from a new perspective, focusing on the ideological connection between the argument and its supposed economic advantages, instead of using the existing dichotomy framework of party politics and war strategy. Second, the book also examines variation within the argument and its different political functions. Third, it reveals the relationship between the argument and reality, such as its impact on naval policy and legislation, in addition to the type of political and commercial interests that were involved in the promotion of maritime war. Lastly, this book analyses the transformation of the argument and change in the naval policy towards Spanish America in the period after the War of the Spanish Succession.

In a wider historical context, this analysis of discourse on maritime war and its alleged economic advantages will provide new insights into the relations between war, especially maritime war, and profit in early modern Europe. Rodger has divided medieval naval warfare into two broad categories: public, military warfare and private, commercial warfare. In the former type of warfare, ships played just a subsidiary role and were mainly used for transportation of the troops or for the assistance of the operations of the armies on land. This type of warfare was

27 Pares, 'American versus Continental Warfare'; Woodfine, 'Ideas of Naval Power'; Woodfine, *Britannia's Glories*.

normally conducted during a declared war between kingdoms. By contrast, the latter type of warfare – private and commercial naval warfare – was carried out against vessels of other nations or ports with the purpose of making profit by seizing their cargoes, sometimes under a legal cover of the doctrine of 'reprisal'.[28] This could take place at all times. The latter type of naval warfare combined with the economic motives was a normal form of war at sea up to the sixteenth century. However, as the seventeenth century went on and as war increasingly became an exclusive activity of state that was fought for a limited period, this type of warfare was reorganised into privateering – an attack conducted by privately owned ships on the enemy vessels with licences from the state, but confined to war time.[29]

Thus, in the medieval period, war at sea was fought not only for public ends but also for private profit, and this characteristic was passed down to privateering, a more regularised form of commerce raiding in the early modern period. Yet, one thing should not be forgotten: in early modern maritime war, the private and commercial character of the medieval maritime war was inherited not only by privateers but also by the naval vessels, which is shown by the fact that men of war as well as privateers had the right to capture enemy vessels as legitimate prizes in war time. Thus, the private and commercial character of the medieval maritime war still had resonance in early modern maritime war, and it can be argued that, to a certain extent, the idea of the economically advantageous maritime war reflected this medieval concept of private and commercial warfare conducted with the purpose of making profit.

It should also be noted that this ideological tie between maritime war and profit inherited from the medieval age was given a new life in a new setting: the Atlantic. The medieval private and commercial warfare in peace time had mostly disappeared in European waters by the mid seventeenth century. However, as Rodger has pointed out, the expansion of the South and North Western European powers into the Americas allowed this form of warfare to survive in the Atlantic. There, Spain attempted not only to limit her colonial trade to her own shipping, as other colonial powers were to do, but also to ban all foreign presence. This Spanish policy provoked the Dutch and English to engage in plunder, which was sometimes combined with illicit trade.[30] As the following chapters will show, the ideological connection between maritime war and profit was often most clearly observable in the argument for maritime war in America. This was partly because this particular circumstance surrounded Spanish America and its wealth. Thus, the pro-maritime war argument with an emphasis on the economic advantages of

[28] The 'reprisal' was a customary practice that was seen in early modern Europe. This allowed a ship owner who had been a victim of the attack by foreign vessels to make a retaliatory capture on ships belonging to the same nations as that of the aggressor in order to recoup his losses.

[29] N.A.M. Rodger, 'The New Atlantic: Naval Warfare in the Sixteenth Century', *War at Sea in the Middle Ages and the Renaissance*, ed. John B. Hattendorf and Richard W. Unger (Woodbridge, 2003), pp. 237–8, 240–1.

[30] *Ibid.*, pp. 241–3.

war at sea, which was seen in the early modern period, was an idea that had part of its origin in the medieval concept but was transplanted in a new theatre: the Atlantic world.

This ideological connection between war at sea and profit, however, has not attracted sufficient attention from naval historians. This might be partly due to a tendency in the study of the eighteenth-century British naval history to focus on institutional and administrative development, which contributed to the success of the British navy in the eighteenth century, especially in the latter half of the century. This tendency is still noticeable in recent writing.[31] This is understandable given the achievement of the British navy in the Seven Years War and, later, in the French Revolutionary and Napoleonic wars. Yet, it also entails a certain weakness, because it could underestimate the importance of such an aspect that historians have not regarded as a contributing factor to the success of the British navy, such as pursuit of profit at sea.[32] To make little contribution to the navy's success, however, does not mean that the aspect was historically insignificant. Sometimes it could have and did have influence on the course of history. Therefore, the connection between maritime war and profit is well worth examining as a significant aspect of early modern maritime war.

Through the analysis of the pro-maritime war argument in early eighteenth-century Britain, this book attempts to reveal how war at sea and economic considerations were interrelated, and what impact the concept of economically advantageous war had on reality. It can give us further insight into the ideological as well as the actual relationships between violence, the economy and colonies in the early modern Atlantic world.

Sources

Some explanation is necessary about the nature of the sources used in this study, especially pamphlets and periodicals. It goes without saying that these sources should always be treated with some caution. First of all, there is a question of the accuracy of their content. In many cases, what was written in these publications was not an accurate analysis of reality, or proposals based on solid evidence. As William A. Speck states, the purpose of these publications was to convince contemporary citizens; in gauging their effectiveness, we must not evaluate it according to the modern standard of 'objectivity' but according to how far they convinced their

31 For example, see Roger Morriss, *The Foundations of British Maritime Ascendancy: Resources, Logistics and the States, 1755–1815* (Cambridge, 2011).

32 It should be noted that, in economic history, there have recently appeared studies that see prize money as part of the incentive system in the British navy, which contributed to the success of the British navy in the eighteenth century. This is in tandem with other systems for governance on ships, such as the articles of war that regulated the behaviour of captains and the hierarchical structure of the navy. For example, see Douglas W. Allen, 'The British Navy Rules: Monitoring and Incompatible Incentives in the Age of Fighting Sail', *Explorations in Economic History* 39 (2002), 204–31.

audience.[33] Because of this characteristic as propaganda, these sources are not necessarily useful in knowing the reality of maritime affairs at that time. However, they at least reveal the contemporary perception of maritime war and its supposed economic advantages.

The second problem with these sources is the difficulty in discerning whose opinions these publications actually represented. It would be dangerous to equate the ideas that appeared in the publications with what we call 'public opinion' at that time. Pamphlets and periodicals could be a tool for politicians and, as was exemplified in the relationships between Robert Harley and pamphleteers such as Daniel Defoe and Jonathan Swift, they were often produced under the strong influence of politicians on both the government's and opposition's side.[34] Therefore, we should not naively regard the pro-maritime war argument stated in the pamphlets and periodicals as an expression of 'public opinion'. Nevertheless, given the very fact that they were used in contemporary political campaigns, it is also extreme to say that these ideas were completely irrelevant to their perception. It would be more appropriate to think that the support for maritime war expressed in these sources reflected the opinion of at least part of contemporary society that was receptive to these discourses.

Thirdly, even if these publications reflected 'public opinion' to a certain degree, there is another tricky question regarding the impact of 'public opinion' on politics in the first half of the eighteenth century, whether or not that 'public opinion' was manipulated by political elites. According to Jeremy Black, regarding the extent of public interest in politics, there has been no consensus yet between the view that places emphasis on radicalism and modernity and the view that stresses deference and conservatism.[35] The evaluation of the extent of the influence that 'public opinion' could exert upon politics seems to vary according to historians. For example, for the age of Walpole, Black is somewhat sceptical about its impact, and argues that, 'Popular opinion could only be effective if harnessed by powerful parliamentary or ministerial groups, and the absence of an effective representative system meant that these groups were not obliged to respond to popular campaigns.'[36] On the other hand, some admit its significance with reservations. Hannah Barker claims that, although the impact of popular sentiment on government policy was limited in the first half of the eighteenth century, popular protests and newspapers had a decisive impact on government policy on a few occasions.[37]

[33] William A. Speck, 'Political Propaganda in Augustan England', *TRHS*, 5th ser, 22 (1972), 27.

[34] For relationships between Harley and the writers, see James A. Downie, *Robert Harley and the Press: Propaganda and Public Opinion in the Age of Swift and Defoe* (Cambridge, 1979).

[35] Jeremy Black, *The English Press in the Eighteenth Century* (London and Sydney, 1987), p. 303.

[36] Jeremy Black, 'Foreign Policy in the Age of Walpole', *Britain in the Age of Walpole*, ed. Jeremy Black (London, 1984), pp. 162–3.

[37] Hannah Barker, *Newspapers, Politics and English Society, 1695–1855* (Harlow, 2000), p. 128.

To be sure, we cannot ignore the fact that the electorate (which overlapped with 'public opinion' to a certain degree) could exert influence upon politics through Members of Parliament, especially for the period up to the early 1720s. As Holmes has pointed out, in the period between the Glorious Revolution and the early 1720s, the electorate as well as political parties increasingly emerged as a decisive force in politics. This was also a period in which the English electorate grew exceedingly rapidly in relation to the growth of the population.[38] Frequent elections that were held in accordance with the Triennial Act also provided political elites with opportunities to make use of the influence of the electorate through propaganda campaigns. From the large floating vote between elections in this period, Speck has guessed that electoral propaganda had some impact on the outcome of the election under the Triennial Act, at least in large constituencies.[39] Even for the period of the Walpole ministry, which showed a tendency towards oligarchy under conditions of growing political stability, Harry T. Dickinson warns against neglecting the influence that extra-parliamentary groups and public opinion could have on the ruling oligarchy through several means such as lobbying, petitioning and instruction campaigns, riots and the press.[40]

Nevertheless, as far as strategic issues are concerned, it would be more difficult to say that public opinion or the electorate could have a direct impact in the early eighteenth century. During this period, decisions concerning war strategy were still made by a small group including the king, the secretaries of state and other chief ministers, although Parliament's control over financial matters also began to increase at the same time. This limitation of the influence of public opinion on strategic issues was also true for the period of the War of the Spanish Succession. In his detailed study of the War of the Spanish Succession, John B. Hattendorf denies the impact of the public debate on the government's broad concept of war strategy in that period.[41]

38 Geoffrey S. Holmes, *The Electorate and the National Will in the First Age of Party* (Lancaster, 1976), pp. 2, 14–15.

39 Speck, 'Political Propaganda', 28.

40 Harry T. Dickinson, 'Popular Politics in the Age of Walpole', *Britain in the Age of Walpole*, ed. Jeremy Black (London, 1984), pp. 45–8.

41 John B. Hattendorf, *England in the War of the Spanish Succession: A Study of the English View and Conduct of Grand Strategy, 1702–1712* (New York and London, 1987), p. 219. It is true that, in some instances, pressure from the extra-parliamentary groups had a certain impact on politics even in this period, as was seen in the case of the Kentish Petition and Defoe's 'Legion's memorial', which called for more vigorous actions against France and was submitted to the House of Commons in May 1701. This prompted the Tory-dominated Commons, which had been reluctant to enter the war, to make a resolution that demonstrated its support for the alliance with the emperor and the Dutch against France, as Baron Godolphin proposed. Henry Horwitz, *Parliament, Policy and Politics in the Reign of William III* (Manchester, 1977), pp. 289–1. This can be regarded as an example of how pressure from extra-parliamentary groups – in this case, possibly incited by the Junto Whigs – had some influence on war policy. However, even in this case, it would be difficult to say that this had a decisive impact on the government's war policy.

It should be noted, however, that it was not only 'public opinion' that these pamphlets and periodicals targeted. As Downie has pointed out, the audiences with which Robert Harley was concerned in his propaganda campaign during the War of the Spanish Succession were MPs as well as 'public opinion'.[42] Some publications on foreign affairs or war, such as *The Conduct of the Allies* written by Swift, obviously targeted a wider audience than MPs, as is shown by the fact that *The Conduct of the Allies* sold 11,000 copies in a month. It should be remembered that politicians were among the readership of those pamphlets. In particular, as Johnston has stated, many of the pamphlets about naval matters were specifically addressed to Parliament, not least the members of the House of Commons, and were certainly distributed and read by MPs.[43] Those politicians also could be swayed by the publications. For instance, in 1739, the Duke of Newcastle became a supporter of West Indian expeditions after reading Swift's *Conduct of the Allies*.[44] For most politicians in those days, who had little knowledge of the practicalities of naval operations, these publications on war policy or maritime affairs could be valuable sources of information.

With these points in mind, this book is not concerned with how widely the pro-maritime war argument was accepted by 'public opinion' and how 'public opinion' tried to exert influence upon government policy, which is difficult to gauge and was probably more limited in strategic issues than in domestic issues in the early eighteenth century. Instead, what it examines is the impact of the pro-maritime war argument on those who were in a position to have influence on decision-making in maritime affairs and legislation, such as leading politicians within and outside the government, administrators, some flag officers and leading West Indian merchants. The book also investigates the extent to which they tried to put the ideas of the pro-maritime war argument into practice.

In order to examine the attitudes of these people in power towards the pro-maritime war argument, this book uses the correspondence of politicians and naval officers along with the pamphlets and periodicals. Moreover, to investigate how the pro-maritime war argument was translated into the reality of naval operations and legislation, administrative sources and the parliamentary sources are used. By combining these different types of sources, this book analyses not only the discourses on maritime war but also its relationship with reality – especially its influence on actual politics and naval policy and its relationship with the political and commercial interests.

Structure

The structure of the book is as follows: Chapter 1 places the pro-maritime war argument in a longer historical context. It examines the history of the English penetration into the Americas from the sixteenth century to the late seventeenth

42 Downie, *Harley and the Press*, p. 7.

43 Johnston, 'Parliament and the Navy', p. 59.

44 Woodfine, 'Ideas of Naval Power', pp. 85–6.

century and describes how the pro-maritime war argument developed under the political and economic situations of each period.

Part I (Chapters 2 and 3) examines the content of the pro-maritime war argument during the War of the Spanish Succession. Chapter 2 analyses the relationship between maritime war and its economic advantages in the pro-maritime war argument, especially its connection with the struggle with France over the Spanish-American market. Chapter 3 examines several types of the pro-maritime war arguments and points out their differences in terms of content and political functions.

Part II (Chapters 4, 5 and 6) examines the interaction between the pro-maritime war argument and reality. Chapter 4 focuses on the impact on naval policy during the war. In particular, it examines the government's commitment to two major means of maritime war in Spanish America: the interception of Spanish silver fleets and colonial expeditions. Chapter 5 deals with the impact on legislation, with special reference to the enactment of the American Act of 1708. Through the analysis of the process of the legislation, it also reveals relationships between political and vested interests and the pro-maritime war policy. Chapter 6 examines a plan for a naval expedition of 1712 by the South Sea Company as the last attempt of a colonial expedition to recover the Spanish-American trade during the war. It also sheds light on conflict of interests between the West Indian merchants and the directors of the South Sea Company over the Spanish-American trade.

Part III (Chapters 7 and 8) analyses the transformation of the argument after the War of the Spanish Succession. It examines the pro-maritime war arguments during the period between 1714 and 1729, particularly the argument regarding two conflicts with Spain in which Britain was involved: the War of the Quadruple Alliance of 1718–20 and the Anglo-Spanish War of 1726–29. Chapter 7 analyses debates in the press and Parliament over the two conflicts and reveals how the role of the government and the opposition in using the pro-maritime war argument alternated in the 1710s and 1720s. Chapter 8 examines how Britain's naval policy in Spanish America changed, especially in consideration of the trade of the South Sea Company, which started on the basis of the Asiento Treaty of 1713.

– 1 –

English Expansion into Spanish America and the Development of a Pro-maritime War Argument

Elizabethan Ventures into the 'New World': The Starting Point

The pro-maritime war argument that this book examines can be placed in the wider context of the history of English expansion into the Americas, especially Spanish America, which is one of the most important aspects of English expansion into the world outside Europe. From the early sixteenth century, several European powers, such as the French, English and Dutch, intruded into South America to obtain a slice of the wealth produced in the 'New World', first by depredation and illicit trade, and later by also establishing new colonies in the Caribbean and North America.[1] In the case of England, this undertaking began in the early sixteenth century. The English had established a commercial link with Spanish America by the 1520s, and were engaged in trans-Atlantic trade with Spanish American colonies through Seville. In the 1530s, some of those with Iberian interests, such as William Hawkins of Plymouth, also initiated direct trade with Guinea and Brazil, though this often caused tension with the Portuguese. This direct trade was undertaken again in the 1550s and 1560s, when English traders, such as John Hawkins of Plymouth – a son of William – and the Fenners of Sussex, conducted slaving voyages to West Africa and Spanish America.[2]

Hawkins made two successful voyages in the first half of the 1560s, but in his third voyage, he met with a severe setback. In September 1568, Hawkins' vessels

[1] A large number of books have been written about the history of intrusion of the European powers into Spanish America. For overviews, see Kris E. Lane, *Pillaging the Empire: Piracy in the Americas, 1500–1750* (New York, 1998) and Peter T. Bradley, *British Maritime Enterprise in the New World: From the Late Fifteenth to the Mid-Eighteenth Century* (Lewiston, NY, 1999).

[2] The account in this section mainly draws on works by Kenneth Andrews, such as *Elizabethan Privateering: English Privateering during the Spanish War 1585–1603* (Cambridge, 1964); *The Spanish Caribbean: The Trade and Plunder 1530–1630* (New Haven and London, 1978); and *Trade, Plunder and Settlement, Maritime Enterprise and the Genesis of the British Empire, 1480–1630* (Cambridge, 1984). For English maritime activities in the Americas in the Tudor period, see also Neville Williams, *The Sea Dogs: Privateers, Plunder & Piracy in the Elizabethan Age* (London, 1975), Chapters 4–5, 7–8; and David B. Quinn and A.N. Ryan, *England's Sea Empire, 1550–1642* (London, 1983), Chapters 1, 3–5.

encountered the Spanish silver fleet at San Juan de Ulúa (the port for Vera Cruz), which roundly defeated his vessels. After this event, the English gradually withdrew from trade with Spanish colonies. The reason was economic as well as political. The increasing costs of armament for protection and competition with other rivals, such as the Portuguese and French, made the trade less profitable for investors and merchants. Moreover, by this time, Anglo-Spanish relations had deteriorated owing to events, such as the exile of Mary Stuart to England and suppression of the rebels in the Netherlands by the Spanish forces under the command of the Duke of Alba, and these relations were worsened by the defeat of Hawkins' fleet at San Juan de Ulúa.[3]

Under these circumstances, some English seamen switched their activities from smuggling to plundering Spanish colonies and vessels. Among them was Francis Drake, a cousin of John Hawkins, who had experienced a humiliating defeat at San Juan de Ulúa. In collaboration with the Huguenot privateers and *cimarrones,* a group of runaway African slaves, Drake launched a series of raiding expeditions against Spanish American colonies. The most noted one was his circumnavigation between 1577 and 1580 in which he succeeded in capturing the *Nuestra Señora de Conceptión*, a rich Spanish vessel laden with silver and gold. Legally speaking, these activities were piracy, as they were conducted without any official commission to authorise the attacks. However, Queen Elizabeth and some of her courtiers with anti-Spanish and Protestant inclinations, such as Sir Francis Walsingham, Sir Christopher Hatton and the Earls of Leicester and Lincoln, tacitly backed them by conniving at their actions or by investing in the ventures.

Closely connected with this unauthorised plunder against Spain's overseas possession was a plan for creating an English settlement in South America in the 1570s.[4] In 1574, Richard Grenville, with other gentlemen of the West Country, submitted to the queen a plan to establish a colony in the area in South America that was not yet effectively occupied by the Spaniards and Portuguese.[5] Although this plan was not adopted, the idea of colonisation was partly inherited by Drake in his plan for circumnavigation in 1577–80, as Andrews has suggested.[6] Elizabeth, however, was not enthusiastic about a new territorial acquisition in the area under Spanish influence, for fear of offending Philip II of Spain, so she did not openly support such schemes.

Instead, from around 1583, the focus of the English colonising attempt shifted to North America, an area outside Spanish influence. The best-known example of such schemes is Walter Raleigh's project to establish a colony in Virginia between

[3] Andrews, *Trade, Plunder and Settlement*, pp. 127–9.

[4] On the English interest in South America in this period, see Kenneth R. Andrews, 'Beyond the Equinoctial: England and South America in the Sixteenth Century', *JICH* 10:1 (1981), 4–24; Andrews, *Elizabethan Privateering*, Chapter 9; Andrews, *Trade, Plunder and Settlement*, Chapter 7.

[5] Andrews, 'Beyond the Equinoctial', 8–10. Although Grenville did not specify his objectives in his proposal, Andrews guesses that Grenville's targets were the River Plate and Chile.

[6] *Ibid.*, 11–12, 20–1.

1584 and 1590, which was intended to be used as a privateering base against the Spaniards as well as a colony for producing commodities that had been hitherto imported from the Iberian countries, such as oils, fruits and dyestuffs. Although he received ideological support from Richard Hakluyt the younger, who wrote *Discourse of Western Planting* for him in 1584, Raleigh could not obtain the queen's financial support, and this sealed the fate of the colony.[7] In 1595, he also attempted a colonising project in Guiana, but this did not bear fruit either. All in all, the primary concern of Elizabeth and her government in those days was the defence of the realm and the power politics of Western Europe, and they were not interested in obtaining a new territory in America. As in the similar attempts in the early Stuart period, colonising projects at that time were conducted on a private initiative, and even when the crown backed such plans, its support was limited.[8]

The deteriorating relations with Spain made war inevitable, and in the summer of 1585, tension finally turned into open hostility. From this time onwards, piracy gave way to privateering, and a number of private expeditions were fitted out with letters of reprisal or other official commissions, while semi-official expeditions were sent both to the Iberian Peninsula and American waters. After the battle with the Spanish Armada in 1588 and the failure of expeditions under Drake and Sir John Norris in 1589, privateering ventures became a dominant form of war at sea. Although its main theatre during the war was in the eastern Atlantic and around the British Isles, at least 150 privateering expeditions were also dispatched to American waters with the aim of intercepting Spanish and Portuguese ships and attacking their American possessions.[9] These expeditionary forces, which sometimes included several royal warships, were led by experienced seamen and gentry, such as Drake, Hawkins, Thomas Cavendish (the second English circumnavigator), Christopher Newport and even prominent aristocrats, such as George Clifford, the third Earl of Cumberland.[10] In addition to the prospect of a hefty prize, widespread anti-Spanish and Protestant sentiments, as well as nationalistic attitude, encouraged these ventures.[11]

It was not only seamen and landowning gentry who participated in privateering. As war continued, overseas merchants, especially great London merchants became deeply involved in the business as promoters. In particular, those who traded with the Iberian Peninsula and the Mediterranean played an important role. Even after some of those with Iberian interests, such as Hawkins and Drake, turned to plunder, the majority of the leading Iberian merchants desired to maintain good relations with Spain, as they preferred safe and steady trade to plunder. However, the outbreak of the war forced those merchants to abandon their business, while also giving them a chance to gain by force the commodities they had been importing. As a result,

[7] On this project, see Andrews, *Trade, Plunder and Settlement*, Chapter 10.

[8] Andrews, *Trade, Plunder and Settlement*, pp. 10–11.

[9] N.A.M. Rodger, *The Safeguard of the Sea: A Naval History of Britain, 660–1649* (New York and London, 1998), pp. 294–5.

[10] On the Earl of Cumberland, see Richard T. Spence, *The Privateering Earl: George Clifford, 3rd Earl of Cumberland, 1558–1605* (Stroud, 1995), Chapters 5–10.

[11] Andrews, *Trade, Plunder and Settlement*, pp. 247–8.

some of the leading Iberian and Mediterranean merchants, such as John Watts and Paul Bayning, became leading promoters of privateering ventures, in which plunder was sometimes combined with trade in the same voyage.[12] This privateering war against Spanish and Portuguese vessels and Iberian overseas possessions continued until James I's accession to the English throne in 1603. It was this experience of maritime war against Spain for nearly two decades that formed the foundation from which the pro-maritime war argument in the later periods evolved.[13]

Spanish War, Colonisation and the Emergence of the 'New Merchants'

As soon as James I came to the English throne in 1603, he declared an end to privateering, and, accordingly, direct trade with Spain was resumed.[14] Nevertheless, a new war with Spain in the latter half of the 1620s led to the revival of the argument supporting vigorous maritime war in the Caribbean.[15] The background of this Spanish war was the outbreak of the Thirty Years War caused by the revolt of the Protestants in Bohemia in 1618, who refused to admit Emperor Ferdinand II as their king. Instead, the Protestant rebels nominated Frederick V, elector of the Palatinate and a Calvinist, as their new king. Frederick's acceptance of the Bohemian throne provoked the invasion of the imperial forces and the subsequent expulsion of Frederick V from Prague in 1620, while Spanish troops invaded the Palatinate to assist the emperor.

This series of events obliged James I to take some action to protect the interests of his son-in-law Frederick. However, James, who had taken a pro-Spanish stance, was reluctant to get involved in open war against the two Habsburg monarchs, the emperor and Philip III of Spain, and tried to limit his response to the defence and later recovery of the Palatinate rather than Bohemia, preferably by diplomatic means, such as Prince Charles' marriage with a Spanish princess. The policy of alliance with Spain and maintenance of peace was strongly advocated by the Spanish faction of the Court, including Sir George Calvert and Sir John Digby (later Earl of Bristol).

By contrast, there was a faction in Parliament that took a firm anti-Spanish and pro-Dutch stance, and desired a break of the Spanish match and a war with Spain. The most influential group in this Puritan faction was led by a powerful aristocrat, the third Earl of Pembroke (William Herbert), and included Archbishop of Canterbury George Abbot, Sir Benjamin Rudyerd and the Countess of Bedford. There was also another group with less political influence made up of the third Earl of Southampton and the third Earl of Essex. Lastly, there was a group of East Anglian Puritans led by the second Earl of Warwick (Robert Rich) and his associates, such as Sir Nathaniel Rich, a kinsman of

12 Andrews, *Elizabethan Privateering*, pp. 13–15, 104–12; Andrews, *Trade, Plunder and Settlement*, pp. 250–1.

13 Rodger, 'Queen Elizabeth and the Myth of Sea-Power', 156–7.

14 Andrews, *Trade, Plunder and Settlement*, p. 286.

15 Denman, 'Political Debate', p. 7.

Warwick, and John Pym, many of whom later became parliamentary leaders in the Civil War.[16] Unlike James, whose concern was limited to protecting Frederick's hereditary rights in the Palatinate, this Puritan faction placed the conflict over Bohemia in the context of the general struggle between the Protestants and the Catholics. The strategy they formulated to win this struggle was a 'war by diversion' that entailed the exertion of maritime as well as land forces. In this strategy, in collaboration with the United Provinces, England was to attack the Spanish Netherlands with land forces, and Spanish American colonies and seaborne commerce with naval forces, by which it was expected that Spain would be forced to divert her troops from the military campaigns against the Palatinate to the defence of her own territories.[17]

This Puritan and anti-Spanish faction was joined by Prince Charles and his right-hand man, George Villiers (the first Duke of Buckingham) in 1623–24. After the breakdown of the negotiations for the Spanish match, they realised that the recovery of the Palatinate was unlikely to be achieved by diplomatic means, and gathered the peers and MPs who desired war with Spain in the Court and Parliament, including Pembroke and Warwick, to persuade James and Parliament to prepare for the Spanish war.[18] As Thomas Cogswell has pointed out, one of the main cohesive forces in this coalition was their support for the 'diversionary war'.[19] Around 1623 and 1624, Sir Edward Conway, a protégé of Buckingham, proposed plans for Anglo-Dutch naval offensives against the Spanish silver fleet and her colonies while helping the Dutch in Flanders with land forces. Moreover, in the Parliament of 1624, Buckingham himself expressed his support for maritime war in Spanish America to deprive Spain of her money.[20]

This 'Patriot' coalition succeeded in pushing the nation towards a Spanish war. Nevertheless, the diplomatic and war policy that Buckingham eventually adopted, such as an abortive Anglo-French joint expedition under the command of the Count of Mansfeld to regain the Palatinate, was not what the supporters of the Spanish war had desired.[21] The disappointment of the Puritan faction at the

[16] S.L. Adams, 'Foreign Policy and the Parliaments of 1621 and 1624', *Faction and Parliament: Essays on Early Stuart History*, ed. Kevin Sharpe (Oxford, 1978), pp. 141–6.

[17] *Ibid.*, pp. 146–52; S.L. Adams, 'Spain or the Netherlands? The Dilemmas of Early Stuart Foreign Policy', *Before the English Civil War*, ed. Howard Tomlinson (London, 1983), pp. 86–93; Robert Brenner, *Merchants and Revolution: Commercial Change, Political Conflict, and London's Overseas Traders, 1550–1653* (Princeton, NJ, 1993, repr. London and New York, 2003), pp. 244, 250.

[18] On the process of the formation of this 'Patriot' coalition in 1624, see Thomas Cogswell, *The Blessed Revolution: English Politics and the Coming of War, 1621–1624* (Cambridge, 1989).

[19] *Ibid.*, p. 153.

[20] John C. Appleby, 'An Association for the West Indies? English Plans for a West India Company 1621–29', *JICH* 15, no. 3 (May 1987), 219–20; Brenner, *Merchants and Revolution*, pp. 253–4.

[21] Cogswell has attributed the reason for Buckingham's failure to fulfil his initial policy to the fact that Buckingham had to consider James' will. Cogswell, *Blessed Revolution*, pp. 314–16. However, it seems that Buckingham retained his interests in the West Indian operations

government's war policy was deepened after the succession of Charles I to the English throne in March 1625. In the same year, a Spanish war began. Two years later, however, Buckingham also declared war on France, with which he had failed to forge an alliance. This two-front strategy soon proved disastrous. Buckingham's Cadiz expedition in October 1625, and expeditions against La Rochelle in 1626 and 1627, ended in failure, and Buckingham himself was assassinated in 1628 when preparing for the third expedition to La Rochelle.

This catastrophic strategy, along with Charles' religious policy to enforce Arminianism, alienated the Puritan faction, including Warwick and his circle, from the prince and Buckingham by 1626. Instead of Buckingham's two-front war, they demanded a maritime war against Spanish colonies in the West Indies to cut off the source of Spain's power, following in the footsteps of the Elizabethan sea dogs, such as Drake and Cavendish – an argument that bore a close resemblance to the pro-colonial maritime war argument during the War of the Spanish Succession. In particular, the Earl of Warwick was an enthusiastic supporter of maritime war against Spain, and as early as 1616, he sent out ships to attack the Spaniards and capture pirates with commissions from foreign princes such as the Duke of Savoy.[22]

In order to pursue this colonial maritime war, Warwick's circle made several proposals for establishing a joint-stock company to conduct privateering ventures as well as trade on the model of the Dutch West India Company founded in 1621.[23] In 1626, Sir Dudley Digges, a member of Warwick's circle, submitted to the Commons a plan for a joint-stock company designed to attack the Spanish silver fleet and her colonies, which was also meant to obtain the right to free trade and a base in Spanish America after peace was concluded with Spain. A similar plan was proposed by Sir Nathaniel Rich in 1628. Also, in 1629, stimulated by the capture of the Spanish silver fleet by the Dutch West India Company in the summer of the previous year, the proposal of 1626 was again

until a very late stage of his life. In March 1628, he made a secret agreement with Gustavus Adolphus, king of Sweden, for an Anglo-Swedish joint expedition to the West Indies, though how seriously he committed to this plan is debatable. Appleby, 'An Association for the West Indies?', 231–2.

22 W. Frank Craven, 'The Earl of Warwick, a Speculator in Piracy', *HAHR* 10, no. 4 (November 1930), 461.

23 It should be noted that support for the establishment of the West Indian Company was not confined to Warwick's circle, but was present in the government as well. In 1625, Sir John Coke submitted to Buckingham a plan for a separate English West India Company to attack Spanish vessels and territories in the West Indies and to establish a footing for trade there. This idea of establishing the West India Company was revived in the government in the late 1630s. In 1637, the Privy Council appointed advocates of the West Indian operations in the Court and Parliament, such as Sir Thomas Roe, Sir Edward Conway and Sir Dudley Digges, to a committee to consider establishment of a West India Company to seize a port in Spanish America and plunder the region, though this plan did not materialise. Timothy Venning, *Cromwellian Foreign Policy* (New York, 1995), pp. 75–6; Brenner, *Merchants and Revolution*, p. 301.

prepared to be submitted to the Commons, though none of these plans materialised in the end.[24]

Undaunted by the failure of the plans for a West India Company, Warwick and his associates, such as Pym, Lord Saye and Sele, and Rudyerd, launched a new colonising scheme. As early as 1619, Warwick founded the Amazon Company along with Roger North, who sailed to the Amazon the next year to establish an English settlement there. However, in the face of strong pressure from Spain, the plan was abandoned. After war with Spain began, Warwick himself sailed to Brazil in 1627 to capture the Spanish silver fleet with a commission from Charles I, though this attempt was also frustrated by the Spanish attack on his ships.[25]

These failures did not dampen the enthusiasm of Warwick and his circle for colonising enterprise. In 1628, they gained control of the Bermuda Company, and in 1629 and 1630, they helped with the creation of the Massachusetts Bay Company.[26] Furthermore, in late 1629, they founded the Providence Island Company to settle several uninhabited islands in the middle of the Caribbean: Santa Catalina and Henrietta, and later the island of Tortuga near the north-western shore of Hispaniola. Their aim was to use these islands as a base for operations against Spanish America, as well as a place to found their ideal godly society. Moreover, it was also expected that this colony would be a stepping-stone for another colony they planned to establish in Spanish America. After the Spaniards attacked the Providence Island colony in 1635, the main business of the colony shifted to plunder. From that point on, the colony became a privateering base, and a series of raiding voyages on the Spanish colonies on the Spanish Main was launched with letters of reprisal from Charles I, which continued until 1641, when the island was overrun by Spanish forces.[27]

These colonising projects were undertaken in collaboration with the emerging groups of merchants engaged in American colonial trade, which Robert Brenner has named the 'new merchants'.[28] By the end of the first quarter of the seventeenth century, especially after the dissolution of the Virginia Company in 1624, the City's company merchants, such as the East India and Levant merchants, had withdrawn from American colonial trade, especially the tobacco trade, in which they were required to make a huge and constant investment in the development of

[24] Brenner, *Merchants and Revolution*, pp. 258–60, 266–8; Appleby, 'An Association for the West Indies?', 223–6, 232.

[25] Andrews, *Trade, Plunder and Settlement*, p. 299; Brenner, *Merchants and Revolution*, p. 265.

[26] Brenner, *Merchants and Revolution*, pp. 148–9.

[27] For the Providence Island colony, see Karen O. Kupperman, 'Errand to the Indies: Puritan Colonization from Providence Island through the Western Design', *WMQ*, 3rd ser, 45, no. 1 (January 1988), 70–99; Karen O. Kupperman, *Providence Island, 1630–1641: The Other Puritan Colony* (Cambridge, 1993, repr. Cambridge, 1995).

[28] My account of the next few paragraphs is largely based on Brenner's *Merchants and Revolution*.

plantations and could not expect the same monopoly as in their other trades. These company merchants, particularly the Levant–East India merchants, were also hesitant to enter into war against Spain, as it could disrupt their established and lucrative trade with the Mediterranean, Near East and Far East. In fact, the war with Spain and France pursued by Charles and Buckingham proved damaging to these merchants as well as to the merchants trading with Spain and France, and this war policy became one of the causes that temporarily moved them to oppose the crown in the late 1620s.[29]

In contrast to these company merchants, the 'new merchants' came to participate in the American colonial trade and supported a more aggressive policy towards the Spanish colonies. Their social origins were diverse, but many of them came from outside the rank of the London elite overseas merchants. Some of them had started their careers as planters in the colonies, and, after returning to London, had begun colonial trade, making use of the profits from the plantations and strong connections with the colonies. Others were domestic traders, sea captains or shopkeepers in London who became engaged in colonial trade, such as the tobacco trade, with American colonies, sometimes to eliminate the middleman's cut.[30]

These 'new merchants' also came to forge close links with the Puritan magnates led by Warwick through the merchants' involvement in commercial activities in the colonies, such as Bermuda and Providence Island, which were founded and assisted by the Puritan faction. Among the leading members of these 'new merchants' were Maurice Thomson and William Pennoyer. They were also engaged in colonial raids on the Spanish American colonies, and, between 1638 and 1641, Thomson, Pennoyer and some West Country merchants fitted out a private expedition against Spain under the command of Captain William Jackson. Again between 1642 and 1645, with support from Warwick and other members of the Providence Island Company, the same group dispatched Jackson, who raided Maracaibo and succeeded in occupying Jamaica temporarily.[31] As Brenner has shown, by the eve of the Civil War, these 'new merchants' had become close allies of the leaders of the parliamentary opposition in the Commons headed by Pym, and they called for a tougher policy against Spain in the Caribbean and the formation of a West Indian Company to protect and encourage their commercial interests there.[32] Under the Commonwealth, they came to have strong ties with the republican element in the Rump Parliament, such as Thomas Scot, Thomas Chaloner and Henry Marten,

29 Brenner, *Merchants and Revolution*, pp. 102–6, 223–4.

30 *Ibid*,, pp. 114–15.

31 Kupperman, *Providence Island*, p. 347; Brenner, *Merchants and Revolution*, pp. 410–11.

32 Brenner, *Merchants and Revolution*, pp. 325–6, 350–1.The demand for a more vigorous war in Spanish America also appeared in the Grand Remonstrance submitted in November 1641 by Pym and his colleagues. One of their protests was the government's supposed shift of its focus in war against Spain from the West Indian operations, which, they claimed, was 'the most facile and hopeful way' to defeat the Spaniards, to an expedition to Cadiz, which was an 'expenceful and successless' operation. Brenner, *Merchants and Revolution*, p. 358; See also *Cobbett*, II, col. 948.

and they played an important role in the commercial, foreign and naval policy-making of the Commonwealth.[33]

Cromwell's 'Western Design'

The period of the Civil War and the Commonwealth marked a turning point in the history of English maritime activities in Spanish America. Although the attempts by Warwick's circle to secure a base in the middle of Spanish America from which to launch an attack on the Spanish empire did not bear fruit, their ambitious vision was inherited by Oliver Cromwell and some of his advisers. In mid 1654, after wavering between France and Spain as a possible target to attack, Cromwell adopted a plan for fighting against the latter in her American colonies. This 'Western Design' was, in a sense, the culmination of the thirty-year effort of the aristocratic English puritans to strike Spain in America and to take away her financial resources, which would also help to protect England from Spanish invasion.[34]

On the other hand, it should also be stressed that this project had significant new features compared with the similar preceding attempts. Importantly, it was the first state-directed expedition with the intention of taking a part of Spanish America. As Timothy Venning has pointed out, while preceding expeditions against Spanish America had been attempted on private initiative, the state was more directly involved in this 'Western Design'.[35] Moreover, John F. Battick has argued that this project was intended not just as an expedition for plunder, but as part of a grand scheme to take control of Spanish colonial trade by seizing key points in Spanish America, an important feature that was also present in the pro-maritime war argument during the War of the Spanish Succession.[36]

The decision to fight with Spain in her American colonies was not, however, a foregone conclusion for Cromwell and his advisers in the Council of State. England had two candidates for possible allies at that time – Bourbon France and Habsburg Spain – and opinions in the council were divided between a pro-French faction and a pro-Spanish faction. The former, led by Sir Gilbert Pickering, supported open war with Spain and alliance with France, claiming that those options would encourage Franco-Spanish war and could improve the situation of

33 Brenner, *Merchants and Revolution*, pp. 577–84.

34 Kupperman suggests that the continuity between this 'Western Design' and the preceding attempts by Warwick's circle can be glimpsed from several facts: the committee chairman who wrote the declaration for war against Spain was Nathaniel Fiennes, the second son of Lord Saye and Sele who was one of the key members of Warwick's circle; and William Jessop, secretary of the Providence Island Company, served as clerk to the council. Moreover, in the declaration, the assault on Providence Island by the Spaniards was invoked to justify war against Spain. See Kupperman, *Providence Island*, p. 351; Kupperman, 'Errand to the Indies', 94.

35 Timothy Venning, *Cromwellian Foreign Policy* (New York, 1995), pp. 74–6.

36 John F. Battick, 'A New Interpretation of Cromwell's Western Design', *Journal of the Barbados Museum and Historical Society* 34 (1972), 76, 82.

the Huguenots in France. On the other hand, the latter faction, led by General John Lambert, was against the Spanish war on the grounds that war might have negative effects on English trade with Spain. In addition, a third group led by John Thurloe believed that England should stay aloof from the conflict on the continent, while setting France against Spain.[37]

In the end, as mentioned, Cromwell chose war with Spain, though he limited the theatre of the war to Spanish America, believing this would prevent the conflict from developing into an open war in Europe. It is difficult to know what drove him to this decision. Kupperman stresses his zeal for defence of Protestantism from the threat of Catholic Spain as one of the main factors that influenced his decision.[38] However, religious zeal would not be a sufficient reason to explain why he chose Spain, not France, especially given that Cromwell was still searching for a way to ally with Spain in 1654. On the other hand, Venning has put more emphasis on pragmatic considerations as one of the reasons for Cromwell's decision: the necessity to give employment to the armed forces after the end of the Dutch war, and the alleged remunerative nature of war against the rich Spanish colonies.[39] Although the importance of the religious factor was undeniable, it can be also said that these strategic and economic considerations were as important as religious zeal in his decision to fight with Spain.

In December 1654, Cromwell sent out an expeditionary force under the command of Admiral William Penn and General Robert Venables to the West Indies, though war had not yet been declared against Spain and there was strong opposition from General Lambert, a leader of the pro-Spanish faction. The expeditionary force arrived in the West Indies in March or April of the next year. Nevertheless, the attack on Hispaniola, their main target, was repelled by the Spanish forces. To make up for this failure, Penn and Venables assaulted Jamaica, a Spanish colony of much lesser significance at that time, and succeeded in capturing it. In spite of the resistance of Spanish guerrillas and expeditions from Cuba to recapture Jamaica, the English forces managed to hold the island, and by 1660, had established a secure footing there.[40]

In retaliation for the English attack on its West Indian possession, the Spanish government confiscated the properties of the English in Spain, which increased the tension between the two countries. In October 1655, England finally declared war on Spain while concluding an offensive and defensive treaty of alliance with France.

[37] Venning, *Cromwellian Foreign Policy*, pp. 44, 47–8.

[38] Kupperman, 'Errand to the Indies', 90.

[39] Venning, *Cromwellian Foreign Policy*, pp. 72–3. Venning also mentioned several other considerations as factors that affected Cromwell's decision, such as having little prospect of gaining a subsidy from Spain for the continental campaign and of receiving assistance from the Huguenot rebels in case of French war, as well as the expectation that a limited war against Spain in the Caribbean would not cause open war with her in Europe.

[40] For the capture of Jamaica and the struggle of the English forces to secure the island after the initial conquest, see S.A.G. Taylor, *The Western Design: An Account of Cromwell's Expedition to the Caribbean* (Kingston, Jamaica, 1965, repr. London, 1969).

After the declaration of war, the theatre of war expanded into Europe, and English squadrons cruised in European waters as well as in the Caribbean in search of Spanish silver fleets carrying cargoes from the Spanish colonies.

These operations enjoyed several successes. In September 1656, Captain Richard Stayner encountered a Spanish silver fleet off Cadiz. He captured two vessels laden with approximately 2,600,000 pieces of eight and 7,000 or 8,000 silver bars, while sinking two vessels with about 1,100,000 pieces of eight and grounding one. The following spring, Robert Blake assaulted another Spanish silver fleet in the harbour of Santa Cruz at Teneriffe in the Canary Islands, sinking sixteen ships with treasure on board. Although these blows did not ruin Spanish finances, they contributed to the failure of the Spanish campaigns in Flanders by depriving them of their sinews of war; encouraged France, England's ally, to continue the war; and restored English morale.[41] The Spanish war continued until September 1660, when Charles II, who came back to England after his exile on the continent, made a peace with Spain.

One question regarding this 'Western Design' in connection with the pro-maritime war argument is to what extent Cromwell was aiming for promotion of trade with Spanish America when he planned the expedition. It is true that he acknowledged the importance of colonial commerce. Cromwell had a personal connection with some groups of London merchants who had interests in West Indian trade, such as Martin Noell and Thomas Povey. Furthermore, during the Protectorate, several committees were set up to supervise West Indian affairs, one of which included Maurice Thomson, who was one of the leading figures of the 'new merchants' and who continued to play an important role in commercial and colonial affairs under the Rump and the Protectorate.[42] Nevertheless, it should be noted that Cromwell did not always heed these merchants' opinions. He ignored the two projects proposed by several merchants, including Noell and Povey, which aimed to enhance English trade in the Caribbean – establishment of a West India Company and an expedition to Florida to assist the rebellion of the local tribal groups against the Spaniards and to set up a base for intercepting Spanish shipping in the Bahamas.[43] Furthermore, it should be also pointed out that the war with Spain was not welcomed by some sections of the mercantile community in England. In particular, merchants trading with Spain were opposed to the war because it could severely disrupt their business.[44] Taking these factors into consideration, it seems that commercial motive was not Cromwell's top priority, and that he supported mercantile interests only if it suited his war policy, which was mainly based on religious and strategic considerations. Rather ironically, however, it was the capture

[41] Venning, *Cromwellian Foreign Policy*, pp. 120–1, 140.

[42] *Ibid.*, pp. 29–30, 231, 242–3; Valerie Pearl, 'Thomson [Thompson], Maurice (1604–1676)', rev., *ODNB*.

[43] Venning, *Cromwellian Foreign Policy*, pp. 84–5, 243–4.

[44] Jean O. McLachlan, *Trade and Peace with Old Spain 1667–1750: A Study of Commerce on Anglo-Spanish Diplomacy in the First Half of the Eighteenth Century* (Cambridge, 1940), pp. 19–20.

of Jamaica, brought about by his 'Western Design', which came to contribute hugely to the development of the economy of the English West Indian colonies in the subsequent period.

Buccaneers on the Rampage

After the Restoration, Spain and England did not go to war with each other in Europe until the beginning of the War of the Spanish Succession, except for a brief period of hostilities at the end of the third Anglo-Dutch War. Accordingly, demand for vigorous maritime war against Spanish America was muted. Nevertheless, the situation was different in the Caribbean. The governor of Jamaica waged unofficial warfare against the Spanish colonies, and this provided further material on which the discourse about the alleged vulnerability of the Spanish colonies and prospects of seizing Spain's wealth was expanded.

The capture of Jamaica in 1655 allowed England to gain its first footing in the Greater Antilles. However, the very proximity of the island to the Spanish colonies exposed the English settlers there to the danger of attack by the Spaniards. Moreover, after the conquest, the naval ships that joined the 'Western Design' had gradually disappeared, returning to England or leaving for the other English stations on government orders. Under these circumstances, for the defence of the colony as well as to weaken the enemy, Governor Edward D'Oyley and subsequent governors of Jamaica were obliged to turn to 'buccaneers' – semi-piratical raiders based at that time on the island of Tortuga – and invite them to the colony by issuing letters of marque. As a consequence, Jamaica soon became one of the main bases for the buccaneers, who carried out raids on Spanish colonies with commissions from the governors of Jamaica throughout the 1660s.[45]

The necessity of the defence of the island also obliged Sir Thomas Modyford, Governor of Jamaica from 1664, to rely on these buccaneers. In accordance with instructions from the English government, Modyford initially tried to repress their activities to establish a peaceful trading link with Spanish colonies. However, he soon came to recognise that it was unavoidable for the security of the colony to give some encouragement to these marauders in order to keep them in the island. As a result, in March 1666, Modyford issued commissions against the Spaniards to the

[45] Peter Earle, *The Sack of Panama: Sir Henry Morgan's Adventures on the Spanish Main* (New York, 1981), p. 47. The 'buccaneers' were originally a group of hunters chiefly of French, English and Dutch origins, who settled in the north and north-western part of Hispaniola (modern Haiti). They made a living by hunting cattle and pigs, which were brought to the island by the Spaniards, and selling their meat and hide to vessels of interlopers that visited the region. However, the campaign by the Spanish colonial authority to drive these hunters out of Hispaniola in the late 1630s forced them to move to the island of Tortuga, located in north-west Hispaniola, and these hunters began to take up plunder of Spanish colonies as their new business. Clarence H. Haring, *The Buccaneers in the West Indies in the XVII Century* (New York, 1910, repr. Hamden, CT, 1966), Chapter 2. As the buccaneers often worked as privateers in war time, in this book I also use the words 'Jamaican privateers' to refer to those buccaneers who were based in Jamaica.

buccaneers, with tacit approval of the first Duke of Albemarle, George Monck, a cousin of Modyford and an anti-Spanish politician in the court.[46]

One of the leaders of the Jamaican buccaneers was a Welshman, Henry Morgan. In July 1668, Morgan attacked Porto Bello, a port of call for the Spanish silver fleet, and captured it. This action, however, ran almost directly counter to the trend in Anglo-Spanish relations in Europe at the time. In May of the previous year, faced with the threat of a French invasion of the Spanish Netherlands, Spain had signed a treaty with England that granted her generous commercial privileges, including most-favoured-nation terms. Morgan's raid on Porto Bello after the conclusion of the treaty naturally provoked strong protests from the Spanish ambassador in London. Nevertheless, the English government refused to take any responsibility for the raid conducted by the buccaneers 'beyond the line', and instead even shifted the blame for the attack on to the Spaniards, claiming their refusal to give the English the right to open trade with the Spanish colonies invited this attack.[47]

As Peter Earle has suggested, one of the factors that allowed this expedition against a friendly nation to be carried out was the political difference in the English government between the anti-Spanish faction led by Albemarle and pro-Spanish politicians like the Earl of Arlington, Henry Bennet, which probably gave Modyford and Morgan room to manoeuvre. Earle has also suggested that there seems to have been an interest in Spanish American expeditions, which could be conducted with France, among the members of the royal family, such as Charles II, the Duke of York (the future King James II), and Prince Rupert. In particular, the Duke of York, Charles' brother and Lord High Admiral, was reputedly involved in a plan to establish a West India Company, a revival of the similar plans in the preceding periods that we have already seen.[48]

While England and Spain were still at peace in Europe, the tension between Jamaica and the Spanish colonies continued. In retaliation for a Spanish raid on the northern coast of Jamaica in June 1670, an expedition against the Spanish colonies on the Spanish Main was prepared, and in July Morgan was appointed as Admiral and Commander in Chief of the expeditionary forces. In the beginning of 1671, with more than two thousand English and French buccaneers, he marched through the dense jungle of the Isthmus of Panama and sacked the city of Panama.[49] Prior

46 A.P. Thornton, *West-India Policy under the Restoration* (Oxford, 1956), pp. 83–5, 93–4.

47 *Ibid.*, pp. 97–8, 101–4, 107–8; Keith Feiling, *British Foreign Policy, 1660–1672* (London, 1930), pp. 232–3.

48 Earle, *Sack of Panama*, pp. 95–7. It is also worth noting that James and his associates keenly supported the second Dutch War, partly for the mercantilist considerations that they had acquired through their personal experience of fighting at sea against the Commonwealth and Cromwellian regime during the late 1640s and 1650s. They believed that the war with the Dutch, a main trading rival of England, could be easily won, and that it would lead to marked increases in the power and wealth of England as well as provide employment in the navy, opportunity for promotions and prize money. J.R. Jones, *The Anglo-Dutch Wars of the Seventeenth Century* (London and New York, 1996), p. 146.

49 A detailed account of this expedition is in Earle, *Sack of Panama*, Chapters 4–6, 12–20.

to this raid, a treaty with Spain was signed in Madrid in July 1670, by which Spain recognised all of the English possessions in the Americas, and in return, England agreed to cease hostilities and recall the privateers there. Morgan's raid on Panama after the conclusion of this treaty again caused fury in the Spanish government, and retaliatory expeditions were seriously considered in Spain. Consequently, to assuage the Spaniards' anger, Morgan and Modyford were arrested and extradited to England as a sop to the Spaniards. In reality, this was a political gesture. The English government rewarded Morgan for his action by granting him a knighthood and sent him back to Jamaica in 1675 as its deputy governor.[50]

Morgan's expedition to Panama was one of the most successful operations of the buccaneers, but this also marked the beginning of an end to private warfare in peace time, which had been a characteristic aspect of the English expansion into the Caribbean since the Elizabethan period. Although Morgan escaped punishment, by this time, the policy of the English government towards the Spanish American colonies and buccaneers had begun to change, which was reflected in the conclusion of the Treaty of Madrid.[51] It is true that the conclusion of this treaty did not bring an immediate end to the depredations by the buccaneers. In the 1670s and 1680s, some buccaneers moved to French colonies, such as Tortuga or Petit-Goâve, and continued their attacks with letters of marque from the French governors, while others ventured into the Pacific and raided Spanish colonies on the western coast of South America without any commission.[52] However, the general trend was irreversible. For the English colonists as well as the English government, trade and sugar plantations increasingly came to be seen as more steady and reliable means to accumulate profit in the West Indies than buccaneering.

Behind this shift were a growing weariness of buccaneering among mercantile and colonial interests in England and an increasing development of direct trade with Spanish colonies via English West Indian colonies, especially Jamaica. While buccaneers' raids were rampant in the West Indies, there was also criticism against their activities in the West Indies in the 1660s. Some Jamaican merchants and planters vehemently criticised buccaneers, claiming that they could ruin and depopulate the island. Traders to 'Old Spain' and English merchants residing in Spain also attested that their raiding was detrimental to England's trade and reputation.[53] On the other hand, there was an ongoing scheme to turn Jamaica into a base for the slave trade with the Spaniards who did not have settlements on the coast of West Africa and therefore had to rely on middlemen for the supply of slaves. This plan received support from the royal family, which was involved in the

50 *Ibid.*, pp. 170–1, 250–3, 261; Thornton, *West-India Policy*, pp. 111–22.

51 Also, in August 1680, England concluded the Treaty of Windsor with Spain, which stipulated a mutual defence against French attacks in America. This shows a further move of the English government towards establishing amicable commercial relations with Spain in America. Thornton, *West-India Policy*, p. 230.

52 Peter Earle, *The Pirate Wars* (London, 2003, repr. London 2004), pp. 97–9; Bradley, *Lure of Peru*, Chapters 6 and 7.

53 Thornton, *West-India Policy*, pp. 79–80.

English African Company. In 1663, while giving orders to stop privateering in order to establish more amicable relations with the Spanish colonists, Charles II gave permission to the Spaniards to come to the English colonies for the purchase of slaves, though strictly speaking, this was a breach of the Navigation Act. This plan finally got on the right track by the 1680s, and the Spanish vessels came to visit Jamaica to buy slaves that were provided by the reconstituted Royal African Company as well as interlopers.[54] In this way the supply of African slaves for the assientists (private contractors who made contracts with Spanish monarchs to supply their colonies with slaves) and their agents became an important business of the island.[55]

A small group of merchants gradually came to control this developing trade in Jamaica. After the Restoration, in the absence of a dominant monopoly company, trade with the American colonies was relatively open compared with other fields of trade, and the low barriers to entry and hope of high returns attracted a wide range of investors who put their money into the trade to diversify their business interests. However, towards the end of the seventeenth century, colonial trade was increasingly concentrated in the hands of fewer numbers of powerful colonial merchants. They included Gilbert Heathcote and Bartholomew Gracedieu, who would play an important role in West Indian trade during the period of the War of Spanish Succession, as we shall see later. These merchants usually specialised in a specific area in America or in specific commodities, although they also often combined their American trade with that of other regions, such as Spain and the Baltic.[56] In the case of Jamaica, after the Restoration, a clique of Whig Asiento traders came to control the lucrative Spanish-American trade, especially the slave trade, though their monopoly caused hostility among small planters and merchants who were excluded from this circle.[57]

Thus, in addition to the existing trade with the Spanish colonies via Cadiz, a new trading channel – direct trade via the English West Indian colonies with Jamaica as its main base – was established by the last quarter of the seventeenth century, and this was increasingly dominated by a handful of Whig magnates and their associates in the colonies. While this process went on, the tendency grew towards tighter regulation of privateering in war time and the suppression of

[54] Nuala Zahedieh, 'The Merchants of Port Royal, Jamaica, and the Spanish Contraband Trade, 1655–1692', *WMQ*, 3rd ser, 43 (1986), 589–91.

[55] The 'Asiento' (or 'Assiento'), which originally referred to every contract made for the public utility, was the exclusive contract to supply Spanish American colonies with slaves. For its history, see Georges Scelle, 'The Slave-Trade in Spanish Colonies of America: The Assiento', *American Journal of International Law* 4 (1910), 612–61.

[56] Nuala Zahedieh, *The Capital and the Colonies: London and the Atlantic Economy, 1660–1700* (Cambridge, 2010), pp. 8, 57–63. According to Zahedieh, many of them increasingly came to support the Whigs in the political turbulence of the late 1670s and 1680s, probably reflecting the antipathy towards Stuart Monarchs' attempt to control the City, Parliament and colonial government. *Ibid.*, pp. 113–16.

[57] Nuala Zahedieh, 'Regulation, Rent-seeking, and the Glorious Revolution in the English Atlantic Economy', *EcHR* 63, no. 4 (2010), 877–9.

unauthorised plundering by private individuals in peace time. Nevertheless, this shift from plunder to trade did not lead to evaporation of the pro-maritime war argument combined with the expectation of making profit. The undercurrent of the idea of colonial maritime war ran deeply, waiting for a time to resurface.

The Nine Years War and Protection of English Interests in the Caribbean

With the outbreak of the Nine Years War in 1689, England faced a new strategic situation. William's intention to check the growth of French power embroiled England in the land war on the continent from which she had stayed aloof since the 1620s. This direct involvement in continental warfare provoked a heated debate on war strategy in Parliament. As far as the use of naval power was concerned, the argument largely concentrated on two issues that mainly involved European waters.[58] The first was a plan for descents on the French coast by Anglo-Dutch naval and land forces, with the expectation that a revolt, especially among the Huguenots, would break out in France, an idea that harks back to Buckingham's expedition to La Rochelle in 1629.[59] During the Nine Years War, these tactics were favoured by William and those who were in charge of the naval affairs of the government in the early years of the war, such as the Earl of Nottingham and Edward Russell (the Earl of Orford from 1697). Plans for descents were also proposed by some of the Court politicians to secure military supplies for war.

The second issue was defence of English seaborne trade from the increasing threat of the French *guerre de course*. From 1694, in response to the financial crisis of the same year, France increasingly shifted its main naval policy from fleet battles to war on enemy commerce, which was conducted by privateers from Dunkirk and St Malo as well as naval ships.[60] On the other hand, from the early years of the war, English merchants kept complaining about the loss of their ships through lack of naval protection. The worst case came in June 1693, when allied merchantmen bound for the Mediterranean were ambushed and part of the convoy was sunk or captured by the French.[61] This disaster of the Smyrna fleet caused anger among the

[58] My account of the debates on war strategy during the Nine Years War in these two paragraphs is largely based on Denman, 'Political Debate', Part One: 'The Nine Years' War, 1689–97'.

[59] *Ibid.*, pp. 42–6.

[60] Compared with English commerce raiding, the navy and privateers were more closely related with each other in this French *guerre de course*. For example, lease of warships and arms to privateers and participation of unemployed naval officers were not unusual. This *guerre de course* was again adopted in the War of the Spanish Succession as one of France's main naval strategies. Geoffrey Symcox, *The Crisis of French Sea Power, 1688–1697: From the Guerre d'Escadre to the Guerre de Course* (The Hague, 1974), pp. 6–8; John S. Bromley, 'The French Privateering War, 1702–13', *Corsairs and Navies, 1660–1760*, ed. John S. Bromley (London and Ronceverte, 1987), pp. 215–16.

[61] John Ehrman, *The Navy in the War of William III, 1689–1697: Its State and Direction* (Cambridge, 1953), pp. 501–2.

mercantile community, which strongly demanded better trade protection.

The issue of trade protection was also taken up by the 'Country' MPs, such as Paul Foley, Robert Harley, Sir Thomas Clarges and Sir Christopher Musgrave, to criticise the government's policy of commitment to costly and lingering continental warfare. They claimed that England should instead concentrate its war effort at sea, especially in defence of trade and in attack of French marine commerce, while throwing doubts on the plans for descents.[62] After the disaster of the Smyrna fleet, the Country MPs in the Commons brought up this issue in 1694, and they succeeded in tacking to the land tax bill a clause for securing forty-three naval ships for trade protection.[63] However, the new act seems to have failed to achieve its end, and the issue of trade defence continued to be exploited by the Country MPs.

On the other hand, during the Nine Years War, maritime war in American waters attracted little attention in parliamentary debate. As far as Spanish colonies were concerned, the argument supporting maritime war in the Americas lay dormant, as Spain was an ally of England in this war. Rather, the main enemy of England was France, and the English government launched several expeditions against the French West Indian and North American colonies.[64] One such expedition was carried out in 1690–91 under Commodore Lawrence Wright and Governor Christopher Codrington of the Leeward Islands, which resulted in the recapture of St Kitts and the Dutch colony St Eustatius from the French, although the subsequent attempt to seize the larger French colony of Guadeloupe failed. Also, in the spring of 1695, together with Spanish forces, English forces under Captain Robert Wilmot and Colonel Luke Lillingston attacked French colonies on Hispaniola and managed to occupy Cap François and Port-de-Paix. However, an outbreak of yellow fever and discord between the English and Spanish forces

[62] The 'Country' MPs in this period can be defined as those who shared a common concern about a growing power of the government over Parliament and tried to limit its power by several measures, such as removal of the public office holders ('placemen') from the Commons, close scrutiny of the government's spending and reduction or total abolition of the standing army. They were found in the Whigs as well as in the Tories, and used the Commission of Public Accounts, an audit body in Parliament, as their main base from which to launch an attack on the government. On the 'Country' attitudes, see Dennis Rubini, *Court and Country, 1688–1702* (London, 1967), especially pp. 23–30, 36–8; David Hayton, 'The "Country" Interest and the Party System, 1689–c.1720', *Party and Management in Parliament, 1660–1784*, ed. Clyve Jones (Leicester, 1984), pp. 42–5. For the Commission of Public Accounts during the reign of William III, see James Alan Downie, 'The Commissioners of Public Accounts and the Formation of the Country Party', *EHR* 91, no. 358 (January 1976), 33–51.

[63] J.A. Johnston, 'Parliament and the Protection of Trade, 1689–94', *MM* 57, no. 4 (November 1971), 408–12; Ehrman, *Navy in the War of William III*, pp. 505–8.

[64] For the West Indian operations during the Nine Years War, see William T. Morgan, 'The British West Indies during the King William's War (1689–97)', *JMH* 2 (1930), 378–409; Norton H. Moses, 'The British Navy and the Caribbean, 1689–1697', *MM* 52 (1966), 13–40.

as well as between Wilmot and Lillingston prevented them from pushing ahead with further conquest, and the expeditionary forces withdrew from the island.[65]

From 1693, it was the French who went on the offensive against Spanish and English colonies. These were not purely naval operations, but were often conducted by a combined force of naval warships and armed private vessels, and were intended for the private profit of investors who financed the expeditions.[66] In 1696, France dispatched two naval squadrons to the Caribbean and the Spanish coast with the intention of intercepting the Spanish silver fleet that was returning from the colonies, as England and the Netherlands had done in the former wars against Spain.[67] A large-scale offensive operation was also launched against the Spanish Main. In April 1697, with the approval of Louis XIV, Baron de Pointis sailed to the Caribbean to attack Spanish colonies. In collaboration with the *flibustiers* [i.e. French buccaneers] led by Governor Du Casse of Saint-Domingue, Pointis raided Cartagena and forced the inhabitants to pay an enormous sum in ransom, which was estimated from eight to forty million livres, although disagreement over the division of the booty created serious friction between Pointis and the buccaneers. Skilfully eluding several English squadrons dispatched to intercept him, Pointis returned to Brest in August with the booty and prizes.[68]

In the face of these French offensives, protection of the wealth of Spanish America from France became a concern of the English government, and the government used naval force for this purpose. In 1697, on receiving the news of large-scale French preparations for a West Indian expedition, the government decided to divert an Anglo-Dutch squadron under Vice-Admiral John Neville from the Mediterranean to the Caribbean in order to stop this attempt, though Neville failed to prevent Pointis' return to France.[69] The English government also tried to keep the Spanish silver fleet from falling into the hands of Louis XIV, lest the silver on board the fleet be used for his war effort. This was also significant for the English merchants trading with Spain, because the silver fleet carried the cargoes of the English as well as the Spanish merchants. As a result, orders to the naval commanders dispatched to European and American waters often included instructions to protect the silver fleet.[70]

The security of the English colonies was another issue that the government had to consider. After the Glorious Revolution, the Whig elite colonial merchants recovered the control of colonial trade that had been temporarily threatened by an

65 Ehrman mentions that, during the war, there was also a proposal from the Dutch for an Anglo-Dutch joint expedition to America for the protection of the colonies and the interests of both countries in the area. However, England did not accept the proposal. Ehrman, *Navy in the War of William III*, p. 252.

66 Pritchard, *In Search of Empire*, p. 312.

67 *Ibid.*, pp. 321–6.

68 Regarding this expedition, see William T. Morgan, 'The Expedition of Baron de Pointis against Cartagena', *AHR* 37, no. 2 (January 1932), 237–54; Symcox, *Crisis of French Sea Power*, pp. 218–19.

69 Pritchard, *In Search of Empire*, pp. 330–1.

70 Ehrman, *Navy in the War of William III*, pp. 499, 503–4, 509, 610–11.

opposing group in the colonies and by the Stuart colonial policy in the 1680s. Moreover, the new war with France and the 'Financial Revolution' provided those Whig colonial merchants such as Heathcote with an opportunity to generate profit through government supply contracts and investment in the national debt.[71] However, the war also posed a threat to their trade with Spanish America and English colonies, especially Jamaica, a gateway in the Caribbean to the Spanish American market. In fact, in 1694, Jamaica was attacked by Du Casse, who landed on the eastern coast of the island with 1,500 men, plundered the island for six or seven weeks, and carried away about 1,300 to 3,000 slaves.[72] In April 1696, fear of French attack urged Heathcote and other merchants to ask the Lords of Trade to send a speedy ship to Jamaica to give them warnings about possible French attack of the colony and to dispatch forces for colonial defence.[73]

The Nine Years War ended with the Peace of Ryswick in September 1697. However, the English government knew that this would be just a brief respite from conflict with France. On the other hand, increasing awareness of the importance of the Caribbean urged the government to dispatch a reconnaissance expedition to the region. In late 1698, Rear Admiral John Benbow was sent there with astronomer Edmund Halley to gather hydrographical and military information about the Spanish West Indies as well as to hunt pirates.[74] Benbow's report submitted to the government pointed out the vulnerability of English colonies to attacks from the enemy and called attention to the issue of how to protect or secure the Spanish silver fleet, which would be the first target when a war broke out.[75] Thus, by the period before the War of the Spanish Succession, the Caribbean had ceased to be a theatre for mere plunder for England. Instead, the protection of the existing interests in that region in war time became an urgent issue for the English government.

Since the late sixteenth century, maritime war in the Caribbean, especially that against Spanish America, had constituted an important element of English expansion into the Americas. The brief survey of the history of colonial maritime war in this chapter reveals three important points: First, the main actor of colonial maritime war shifted from privateers and semi-piratical raiders to the navy. From the mid seventeenth century onwards, as was seen in Cromwell's 'Western Design', the state grew more directly involved in colonial maritime war, which so far had been carried out chiefly on private initiative and with private capital. This probably reflected the increasing interest of the English government in the Caribbean as an

[71] Zahedieh, *Capital and the Colonies*, pp. 121–7; Zahedieh, 'Regulation', 879–81, 883–7.
[72] Pritchard, *In Search of Empire*, pp. 317–18.
[73] Morgan, 'British West Indies', pp. 403–4. For the government's policy of the defence of the English North American and West Indian colonies and the difficulties caused by the uncooperativeness of the colonial assemblies, see G.H. Guttridge, *The Colonial Policy of William III* (Cambridge, 1922, repr. London, 1966), Chapter 3.
[74] On this voyage, see Sam Willis, *The Admiral Benbow: The Life and Times of a Naval Legend* (London, 2010, repr. London, 2011), Chapter 16.
[75] *Ibid.*, pp. 273–4.

area suitable for establishing naval and trading bases and plantations, as well as its improved ability to mobilise resources for naval operations outside European waters. From this time, the navy became a prime agent of the state in the colonial maritime war, though privateers continued to be seen as an important auxiliary force in it.

The second important point is that colonial maritime ventures, including plundering expeditions as well as colonisation, were carried out by or (more often) in collaboration with overseas merchants. These merchants can be divided mainly into two groups. The first included the merchants who were outside the ranks of the elite merchants in the City and were excluded from the established trading channels. They tried to penetrate the Spanish American market not by trade via Cadiz, but by risky and profitable direct trade with the Spanish colonies. As a means to achieve this end, they conducted or invested in colonial maritime enterprises, which also enabled them to secure a trading base in the Caribbean. During the Elizabethan period, this group was represented by the West Country merchants, such as Hawkins and Drake, and from the 1620s to the 1650s by the 'new merchants'. On the other hand, those merchants who already had an established commercial link with Spain or the Mediterranean invested in the colonial maritime war only when their existing trading channel was severed by the outbreak of hostilities. For them, however, this was just a second-best option for investment during war time, and they tended to return to their original safer and steadier channel of trade as soon as it was recovered. In Chapter 5, we will see a similar pattern in Spanish American trade during the War of Spanish Succession.

The third point to note is that, from the late seventeenth century, there was a gradual shift of emphasis from plunder, often combined with trade by force, to peaceful but not necessarily legal trade in the Caribbean. After England secured trading bases in the region, direct trade via the English West Indian colonies gradually emerged as a new channel for Spanish American trade in addition to the existing indirect trade via Cadiz. In particular, after its capture in 1655, Jamaica rapidly became a centre of smuggling with the Spanish colonies as well as a base for privateers. As this new trading channel developed, its protection came to take precedence over plundering, since direct trade was regarded as a more efficient means of extracting wealth from Spanish America than plunder. It should be stressed, however, that exertion of force continued to exist as an important option by which to recover channels of trade when they were cut off.

Running parallel to this process of English intrusion into Spanish America was the development of an argument supporting maritime war against Spanish America. This pro-maritime war argument provided a driving force for intrusion and was strengthened by the occasional successes of raids on the Spanish colonies, which brought tangible profit to England in the form of bullion and other colonial produce. From the late sixteenth century, this idea of supporting maritime war in Spanish America surfaced repeatedly when a conflict with Spain occurred.

The strategy of striking Spain in the West Indies first emerged during the Elizabethan period and was put into practice by English seamen and gentry, sometimes in cooperation with London merchants. After the advent of peace with

Spain in 1603, the hostilities in the Americas temporarily ceased. In the 1620s, however, with the outbreak of the Thirty Years War, the argument for colonial maritime war was brought up by a Puritan faction in the Court and Parliament, including the Earl of Warwick and his associates, in the debate over the English policy towards European conflict. The enthusiasm of Warwick's circle for colonial maritime war was inherited by Oliver Cromwell. He carried out the 'Western Design', which resulted in the capture of Jamaica in 1655. After the Restoration, though occasional raids on Spanish colonies by buccaneers continued to cause diplomatic embarrassment, considerations for stable trade with Spanish America increasingly gained the upper hand over plundering in English foreign policy towards Spain, and arguments supporting war against Spanish America subsided. The pro-maritime war argument remained dormant throughout the Nine Years War, in which Spain was an ally of England. However, when war with Spain broke out in 1702, and the English share in the Spanish American trade was threatened by the advance of the French merchants, the argument surfaced again, as we shall see in the following chapters.

PART I

Pro-maritime War Arguments during the War of the Spanish Succession

– 2 –

The Idea of Economic Advantages of Maritime War in Spanish America

The emphasis on the alleged economic advantages of maritime war, especially that against Spanish America, in the pro-maritime war argument has been pointed out by historians who have examined relations between politics and war in the period of the Nine Years War and the War of the Spanish Succession. For example, Terence J. Denman has summed up the character of the argument supporting war at sea (which he calls the 'Country strategic argument'), which had its origin in the Elizabethan war at sea and had developed by the late seventeenth century, as follows: 'maritime attacks on an enemy's colonies and trading routes were the best method of bringing a power, such as Spain low, and that such attacks would make a war a profitable or self-financing enterprise'.[1] Likewise, J.A. Johnston describes the convictions regarding naval power, which were often expressed in Parliament in the period between 1688 and 1714, as follows: 'England was by tradition, if not by right, a great sea power', and 'Englishmen instinctively understood the management of a sea war, and that properly managed, a sea war should largely pay for itself out of the spoils of the enemy.'[2]

Thus, the emphasis on the economic advantages of war at sea has been mentioned by historians as one of the main features of the pro-maritime war argument in the period of the War of the Spanish Succession. Nevertheless, it has not been fully explained why exactly maritime war, not least that in Spanish America, was believed to be economically advantageous in this period and what measures were proposed to gain those advantages. To answer these questions, this chapter examines, in detail, the pro-maritime war argument during the War of the Spanish Succession that appeared in contemporary pamphlets, periodicals and proposals for colonial expeditions submitted to the government. This chapter will reveal that there were chiefly two alleged economic advantages of maritime war:

[1] Denman, 'Political Debate', p. 7.

[2] Johnston, 'Parliament and the Navy', p. 14. Johnston regards the identification of the navy with national security as the central tenet of the English belief in naval power. *Ibid.*, pp. 15–16. It is true that the Tory pro-maritime war argument that appeared in the beginning of the war had this defensive character. However, other pro-maritime war arguments often emphasised more positive economic advantages too, such as territorial acquisition and enhancement of trade with the Spanish American colonies, which will be examined in the next chapters.

one closely intertwined with strategic considerations and one connected with commercial consideration, not the least of which was the recovery of the Spanish-American market.

Wealth of Spanish America and Maritime War

According to Laurence Dickey, at least from the beginning of the seventeenth century, one idea began to permeate English political thought: one of the decisive factors in modern warfare was the nation's economic prosperity brought about by trade, a lesson learnt from the successful Dutch revolt against the Habsburgs.[3] This idea can be seen in one pamphlet published in 1711. The author stressed the absolute necessity of trade to all the Europeans not only for their present way of living but also for their defence against the encroachment of ambitious neighbouring countries. 'For', the author claimed, 'War in the late Ages of the World, both offensive and defensive, hath been, and is carried on by Force of Gold and Silver, and whatever be the Virtue of a Nation, if Treasure be wanting, it is in Danger of being overrun by its Neighbours.'[4] Thus, as one anonymous writer wrote in 1701, 'whatever might bee formerly; yett, the Warrs of those times are rather to be waged wth Gold then wth Iron'.[5]

Defoe marvelled at this power of money in modern warfare:

> O Money, Money! What an Influence hast thou on all the Affairs of the quarrelling, huffing Part of this World, as well as upon the most plodding Part of it! Without Thee Parliaments may meet; and Councils sit, and Kings contrive, but it will all be to no Purpose, their Councils and Conclusions can never be put in Execution! Thou raisest Armies, fightest Battles, fittest out Fleets, takest Towns, Kingdoms, and carriest on the great Affairs of the War; All Power, all Policy is supported by Thee, even Vice and Vertue act by thy Assistance, by Thee all the great things in the World are done, Thou makest Heroes, and Crown'st the Actions of the mighty; By *thee*, in one Sence Kings reign, Armies conquer, Princes grow Great, and Nations flourish.[6]

From this idea about the importance of economic power to the nation's ability to conduct war, it was only a short step to another idea that the most effectual means of warfare was to attack the core of the enemy's financial resources by force. As the author of *The Duke of Anjou's Succession Further Consider'd* put it, 'The most speedy and effectual Method to reduce our Enemies is to stop the Fountain of their Money, and obstruct their Commerce.'[7]

3 Laurence Dickey, 'Power, Commerce, and Natural Law in Daniel Defoe's Political Writings, 1698–1707', *A Union for Empire: Political Thought and the British Union of 1707*, ed. John Robertson (Cambridge and Washington, DC, 1995), pp. 67–8.

4 *A Letter to a Member of Parliament, on the Settling a Trade to the South-Sea of America* ([London], [1711]), pp. 7–8.

5 BL, Add MS 70164, p. 7 [no title], 12 December 1701.

6 *Review*, IV, p. 422, no. 106, 16 October 1707.

7 *The Duke of Anjou's Succession Further Consider'd, as to the Danger That May Arise from It to Europe in General; but More Particularly to England* ... (London, 1701), p. 54.

In the case of Spain, it was her American colonies that were regarded as the source of her financial power. Those colonies supplied their mother country with bullion and other colonial produce, such as cacao, sugar and cotton, in exchange for European merchandise shipped from Cadiz. This trade was mainly carried out by two fleets called the *Flotas*, which were bound for New Spain (modern Mexico), and the *Galeones*, which were bound for the Spanish Main and Portobello on the Isthmus of Panama.[8] These Spanish-American colonies, with their mines, were thought to be a source of wealth for Spain and were sometimes described as 'the only Fountain of Gold and Silver'.[9]

It should be stressed that the wealth of Spanish America has further significance during the War of the Spanish Succession. In this war, this was believed to be a financial source not only for Spain but also for France, which became her ally in 1701. It was believed that this very supply of bullion and the merchandise shipped from the colonies by the Spanish silver fleets ('Floating Warehouses of Silver and rich Merchandizes')[10] enabled France to pursue the war. In 1702, the author of the pamphlet entitled *The Dangers of Europe* argued that, because it was evident that men and money were the sinews of war and those who had money would, therefore, never lack men, if the French king was allowed to take control of the Spanish-American colonies, he would 'be thereby enabled to carry on a War with great probability of Success against the rest of Europe'.[11] Likewise, in 1707, the author of *An Account of What Will Do* stated that the mines of Spanish America were 'the Fountain of that Treasure, by which the *French* King is Enable to Carry on his Arbitrary Designs'.[12]

There was an element of truth in this belief. Kamen claimed that the French crown probably gained much more benefit from the Spanish silver fleet than Spain did by several means, such as trade in the Indies, smuggling of bullion via Bayonne and payment for war materials in France by the king of Spain.[13] On the other

[8] Geoffrey J. Walker, *Spanish Politics and Imperial Trade, 1700–1789* (Bloomington and London, 1979), p. 4.

[9] *An Account of What Will Do; or An Equivalent for Thoulon* ... (London, 1707), p. 3. In reality, it is difficult to estimate the degree of financial contribution of the Spanish colonies to their mother country. According to Henry Kamen, shipments of bullion made hardly any significant financial impact on Spanish finances. The only exception is the case of the Spanish silver fleet from New Spain under the escort of a French admiral, the Comte de Château-Renault, which was captured by the Anglo-Dutch fleet under Sir George Rooke in Vigo in 1702, as we will see in Chapter 4. Although the Spanish crown's income increased during the war, this was mainly achieved by exploitation of new sources of revenue, including the Church, confiscation of property of traitors, and impositions. Henry Kamen, *The War of Spanish Succession in Spain, 1700–15* (London, 1969), pp. 215–24.

[10] Josiah Burchett, *Mr. Burchett's Justification of His Naval-memoirs. In Answer to Reflections Made by Col. Lillingston* ... ([London], 1704), p. 152.

[11] *The Dangers of Europe, from the Growing Power of France. With Some Free Thoughts on Remedies .... By the Author of, The Duke of Anjou's Succession Considered* (London, 1702), p. 14.

[12] *An Account of What Will Do*, p. 7.

[13] Kamen, *War of Spanish Succession*, pp. 172–3, 193–5.

hand, Malamud Rikles emphasises that it was private individuals who financed commercial operations with Spanish colonies, rather than the French crown, who profited from the return of bullion.[14] In any case, it was likely that the French economy indeed benefited from the bullion from the Spanish colonies.

This supply of bullion, especially silver, had further significance for England from a financial viewpoint. Although it was common to use bills of exchange as a means of international transfer of credit in those days, it was in bullion that the debts contracted on the bills were ultimately settled. Thanks to her alliance with Spain, France got access to Spanish bullion through payment for war supplies by Spain or through smuggling with the Spanish-American colonies. On the other hand, England was obliged to depend for the settlement of payments entirely upon its trade balance, which was not necessarily favourable in war time.[15] Thus, the French control of this wealth of Spanish America was considered to be a serious threat to the safety and economy of England.

As the author of *Europa Libera* claimed, it was believed that the possession of the wealth of Spanish America would be a decisive factor in the war:

> 'twill not be so much the longest Sword, as the deepest Purse (which are the *American Mines*, litterally and effectually) that will be like to carry it; if a new *War* shall be resolved on: This Fund of Treasure … will be the dead weight to cast the Scale on the *Possessors* side, if there shall be any thing of an equality in other Respects; nay even with some material disadvantage on the *Possessors* side.[16]

Similarly, in 1708, Joseph Addison claimed as follows:

> But if he once engrosses the Commerce of the *Spanish Indies*, whatever Quantities of Gold and Silver stagnate in his private Coffers, there will be still enough to carry on the Circulation among his Subjects. By this means in a short space of time he may heap up greater Wealth than the all the Princes of *Europe* join'd together; and in the present Constitution of the World, Wealth and Power are but different Names for the same thing.[17]

Given this contemporary perception of the importance of the wealth of Spanish America for France, it is little wonder that it was thought necessary to take some

14 Carlos Daniel Malamud Rikles, *Cádiz y Saint Malo en el Comercio Colonial Peruano (1698–1725)* (Cádiz, 1986), p. 114.

15 Dwyryd W. Jones, *War and Economy in the Age of William III and Marlborough* (Oxford, 1988), pp. 39–43. Silver was also necessary for running the East India trade; though, in this trade, purchase of silver in Amsterdam increasingly became more important for the East India Company after 1695. Zahedieh, *Capital and the Colonies*, p. 233.

16 *Europa Libera: or, A Probable Expedient (the like Scarce Ever to be Hop'd for Again) to Restore and Secure the Publick Peace of Europe, for this* … (London, 1703), pp. 2–3. Although this pamphlet was published in 1703, according to its preface, the former part had been already written fourteen or fifteen months prior to the conclusion of the Grand Alliance in September 1701. However, because of the need for the secrecy about similar projects, such as Benbow's expedition, the author held off publishing. *Ibid.*, 'The Preface to the Reader'.

17 Joseph Addison, *The Present State of the War, and the Necessity of an Augmentation, Consider'd* (London, 1708), p. 11.

measures against 'this formidable Conjunction of the Sword of *France* and the Purse of *Spain*'.[18]

Since the wealth from the Spanish-American colonies was regarded as the very source of power for both Spain and France, it was argued that the most effective way to subdue them was by attacking and cutting off supply route.[19] In 1703, the author of *The Dangers of Europe* argued that the war in the West Indies gave England 'a Prospect of most Advantage' and 'an Opportunity of annoying the Enemy in the most sensible part'. According to the author, the French king needed the treasure of the Spanish West Indies more than Spanish forces in Europe to become a 'Universal Monarchy'. By preventing his acquisition of the treasure, 'we cut off the Sinews of his War, and shall quickly oblige him to drop his Sword'.[20]

This attack on the Spanish colonies was expected not only to deprive the enemies of their power, but also to allow England and her allies to use those resources to their own advantage. In 1701, Sir Edward Coke claimed 'the onely way to pinch and stress him will be by the united naval strength of England and Holland to make desultory war on the Spanish Coast and to seize the Spanish mines in the West Indies and to turn that immense treasure against the King of France'.[21] Likewise the author of *Europa Libera* asserted that if England and her allies 'could once turn these Springs of *Treasure* into their Channel, to be a Supply to them, this alone would soon cause the King of *France*'s already blooming Lawrels of Triumph to wither and decay'.[22] As a result, it was believed that this operation

18 *The Duke of Anjou's Succession Considered, as to Its Legality and Consequences* ... 2nd edn (Dublin, 1701), p. 6. Similarly, in 1701, William Paterson warned of the danger of the attempt by the House of Bourbon 'to unite the Purse of the world to the Sword of France'. BL, Add MS 12437, fol. 13v [William Paterson], 'Proposal for settleing on ye Isthmus of Darien...', 1 January 1701.

19 In this book, I focus mainly on expeditions against the Spanish-American colonies, which were more closely associated with the idea of economic advantage of maritime war than those against the French colonies in America were. In the late eighteenth century, the French colonies in America contributed significantly to French foreign commerce and wealth. By the 1780s, as a consequence of the growing economy of Saint Domingue, direct trade with those colonies approached a third of all French trade, and re-export of West Indian produce to other parts of Europe had also risen up to 34.7 per cent by 1787. Michael Duffy, *Soldiers, Sugar, and Seapower: The British Expeditions to the West Indies and the War against Revolutionary War* (Oxford, 1987), pp. 11–13. However, in the early eighteenth century, the French colonies in America were not yet very important economically, and it seems that proposals to attack the French colonies in this period were made mainly out of purely strategic considerations, especially the protection of British West Indian colonies and trade against attack by French privateers, rather than in expectation of economic benefits.

20 *Dangers of Europe*, p. 61.

21 BL, Add MS 69938, fol. 57, Sir Edward Coke to Thomas Coke, 3 February 1700/1. It should be noted that he also emphasised the importance of preventing Flanders from falling into French hands and of securing safety of trade with the Mediterranean, East Indies and the Levant.

22 *Europa Libera*, p. 5.

could enrich England herself. In a proposal submitted in 1711 to the Earl of Oxford, Mitford Crowe, the former governor of Barbados, emphasised the effectiveness of the expedition to the West Indies, and asserted that since the Castilians wholly depended on the West Indian trade, attacking them there was 'the best way to Reduce them and Inrich Our selves'.[23]

It was also maintained that England would be able to cover the war's cost by profit earned through maritime war. This notion of 'self-financing war' was especially noticeable in the early stage of the war. For example, the author of *Proposals for Carrying on an Effectual War in America* insisted that a war in America might be conducted at very little cost 'by managing the Plunder and other Things of that Nature, in such a manner as the proposed War should feed and maintain it self'. The author also expected that, by waging war in a rich country, it might be possible to make the conquered people pay the expenses of the war, and consequently, 'the War will be enabled to support and maintain it self'.[24] Similarly, in *An Essay upon the Present Interest of England*, George Stepney, envoy extraordinary at Vienna, claimed that 'a moderate strength well Managed in *America*' would compensate for the loss caused by interruption of the Spanish trade. Moreover, the wealth which England would acquire by maritime war in Spanish America would not only defray the expense of forces there but also, with good management, might 'go a great way towards the Charge of the whole War'.[25]

Thus it was argued that colonial maritime war was an inexpensive and efficient, or even a profitable means of warfare for England. However, it should be noted that these economic advantages were not necessarily real ones. In fact, the maintenance of naval forces placed a heavy financial burden on the nation. As Hattendorf has pointed out, the chief cause of the war debts incurred during the war were expenses for the navy.[26] But, in the pro-maritime war argument, there was hardly any analysis of the advantages of colonial maritime war from the perspective of cost-effectiveness, and instead the economic advantages of colonial maritime war, which was mainly based on the wishful thinking on the wealth of Spanish America and easiness to capture it, were repeatedly emphasised.

This emphasis on the supposed economic advantages of war at sea was often reinforced by use of historical precedents, in particular, the glorious memory of the reign of Queen Elizabeth I. As N.A.M. Rodger has pointed out, the origin of the 'English national myth about sea-power' can be traced back to the memory of the maritime war against Catholic powers during the reign of Elizabeth,

23 BL, Add MS 70164 [no title], Mitford Crowe to [the Earl of Oxford], 11 June 1711. According to J.G. Davies, Crowe seems to have become acquainted with Jonathan Swift after returning from Barbados in 1710. J.D. Davies, 'Crowe, Mitford (*bap.* 1669, *d.* 1719)', *ODNB*.

24 *Proposals for Carrying on an Effectual War in America, against the French and Spaniards* (London, 1702), p. 8.

25 George Stepney, *An Essay upon the Present Interest of England. To which are Added, the Proceedings of the House of Commons in 1677 …* (London, 1701), pp. 64–5.

26 Hattendorf, *England in the War of the Spanish Succession*, pp. 130–2.

especially in the English cooperation with the French Huguenots in 1560s.[27] This memory of maritime war during the Elizabethan period became a reference point for advocates of maritime war against Spain and her colonies, and pro-maritime war arguments in the succeeding period often alluded to the glorified memory of maritime war conducted by Elizabethan 'sea dogs' such as Drake and Cavendish.

This reference to Elizabethan maritime war was also present in pro-maritime war argument during the War of the Spanish Succession. For example, in the *Review* of 1707, Defoe stressed the profitability of that sort of war by invoking the brilliant successes of Drake's colonial expeditions:

> how often in a War with *Spain*, did Queen *Elizabeth* enrich her self, and furnish not her own Coffers only, but the whole Nation with Treasure, from the *Spanish West-Indies*, how did Sir Francis *Drake* plunder the Coasts, take their Towns, and even load his Vessels Home with their Spoils...[28]

Likewise, when explaining the project of the expedition to the West Indies, the author of *An Account of What Will Do* pointed out 'a Semblance in the Growing Profits that would arise by such an Expedition', and reminded readers of a huge profit made by the expeditions in the Elizabethan period: ''tis undeniable so Immense and valuable Treasure Q. Elizabeth had by it, that she Enrich'd her subjects at home, planted Collonies abroad, and supported the States of *Holland*, when at the lowest Ebb'.[29]

There was also a new feature in references to the Elizabethan maritime war in this period. The memory of Queen Elizabeth's reign was not simply quoted, but was also compared to the reign of Queen Anne, and war against the House of Habsburg at that time was likened to the war against the House of Bourbon – France under the new 'Universal Monarch', Louis XIV.[30] The author of *Europa Libera* drew parallels between the reigns of both monarchs as follows:

> we have more than common Grounds of Hopes at least, that Her Majesties Reign, for *Conduct* and *Success*, and *Love to her People*, may be as a Counterpart of that Prosperous and *true* English *Reign* of Queen *Elizabeth*. And that our Queen *Anne*, as the Chief Instrument, under God, amongst the Allies, may

27 Rodger, 'Queen Elizabeth and the Myth of Sea-Power', 153–4.

28 *Review*, IV, p. 437, no. 110, 25 October 1707.

29 *An Account of What Will Do*, pp. 14–15.

30 Steven Pincus argues that, by the time of Restoration, preoccupation with 'universal monarchy', that is, super-power in Europe, rather than religion, had become the central focus of the political debate in England and in Europe, though the powers criticised for harbouring the ambition of 'universal monarchy' changed according to the political and economic situation from the Habsburgs to the Dutch Republic. After 1670s, it was France under Louis XIV that came to be regarded as a possible candidate for universal monarchy. According to Pincus, for Englishmen after the Restoration, the role of England was to prevent these other powers from fulfilling the ambition of the universal monarchy. Steven Pincus, 'The English Debate over Universal Monarchy', *A Union for Empire: Political Thought and the British Union of 1707*, ed. John Robertson (Cambridge, 1995), pp. 38–54.

> reduce this *French Disturber of* Europe to such a Level, as Queen *Elizabeth* did that Haughty Monarch of *Spain*.[31]

Similarly, *The Dangers of Europe* compared Anne's reign with that of Elizabeth, when England fought against the Habsburgs in cooperation with the Dutch, who were also one of the chief allies in the current war. It argued that England was in a more advantageous position than in the Elizabethan period in terms of her economic and naval power, as well as the prosperity of the West Indian colonies, which would enable the English to take control of the French and Spanish treasure.[32]

The war at sea during the Elizabethan period was not the only historical precedence that was alluded to in pro-maritime war arguments. Other historical examples, such as the West Indian expedition of 1655 dispatched by the Cromwell and raids on the Spanish colonies by buccaneers during the latter half of the seventeenth century, were sometimes mentioned to show the good prospects of colonial maritime war.[33] In 1701, in a pamphlet that recommended fighting war with Spain, Defoe maintained as follows:

> Why should we fancy to our selves, that we shall be less able to make a profit of them now, than in *Oliver*'s time, or in Queen *Elizabeth*'s time. Or why must a Royal fleet be less able to Inure the *Spanyard*, in the *West-Indies*, than *Monsieur Pointi*'s little Squadron, or than a few Buccaneers have often done.[34]

Thus, arguments supporting colonial maritime war were often embroidered with glorified memories of English naval victories in the preceding periods.

As we have seen so far, it was war against the Spanish colonies that was most often advocated in the pro-maritime war argument during the War of the Spanish Succession. However, it should be noted that other ways of deploying British naval force were proposed during the war. In *Reasons for a War with France and Spain*, one anonymous author suggested an attempt on the French colonies as an alternative to those in the Spanish West Indies. However, the author argued that unlike the reign of Queen Elizabeth and Cromwell's days, when England 'made what Profit we pleas'd of Poor *Jack Spaniard*', such conquest of the enemy

31 *Europa Libera*, p. 58.

32 *Dangers of Europe*, p. 67.

33 Even the Tory *Examiner* admitted the achievements of the navy during the Civil War to a certain extent: 'If I were to recommend even to them, any one Principle from the Conduct of their *Favourite Times* in *Forty One*, it should be this, of providing well for the Honour and Strength of the *British Navy*.' *Examiner*, IV, no. 39, 19 October 1713. However, compared with the widely accepted memory of the Elizabethan period, it seems to have been far less popular as a historical precedent to be invoked.

34 Daniel Defoe, *Reasons against a War with France, or an Argument Shewing that the French King's Owning the Prince of Wales as King of England, Scotland and Ireland; is no Sufficient Ground of a War* (London, 1701), p. 28. As is seen here, an attack on Cartagena by Pointis with *flibustiers* [French buccaneers] in April 1697 was also sometimes referred to as a successful operation against the Spanish colonies.

colonies in America would not be as easy as was talked of, because France would try to hinder any such attempt. Therefore, he proposed attacking the French at home so that they could not send their fleet abroad and obstruct the English design.[35]

Also, in addition to attacks on Spanish-American colonies, the author of *The Dangers of Europe* suggested a descent on the French coast, a revival of a similar plan proposed during the Nine Years War. The author claimed that frequent descents on the French coast from the Channel would put pressure on France and oblige them to keep part of their fleet in the Channel; this would hinder French naval operations in the Mediterranean and the West Indies and their land operations in the Netherlands, Germany and Italy. The author also recommended attacks on the Mediterranean side of the French coast, which could induce revolt in Italy, interrupt French commerce in that region, protect English trade there and relieve the emperor's military burden in Italy.[36]

Thus, some alternative ways of using naval force were also proposed during the war, though they were not always thought incompatible with the West Indian operations. From a strategic viewpoint, these alternatives might be sounder plans than expeditions against Spanish America. However, maritime war in Spanish America was depicted as the most economically advantageous means of warfare, because it was believed that such operations could strike at the heart of enemy financial resources. Then, what means were proposed to achieve this objective? We shall examine them next.

Attacking the Enemy's Financial Resources

Capture of Spanish Silver Fleets

During the War of the Spanish Succession, two options were chiefly considered for depriving the enemy of their means of financing the war: the capture of Spanish silver fleets and colonial expeditions. The first means, the capture of silver fleets that conveyed bullion from the Spanish colonies, was regarded as a direct way to bring England ready money that would help to solve her financial problem as well as destroy her enemy's economic power.

The interception of incoming Spanish silver fleets, especially in the Azores, had already been proposed during the Elizabethan period, though it was difficult to achieve at that time owing to the existence of a strong Spanish fleet in European waters that could have been used for invading England as well as protecting the silver fleet.[37] By the early eighteenth century, however, England was in a far more advantageous position to carry out this operation because of two factors: possession of colonies in the West Indies and superiority over Spain in naval power both in

[35] *Reasons for a War with France and Spain, wherein Some Late Arguments against It are Consider'd* (London, 1702), pp. 30–1.

[36] *Dangers of Europe*, p. 63.

[37] R.B. Wernham, 'Elizabethan War Strategy', *Elizabethan Government and Society*, ed. S.T. Bindoff et al. (London, 1961), pp. 357–9.

Europe and America. Under these more favourable conditions, during the period of the War of the Spanish Succession, interception was attempted on the both side of the Atlantic.[38]

At the beginning of the war, there was an expectation that fortunes might be made at a stroke by capturing the silver fleet and that the national debt could be reduced accordingly. In a poem entitled 'The Spanish Descent', with a touch of irony, Daniel Defoe referred to such an expectation, which the English had of the Cadiz expedition of 1702:

> Other's describe the Castle and *Puntalls*
> And tell how easie 'tis to Conquer *Cales*;
> Wisely propose to let the Silver come,
> And help to Pay the Nation's Debts at Home.
> But still they count the Spoils without the Cost,
> And still the News comes faster than the Post.[39]

Capture of the Spanish silver fleet by Sir George Rooke at Vigo, Spain, in October 1702 was to a certain extent the realisation of this dream. The congratulatory speech in the House of Commons delivered by Speaker Robert Harley encapsulated the contemporary perception of the economic advantages of taking a Spanish silver fleet:

> you have not only Spoiled our enemies, but you have also inriched your own Country; Common Victories bring terror to the conquered, but you have brought Destruction upon them, & additional Strength to England: France had endeavoured to support its Ambition by the Riches of India; your Success, Sir, hath only left them the Burden of Spain, & stripp'd them of the ascistance of it: The Wealth of Spain & Ships of France are by this Victory brought over to our juster Cause.[40]

In the middle stage of the war, there was still strong support for this policy. In the *Review* of October 1707, Defoe encouraged readers to take the fleet as a 'prize': 'Now, Gentlemen, here is a Booty worth taking, here is a Prize worth Fetching.' He claimed that the capture would 'save *England* the Trouble of raising next Year, about six Millions and a half, *Sterling*' and at the same time, would give 'a blow superior to *Hockstedt* or *Rammillies*' to France and Spain. He went on to say 'it would be a perfect Amputation of Members to their whole Body, cutting the Sinews of both their Arms'.[41]

This policy got a further boost from another capture of the silver fleet by Sir Charles Wager in 28 May 1708. Upon hearing this news, the *Observator* acclaimed this capture as 'a Wound to the French King, in the most sensible Part'. According

38 Hattendorf, *England in the War of the Spanish Succession*, pp. 185–6.

39 Daniel Defoe 'The Spanish Descent' (December [?] 1702), *Poems on Affairs of State: Augustan Political Verse 1660–1714*, VI 1697–1704, ed. Frank H. Ellis (New Haven and London, 1970), p. 470.

40 Portland Papers [Microfilm], PO/VOL XVII, fol. 50v, 'Minutes of proceedings in the House of Commons on thanks being given to Sir George Rooke', 21 November 1702.

41 *Review*, IV, p. 422, no. 106, 16 October 1707.

to the *Observator*, ''tis so much Money lost to the Enemy, and so much gain'd by us; so that it affects him doubly, besides the Disrepute it brings to his Affairs'. The *Observator* hoped that this success would encourage merchants and adventurers to launch a further project to harass the enemy and to enlarge trade with the Spanish colonies both in the Caribbean and the Pacific.[42] Likewise, in the *Review* of July 1708, in his analysis of the war situation, Defoe maintained that want of money and the delayed arrival of the galleons thwarted all the prospect of the Spaniards and their plans. Then he urged on the readers: 'Would you have Victory, then you have nothing to do but go fetch home the Galeons, and you fetch Victory; get but their Silver, you defeat all their Projects, and prevent all their Conquests', by which Britain would recover Spain in two years, while France could not support Spain and Spain could not defend herself. He asserted, 'the Money is the Victory, and without you do nothing'.[43]

Another capture of a silver fleet was made in December 1709 by Captain Woodes Rogers, a Bristol privateer, during his circumnavigation between 1708 and 1711. In *The Conduct of the Allies*, published in 1711, with the intention of criticising neglect of naval operations by the former ministry and winning support for a similar plan by the navy, Jonathan Swift referred to Rogers' voyage as an exceptional attempt to hinder the profitable French trade with Peru. He argued that Rogers and his crew, 'who inflamed by a true Spirit of Courage and Industry', fitted out a few ships at their own cost, succeeded in taking one of the Manila galleons, and returned with some wealth, 'to shew us what might have been done with the like Management, by a publick Undertaking'.[44]

Various methods were proposed to increase the chance of capture. Defoe recommended waiting in ambush in the latitude in which the fleet usually arrived, instead of dispatching forces to Havana or plying the ocean in search of the fleet.[45] On the other hand, one pamphleteer believed that the Bahamas, which was on the way home for Spanish treasure fleets, was a suitable place for such interception. He lamented that England did not send a squadron there at the beginning of the war, which, he claimed, might have prevented the silver plate from being unloaded and would have been far more advantageous than Sir George Rooke's accidental encounter with the silver fleet at Vigo in October 1702.[46] Thus, capturing the silver fleet was proposed as a direct way to obtain the wealth of Spanish America, and several successes raised the hopes of further captures. However, just as in a plan for naval expeditions which we see next, supporters of this tactics seem to have been somewhat over-optimistic about its prospect. When Sir Charles Wager failed to intercept a *flota* escorted by the squadron of Admiral Gaztañeta in 1727, he

42 *Observator*, no. 49, 4 August 1708.

43 *Review*, V, p. 170, no. 43, 6 July 1708.

44 Jonathan Swift, *The Conduct of the Allies, and of the Late Ministry, in Beginning and Carrying on the Present War* (London, 1711), p. 31.

45 *Review*, IV, p. 422, no. 106, 16 October 1707.

46 *An Inquiry into the Causes of Our Naval Miscarriages: with Some Thoughts on the Interest of This Nation as to a Naval War…*, 2nd edn (London, 1707), p. vi.

grumbled that people generally supposed that intercepting ships at sea was as easy 'as to stop a Coach at the end of a Street'.[47]

Colonial Expeditions

Another means that the supporters of pro-maritime war argument often proposed to deprive the enemy of its financial resources was to send expeditions to Spanish America. The view that such expeditions had economic advantages was well expressed in the Queen's instruction of 9 July 1702 to Sir David Mitchell, who was negotiating with the Grand Pensionary Heinsius of the Netherlands as the Admiralty's representative, to ask for assistance with a West Indian expedition:

> wee think an Attempt on the Spanish West Indies to be of very great importance both for Our Common Interest and in prejudice of our Enemys, by depriving them of the supply of money and plate to wch they seem to rely on for the Support of Warr, and that this is a probable means of inducing the Spaniards in other parts of the world to submit to the House of Austria.[48]

This support for Spanish-American expeditions continued to exist throughout the war. In August 1708, the *Observator* argued that a naval war in the West Indies would be the most effectual and speedy way to rescue the Spanish monarchy from French hands, because if England 'could once be Masters of the *French* King's Purse, he must of Course drop his Sword'.[49] Also in the *Review* of January 1711, in response to the public's pessimistic view of the war situation after the British defeat in Spain in December of the previous year, Defoe claimed, '*the War is but now begun*'. He doubted that Britain could obtain peace with the restitution of the Spanish monarchy through war in Spain, and instead supported an expedition to the Spanish West Indies. He lamented that British forces had not been employed there to seize the centres of Spanish-American commerce, such as Havana and Cartagena, and to stop the enemy's source of money, which would have subdued France and Spain much earlier.[50]

In this colonial maritime war, it was expected that Jamaican privateers could be an auxiliary force. In 1702, the author of *Proposals for Carrying on an Effectual War in America* proposed the offer of a general pardon to the buccaneers so that they could be used as an auxiliary force for Spanish-American expeditions.[51] Likewise, considering Britain's limited manpower and financial resources for these expeditions, one Captain Martin Laywike proposed seeking the assistance of these

47 Ch (H) MSS Correspondence 1, 1410, fol. 1v, Wager to Sir Robert Walpole, 14 March 1726/7.

48 FH MSS 275, p. 48, Instruction for Sir David Mitchell, 9 July 1702.

49 *Observator*, no. 49, 4 August 1708.

50 *Review*, VII, pp. 510–11, no. 128, 18 January 1711. As we shall see in Chapter 4, at that time, the Harley ministry planned an Anglo-Dutch joint expedition to Spanish America, though it did not materialise in the end owing to the Dutch refusal to join. It is possible that Defoe wrote this article to support the plan for his patron, Harley.

51 *Proposals for Carrying on an Effectual War in America*, p. 14. The author estimated their number at one thousand.

buccaneers, who were versed in the country and acclimatised to that region, and were dreaded by the Spaniards. He expected that, if pardon was given, they would join with a tribe of the Native Americans under 'Sachem Dego' in order to take the mines out of the hands of the French and Spaniards, and also help the English to secure the trade to Darien [modern Panama] and Madagascar.[52] Thus, supporters of the pro-maritime war policy claimed that Spanish-American expeditions, with the assistance of Jamaican privateers, could strike a fatal blow to the enemy by destroying the source of wealth.

It should be noted, however, that there was also strong criticism against colonial expeditions from a strategic viewpoint. The Duke of Marlborough, who commanded land forces in Flanders and Germany, consistently denounced the projects, which could deprive him of his land forces. From the early stage of the war, he questioned the idea of the expeditions and regarded it as 'not reasonable'.[53] Again in 1710, in a letter to Godolphin, he emphasised the uselessness of such expeditions, learnt from his past experiences, and maintained, 'it is next to impossible that this can end in anything but an expence to make you uneasy, the ruining of the redgiments, and the encreasing the dept [i.e. debt] of the Ordenance'.[54]

Harsh criticism also came from naval experts, such as Josiah Burchett, secretary of the Board of Admiralty. He deplored the 'great Charge' and 'little benefit' of the foreign expeditions, especially those to the West Indies. He was dismissive of almost all the operations that had been carried out there so far, such as Sir Francis Wheeler's expedition in 1693, and the unsuccessful chase of Baron de Pointis' French fleet by Rear-Admiral John Nevill in 1697. He went so far as to say, 'I cannot recollect that one beneficial Service hath been performed in *America* for many Years past, either by our Squadrons or Land-Forces; at least not any that hath in any measure been answerable to the Expence, and other Misfortunes.' Although he recognised the necessity of colonial defence and admitted that several ships should be stationed in the colonies for that purpose, he preferred further fortification of the colonies as a more effective means of defence.[55] Thus, while the support for colonial expeditions recurrently appeared during the war, there was also strong criticism levelled at the plans.

[52] BL, Add MS 70164, Captain Martin Laywike, 'An Essay to demonstrate an Easie Aquisition of the Spanish West India trade to the English Govenrment…', 10 November 1702 [not foliated]. 'Sachem Dego' seems to refer to Diego, who was one of the newly emerging leaders of the Tule, indigenous people living there, and a governor of the Gulf of Urabá. In 1698, Diego had a meeting with Richard Long, an English captain who visited the gulf to gain a foothold in the region for England, though, in February 1699, Diego also signed a treaty with the Scottish, who tried to establish a new colony there. James S. Barbour, *A History of William Paterson and the Darien Company* (Edinburgh and London, 1907), p. 103. Ignacio Gallup-Diaz, *The Door of the Seas and Key to the Universe: Indian Politics and Imperial Rivalry in the Darién, 1640–1750* (New York, 2004), pp. 114–16.

[53] *Marlborough–Godolphin Correspondence*, I, no. 377, p. 370, Marlborough to Godolphin, 8/19 September 1704.

[54] *Ibid.*, III, no. 1524, p. 1485, Marlborough to Godolphin, 8/19 May 1710.

[55] Burchett, *Mr. Burchett's Justification of His Naval-memoirs*, pp. 153–4.

Persuasion of the Spanish Colonists

As we have seen so far, in the pro-maritime war argument, two primary measures were proposed to deprive the enemy of the wealth of Spanish America: interception of the silver fleet and colonial expeditions. In addition, it was also considered possible to persuade the Spanish colonists to defect from France and Philip V, the French candidate for the Spanish crown, and come over to the side of Archduke Charles ('Charles III'), the Austrian candidate. It is worth noting that, especially in the early stage of the war, the Spaniards were regarded as potential supporters of Archduke Charles; it was argued that they were suffering from French rule and keen to be liberated from it, and that an expeditionary force sent by England could be a godsend to them.[56] For example, in answer to the objection that the expedition to Spanish America might create antipathy among the Spaniards, the author of *Europa Libera* asserted that they could be rescued from the yoke of France only by such an expedition by the emperor and the allies, who alone were 'able to give *Liberty*, and *Enfranchise* their *Captive Monarchy*'. If England and Holland could make conquests in the West Indies, they could be '*Guarrantees* to the *Spaniards*', protecting the rest of their monarchy from being absorbed into France or any other country. The author also claimed that there was still enough room and territory in Spanish America for both the Spaniards and the allies, because that region only had a small population in proportion to its area.[57]

Encouraged by such an optimistic view, there was an expectation that the Spanish colonists might voluntarily come to help the English operations in Spanish America. It was expected that they might turn over silver fleets to England to have the fleets convoyed, just as they did to France at the beginning of the war. In 1707, *An Inquiry into the Causes of Our Naval Miscarriages* claimed that there was no reason 'why we should not rather be intrusted to convey and bring home their plate, to be made use of for our mutual Wealth and Defence, than that it should be suffered to come under the *French* King's Management, to be made use of against us both'.[58]

It was also believed that, if help was given, the Spaniards might stand up for the House of Austria and fight with the allies.[59] This idea was well represented in

56 This belief was not completely unfounded. The growing influence of France upon Spanish colonial trade made relations tense between the two countries. In August 1706, there was even a skirmish between them in Havana. *Ibid.*, p. 32. This Spanish colonists' discontent with the advance of the French can be glimpsed from the extract of Spanish letters sent by Charles Wager, whose original was intercepted by Jamaican privateers. BL, Add MS 61583, fols 210–11, 'Extract of some Spanish letters from Wager, June–July 1708'. Also in the mother country, anti-French sentiment began to grow after the withdrawal of French troops from the Iberian Peninsula in 1709. Kamen, *War of Spanish Succession*, pp. 20–1.

57 *Europa Libera*, pp. 33–6.

58 *An Inquiry into the Causes of Our Naval Miscarriages*, p. 24.

59 At the beginning of the war, Habsburg agents actually attempted to win over the colonists in Venezuela and Mexico to the side of 'Charles III'. Also, there were some foreign Jesuits who were sympathetic to the Habsburg cause and established contacts with the Dutch

instructions to the Earl of Peterborough, who was appointed as captain general and commander in chief of the forces for the West Indian expedition planned between 1702 and 1703. The instructions stated that the Spaniards who were concerned about French rule were eager to free themselves from 'the Tyranny and apprehension of a rival Nation'. Therefore, Peterborough was directed to attempt to draw off the Spaniards from the French interest 'by fair means and perswasion', and to induce them to declare for the emperor and join the allies by offering them assurance of protection and advantages. At the same time, however, the option of using force was kept open. The instruction also directed him to 'employ Our Arms under your Command to reduce them by force, annoying and destroying them pursuant to the Law of Arms', if persuasion failed.[60]

Internal conflict in the Spanish colonies was also regarded as exploitable asset for England. John Pullen, ex-governor of Bermuda, suggested making use of a conflict between the Spaniards who came from the mother country and the 'Criollos', colonial-born Spaniards, who were frustrated at their exclusion from any military post or civil office. Pullen claimed that 'Charles III' could easily win the support of the latter, by promising them an equal share in the administration, and privileges.[61] On the other hand, Lionel Wafer, a surgeon and ex-buccaneer with experience of living with the Cuna Indians in Panama, expected to win the support of Native Americans in Chile who were 'inveterate Enemies' of the Spaniards, if England could establish a settlement there.[62] Likewise, the author of *Europa Libera* expected that England would be assisted by both Spanish colonists and the Native Americans, since the former were suffering from discrimination in terms of offices in the government, and the latter was seeking revenge for the cruel treatment that their ancestors received from the Spaniards.[63]

contrabandists. However, the majority of the colonial administrators were loyal to Philip V. John Lynch, *Bourbon Spain, 1700–1808* (Oxford, 1989), pp. 52–4. Linda M. Rupert, 'Contraband Trade and the Shaping of Colonial Societies in Curaçao and Tierra Firme', *Itinerario* 30, issue 3 (2006), 42–3.

60 FH MSS 275, p. 251, 'INSTRUCTIONS for Our right trusty & right wellbeloved Cousin Charles Earl of Peterborough & Monmouth…', 17 December 1702.

61 BL, Add MS 70311, fols 315v–316 [John Pullen], 'Memo on the West India expedition and South Sea trade' [n.d., but c. 1711].

62 BL, Add MS 70163, fol. 231, Lionel Wafer, 'An account of the places and Ports which are most proper to make a settlement, and also which are not, in the South Sea' [n.d.]. For another example of the expectation of assistance from the native populations, see BL, Add MS 28140, fol. 29v, 'An Account of ye Places which ye Duke and Dutchess anchor'd at in ye South Seas wrote by Edw: Cook, Commander of ye Marquess Prize' [n.d., but c. 1711].

63 *Europa Libera*, pp. 21–2. This idea of gaining support from various groups within Spanish America, such as the Native Americans, *cimarones* (escaped slaves) and Criollos, had a long history. Its origin can be traced back to the Elizabethan period; thereafter, it recurrently appeared, with some variations as a possible candidate for an ally. In 1584, in his *Discourse of Western Planting*, the younger Richard Hakluyt mentioned the possibility of the alliance with the indigenous populations as well as with *cimarones*. The expectation of gaining assistance from indigenous populations also appeared in the 1620s. Furthermore, in his proposal concerning a Spanish American expedition submitted to John Thurloe in 1654,

As we have seen, there were two main ways of depriving the enemy of the wealth of Spanish America by force: intercepting silver fleets and sending military expeditions. In addition, especially during the early stage of the war, persuading Spanish colonists to come over to the allies' side or fomenting revolts in their colonies were also considered as possible options to take away the financial resources of the enemy without direct exertion of force. As we shall see in Chapter 4, these options were actually exercised during the War of the Spanish Succession, albeit with mixed results

Struggle over Spanish-American Trade

As we have seen, maritime war in Spanish America was regarded as an effective means to subdue the enemy by attacking its source of wealth. However, in addition to economic advantages closely connected with strategic considerations, there was another alleged economic advantage that colonial maritime war – especially colonial expeditions against Spanish America – was believed to possess.

One of the motivations of colonial expeditions was acquisition of the wealth of Spanish America in the form of bullion and other colonial produce. The author of *Proposals for Carrying on an Effectual War in America* claimed, 'The *Spaniards* have possess'd the Fountains of Gold and Silver long enough, 'tis high time they shou'd pass into the Hands of the *English*.'[64] He explained that success in American expeditions would enrich England, making her mistress of gold and silver mines as well as other colonial produce, such as sugar, cocoa, cotton and indigo. Moreover it was expected that all merchant ships would be built in North America or with timber from there, while English oak could be kept for building men of war.[65]

In addition to these direct gains, however, there was another economic incentive to the colonial expeditions that was more important for the long-term interest of the British economy: expectation of the recovery of the trade with Spanish colonies. This expectation should be understood against the background of growth of French influence on the trade with the Spanish colonies, especially those on the coast of the South Sea (i.e. the Pacific Ocean).

As explained in Chapter 1, by the end of the seventeenth century, England had established two channels for trade with Spanish-American colonies. The first was the trade through Cadiz in Spain.[66] Spain was significant for England as a market

Thomas Gage, one of Cromwell's main advisers, suggested that England should make use of the various disaffected groups in the Spanish colonies. This idea was still present in the late 1730s. Andrews, *Trade, Plunder and Settlement*, p. 204; Venning, *Cromwellian Foreign Policy*, pp. 78–9; John C. Appleby, 'An Association for the West Indies? English Plans for a West India Company 1621–29', *Journal of Imperial and Commonwealth History* 15, no. 3 (May 1987), 219–20, 223; Woodfine, *Britannia's Glories*, pp. 176–7.

64 *Proposals for Carrying on an Effectual War in America*, pp. 6–7.

65 *Ibid.*, p. 24.

66 For the trade with Spain, see Jean O. McLachlan, *Trade and Peace with Old Spain 1667–1750: A Study of Commerce on Anglo-Spanish Diplomacy in the First Half of the Eighteenth Century* (Cambridge, 1940), Chapter 1.

for English staples, such as woollens, fish, lead and tin, and as a source for raw material, such as wool and Castile soap. It was also important as a channel of bullion, which could be obtained at Cadiz through the sale of merchandise there or through trade with Spanish colonies under the names of Spanish merchants.

The importance of the Spanish trade was often emphasised by contemporaries. In 1702, Solomon Merrett, a supporter of the Newfoundland fishery, stated that trade with Spain was 'the Only way to keep our Woollen Manufactury and ffishery in Use, and to Vend ye Same'.[67] Likewise, the author of one tract, which lamented the scarcity of bullion and criticised war in Germany, claimed that, even when Britain conquered all Flanders, 'they would not take of from us soe much of our Manufactoryes, as halfe the Kindome of Spain will, neither will they returne us any Bullion for it, but such goods p[er]haps as we have noe need of'.[68]

The other important channel was the clandestine trade via the English West Indian colonies, particularly Jamaica, and this had been the only way to trade directly with the Spanish colonies until 1713. As explained in Chapter 1, after Jamaica was captured by England in 1655, it rapidly became a thriving centre of smuggling to and from Spanish colonies as well as a base of buccaneers.[69] One of its main businesses was the slave trade, which started in the 1660s and had become an important branch of the trade of the island by the 1680s. European and Mediterranean goods, such as linen and silk, and provisions from North American colonies, especially flour, also constituted other important exports in the trade. In return, Jamaica received various commodities, such as hides, cattle and logwood. However, the most important and most coveted return was, as in the case of trade via Cadiz, silver coin and bullion, which was in turn exported to England and North American colonies.

Thus, for England, trade with the Spanish colonies was 'both the Life of our Manufactures, and the Fountain of our Bullion'.[70] Although England was not permitted direct trade, she had been able to receive a slice of the wealth of the Spanish empire through the above two channels. At the turn of the eighteenth century, however, England faced the emergence of a new rival, France.

Even before the declaration of war, the possibility of the accession of the Bourbon king to the Spanish throne had already caused apprehension among the English

[67] TNA, CO194/2, no. 55, p. 206, Solomon Merrett to Board of Trade, 29 January 1701/2. However, Merrett himself was optimistic that the trade could be carried on in spite of the war under the guise of neutral ships, because the war would not be so directly targeted at the Spaniards as the French, and because the trade was beneficial for both England and Spain.

[68] BL, Add MS 70277, p. 3, 'The Countrey mans Complaint', 9 April 1709.

[69] For the trade with the Spanish colonies through Jamaica, see Curtis Nettels, 'England and Spanish-American Trade, 1680–1715', *JMH* 3 (1931), 1–32; Zahedieh, 'Merchants of Port Royal', 570–93; G.V. Scammell, '"A Very Profitable and Advantageous Trade": British Smuggling in the Iberian Americas circa 1500–1750', *Itinerario* 24, issue 3–4 (2000), 135–72.

[70] *Review*, IV, p. 438, no. 110, 25 October 1707.

over a French monopoly of Spanish colonial trade.[71] The French had been one of the main participants in Spanish-American trade via Cadiz, as well as the English and the Dutch. However, by the end of the seventeenth century, the situation surrounding the trade via Cadiz had deteriorated owing to the Spanish government's weakening control on her colonies, growing direct trade with the Spanish colonies by foreign interlopers, such as the Dutch and English, and decline in trade with the Spanish silver fleet, whose voyages became more prolonged and less frequent. These changes persuaded French merchants, financiers and some of the leading ministers, such as the Marquis de Seignelay and Comte de Pontchartrain, to turn their attention to direct penetration into Spanish America, either by trade or by force, as a new channel to gain bullion.[72]

After the Nine Years War ended in 1697, the French attempts to open a direct trade with Spanish America gained momentum. In particular, the merchants of St Malo, who had to cease privateering after the Peace of Ryswick and who needed to find a new use for its capital, vessels and labour, were enthusiastic about this direct trade with the Spanish colonies, especially those on the Pacific coast.[73] In August 1698, with the backing of the Comte de Pontchartrain, who aimed to increase French influence in the Spanish-American trade, Noël Danican de L'Epine, one of the leading merchants of St Malo, created the company to trade with the Pacific coast of South America, with Jean Jourdan de Grocey of Paris. Subsequently, in December, Jacques de Beauchesne-Gouin, a Malouin privateer-entrepreneur, set sail from La Rochelle for the Pacific coast of Spanish America to trade with the Spanish colonies there. Although this was not necessarily commercially successful, it demonstrated the possibility of future success in the trade.[74]

By the beginning of the eighteenth century, St Malo's merchants had vigorously participated in the direct Spanish-American trade. The merchants of St Malo together with those of other ports in Brittany soon came to play a leading role in the trade between 1701 and 1716, the heyday of this trade. The investment made by them accounted for nearly three-quarters of the entire investment made by the French merchants in the trade during that period.[75] Furthermore, in 1701, French merchants obtained a legal access to the Spanish-American market. In August of that year, the French Guinea Company (Compagnie de Guinée) took over the

71 Walker, *Spanish Politics and Imperial Trade*, pp. 19–20.

72 Malamud Rikles, *Cádiz y Saint Malo*, pp. 97–8; Andreé Lespagnol, *Messieurs de Saint Malo: Une Élite Negociante au Temps de Louis XIV*, II (Rennes, 1997), pp. 496–506.

73 Malamud Rikles, *Cádiz y Saint Malo*, p. 56; Lespagnol, *Messieurs de Saint Malo*, II, pp. 518–19.

74 Pritchard, *In Search of Empire*, pp. 362–3; Charles Frostin, 'Les Ponchartrain et la Pénétration Commercial Française en Amérique Espagnole (1690–1715)', *Revue Historique*, no. 498 (Avril–Juin 1971), 320–2. In France, before Beauchesne's voyage, Jean Baptiste de Gennes, a naval officer, had already attempted a similar trading voyage to the Pacific in 1695–97. Although this voyage ended in total failure, it provided valuable information about the difficulties in navigating into that region. John Dunmore, *French Explorers in the Pacific: I. The Eighteenth Century* (Oxford, 1965), pp. 10–11.

75 Lespagnol, *Messieurs de Saint Malo*, II, p. 555.

Asiento, the contract for the exclusive supply of slaves to Spanish colonies, from the Portuguese Cacheu Company.[76]

The possible French accession to the Spanish throne and the increasing presence of the French in Spanish-American market posed a serious threat to the English economy. It not only endangered English trade to Spanish America but also her trade with other regions, such as Old Spain, the Netherlands, the Mediterranean and the Levant.[77] It also had an impact on England's financial system. About 1711, John Pullen, ex-governor of Bermuda, lamented that the French dominance in the Spanish-American market in both the Caribbean and in the Pacific caused severe damage to the Spanish-American trade that had been conducted by British merchants. According to Pullen, it was this trade that enabled England to raise immense sums of money, which in turn made it possible for her to fight the last war and this war so far. However, he argued, 'now wee are spending upon the Capitall Stock which all wise men know will soon be exhausted if wee cann't find a means of retrieveing Our lost trade to Peru, and New Spaine, and Ruineing that of the French in those parts'.[78] The financial ramification of the loss of the Spanish-American trade was felt in England in a quite noticeable way: shortage of coin. In 1706, James Vernon grumbled, 'money is so scarce that unless a trade be opened with the Spanish West Indies, and that we can have bullion, we shall be reduced to barter comoditys for want of current coine in the market to sell them with'.[79]

Moreover, in a wider European context, this French advance in Spanish colonial trade clashed with the commercial interests of the other countries as well as that of England. According to Stanley and Barbara Stein, the struggle over Spanish-American market was fought between two groups. One was constituted of a Catalan and Anglo-Dutch interest, in alliance with Spanish privilege holders who supported the Austrian Habsburgs. The other group was made up of an Aragonese, Navarresse and Lower Andalusian faction that hoped to protect and carry on colonial trade in collaboration with France. For the Anglo-Dutch merchants who had been conducting trade, not least slave trade, with Spanish-American colonies through their West Indian colonies as well as through Cadiz, the ascendance of the French interests at Madrid caused serious concern, and the award of the Asiento to the French Guinea Company confirmed their fear that the French might dominate the Spanish-American trade at the expense of the English and the Dutch.[80]

76 The Earl of Manchester, ambassador-extraordinary to Paris at that time, reported projects for several joint ventures in the trade to Spanish America by France and Spain. BL, Add MS 34348, fol. 128v, Copy of a letter from the Earl of Manchester to Secretary Vernon, 13 July 1701.

77 McLachlan, *Trade and Peace with Old Spain*, pp. 39–42.

78 BL, Add MS 70311, fols 305–306v [John Pullen], 'Memo on the West India expedition and South Sea trade' [n.d., but c. 1711].

79 BL, Add MS 40776, fol. 11, James Vernon to the Duke of Shrewsbury, 28 October 1706.

80 Stanley J. Stein, and Barbara H. Stein, *Silver, Trade, and War: Spain and America in the Making of Early Modern Europe* (Baltimore and London, 2000), pp. 119–21.

Considering the wide repercussions that the loss of Spanish-American market could cause, it was no wonder that the recovery of trade with Spanish America became a matter of great importance for England and that colonial maritime war was thought an effective way to achieve it. In August 1708, the *Observator* argued that a naval war in the West Indies would be 'the best and speediest Way for us to retrieve our Trade, in which we have suffer'd so much by a tedious and expensive War'.[81] Thus, Spanish-American expeditions were not only aimed at inflicting direct damage on the enemy source of power. The control of trade with Spanish colonies and access to the Spanish-American market was also at stake.

There were two ways in which an expeditionary force was expected to contribute to the recovery of the Spanish-American trade. The first was to carry merchandise on board and coerce the Spanish colonists to trade, tactics that had often been adopted by privateers in the face of blunt refusal by the Spanish authorities to condone direct trade with their colonies by foreigners. For example, in explaining the plan of trading to the South Sea, one Dummer proposed that the first enterprise on trade should be done 'more By Power, than Charge of Comoditys', considering a possible glut of French goods, and the necessity of avoiding the risk of losing too many commodities on the first voyage, which was usually accompanied by many accidents.[82] An expeditionary force could maintain the option of attacking Spanish colonies in case trade proved to be unsuccessful. This practice was not uncommon in the history of the Caribbean. As Nuala Zahedieh states, in the Caribbean, commerce and plunder had been long interchangeable, and unsuccessful trading ventures often turned into a piratical raid.[83]

In the *Review* of October of 1707, Defoe urged his readers that, instead of complaining about the loss of Spanish trade, they should make the 'Attempt both of War and Trade' with the assistance of the Royal Navy. He believed that a squadron of ten or twelve well-armed ships would have driven the French out of the South Seas, and have plundered rich Spanish cities. On the other hand, if these ships had carried English goods, the Spanish colonists, who in their hearts desired to trade with the English at cheaper prices, would have happily agreed to trade on favourable terms under the protection of English ships provided the English had declared freedom of trade, which would also solve the scarcity of bullion.[84]

This 'trade by force', however, was just a temporary measure. For a more stable and long-lasting trade with Spanish colonies, it was often proposed that expeditionary forces should seize a part of Spanish America in order to control the Spanish-American trade or to use them as trading bases. The *Observator* of 25 October 1707 claimed that dispatch of a strong squadron to the West Indies under a brave and trustworthy admiral was 'the speediest Way to ruin our common

[81] *Observator*, no. 49, 4 August 1708.
[82] BL, Add MS 70163, fol. 175v [Edmund?] Dummer to [Robert Harley?], 20 June 1711.
[83] Zahedieh, 'Merchants of Port Royal', 587.
[84] *Review*, IV, p. 438, no. 110, 25 October 1707.

Enemy, to fill us with Money, and to raise our sinking Trade'. Then he mentioned seizure of part of Spanish America as one of the main benefits that such expeditions could bring. The *Observator* stated, 'This would effectually secure us from all those Dangers and Vexations that our Traders to the *Spanish West Indies* were formerly subject to.'[85]

Several regions were proposed as possible targets for such expeditions. Among them was Havana. One anonymous writer proposed capturing this place as well as Gibraltar, on the ground of its geographical advantage in controlling the colonial trade and the security of other English colonies. As Havana was the rendezvous of all Spanish ships from most parts of Spanish America, the writer claimed, 'if this Port were in possession of ye English, & that passage well guarded, it would putt a Totall stopp to trade from Spaine to the Kingdome of Peru & Mexico, & consequently make those People freely traffick with us & other Europeans'. Furthermore, possession of the port would be useful for the security of English West Indian colonies and North American colonies, particularly Carolina.[86] Another anonymous writer also advocated capture of Havana as well as St Augustine (San Agustin) because of its strategic value. As both were conveniently situated to take control over the 'Gulf of Florida' (i.e. the Florida Straits), the only passage through which ships from the West Indies sailed, he argued that the possessor of this 'gate from the Indies', would 'be able to give Terms to all the Spanish Trade in that part of the World'.[87]

The second place which was often proposed was the Isthmus of Panama, including Darien, where the Scots' attempt to establish a colony failed between 1698 and 1699.[88] In 1704, one Captain Richard Long recommended taking this place, claiming, 'Whoever can block up the Mouth of the great river will in a great measure command the Empire of Perew [Peru], Portobell, Carthagena'. He also presumed the existence of 'some Tunns of Gold within the Gulph of Darien and the Land adjoinying thereunto'.[89] Captain Long believed that this lure of gold would attract many settlers from North American colonies if the Crown gave them liberty of work in return for a certain amount of tribute.[90] Likewise, one anonymous writer proposed capturing Panama and Porto Bello

85 *Observator*, no. 69, 25 October 1707.

86 BL, Add MS 28058, fols 31–31v, 'Memorandum advocating the occupation by the English of Gibraltar and the Havana' [n.d.].

87 BL, Add MS 70049, fol. 182v, 'Some considerations about forming a Descent in the Spanish West Indies'.

88 On this Scottish Darien project, see Douglas Watt, *The Price of Scotland: Darien, Union and the Wealth of Nations* (Edinburgh, 2007).

89 BL, Add MS 70164 [not foliated], Richard Long to Thomas Handasyd, 13 March 1703/4. In 1697, Captain Long was sent out to Darien by Secretary of State James Vernon to discover gold mines and wrecks, and to secure the region as an English territory before other nations did, but only to find the Scots had already established a colony there. Barbour, *A History of William Paterson*, p. 118, note 1; John Prebble, *The Darien Disaster* (London, 1968), pp. 147–8; Gallup-Diaz, *The Door of the Seas*, pp. 92–101.

90 BL, Add MS 70164 [not foliated], Richard Long to Harley, 16 May 1704.

by naval and land forces in order to take control of the Spanish-American trade on the Pacific coast and gold mines, and thereby reduce the French influence there.[91]

It was William Paterson, one of the founders of the Bank of England, who was the keenest supporter of the plan to establish a colony at Darien. Even after the disastrous failure of the Darien Company of Scotland, this indefatigable man did not give up hope, and submitted a new project to William III. In this plan, he proposed capturing Darien, 'the Keys of the Indies, and door of the world' as well as the other key point in Spanish America, Havana.[92] By allowing general naturalisation and permitting trade and liberty of conscience to people of other countries, these colonies were to be the centre of trade not only for the West Indies but also the East Indies, with England as its keeper.

The profit expected from this new colony was enormous. By securing Darien, England was able to get access to the South Sea, which was 'by far the richest side of the World'. This was expected to cause an influx of immense amount of wealth, 'at least two thirds, of whatever both Indies is Capable of yielding to Christendom' in the form of various products, such as gold, silver and copper, which would amount to no less than thirty million pounds per year. The colony could also save time and money in the voyage to some countries in the East Indies, such as China and Japan, and enable the doubling of consumption of European commodities there.[93] He claimed, 'Thus these doors of the seas, and keys of the Universe would of Course be Capable of enabling their possessors, to Give Laws to both oceans, and to become the Arbitrators of the Comercial World' without being subject to the harm, expenses and dangers that were usually involved in the building of empire.[94]

The western coast of South America is another place that was often mentioned in the plan for colonial expeditions. As has already been explained, increasing presence of the French merchants there caused great concern to Britain. At the same time, there was an expectation that Britain might be able to imitate France's success if she could secure a footing there and drive out the French. Against this backdrop, during the last years of the war, a number of proposals for making a new settlement for direct trade with the Spanish colonies on the Pacific coast were

91 BL, Add MS 61644A, fols 59–64, 'Proposal for carrying on the War with more Vigour in America', 1708 [?].

92 BL, Add MS 12437, fol. 22 [William Paterson], 'Proposal for settleing on ye Isthmus of Darien', 1 January 1701.

93 BL, Add MS 12437, fols 29v–30. As is seen in this case, some writers stressed the benefit of seizing part of Spanish America, especially Darien, for the East Indian trade. For instance, the author of *The Dangers of Europe* claimed that seizure of some parts of Spanish America would give the English a source of supply of bullion, which was necessary for the East Indian trade, and that a new colony at Darien would disrupt French East Indian trade, shorten voyages to the East Indies and reduce its costs. *Dangers of Europe*, p. 61.

94 BL, Add MS 12437, fols 30–30v [William Paterson], 'Proposal for settleing on ye Isthmus of Darien', 1 January 1701.

made to Robert Harley, who proposed the establishment of the South Sea Company in May 1711.[95]

It was especially Valdivia in southern Chile that was often named as a suitable place for the settlement in these proposals. For example, in September 1711, Thomas Bowrey proposed setting up a colony there. According to him, there were a number of advantages in this place, such as its remoteness from Lima, whence the Spaniards could summon forces, production of gold, and the existence of friendly Native Americans, whose help Britain could expect and to whom she could sell woollen goods. Moreover, having a stronghold there would help Britain to interrupt the French ships coming to Peru, which would eventually persuade the Spaniards to start trading with Britain.[96] In his plan, this colony in Valdivia was to be linked with another colony on the south-east coast of South America. In fact, in another proposal, he suggested establishing a settlement in the region between Rio de la Plata and the Strait of Magellan, where ships could be supplied with provisions before their voyage into the South Sea.[97]

Likewise, Defoe submitted a proposal to Harley for establishing colonies in Chile, especially in Valdivia. This plan was, according to him, originally presented to William III, and 'had Not Death prevented him, had been Then Put in Practice'.[98] Defoe's proposal bore a close resemblance to that of Bowrey's. As for the advantages of the place, he mentioned they were its mild climate, fertility, remoteness from the other Spanish settlements and the existence of friendly natives who could also provide markets for manufactures. Trade with Peru and Spanish colonies on the eastern coast of South America and abundance of gold were other great attractions. Like Bowrey, Defoe proposed establishing a settlement on the

[95] In 1712, the South Sea Company founded by Harley planned an expedition to the Spanish colonies on the Pacific coast. This plan by the South Sea Company will be dealt with in Chapter 6.

[96] BL, Add MS 28140, fols 31–31v, 'Proposal for taking Baldivia in ye So: Seas by Thos Bowrey', Thomas Bowrey to [Robert Harley?], 10 September 1711. The copy of the same proposal was delivered to Robert Harley. BL, Add MS 70163, fols 196–7, 'Proposal for Taking Baldivia in ye South Seas by Thos Bowrey'. Bowrey was a merchant who was versed in the East Indies in particular. However he seems to have been also interested in the trade to Spanish America, and owned shares in the South Sea Company as well as the East India Company. Margaret R. Hunt, 'Bowrey, Thomas (*d.* 1713)', *ODNB*.

[97] BL, Add MS 28140, fols 31v–32, 'Proposal for a Settlement in ye way to ye So Seas' by Thos Bowrey, 11 September, 1711.

[98] BL, Add MS 70291, fol. 19, Daniel Defoe, 'Proposall for a Settlement Upon The Coast of America', 23 July 1711. Defoe claimed that only William III and the first Earl of Portland (Hans Willem Bentinck, 1648–1709) had seen the draft of this proposal, but he was forced to burn it along with other papers by order from the Earl of Nottingham, who was then interrogating him about a controversial pamphlet, *Shortest Way with the Dissenters*. BL, Add MS 70291, fol. 17, Defoe to Harley, 23 July 1711. However, Furbank and Owens have denied Defoe's claim of friendship with William III, and suggested that Defoe might have invented the story about the submission of the proposal to William, inspired by a similar proposal made by William Paterson. P.N. Furbank and W.R. Owens, *A Political Biography of Daniel Defoe* (London, 2006), pp. 26–32.

eastern coast of South America as well, which would be useful as a source of food supply to the colony in Chile and also to the fleet from Europe.[99]

The southern part of the eastern coast of South America, another region where the South Sea Company was given a monopoly by its charter, was also named as a possible place for conquest. Among the possible locations was the region around the River Plate (Rio de la Plata), including Buenos Aires. In June 1711, Thomas Pindar proposed sending an expedition there, where Britain could expect to trade with Spanish colonies on the Pacific side, such as Peru and Chile. He also planned to link this new settlement with the British settlement in Africa and bring slaves to sell to Peruvian merchants.[100] Likewise, one anonymous author proposed sending warships with 2,500 men to attack Buenos Aires. In this proposal, Buenos Aires, from which Britain could obtain access to the southern province of Peru and a rich mine in Potosi, was to be used as a base for trade with other Spanish colonies in South America. By using this route, it was expected that England could supply the colonies with merchandise and African slaves at a much cheaper price and more quickly than trading via Cadiz and by using English ships. The author asserted that if Britain secured a colony there, 'Wee would in Despite both of French and Spaniards tho Phillip kep'd the throne of Spain enjoy a more Beneficiall Trade then ever with So [South] America.' The author also emphasised that there was a strategic advantage in establishing a settlement in Buenos Aires over other projects, especially sending trading vessels directly to the South Sea where the traders could not rely on assistance from British colonies, such as Jamaica, even if they were attacked by Spanish colonists.[101]

This idea of establishing a settlement at the River Plate was sometimes combined with considerations of trade with Brazil as well as the South Sea. According to Dwyryd W. Jones, what was at the stake in the War of the Spanish Succession was not only the Spanish and Spanish-American market, but also the market in Portugal and her colony Brazil, where the discovery of gold mines around 1700 instigated a sustained economic boom.[102] In August 1711, one anonymous writer expressed concern that the French squadron of René Duguay-Trouin from St Malo might take control of a great part of Brazil and her gold mines or make colonies there, which might cause trade to Brazil to fall into French hands.[103] In order to counter this French movement, the author proposed the dispatch of two squadrons: the first was to sail to West Africa to expel the French and purchase slaves to sell in Brazil. The second, with land forces, was to sail from Portugal. After obtaining promises of assistance and privileges in importing slaves and other

99 BL, Add MS 70291, fols 19–21, Daniel Defoe, 'Proposall for a Settlement Upon The Coast of America', 23 July 1711.

100 BL, Add MS 70164 [not foliated], 'A Scheme for improvemt of the trade to the South Parts of America', Thomas Pindar to Oxford, June 1711.

101 BL, Add MS 70164 [not foliated] [no title (A plan to attack Buenos Aires)] [n.d., but 1711?].

102 Jones, *War and Economy*, p. 4.

103 The author's concern proved correct. Rio de Janeiro was captured by Dagnay-Trouin on 11 September 1711.

goods into Brazil from the court of Portugal, this squadron was to proceed to South America with the first squadron, where they were to oust the French and establish a settlement in the River Plate. If this succeeded, he claimed, 'the Extraordinary Charge will be Thankfulley repaid by ye South Sea Company, Those whoe shall have ye Affrican Trade, and those whoe shall have ye Assiento'.[104]

As is seen in this plan, capturing some parts of Spanish America and trading with Spanish colonists from there was sometimes also coupled with consideration of the African slave trade. For example, one anonymous writer who proposed taking Buenos Aires argued that the supply of slaves to other Spanish colonies via Buenos Aires could contribute greatly to the development of African trade by the Royal African Company.[105] Also in 1711, one John Chidley proposed seizing the French forts at Gorée Island off the West African coast (near modern Senegal). This was an important base for French traders replenishing water and provisions. Chidley claimed that this capture would drive the French out of the African trade and, at the same time, facilitate voyages to the South Sea by the British.[106]

Thus, plans for taking Spanish colonies or making new colonies in South America were closely intertwined with various commercial as well as strategic considerations. Colonies made as a result of expeditions were thought beneficial not only for their colonial produce, but also for a role as a base for trade with other Spanish-American colonies.

Ground for Conquest

The Sixth Article of the Treaty of the Grand Alliance and Colonial Conquest

The projects to establish a new colony in Spanish America were often defended on the grounds of supposed 'right' of conquest that England obtained as a result of her alliance with Austria. In September 1701, in response to the acceptance of the will of Charles II of Spain by Louis XIV, England concluded the Treaty of the second Grand Alliance (the Treaty of The Hague) with the Netherlands and Austria. The sixth article of this treaty allowed England and the Netherlands to capture any territory in Spanish America and retain it.[107]

The idea of granting some places in Spanish America to the two maritime

104 BL, Add MS 70310 [not foliated], 'Some thoughts about an Expedition', 21 August 1711.

105 BL, Add MS 70164 [not foliated] [no title (A plan to attack Buenos Aires)] [n.d., but 1711?].

106 BL, Add MS 70163, fols 183–4, 'The humble proposal of John Chidley relating to the South Sea trade', 6 July 1711; fols 185–6, 'The Humble representation of John Chidley relating to ye South Sea Trade and to ye African Trade', 1711; and fol. 187, John Chidley to ? , 12 July 1711.

107 The original text of this sixth article of the Treaty of the Grand Alliance is as follows: 'Pourront le Roi de la Grande-Bretagne, & les Seigneurs Etats Generaux, conquerir à force d'Armes, selon qu'ils auront concerté entr'eux, pour l'utilité & la commodité de la Navigation & du Commerce de leurs Sujets, les Païs & les Villes que les Espagols ont dans les

powers had already appeared in negotiations for the first partition treaty with France. In the negotiations, William III demanded some ports in Spanish America as well as in the Mediterranean for the security of the trade by the English and Dutch there.[108] However, Louis XIV was strongly opposed to this proposal, claiming that Spain without the Indies 'would be too inconsiderable, and that the king of Spain could never call himself master of that part of the new world, if he shared it in any way with the English and the Dutch'.[109] In the process of negotiations, William mentioned Havana as a place to be ceded in the West Indies, while Louis reluctantly offered a Spanish part of Santo Domingo. In the end, the two sides could not come to terms and this demand seems to have been dropped.[110]

The sixth article of the Treaty of the Grand Alliance was, in a sense, a revival of the idea of securing some parts of Spanish America to protect the commercial interests of England and the Netherlands there. According to George Stepney, envoy extraordinary to the emperor, this article was proposed during the negotiations for the treaty as a reward for the war effort that England and the Netherlands would make to procure several regions for the emperor, such as the Spanish Netherlands, Milan and Naples, if ongoing negotiations with France broke off and if the allies could not obtain reasonable security and satisfaction for themselves.[111]

This article was often invoked as legal grounds for the conquest in the pro-maritime war argument.[112] For example, the author of *The Dangers of Europe* claimed, 'by the Sixth Article of our Treaty with the Emperor, the *Dutch* and we are impowered to keep to our selves what we conquer in the West Indies'.[113] Similarly, the address of the House of Lords regarding privateers, which was delivered on 23 May 1702, stipulated that, by the sixth article, 'Your Majesty is at Liberty to take and seize Lands and Cities belonging to the *Spanish* Dominions

Indes, & tout ce qu'ils pourront y prendre sera pour eux, & leur demeurera.' G.M. Trevelyan, ed., *Select Documents for Queen Anne's Reign: Down to the Union with Scotland, 1702–7* (London, 1929, repr. Wilmington, DL and London, 1973), p. 7.

108 *Letters of William III and Louis XIV*, I, p. 360, William III to Heinsius, 1/11 April 1698; TNA, SP 8/18, pp. 242–4, Portland to William III, 6/16 April 1698.

109 *Letters of William III and Louis XIV*, I, pp. 390–1, Louis XIV to Count of Tallard, 17 April 1698.

110 *Ibid.*, I, p. 473, William III to Portland, 2/12 May 1698; TNA, SP 8/18, pp. 323–4, Portland to William III, 7/17 May 1698; *Letters of William III and Louis XIV*, II, p. 10, Louis XIV to Tallard, 29 May 1698, and pp. 19–20, Portland to William III, 4 June 1698.

111 TNA, SP105/63, pp. 152–3, Stepney to Blathwayt, 10 August 1701.

112 Apart from the legal ground, some invoked other reasons to justify the expeditions to Spanish America. For example, the author of *Europa Libera*, by quoting a work of Francis Bacon, claimed that fear of being oppressed could be a just cause of war and advocated a pre-emptive attack as a means of self-defence. Referring to the failure of the Spaniards to convert the native people to Christianity and ill-usage of them, he also questioned the legitimacy of conquests by the Spaniards and asserted that, 'if a Conquest was made by Protestant States, they would then be instructed in the true Principles of Religion, and be drawn off from the Idolatrous Worship they remain in still'. *Europa Libera*, pp. 14–16.

113 *Dangers of Europe*, p. 60.

in *The Indies*, and retain the same as Your own.'[114] Thus, from the English viewpoint, England, as well as the Netherlands, was legally entitled to seize parts of Spanish America by virtue of the sixth article of the Treaty of the Grand Alliance.

Conquest and Free Trade

This idea of conquest in Spanish America on the basis of the sixth article of the Treaty of the Grand Alliance, however, did not go unopposed. The imperialists were uneasy about conquest on the grounds of the sixth article. After England and the Netherlands joined the war, they soon came to realise that the sixth article was an excessive privilege and tried to restrain Britain from making use of it. In 1702, Godolphin reported that Count Wratislaw, Imperial Ambassador Extraordinary in England, showed an unfavourable attitude to this article, claiming that it would offend the Pope.[115] Instead of the right of conquest, the imperialists proposed offering a right to free trade with Spanish America as a reward for the English and Dutch assistance in the war.[116] According to Vernon, the imperialists repented that they had granted the right of conquest to England and the Netherlands. In their interpretation, the two maritime powers were supposed just to make the Spanish colonists submit to the rule of the House of Habsburg; and, in return, they were to be allowed liberty of trade, that is, a right to trade with Spanish colonies as freely as Spanish subjects did. Vernon thought that this was not necessarily a bad bargain, and stated that this might be 'much more advantageous to us than any thing got by rapine or buccaneering'. However, he thought that the actual use of force would be inevitable in subjecting the Spanish colonists, and it would also be difficult to persuade Parliament to renounce its right to conquest, for many people were pleased with this article and would strongly oppose its

[114] *L.J.*, XVII, p. 147, 23 May 1702.

[115] BL, Add MS 29588, fols 233–4, Godolphin to Nottingham, 17 September 1702. The grounds of Count Wratislaw's argument are not clear, but this might be relevant to concern among the Roman Catholics in Austria about possible promulgation of Protestantism in new territories that England and the Netherlands would acquire by virtue of the sixth article, which was mentioned by George Stepney in August 1701. TNA, SP105/63, pp. 153–4, Stepney to Blathwayt, 10 August 1701.

[116] The concept of 'free trade' had already emerged in the late seventeenth century, albeit with a more relatively limited sense than the one advocated by economic thinkers in the latter half of the eighteenth century such as Adam Smith. According to Peggy K. Liss, in the late seventeenth century the term 'meant more free than the norm, and was a request for unrestricted competition among national carriers within the empire and for open season on foreign markets'. Moreover, by the early eighteenth century, it also became a synonym for smuggling and interloping commerce, which was conducted in defiance of the regulation of the foreign government or monopoly of the chartered companies of their own nation. Peggy K. Liss, *Atlantic Empires: The Network of Trade and Revolution, 1713–1826* (Baltimore, 1983), p. 10. For the impact of this idea of the 'free trade' on the government policy in this period, see George L. Cherry, 'The Development of the English Free-Trade Movement in Parliament, 1689–1702', *JMH* 35, no. 2 (June 1953), 103–19.

abandonment, "till they can be convinced that the nation will reap a greater benefit another way'.[117]

Like Vernon, there were some government officials who favoured the idea of obtaining the right of free trade in place of territorial conquest. Among them was William Blathwayt, a leading member of the Board of Trade. He thought that Spain would never endure England's governance of the West Indies, which was also harmful to England. Instead, he preferred the Spanish-American colonies being in possession of the House of Austria with the right of free trade given to England, rather than England retaining them.[118] George Stepney had a similar opinion. He claimed that, by consenting to neutrality with all the Spanish colonies in America, the Spanish colonists might allow the English free trade with them. This would not only contribute to expelling the French from America, but would also enable England to make far larger profits than through mere plundering, which would 'certainly prove more beneficial to the Trading Interest and Manufactures of *England*'.[119]

In the early stage of the war, the Dutch also demanded this liberty of trade, together with reimbursement of the expense of expeditions, as compensation for carrying out West India expeditions on behalf of the emperor.[120] The Earl of Nottingham, Secretary of State for the South at that time, was sympathetic to this Dutch idea. However, he was not really keen to press at this stage, out of concern that the demand might upset the Spaniards. Instead, Nottingham believed that, after making conquests in Spanish America on the grounds of the sixth article, England could easily exchange them with a right of free trade, which would be more acceptable to the Spaniards.[121] Probably realising the difficulty in retaining those conquests, Nottingham seems to have become increasingly inclined to regard conquest not as an end in itself, but as a stepping-stone to freedom of trade. About three months later, when John Methuen tried to offer ports in Spanish America and freedom of trade to the Portuguese in his negotiations with them, Nottingham strongly opposed the idea, claiming that such cession would alienate the Spaniards

[117] G.P.R. James, ed., *Letters Illustrative of the Reign of William III from 1696 to 1708 addressed to the Duke of Shrewsbury … by J. Vernon, Secretary of State*, III (London, 1841), pp. 176–7, James Vernon to Stepney, 13 February 1701/2.

[118] Denman, 'Political Debate', pp. 141–2; TNA, SP105/63, p. 331, Blathwayt to Stepney, 8/19 August 1701; pp. 346–7, Blathwayt to Stepney, 26 August 1701; pp. 432–3, Blathwayt to Stepney, 9 September 1701.

[119] Stepney, *An Essay upon the Present Interest of England*, p. 66. This request for the right to trade with Spanish colonies was not a new idea, and similar ideas for freer trade had already appeared in the diplomatic negotiations with Spain in the latter half of the seventeenth century. Keith Feiling, *British Foreign Policy, 1660–1672* (London, 1930), pp. 172, 179–80; A.P. Thornton, *West-India Policy under the Restoration* (Oxford, 1956), pp. 103–4.

[120] TNA, SP 84/225, no. 51, fols 183v–184, Sir David Mitchell to [Nottingham], 8 September 1702.

[121] FH MSS 275, p. 116, Nottingham to Richard Warre, under-secretary of state, 16 September 1702.

from the House of Habsburg. He argued that even the sixth article, of which the emperor complained, did not allow England and the Netherlands to have liberty. What England could expect at best was, 'to exchange our Conquests for this liberty of Trade'.[122] Thus, in place of colonial conquest, which could cause disturbance to the allies, the right of free trade with Spanish-American colonies was often discussed as a preferable economic benefit, which England could expect to obtain in return for her assistance to Austria in the war.

Reward for the War Effort

As the war became prolonged, however, this expectation of obtaining new territories or opportunity for trade gradually turned into a sense of entitlement that Britain deserved to receive those benefits as just reward or compensation for her war effort on behalf of her allies. In 1707, the author of *An Inquiry into the Causes of Our Naval Miscarriages* claimed that, by proper management of her fleet, England had the power to subdue France and 'to have had the whole Trade of the Spanish West-Indies as the Reward of the Blood and Treasure we have expended in defence of our own, and the Libertys of Christendom'.[123] Similarly, in 1710, one anonymous writer who proposed taking Havana claimed that the possession of the place would 'doe what ever else may be thought fitt to ask of ye Spanish Government, for all the Treasure, and Blood, this Nation has spent in the Defence of their Liberty, and of all Europe'.[124]

The claim that Britain was entitled to some kind of compensation for her war effort was also present in the peace negotiations with France, which began in 1709 and intermittently continued until the Treaty of Utrecht was finally concluded in March 1713. For example, in a letter to Viscount Townshend, who was negotiating with the Dutch about a preliminary peace treaty at that time, Henry Boyle, Secretary of State for the North, asked him to observe to the Dutch that it was reasonable for Britain and the Netherlands, which had been fighting for the Archduke Charles at great expense, to expect 'some kind of retribution' after a peace, such as commercial privileges in Spanish and Spanish-American trade.[125] William Paterson attached similar meaning to new territories that could be gained through peace with France. In a letter dated September 1710, probably addressed to Robert Harley, who had started the peace negotiations in the previous month, Paterson claimed that Britain should insist on obtaining some territories in Newfoundland and Canada from France, and some places in South America from Spain, until reimbursement of at least part of the vast cost that Britain had borne and would have to bear for recovery of the Spanish monarchy to the House of Habsburg. Together with a commercial treaty regarding America, this would be

122 FH MSS 275, pp. 242–3, Nottingham to Methuen, 22 December 1702.

123 *An Inquiry into the Causes of Our Naval Miscarriages*, p. iii.

124 BL, Add MS 70049, fol. 180, 'Considerations in regard to a proposal for a descent on Havana', 2 September 1710.

125 Bodleian Library, MS Eng. Hist. d. 147, fol. 79v, Henry Boyle to Townshend, 2 September 1709. I am grateful to Professor Steven Pincus for drawing my attention to this source.

'some Acknowledgement, tho' far enough from a Reasonable Compensation, for the Immense Expences & losses of this Nation herein'.[126] Thus, as the war progressed, new conquests and right to free trade that Britain might be able to obtain by force or by peace negotiations came to be seen as just reward or compensation for her war effort.

As we have seen so far, in the pro-maritime war argument in this period, it was claimed that maritime war, particularly maritime war in Spanish America, had several economic advantages. They can be divided roughly into two categories. The first was an economic advantage closely intertwined with strategic considerations. It was believed that the wealth of Spanish America, not least bullion, was the very source of financial power for both Spain and France; and, by cutting off its supply, England could subdue the enemy effectively and, at the same time, use those riches for the benefit of England and her allies. In order to deprive the enemy of the wealth of Spanish America, two options were considered: interception of Spanish silver fleets and colonial expeditions. In addition to the foregoing, especially in the early stages of the war, it was expected that Spanish colonists or native Americans who were discontented with the mother country and French rule might be persuaded to defect to the allies' side and rise in rebellion.

Colonial expeditions were also often supported out of commercial considerations: recovery of the Spanish America market from the French who had made rapid advances in the Spanish-American trade. It was argued that, by sending expeditionary forces, Britain was able to seize and secure some places in Spanish America, such as Havana and Panama, and use them as bases for trade with the Spanish-American colonies. Colonial conquest by such expeditions was defended on the grounds of the sixth article of the Treaty of the Grand Alliance, or, in later periods of the war, was advocated as just reward or compensation for Britain's effort to help her allies. Yet, since such acquisition could cause tension with the allies, such as the Netherlands and Austria, acquisition of the right of free trade with the Spanish colonies in exchange for conquests was also considered. This choice between new territories and right to free trade was a recurring issue in the debate over the British policy towards Spanish America in this period; and, as we shall see in Chapter 6, in a later stage of the war, a similar question reappeared in controversy over the feasibility of trade planned by the South Sea Company.

The economic advantages examined in this chapter were present in most of the pro-maritime war argument during the War of the Spanish Succession, and had a strong appeal to a wide range of people. However, it is not correct to regard the pro-maritime war argument as a single and unitary ideology. The struggle between political parties under the reign of Queen Anne strongly influenced the pro-maritime war argument, and it diversified the contents and functions of the argument, which will be examined in the next chapter.

126 BL, Add MS 70026, fols 146v–147, William Patterson to [Robert Harley?)], 4 September 1710.

– 3 –

Pro-maritime War Arguments and Party Politics

As we have seen in the previous chapter, the argument supporting maritime war emphasis on the economic advantages of war at sea as its key and common feature. However, at the same time, the pro-maritime war argument was also influenced by the contemporary political situation. In the period of the 'rage of party', the political struggle between the Whigs and Tories affected and diversified the content of the argument. By examining the pamphlets and periodicals that appeared during the War of the Spanish Succession, this chapter points out the existence of two different pro-maritime war arguments, which reflected the political struggle between the Whigs and Tories, and by putting them in the political context of the time reveals who was behind these arguments and what political purposes they had.

The Early Stages of the War

Emergence of the First Pro-maritime War Argument

Before analysing several pro-maritime war arguments that appeared during the War of the Spanish Succession, we need to look at the political situations of England and Europe at the time. The brief period of peace after the end of the Nine Years War did not last long, and the hostility that smouldered in Europe was soon rekindled. One of the main issues that triggered a new conflict was the succession of the Spanish monarchy. When it became clear that Charles II of Spain was going to die without issue, the question of the Spanish Succession became the focal centre point of the interests of European powers, as it would also determine into whose hands the vast Spanish empire and its wealth would fall. While Louis XIV claimed a right to the Spanish throne for the House of Bourbon, King William III of England tried to prevent Louis' attempt by concluding two partition treaties (one in 1698, the other in 1700), which were designed to divide Spain and her empire among several powers.

When Charles II died in November 1700, however, it turned out in his will that he had designated the Duke of Anjou, a grandson of Louis XIV, as the sole inheritor of the Spanish monarchy. The acceptance of this will by Louis XIV, in breach of the second partition treaty, caused serious concerns in England. The anxiety of the English was further increased by the advance of French troops into the Spanish Netherlands in February 1701 and Louis' recognition of the son of the exiled James

II as the king of England in September. These events pushed England into joining the second treaty of the Grand Alliance with Austria and the Netherlands in September 1701, and to declare war on France with her allies in May 1702. Thus, the War of the Spanish Succession began, which lasted for nearly twelve years.

As war approached, there occurred a debate over how England should react to the issue of Spanish Succession. In particular, discussion focused on whether England should join the war and how England should fight, if she joined. In this debate, one argument strongly advocated English commitment to the war and emphasised the effectiveness and profitability of maritime war, which was to be conducted in cooperation with the Dutch. This can be called the first pro-maritime war argument.

As early as 1700, when discussing the issue of the partition of the Spanish monarchy, Daniel Defoe had already cautioned that, if France took control of the Spanish empire, it could bring serious consequences to England and the Netherlands, such as an inflow of wealth from the Spanish colonies into France, an increase of French shipping and the destruction of trade with Spain. Defoe argued that, if France breached the partition treaty and claimed the Spanish crown for Louis XIV's grandson, England and the Netherlands should take military action and send a fleet with land forces to the Mediterranean to defend Catalonia. He criticised the complacent attitude about England's naval fleet and safety from invasion, and he emphasised the necessity of preventing France from taking control of the Spanish crown, which would ultimately lead to French supremacy in the fields of trade and naval power.[1]

The French acceptance of Charles II's will in the next year provoked a further outcry about the need to take precautionary measures, in order to prevent a possible union between France and Spain. The author of a pamphlet entitled *The Duke of Anjou's Succession Further Consider'd* warned of France seizing the wealth of Spanish America and enumerated the harmful effects that French control of the Spanish monarchy could have on English overseas trade. In order to stop this, the author stressed the necessity 'to make use of early and forcible Preventions by Alliances abroad, and vigorous Attempts by Sea'.[2] Similarly, the author of *A Debate between Three Ministers of State on the Present Affairs of England* claimed that, given Louis XIV's ambition to expand his territory and the burden of expenditures on defence in peace time, the worst stance that England could take was 'sitting still'. Instead, the author argued that joining the allies in the fight against France was in the interest of England:

> By uniting with *Holland*, we do follow our true Interest, which hath ever been successful to this Nation, which is to be still Masters at Sea, and by Embracing the Emperor's Interest, we may hope for a considerable Portion in the Spoils of the *Spanish Indies*.[3]

[1] Daniel Defoe, *The Two Great Questions Consider'd* ... (London, 1700), pp. 18, 22–6.

[2] *Duke of Anjou's Succession Further Consider'd*, pp. 5–7, 10–13.

[3] *A Debate between Three Ministers of State on the Present Affairs of England* (London, 1702), pp. 16–17.

This first pro-maritime war argument emphasised the economic advantages of maritime war in order to show that participation in the war was not necessarily burdensome, and might even be profitable for England. In response to the argument opposing participation in the approaching new war on financial grounds, the author of *The Duke of Anjou's Succession Further Consider'd* maintained that one half of England's annual income by trade, which was estimated at two millions pounds, would be enough to bring the war 'to a speedy and happy Conclusion'. Moreover, with a far lower sum, England could equip a fleet and send a strong squadron to the West Indies under English commanders, which might 'in all probability soon repay us'. The author asserted that a naval war was 'the likelyest method to quell that *Leviathan* [i.e. France]' and 'a sort of War that we can best manage with the least expense and danger to our Selves'.[4]

It was especially war with Spain that was believed to be profitable.[5] The author of a pamphlet entitled *Europa Libera* emphasised this point by quoting Francis Bacon's words from his essay that justified and encouraged a Spanish war:

> whereas *Wars* are generally Causes of *Poverty*, or Consumption; on the contrary part, the special Nature of this *War* with *Spain*, (if it be made by Sea) is like to be a Lucrative and Restorative War. So that, if we go roundly on at the first, the *War* in continuance will find it self.[6]

The notion of a 'self-financing war', mentioned in the previous chapter, was also present in the first pro-maritime war argument. For example, the author of *The Dangers of Europe, from the Growing Power of France* claimed that England had 'still this Great and Capital Encouragement to go heartily into a War', for England was allowed to retain conquests in the West Indies through the alliance with the emperor. By this, the author claimed, England could certainly carry on this war 'at the Charge of our Enemies', in contrast to the Nine Years War, which England carried out at her own expense without any hope of repayment.[7] Likewise, *A Debate between Three Ministers of State on the Present Affairs of England* claimed that

> a ready Assistance to the Emperor will make the Charge much less, nor, shall we need to be Principal in the War; but, the Prizes to be got at Sea, may, if well manag'd, largely contribute to discharge the Expences both the Naval and Land Forces.[8]

[4] *Duke of Anjou's Succession Further Consider'd*, p. 54.

[5] In 1701, Defoe even argued that England should fight a war not against France, which had not attacked English territory yet and whose privateers would cause severe damage to English commerce in case of war, but only against Spain, which violated the emperor's right to the Spanish crown. He claimed that, from this war against Spain, England could gain benefits from free trade and depredations in Spanish America. Defoe, *Reasons against a War with France*, pp. 18–21.

[6] *Europa Libera*, p. 18. The original text of Bacon's essay, 'Considerations Touching a War with Spain', is included in *Certain Miscellany Works of the Right Honourable Francis Lord Verulam, Viscount St. Alban published by William Rawley* … (London, 1670).

[7] *Dangers of Europe*, pp. 67–8.

[8] *Debate between Three Ministers of State*, p. 18.

The glorious memory of the reign of Queen Elizabeth was also referred to in the first pro-maritime war argument. The author of *Europa Libera* stated that after the defeat of the invincible Spanish Armada, Queen Elizabeth pushed forward with her war with Spain, so that 'the very Names of our Admirals, Generals, and Chief Commanders, struck an *awful Dread* and *Terror* into the *Spaniards* where-ever they came'.[9]

Thus, the first argument emphasised the economic advantages of maritime war to ease English anxiety over the financial burden of a new war, and to dispose opinion towards a war against France. It also invoked the glorious memory of war at sea during the Elizabethan period to encourage the English to enter the war. However, it should be noted that, while this first argument advocated maritime war, the criticism of the continental land war, one of the characteristics of the second argument, was absent. Moreover, unlike the Country Whig's pro-maritime war argument, which we shall see later, the first argument stressed the necessity of maintaining land forces.

For example, while supporting maritime war, in conjunction with a Dutch squadron, because of the rejection of the partition treaty by France, the author of *The Succession of Spain Discuss'd* claimed that 'we cannot be without more Land Troops than are upon the present Establishment'.[10] Likewise, *The Duke of Anjou's Succession Further Consider'd* stressed the necessity of land force, as well as naval force, to protect England from invasions by the enemy and to preserve peace at home. While being sensitive to the anti-standing army feelings in England caused by the historical precedents – particularly Cromwell's army – it claimed that this could be soothed by control of the army, both by the crown and Parliament.[11] One anonymous writer even postulated that, behind this opposition to a standing army, there was a plot by France and her collaborators in England. According to the writer, their aim was, by depriving England of her army, to force the naval fleet to stay in home waters to protect the country from French invasions and to make it

[9] *Europa Libera*, p. 57.

[10] *The Succession of Spain Discuss'd. With a Project of Reconciling all the Present Pretensions to that Crown …* (London, 1701), p. 27.

[11] *Duke of Anjou's Succession Further Consider'd*, p. 26. As far as the attitudes towards the army were concerned, there is a similarity between these arguments and the pro-army argument presented by royal writers, such as Somers and Defoe, in debates on the standing army between 1697 and 1699. Lois G. Schwoerer, *"No Standing Armies!": The Antiarmy Ideology in Seventeenth-Century England* (Baltimore and London, 1974), pp. 184–7. On the other hand, anti-army writers, such as Andrew Fletcher and John Trenchard, denied the necessity of a standing army, claiming that the navy and militia were sufficient to defend England from foreign invasion. Their view towards the naval forces was close to that of the Country Whig or Tory pro-maritime war argument. Andrew Fletcher, *A Discourse concerning Militia's and Standing Armies with relation to the Past and Present Governments of Europe and of England in Particular* (London, 1697), pp. 27–8; John Trenchard, *An Argument, Shewing that a Standing Army is Inconsistent with a Free Government and Absolutely Destructive to the Constitution of the English Monarchy* (London, 1697), pp. 18–20.

impossible for the navy to prevent the return of silver from Spanish America, a source of enemy financing for war.[12] Thus, the first argument also emphasised the need to maintain the army, while praising the advantages of naval force.[13] These were the features that distinguished the first pro-maritime war argument from both the second pro-maritime war argument and the Country Whig pro-maritime war argument, which we shall see later.

The other equally important feature of the first argument is the attitudes towards the allies of England, especially the Dutch. In the case of the first argument, the Netherlands, another great maritime power, was regarded as a necessary and essential ally in the war against France. This emphasis on unity with the Dutch is a distinctive feature of the first argument. The author of *The Duke of Anjou's Succession Considered* stressed that the Dutch, who were 'the great Barrier of the Protestant Interest' and that of 'the Civil Liberties of *Europe*', were now under the threat of an alliance between France and Spain. Considering this situation, the author urged the English to enter into 'a stricter Amity and Friendship with the Dutch than ever', referring to the precedents of the alliance and cooperation in the Elizabethan period and in the Glorious Revolution. This alliance had a strategic advantage, as well. The author claims that 'there is no other Foreign Nation so capable as the Dutch, of giving the French a Diversion by Sea and Land, if they should attempt to invade us'. The author went on to say that it would be in England's interests to keep the war at a distance, in cooperation with the Dutch, whom England could assist with her forces or through foreign troops hired at her expense.[14] The naval strength of the Dutch was thought to be useful for the West India expedition, as well. The author maintained that the naval force of the two countries, when commanded by trustworthy persons, would certainly bring a speedy end to the war by sending 'such Squadrons abroad as may secure the Treasure of the *West Indies* for the Use of the League'.[15]

The importance of unity with the Dutch was repeated in *The Duke of Anjou's Succession Further Consider'd*. It warned of the harmful effect of the division between England and the Netherlands, and it stressed the necessity of an alliance with other Protestant countries, including the Netherlands. This alliance was also important from a naval point of view. The pamphlet claimed that 'We have the noblest Fleet now that any Nation can boast of. … There's nothing humanely speaking, could be able to stand in the way of the united Naval Force of the Protestant Princes and States.'[16]

12 *Division our Destruction: or, a Short History of the French Faction in England* (London, 1702), pp. 11–12.

13 One exception to this is a passage in *The Duke of Anjou's Succession Further Consider'd*. In answering the objection to a new war based upon fear of further economic burdens, the author explained that naval forces could contribute to the consumption of English commodities, whereas keeping armies in foreign countries tended to cause outflow of money from England. *Duke of Anjou's Succession Further Consider'd*, pp. 54–5.

14 *Duke of Anjou's Succession Considered*, pp. 15–17.

15 *Ibid.*, p. 23.

16 *Duke of Anjou's Succession Further Consider'd*, pp. 37, 47–8.

It should be noted that this sympathy with the Dutch was a characteristic feature of the Whig argument. According to Douglas Coombs, while there was a broad consensus among the Englishmen that Dutch commercial methods should be emulated, a fairly clear distinction existed between the 'Tory' and the 'Whig' attitudes towards the Dutch constitution and government, which was also deeply connected to the religious matter. While the Tories abhorred their republicanism and Calvinism, the Whigs praised the Dutch Republic for its religious toleration.[17]

The affinity with the Dutch can be seen also in the Whig argument over foreign policy and economy, often coupled with antipathy towards France, which was regarded as a disturber of the balance of Europe. In the debates over the Anglo-French Treaty of Commerce of 1713, Doohwan Ahn has perceived pro-Dutch attitudes in the Whig argument. According to Ahn, the Whigs regarded the Netherlands as a Protestant ally and saw France as the foremost rival of Britain in foreign trade and diplomacy, whereas Tory thinkers, such as Bolingbroke and Davenant, argued that it was the Dutch, not the French, who were the main threat to the British economy.[18] Thus, the first pro-maritime war argument, which was Whiggish in tone, strongly advocated for an alliance with the Dutch, who were not only regarded as a shield against France on the continent, but also a great asset in naval war.

As we have seen so far, the first pro-maritime war argument emphasised the economic advantages of maritime war, sometimes referring to historical precedents, to dispose the nation towards war, and it stressed the necessity of maintaining the army and cooperation with the Dutch. What, then, was the background of this first argument? Who directed it? What was its purpose? In order to answer these questions, first we have to understand the political situation of England in 1701.

According to Henry Horwitz, the House of Commons, which was newly met in February 1701, was under the influence of three forces. The first was King William III, who was eager to enter into the war against France; at the same time, however, he realised that he needed the backing of Parliament. The second were his new Tory ministers, such as Baron Godolphin and Earl of Rochester, who were keen to consolidate their position in the king's council but also had to consider the attitudes of their fellow Tories, who were reluctant to enter the new war. Thirdly, there were the Junto Whigs, former ministers, and their associates in the Commons, who also supported participation in the war against France.[19]

Of these three political forces, one of the possible backers of the first argument was the king. When the negotiation by the two partition treaties failed and the possibility of union between Spain and France became stronger, William tried to persuade England to prepare for war with the French in alliance with Austria and

17 Douglas Coombs, *The Conduct of the Dutch: British Opinion and the Dutch Alliance during the War of the Spanish Succession* (The Hague, 1958), pp. 7–12.

18 Doohwan Ahn, 'The Anglo-French Treaty of Commerce of 1713: Tory Trade Politics and the Question of Dutch Decline', *History of European Ideas* 36 (2010), 179–80.

19 Horwitz, *Parliament, Policy and Politics*, pp. 280–1.

the Netherlands; the defence of the latter was one of his greatest concerns. For this purpose, the king had to convince the Commons, which could vote to fund the war. However, in contrast to the House of Lords, where William could exert his influence through a large proportion of the peers who owed their title to the king, and where he could count on the Junto's assistance, it was difficult to gain support for his war policy in the Commons, as it was then dominated by the Tories, who were averse to involvement in a new war out of concern for further financial burdens. Considering this situation, it is possible that the first argument was part of a political campaign by William, or those personally working for him, to dispose the MPs in the Commons towards the war.[20]

Another possibility was the Junto Whigs, especially Lord Somers, who was the centre of the Whig propaganda campaign in 1701.[21] According to Horwitz, after the 1701 session was over, the Whigs strove to convince the king to dissolve Parliament and call a new election, in order to change the composition of Tory-dominant Commons. For this purpose, they had recourse to a propaganda campaign that demonstrated popular zeal for the war and attacked the Tory-dominated Commons.[22] Actually, some of the pamphlets that could be categorised into the first argument contained criticisms of the Tories and insinuated their connection with France.[23] Even after the dissolution of Parliament and a new

[20] There is uncertainty about Defoe's role in this period. It is debatable whether Defoe was actually working for William at this time, as Defoe himself often claimed. Frank Bastian states that Defoe began to work for the king from late 1700, while John Robert Moore claims that he became the king's agent from about 1692. Frank Bastian, *Defoe's Early Life* (London, 1981), p. 225; John R. Moore, 'Daniel Defoe: King William's Pamphleteer and Intelligence Agent', *HLQ* 34, no. 3 (May 1971), 25–6. On the other hand, James A. Downie has reservations about the possibility of Defoe working for the king, and Furbank and Owens cast serious doubts upon Defoe's claim. Downie, *Harley and the Press*, pp. 33–4; Furbank and Owens, *Political Biography*, pp. 26–32. However, even if Defoe did not personally know the king, it is still possible that he supported the king's policy independently by pamphleteering.

[21] Downie has suggested that Somers played a significant role in the propaganda campaign for the Whigs in 1701, in cooperation with Halifax, Edward Clarke, John Freke and the publisher Jacob Tonson, just as Harley did with Charles Davenant for the 'New Country Party'. Downie, *Harley and the Press*, pp. 41–2. Also, Bastian claims that there is a possibility that some of the pamphlets attributed to Somers were actually written by Defoe or written in collaboration with him. Bastian, *Defoe's Early Life*, pp. 305–6.

[22] Horwitz, *Parliament, Policy and Politics*, p. 295. One example of the Junto's propaganda campaign is *Jura Populi Anglicani*, written by Somers in 1701, which defended the Kentish petitioners and severely criticised the Tory-dominated House of Commons, which imprisoned them. In this pamphlet, Somers also refuted the isolationist view held by the '*French* Party' (by which terms, he meant the Tories) that naval defence alone was sufficient to secure the safety of England. Instead he argued for immediate preparation for war against France to check the growth of its power, though he did not explain how war should be conducted. John Somers, *Jura Populi Anglicani: or, the subjects right of petitioning set forth. Occasioned by the case of the Kentish petitioners* (London, 1701), pp. 58, 63.

[23] For example, see *Duke of Anjou's Succession Further Consider'd*, p. 56; *Division our Destruction*, p. 4.

election had taken place, they still needed to persuade the Commons to assist the war against France financially. Moreover, as we shall see in Chapters 4 and 5, some of the Junto Whigs themselves, especially Halifax and Somers, were supporters of West Indian expeditions. Given these facts, it is also likely that the first pro-maritime argument was presented by the Junto.

In any case, it seems that one of the main purposes of this first argument was to make the MPs in the Commons inclined towards war. The intention to persuade the MPs can be perceived from a passage of *Europa Libera*. After explaining the advantages and feasibility of Spanish-American expeditions, the author stated:

> And if Success in this *War*, shall be the most probable means for both the Ends and Purposes aforesaid these Considerations will be prevailing Arguments, no doubt (together with hopes of reinbursing us the Charge and Expence of the War) with the Honourable Houses of Parliament to support with seasonable and proportionable Supplies; for as to the Expence, 'twill be but like a Merchant's Adventure by Sea, in hopes of a return with great Encrease: To Spend to Get, is always accounted a prudent piece of Good Husbandry, as 'tis to Sow in hopes to reap a plentiful Harvest, as this is like to prove.[24]

In another section, the author also claimed that, if hints about the expedition to Spanish America were made public, it would help 'to satisfie those who are to raise and pay Taxes, to raise and pay them more readily and chearfully'. He went on to say,

> And when they shall be satisfied in these particulars, their Hearts and their Hands, would freely go along, and assist, and their Purses be almost as inexhaustible, as the Mines we are speaking of.[25]

Thus, this first pro-maritime war argument seems to have been a part of the propaganda campaign by the Court or by the Junto Whigs, especially Somers, or perhaps a cooperation of the both, to pressure the House of Commons into preparing for war.

'Country' Pro-maritime War Argument

In addition to this first argument, in the early stages of the war, there was another argument that also advocated war at sea. While this argument admitted the necessity of entering the war, it also claimed that war should be conducted in a different manner from the Nine Years War. Behind this argument was a 'Country' concern over the growing national debt and taxes caused by wars against France, a concern shared by both some of the Tories and some of the Whigs. As John Brewer has argued, through a series of wars against France that started in the late seventeenth century, England gradually developed into a 'fiscal-military state'. In terms of its financial aspects, what propped up this 'fiscal-military state' was a system of public borrowing based mainly on long-term loans – a result of the 'Financial Revolution' – and an efficient taxation system. Especially in the period

24 *Europa Libera*, p. 23.

25 *Ibid.*, p. 52.

after 1714, indirect taxes, such as excise taxes, guaranteed the payment of the national debt. Because of them, Britain was able to afford the immense costs of the war.[26]

Nevertheless, in spite of their contribution to the rise of Britain in the eighteenth century, these changes were not necessarily welcomed by contemporaries. According to P.G.M. Dickson, public reaction to the 'Financial Revolution' was generally hostile, and there were criticisms from political, social and economic viewpoints.[27] Accusations were also levelled at new financiers who made a huge profit on this new system by acting as undertakers or underwriters of government stock, or by making contracts to supply the British troops.[28]

By the reign of Queen Anne, this 'Country' concern came to be shared mainly by the Tories. Yet, there were still Whigs with Country attitudes too.[29] The character of the pro-maritime war argument presented by Country Whig writers was more defensive than that of the first argument. Although they accepted that war was unavoidable, they opposed war on land, especially war in Flanders, as a costly and lengthy means of warfare; instead, they stressed the significance of trade protection, an argument close to that of the 'Country' opposition in the Commons during the Nine Years War.[30] For example, in a supposed dialogue between two characters named 'Young Fudg of the Admiralty' and 'Capt. Steerwell, an Oliverian Commander', the author of *The Present Condition of the English Navy* claimed that, in the approaching war, the English 'had better spend a little Mony in Booms and Chains to secure our Ships in Harbour, than to send 'em abroad to spend our Mony, lose our Reputation, and not secure our Trade'. He had a negative view towards dispatching England's native strength 'in other Peoples Quarrels' at England's expense, while leaving the liberties of the English at the mercy of the standing army at home. He was also suspicious of the usefulness of colonial expeditions, and he made an ironic remark about Benbow's dispatch to the West Indies in the summer of 1701: 'our modern Whigs boasted of the Conduct and built Castles in the Air to hold the Money they would bring home in the *Spanish* Galleons'. However, in reality, 'in a short time we found them all at *Spithead*, except a few Ships that proceeded with *Benbow* to the *West Indies*'. Instead of embarking

[26] As to the argument concerning the emergence of the fiscal-military state, see John Brewer, *The Sinews of Power: War Money and the English State, 1688–1783* (London, 1988, repr., Cambridge, MA, 1990). Regarding the 'Financial Revolution', see P.G.M. Dickson, *The Financial Revolution in England: A Study in the Development of Public Credit, 1688–1756* (London, 1967).

[27] Dickson, *Financial Revolution in England*, pp. 17–32.

[28] Brewer, *Sinews of Power*, pp. 206–8.

[29] For 'Country' attitudes among MPs during Anne's reign, see Holmes, *British Politics*, Chapter 4. Although Hayton claims that actual number of the MPs who could be regarded as 'Country Whigs' had been reduced to a handful of men by the second half of Anne's reign, he also admits that Whig writers continued to have some influence on the Country ideology through their publications. Hayton, 'The "Country" Interest and the Party System', pp. 54–6.

[30] Denman, 'Political Debate', p. 56.

on such an expedition, he claimed that England should have sent the navy to the Strait of Gibraltar, which would have encouraged the pro-Austria party in Naples.[31] Likewise, a Whig periodical, the *Observator*, explained the value of maritime war in defensive terms. It claimed that men of war were 'our chiefest Security' and argued that, 'In a War at Sea, the chief Care ought to be the Security of our Merchants Ships by providing sufficient Convoys, and next to that, the Encouragement of Privateers.'[32]

After the war began, in 1703, John Dennis, a writer of independent Whig tendencies, advocated maritime war as the most effective means of warfare. He claimed that war at sea would 'be more effectual on our part towards the speedy ending of the war, than the sending formidable Forces to *Flanders*, or any part of the Continent', where the risk would be high and the gains would be small.[33] Dennis argued that, as the only intention of France was to destroy English commerce, England should concentrate her war efforts on trade protection against attack from French privateers and on the destruction of enemy trade.[34] For this purpose, he proposed establishing an auxiliary naval force, composed of two hundred English and two hundred Dutch vessels and maintained at the merchants' expense. With the assistance of naval cruisers, this auxiliary force would be expected to clear the sea of French privateers. Moreover, in cooperation with buccaneers, the fleet could cut off the enemy supply of bullion and seize important places in the Spanish colonies.[35]

As is seen in the above statement, these writers of Country Whig inclination had a strong aversion to the army and war on the continent. However, there was a slightly more qualified version of the 'Country' argument presented by Charles Davenant, a Tory pamphleteer and economist associated with Harley and his 'New Country Party' at the time.[36] Unlike the Country Whig writers noted above, Davenant was more agreeable to England entering the war with a land force, as well as naval force, though he also claimed that the war should be conducted in a more frugal way. In his writings on the balance of power, published in March 1701, Davenant warned of the danger of the union between France and Spain and its harmful consequences, and he argued for joining the war and assisting England's

31 *The Present Condition of the English Navy Set Forth in a Dialogue betwixt Young Fudg of the Admiralty, and Capt. Steerwell, on Oliverian Commander* (London, 1702), pp. 24–5. In the autumn of 1701, Benbow was dispatched to the West Indies to secure the Spanish silver fleet and to take Havana or Cartagena. However, he could not achieve either goal and died in a battle with the French squadron under du Casse in August 1702. As to his dispatch, see Chapter 4.

32 *Observator*, no. 5, 29 April 1702.

33 John Dennis, *A Proposal for Putting a Speedy End to the War, by Ruining the Commerce of the French and Spaniards, and Securing Our Own …* (London, 1703), p. 5. Dennis, who was famous as a critic, also wrote several pamphlets about naval affairs. Jonathan Pritchard, 'Dennis, John (1658–1734)', *ODNB*.

34 Dennis, *Proposal for Putting a Speedy End to the War*, p. v.

35 *Ibid.*, pp. 9–10, 13.

36 Downie, *Harley and the Press*, pp. 37–9.

allies. At the same time, he understood the people's anxiety that a new war might be conducted 'by a numerous Land-Army and with a small Fleet' and might impose further financial burdens on England as in the Nine Years War, when the Junto Whigs who were in power allegedly squandered public money on the war and lined their own pockets. However, he claimed that if these apprehensions were removed through frugal management of the war, people would be willing to join the war using land and naval forces.[37]

Unlike the Country Whig arguments, Davenant did not explicitly criticise land warfare on the continent in his pamphlet. This might partly reflect the fact that Harley and his collaborators, such as Davenant and John Toland, gradually moved towards the court's side at the time, which resulted in Harley's appointment as the Speaker of the Commons with support from the court, as well from the Tories, in February 1701.[38] Given Harley's approach to the court in this period, it is probable that Davenant's aim in this pamphlet was to support the war policy of the court and persuade the MPs in the Commons, not least the Country Tories, towards supporting the war against France, by showing that it could be fought with less expense than the last war. Thus, these arguments, based upon the Country concern, admitted the necessity of fighting a war against France; yet they maintained that the war should be fought in a more frugal and effective manner, not least at sea, in order to avoid putting further financial burden on the country.

Tory Argument: The Navy and Defence of England

The abovementioned argument, based on the 'Country' ethos, was, as T.J. Denman has pointed out, one of the bases of the Tory pro-maritime war argument that flourished in the late stages of the war.[39] However, on the eve of the war, the Tories, who were dominant in the Commons at that time, were opposed to active commitment to the war itself. In their argument, it was claimed that England should stand aloof from the continental war and concentrate on her defence through her naval forces. In countering Defoe's argument, which insisted on taking

[37] Charles Davenant, *Essays upon I. The Ballance of Power. II. The Right of Making War, Peace, and Alliances. III. Universal Monarchy* (London, 1701), pp. 74–85. According to Waddell, this pamphlet was published on 19 March 1701. David Waddell, *The Writings of Charles Davenant* (1656–1714), *Library (1956) s5-XI(3)*, 207.

[38] Downie, *Harley and the Press*, pp. 39–40. According to Downie, the publication of this pamphlet was held over until after the general election of January 1701. It is possible that the original content of Davenant's pamphlet, which might have had more strong Country flavour, was qualified to suit William's policy while it was waiting for publication.

[39] Denman, 'Political Debate', pp. 302–3. J.G.A. Pocock has placed this Country argument, including advocacy of the militia and war at sea, which was represented by Davenant's works, into the context of ideological tradition of Machiavellian political thought. J.G.A. Pocock, *The Machiavellian Moment: Florentine Political Thought and the Atlantic Republican Tradition* (Princeton, NJ, 1975), p. 442. However, as far as support for naval war is concerned, it would be more proper to place it into the context of the English ideological tradition of the pro-maritime war argument, which dates back to the Elizabethan period.

precautionary measures to prevent Spain falling into French hands, one anonymous author maintained:

> I don't know of any League the *English* are enter'd into; and if the *French* king will push for the Whole, that's his own business, and none of ours; let us keep our island safe, and let him push himself to pieces if he pleases.[40]

From this isolationist viewpoint, alliance with other countries on the continent was not necessary for the security of England, which was surrounded by sea and therefore did not need auxiliary forces for her defence, unlike England's neighbours on the continent. Instead, the author argued that the Dutch should assist the emperor, because it was their security, religion and commercial interests that were threatened by France and Spain.[41]

This argument also shared concerns over growth of the national debt and aversion to a standing army with the Country Whig pro-maritime war argument, though the former was initially even more reluctant to join the war than the latter. In reply to Defoe's remark that England was now in the same good condition as that which the last war left her, one anonymous writer argued, 'The War left us abominably in debt, with an Army upon our hands, from which we are not yet wholly freed.' Instead of land forces associated with tyranny and conquest, the writer preferred that the navy, 'the Walls and Bulworks of our Island', ensure the security of England. He claimed that,

> If *France* attack us, if the Lords of Admiralty please, we know how to defend our selves without the Assistance of a Land Force or turning Knights Errant in seeking dangerous Enterprise, and broken Bones abroad, because we are weary of Peace at home.

The writer was reluctant to treat France as an enemy, claiming that France had not yet declared war against England, nor seized any English territory, merchandise or ships. Even if war with France and Spain broke out, the author argued, England did not need to fear, for under a well-managed navy, England would have an opportunity to destroy their shipping and become 'the Carriers of all *European* Commodities'.[42]

This reluctance to participate in a war was an attitude shared by the new Tory ministers. In December 1700, some of the leading Tory politicians, such as Godolphin and Rochester, were bought off by the court, taking office as first Lord of Treasury and Lord Lieutenant of Ireland, respectively. However, to William's dismay, these new ministers were inclined to allow the Duke of Anjou's succession to the Spanish throne, and they were reluctant to take immediate military action to prevent the succession.[43] Their view was well represented in a pamphlet entitled

40 *Remarks upon a Late Pamphlet intitul'd The Two Great Questions Consider'd …* (London, 1700), p. 5.

41 *Remarks upon the Two Great Questions. Part II. Wherein the Grand Question of All is Consider'd, viz. What the Dutch Ought to Do at This Juncture?* (London, 1701), pp. 14–17.

42 *Remarks upon a Late Pamphlet intitul'd The Two Great Questions Consider'd*, pp. 8, 12–13, 16, 22.

43 Horwitz, *Parliament, Policy and Politics*, pp. 277–9.

An Argument against War, which was written in response to the pamphlets supporting participation in the war, such as *The Duke of Anjou's Succession Consider'd*. Its author was opposed to going to war immediately when England was not yet ready for it. Instead, the author tried to reassure his readers by pointing out the possibility of a breach between Spain and France after the Duke of Anjou's accession to the Spanish throne. He also proposed the marriage of the Arch-Duchess of Austria to King of Spain to prevent the union between Spain and France, which could help England to gain time to prepare for war, especially for a maritime war in Spanish America.[44]

However, in the following year, when the possibility of war loomed larger, given the provocative actions by France, Rochester seems to have accepted that English commitment to the war was inevitable. However, he insisted that it should be confined to war at sea. In a preface to his father's *History of the Rebellion and Civil Wars in England*, he deplored that England had concentrated on disadvantageous and expensive war on land, when England could restrain enemy powers without difficulty through naval expeditions. Then, he emphasised that England could help the common cause most through maritime war, not by expensive land warfare in foreign countries, whose burden England and her trade could not bear for long.[45]

Thus, while the first argument supported active engagement in the war and emphasised the positive economic advantages of maritime war, the Tories' support of the navy was initially of a more defensive character. However, in the last years of the war, combined with distrust of their allies, war at sea was depicted by Tory writers as an ideal and winning means of warfare, and it became a powerful weapon to criticise the war conduct of the Marlborough–Godolphin ministry, as we shall see later.

The Middle Stages of the War

The Marlborough–Godolphin Ministry under Attack

The demand for vigorous maritime war was temporarily submerged after the cancellation of the West Indian expedition under the command of the Earl of Peterborough, planned in 1703, which will be examined in the next chapter. However, in the middle stages of the war, debates over maritime affairs emerged again, against the dismal background of England's maritime affairs in 1707. In February, provision ships for the forces in Spain were attacked by Duquesne-Mosnier, and in May, the comte de Forbin attacked Portuguese and West Indian merchant men off Beachy Head and captured more than twenty ships. Also in August, the allied force under the command of Sir Cloudesley Shovell and Prince Eugene failed to seize Toulon, and, in late October, Shovell died in a shipwreck off

[44] *An Argument against War: In Opposition to Some Late Pamphlets, Particularly; the First and Second Part of The Duke of Anjou's Succession* ... (London, 1701), pp. 12–18.

[45] Edward Hyde, Earl of Clarendon, *The History of the Rebellion and Civil Wars in England, Begun in the Year 1641*, I (Oxford, 1702), pp. ix–x.

the Scilly isles on his way back to England.[46] In the same month, the combined squadron of Forbin and Duguay-Trouin assaulted a convoy carrying troops for Portugal off the Lizard, destroying several men of war and taking a dozen merchant men.[47]

This series of failures provoked a storm of criticism about the government's management of naval affairs. In November 1707, an acrimonious debate over the alleged mismanagement of naval affairs occurred in the House of Lords, in which the Junto, as well as the High Tories, severely criticised the government. Outside Parliament, the *Observator*, a Whig periodical, spearheaded the attack on the government. In September 1707, the *Observator* deplored the miserable situation of naval affairs, not least the damage caused by French attacks on British shipping, which brought wealth to the French and enabled them to pay their army at the same time. It claimed that, if Britain had concentrated her war effort on maritime war and assisted her allies in land warfare through subsidies, Britain might have already destroyed the enemy shipping.[48] The *Observator* also lamented that war in Spain and the West Indies had been neglected by Britain and her allies, whereas the French understood the importance of these regions and how to bring bullion from there for the use of the Duke of Anjou.[49] In this respect, the cancellation of Peterborough's expedition at the beginning of the war was a regrettable mistake. The *Observator* wrote:

> could our Circumstances have allow'd the brave Earl of *Peterborough* to have gone to the *West Indies* with a good Squadron, what might we not have expected from his Lordship, when a few of our Buccaneers could take *Panama*, and other Towns, both on the *North* and *South* Sides of *America*?

This support for the West Indian expeditions was connected with the expectation that Spanish-American trade would recover. The *Observator* claimed that such an expedition would frighten the Spaniards into sending the Duke of Anjou back to France and enable England to secure places in the continental part of the Spanish colonies 'as would have commanded a better Share in the Trade of both the *Indies*, than we have had yet', according to the sixth article of the Treaty of the Grand Alliance. The motif of the reign of Queen Elizabeth was used as well. After referring to the victory against the Spanish Armada in the reign of Queen Elizabeth and the battles of Vigo and Malaga in Anne's reign, the *Observator* maintained that, 'a *British* Queen, at the Head of a *British* Parliament,

46 On the failure at Toulon in 1707, see John H. Owen, *War at Sea under Queen Anne, 1702–1708* (Cambridge, 1938), Chapter 6. Although the allies failed to capture Toulon, the expedition contributed to their war effort in that it caused the diversion of French forces employed in other regions and also in that it forced France to scuttle most of its Mediterranean fleet. *Ibid.*, p. 191.

47 In addition to the losses at sea, in April, the allied force under Galway and the marquis of Minas suffered a crushing defeat at Almanza in Spain, from which Britain lost hope for Charles III's immediate accession to the Spanish crown.

48 *Observator*, no. 56, 10 September 1707.

49 *Observator*, no. 67, 18 October 1707.

is capable of taking such Measures, as may retrieve all our Losses; and by the Blessing of God, make her Arms as glorious by Sea, as they have been by Land'.[50]

Similarly, in 1707, the author of *An Inquiry into the Causes of Our Naval Miscarriages* lamented that war on foreign soil had been regarded as England's principal business. The author claimed that naval war was a more suitable means of warfare for England, an island endowed with materials to build ships and good sailors to man them, as well as navigable rivers and safe harbours.[51] After stressing the need to terminate the war soon, the author argued that subjecting the Spanish West Indies to Charles III was the most effectual way of bringing the war to 'a speedy and honourable Conclusion', while giving the English 'an Opportunity of enlarging our Trade in those parts, and of getting some convenient Ports to secure it', on the grounds of the sixth article. The author grumbled about the continuation of Dutch trade with the French and Spanish colonies through Curaçao while England was fighting for them and the emperor. However, in this pamphlet, the Dutch were still regarded as a partner with whom England should share Spanish-American trade, on the basis of privileges that might be granted by Archduke Charles. With regard to the war in the Netherlands, the author suspended his judgement about the need for a reduction of forces there, though he claimed that, if the conflicts between the emperor and the Hungarians and that between Catholic princes and German Protestants were resolved, England and the Netherlands might be able to use part of their forces for the war in Spain and the West Indies.[52]

Who was behind these criticisms of naval affairs is not clear. The writer of the *Observator* was John Tutchin, but he reportedly died in September 1707.[53] Given that his reputed patron, Baron Haversham, was one of the peers who made harsh criticisms of the government's alleged mismanagement of naval affairs in the House of Lords in November 1707, it might be possible that he hired another writer and used the *Observator* to support his attack on the government in Parliament.[54] On the other hand, it seems that *An Inquiry into the Causes of Our Naval Miscarriages* might have been written by a writer with Country Whig inclinations. This can be judged

50 *Observator*, no. 68, 22 October 1707.

51 *An Inquiry into the Causes of Our Naval Miscarriages*, p. iii.

52 *Ibid.*, pp. 23–5.

53 J.A. Downie, 'Tutchin, John (1660x64–1707)', *ODNB*. Also, Horsley has guessed from changes in styles that the *Observator* was taken up by some other writer from the issue of 17 September 1707. Lee S. Horsley, 'The Trial of John Tutchin, Author of the "Observator"', *The Yearbook of English Studies* 3 (1973), 139.

54 John Thompson, First Baron Haversham (1648–1710), was the second son of Maurice Thomson who was one of the leading figures of the 'new merchants' and collaborated with the Puritan faction, led by Warwick, in their West Indian enterprise from the 1620s to the 1630s. According to Downie, Haversham broke with the Junto in 1704. By 1708, he had joined the camp of Harley who increasingly came into antagonism with Godolphin, and as a result, was forced to resign his position as Secretary of State for the North in February 1708 and went into opposition. Downie, *Harley and the Press*, p. 97. Therefore, it is not impossible that Harley was also involved in this campaign.

from the fact that it contained a criticism of the Court's control of Parliament through pensions and places, as well as several arguments that were characteristic of the 'gentlemen versus tarpaulins' controversy, such as a preference for commanders with trading backgrounds over those with gentlemen backgrounds.[55]

By contrast, it does not seem that Junto Whigs, who played a leading role in the attack on the government over naval affairs in the Lords in November 1707, were directly involved in these publications. As we shall in Chapter 5, the purpose of their attacks, at that time, was to force the Marlborough–Godolphin ministry to accept their demands, some posts in the ministry and the removal of their political foe, Harley, by displaying their power in Parliament. In fact, in the debates over the deficiency of English troops in Spain, which took place in the same session, they even came to the rescue of the Court several times.[56]

In 1708, in the process of their attempt to force further concessions from the ministry, it appears that the Junto came to defend the government's continental war policy, to a certain extent. This is reflected in one pamphlet written in 1708 by Joseph Addison, who was, at that time, under-secretary to the Earl of Sunderland, Secretary of the State for the South and one of the members of the Junto Whigs. In this pamphlet, Addison mentioned that many people believed that the most effective way to subdue France was to stop the inflow of Spanish-American wealth into France or to channel it into Britain by attacking the Spanish West Indies. Although not completely dismissive of this idea, which carried 'so promising an appearance', he regarded it as 'a collateral Project, rather than our principal Design'. The reason was simple: 'an Enterprise that carries in it the Fate of *Europe* should not turn upon the Uncertainty of Winds and Waves, and be liable to all the Accidents that may befal a Naval Expedition'. Instead, the tactic that he recommended was 'to throw in Multitudes upon 'em and overpower 'em with Numbers' by land forces.[57] As William L. Sachse has mentioned, it is possible that this pamphlet reflected the views of his patron, Baron Somers, one of the Junto Whigs.[58] If this was the case, this defence of the war on the continent by Addison might have been intended to win the favour of the Marlborough–Godolphin ministry, in the expectation of further concessions from them.

Defoe, who was working as a government agent in Scotland at that time, also

55 *An Inquiry into the Causes of Our Naval Miscarriages*, pp. vi–vii, 8–9. The 'gentlemen versus tarpaulins' controversy was a debate that had its origin in the social tension caused by the return of gentlemen captains to the naval service after the Restoration, though in reality, that tension had already ceased to exist by the beginning of the eighteenth century. In this controversy, in order to criticise the monarchy, the image of corrupt and cowardly gentlemen captains, who were associated with the court, was often set against the image of brave and honest tarpaulins, who were believed to retain the virtues of the navy under the Commonwealth. Robert E. Glass, 'The Image of the Sea Officer in English Literature, 1660–1710', *Albion* 26, no. 4 (Winter 1994), 585.

56 William A. Speck, *The Birth of Britain: A New Nation 1700–1710* (Oxford and Cambridge, MA, 1994), pp. 130, 138.

57 Addison, *The Present State of the War*, pp. 16–18.

58 William L. Sachse, *Lord Somers: A Political Portrait* (Manchester, 1975), p. 258.

came to defend the ministry's war policy.[59] In response to the *Observator*'s argument for a more aggressive naval war against France, while admitting the importance of naval power, he maintained that the only way to defeat France was by war on land. In the *Review* of 6 January 1708, he argued that, 'the best Way to prosecute a War against any Prince, is to fall upon him in that Part, in which his Power does chiefly consist'. In the case of France, it was not at sea, because, for the French king, 'his Naval Strength was an Accident to his Power'. Rather, his power was derived from land forces. Therefore, 'a vigorous Prosecution of the War by Land might ruin him, and within a little had entirely subdued him'.[60] Defoe developed his argument through the following issues. While admitting the significance of the West Indian expeditions in cutting off the enemy supply of money and the necessity of trade protection by using convoys and cruisers, he rejected the idea of the sea and land services as being in rivalry.[61] Thus, in the middle stages of the war, against the criticisms of the mismanagement of naval affairs, those pamphleteers who were close to the Junto or Godolphin tried to defend the continental war, though they did not deny the usefulness of the colonial maritime war.

Projecting a Company for Spanish-American Trade

The middle stages of the war also saw the appearance of several pamphlets proposing means to exclude the French from trade with the Spanish-American colonies. This period falls into the first boom in South Sea trade by French merchants, especially those of St Malo, which continued from May 1705 to the summer of 1708. At the same time, they also penetrated the Spanish-American market from the Caribbean side. Thus, this was a period when the French were making significant inroads into the Spanish-American market through both the Pacific and the Atlantic.[62] In the face of this increasing French presence in the Spanish-American colonies, Britain tried to secure her position by extracting trade privileges from Archduke Charles. In July 1707, James Stanhope, an English diplomat who had been sent to Spain, managed to obtain trade privileges through the treaty signed in Barcelona with Archduke Charles. This included a secret clause that allowed the English to trade with the Spanish-American colonies as freely as the Spaniards until an Anglo-Spanish company could be founded after the war, excluding the French from Spanish-American trade, as well as from the proposed company. The Dutch, however, were indignant about this clause, because they regarded it as a breach of the Treaty of the Grand Alliance.[63]

[59] At this time, Defoe was torn between his patrons Harley and Godolphin, who increasingly came into conflict with each other. However, with Harley's permission, he continued to work for Godolphin and the government. Furbank and Owens, *A Political Biography of Daniel Defoe*, pp. 85–6.

[60] *Review*, IV, pp. 561–3, no. 141, 6 January 1708.

[61] *Review*, IV, p. 567, no. 142, 8 January 1708.

[62] Lespagnol, *Messieurs de Saint Malo*, II, pp. 554, 556. The second and greater boom started in October 1709 and continued until May 1715.

[63] Basil Williams, *Stanhope: A Study in Eighteenth Century War and Diplomacy* (Oxford, 1932), pp. 60–1; Stein and Stein, *Silver, Trade, and War*, pp. 131–2.

Against this background, there appeared to be several proposals promoting a Spanish-American trade. For example, the *Observator* of 29 October 1707 mentioned the French dominance in Spanish-American trade, especially in South Sea trade, and lamented that England had not taken measures to prevent it, in spite of her strong naval forces, while the French achieved success without spending much on a large fleet. The *Observator* claimed that, ''tis in our Power, when we please, to out them of that Trade, both on the *South* side and *North* side of *America*; and if we don't, farewell to our *West India* Trade, which is of the greatest Consequence to the Nation'. Then, the *Observator* proposed making a colony on the Isthmus of Darien, following the example of the Darien scheme by Scotland, with which the England was now united, and to drive the French out of Spanish America by using the colony as a base.[64]

Likewise, in 1707, one anonymous pamphleteer proposed carrying on trade with the Spanish colonies, including those in the South Sea, which would provide a large market for English woollen and linen products and, in return, bring back bullion to England. Moreover, the author implied that there was hope of establishing settlements on the west coast of Spanish America, which would make trade much quicker and easier. This was an attempt to imitate the French success. The author claimed that 'The Benefits the French have found from it already, are but Shadows of what we may from this Undertaking, reasonably expect.' In response to a possible objection that the Spaniards would not allow Britain to share in their trade, the author argued that, in the peace treaty, Britain could demand 'a freedom of Traffick', which was also beneficial for the Spaniards, as it could bring them further income from import duties and would incline other nations to protect their mines from the attacks of marauders.[65]

There were also several proposals to establish a private company to recover Spanish-American trade from the French. They were, in a sense, descendants of the plan for a West India Company, which was proposed several times during the seventeenth century. The author of *An Account of What Will Do; or An Equivalent for Thoulon* put forward a plan for a private company to trade with the Spanish colonies on the Pacific coast, in order to 'put a stop to the growing Trade and Power of the France in the South-West Indies'. This company was to make a settlement at Darien or some other part of Spanish America, which was thought not only rich in its products, such as gold and silver, but also useful as a centre of trade: 'was a *Free Port* settled here, it would Inevitably Draw all the Trade of *Europe* to it Self, which the other part of the World hold now in *America*'. 'And thus', the author claimed, 'we may Secure by a Single Company of Men that *Spanish* Trade, for which We are now Conquering all *Spain*. And to Regain which, we must Conquer the *Politicks* of *France*, after we have Subdued their Force, United with that of *Spain*'. It was further expected that 'Charles III' would allow Britain to keep St Mary [Santa María de la Antigua del Darién], a town near

64 *Observator*, no. 70, 29 October 1707.

65 *A Letter to Sir William Robinson, in Relation to a Proposal for a Trade to the Spanish West-Indies* (London, 1707), pp. 2–3, 5–6.

Darien and a suitable base for South Sea trade, after it was taken.[66] Similarly, *A Letter to a Member of Parliament concerning Trade* deplored the neglect of foreign trade and emphasised the necessity of its promotion. In reference to a proposal by one Mr Puckle to establish a company for Spanish-American trade, it proposed combining the Spanish colonial trade of the projected company with the slave trade of the Royal African Company to make the proposal more practicable.[67] Although none of these proposals were actually put into practice, this idea of establishing a company for Spanish-American trade later culminated in the plan for the South Sea Company proposed by Robert Harley, which will be dealt with in Chapter 6.

As we have seen so far, in the middle stages of the war, against the backdrop of a series of failures at sea, there was criticism of the Marlborough–Godolphin ministry's naval management and a call for a more active maritime war, although the writers who were close to the Junto or Godolphin defended the continental war policy. Furthermore, in the face of the French advance in South Sea trade, several proposals were made to promote Spanish-American trade by establishing a trading company. As we shall see next, these elements converged in the Tory pro-maritime war argument, which appeared in the last years of the war.

The Later Stages of the War

The Harley Ministry and the Second Pro-maritime War Argument

In August 1710, there was a drastic change in the political situation of Britain. The attempt of Queen Anne and Robert Harley to get rid of the influence of 'the family', a core group who had held power, including Marlborough, Godolphin and Sunderland, led to the dismissal of the latter two politicians. Instead, Harley came to the centre of the political stage, together with his political partner, Henry St John. Moreover, in the general election that took place in 1710, the Tories won by a landslide, helped by the Sacheverell affair.[68] Against the background of this Tory resurgence, another pro-maritime war argument increasingly became influential in this period. As in the first argument, emphasis on the economic advantages of maritime war and references to historical precedents were present in this second pro-maritime war argument. However, on closer examination, there were several

66 *An Account of What Will Do*, pp. 3–4, 7–8. There is a pamphlet with quite similar content that was by Captain John Le Wright and published in 1706. This pamphlet seems to have been the basis of *An Account of What Will Do* [John Le Wright], *Two Proposals becoming England at this Juncture to Undertake. One, for Securing a Collony in the West-Indies … And the Other, for Advancing Merchandize, and the Crown-Revenue to at least 40000l. p. an* ([London?] 1706). Judging from close similarities between the arguments in these pamphlets and William Paterson's plan for establishing a free port in Darien, it might be presumed that Le Wright wrote the pamphlet in collaboration with Paterson, or at least, was influenced by him.

67 *A Letter to a Member of Parliament concerning Trade; and Particularly the Trade of the Spanish West-Indies* (London, 1707), pp. 1–2, 4–6.

68 Speck, *Birth of Britain*, pp. 177–83, 188–92.

differences between the first and second arguments, in terms of their contents and political purposes.

There were two factors that helped the rise of this second argument: concern about the growth of public debt and distrust of the allies, especially the Dutch. The anxiety about the public debt, which was already mentioned, increased as the war went on. By 1709, Britain faced the grim prospect of an endless and costly war. Discontent with the war was exacerbated further by a series of events, such as a cold winter in the previous year and a bad harvest in the following summer, the failure of the peace talks in The Hague in August and the Pyrrhic victory at Malplaquet in September.[69]

In the late stage of the war, it was mainly the Tories who criticised Britain's financial situation. They protested that the 'moneyed men' were taking advantage of the new financial system and of the lingering war at the expense of landowners, who bore the burden of the heavy taxation, such as the new land tax.[70] Their criticism was also levelled at the Whigs. The *Examiner*, a Tory periodical, accused the Whig political leaders of increasing the public debt immensely while exploiting the debt to strengthen their political position.[71] The *Examiner* warned that:

> Had they gone on *Fighting* and *Taxing* at this Rate, it is morally impossible but we must have been Ruin'd; tho' France had been Conquer'd at the same time. When we had *Mortgag'd* the *Land* and *Malt-Tax*, and after that a *General Excise*, we must have resorted to some Foreign Country, enrich'd by our Spoils, and there have Pawn'd *Great Britain* for our own Money, to spend it in their Defence.[72]

As is seen in this statement, the concern over the alarming rise of financial burdens was often linked with the second problem, discontent with the allies, who were blamed for being dishonest and self-serving. Of the allies, it was the Dutch who were especially castigated. Contrary to the initial expectation in England that the Dutch would contribute to the war effort as her chief partner, in English eyes, the Dutch looked uncooperative throughout the war. They also did not live up to English expectations in terms of naval assistance. There had been a disagreement over the quota of naval ships to be provided in accordance with the perpetual

69 Dickson, *Financial Revolution in England*, p. 62.

70 On the Tories' hostility to the 'moneyed men' during the reign of Queen Anne, see Holmes, *British Politics*, Chapter 5. Holmes has denied a simple dichotomy between Tory landowners and Whig businessmen by pointing out that some of the Tories had actual interest in foreign trade as well, and some of them, such as Henry St John distinguished overseas merchants from the 'moneyed men'. However, he admits that 'by 1702 the Tory party was already identified with the defence of the special interests of the landed men'. *Ibid.*, p. 170.

71 Between December 1711 and 1714, the main contributor for the *Examiner* was William Oldisworth, who succeeded the previous editors, Jonathan Swift and Delarivier Manley. Abigail Williams, 'Oldisworth, William (1680–1734)', *ODNB*. Robert J. Allen has conjectured that Swift could still have had influence on Oldisworth through John Barber, the Tory printer. Robert J. Allen, 'William Oldisworth: the Author of the *Examiner*', *Philological Quarterly* 26, no. 4 (1947), 172.

72 *Examiner*, V, no. 23, 15 February 1713/14.

alliance signed between the two countries in November 1701.[73] Also, their refusal to agree to England's request to send a squadron to the West Indies, except in 1703, worsened the problem. These led to increasing discontent with and distrust of the Dutch in England. According to Coombs, from about 1707, as war-weariness grew in England, anti-Dutch feeling gradually resurfaced, connected with the suspicion that England had been dragged into the lengthy and costly war in the Low Countries by the Dutch in order to protect Dutch interests, while the Dutch were prospering at England's expense. In particular, the opposition Tories fostered these ideas.[74]

This discontent increasingly became linked with an argument about the proper role of England in the war, which had been seen from the early stages of the conflict. It was debated whether England should fight as a principal in land warfare on the continent, especially in Flanders and Germany, to help her allies, or should play only an auxiliary role and pursue her own interests at sea.[75] Those who made the second pro-maritime war argument insisted that England should choose the latter, instead of wasting money on assisting her faithless allies. As early as 1704, Edward Repington expressed this view in a letter to Thomas Coke. He regarded an expedition to the Spanish West Indies as the only economically promising operation, and he dismissed other 'Transmarine projects', which would 'serve to ruine, rather than enrich the Nation'. Referring to historical precedents, he claimed that England should not naively sacrifice her own interests to help her allies:

> You may say it's Roman like and generous to assist our Allies, perhaps it may be so, but the Romans always made an advantage of their Allies in the conclusion, and were too wise to ruine themselves out of mistaken notions of honor, being ever wel rewarded for the Assistance they sent.[76]

[73] Hattendorf, *England in the War of the Spanish Succession*, pp. 91–2, 155–9. However, this is not necessarily attributable to Dutch negligence. According to Hattendorf, the dispute over the number of ships in fact reflected a disagreement over naval strategy between the two countries. For example, the Dutch preferred the use of convoys to a blockade, on which England insisted.

[74] Coombs, *Conduct of the Dutch*, pp. 158–9. Although the Dutch were the main target of the criticism, other allies were also blamed. In a letter to the Duke of Shrewsbury, James Vernon made the following complaint of the Germans: 'they make war so much at their ease whilst England & Holland pay all, that I believe they rather grow rich than poor I wish we did so too, but that is very farr from our case'. BL, Add MS 40776, fol. 11, James Vernon to the Duke of Shrewsbury, 28 October 1706.

[75] This was not a new debate. How England should meet conflicts on the continent was a recurring question in English foreign policy that had existed since the Elizabethan period. Richmond, *Navy as an Instrument of Policy*, pp. 41–2, 70, 179, 222–3, 235–7.

[76] BL, Add MS 69941, fol. 28v, Edward Repington to Thomas Coke, 1 December 1704. Thomas Coke was originally a Tory with Country tendencies, but around 1704 he turned to the Court. *House of Commons, 1690–1715*, III, 'COKE, Thomas'. Geoffrey Holmes describes Coke as a placeman with inclinations towards the Tories. Holmes, *British Politics*, p. 50.

The frustration with Britain's role in the war became stronger as the war continued. In *A Letter to the Examiner* of 1710, Henry St John maintained:

> We engag'd as *Confederates*, but we have been made to proceed as *Principals*: *Principals* in expence of Blood and of Treasure, whilst hardly a *Second* place in Respect and Dignity is allow'd to us.[77]

Similarly, in 1712, the *Examiner* lamented that Britain had neglected her own interests while taking care of those of other countries; it compared the present role of Britain, which tried to keep the balance of Europe, to 'a Servant in a Shop, who holds the Scales indeed, but it is for others to receive all the Advantage of the Trade'.[78]

These two questions – the growing financial burdens and the proper role in the war – converged in the second pro-maritime war argument. This linkage can be seen in Jonathan Swift's widely read pamphlet, *The Conduct of the Allies*, published in November 1711. In this pamphlet, he deplored how Britain was unnecessarily dragged into the war as a principal actor by political leaders and those who expected to profit from the war, and that Britain was forced to bear the war costs to help her allies, which consequently burdened Britain with an enormous amount of debt.[79] Similarly, the *Examiner* of October 1712 claimed that if Britain had fought only as an auxiliary, she 'might have brought additional Riches into our Country, instead of Poverty, Debts, and Mortgages' from the war. However, the *Examiner* lamented, Britain plunged into the war as a principal actor, and her war efforts ended up only benefiting the allies by gaining new territories for them, even though they had failed to meet their quota of military forces.[80]

Instead of pursuing lengthy and costly continental warfare, which was regarded as the main cause of the increases in debt and taxes, the ministerial writers argued that Britain could have fought a maritime war, which would have been more effective and profitable. The *Examiner* maintained that 'the War at Sea, where it could most successfully have been carry'd on, has been scandalously neglected, and yet our Fleet, which is our greatest Security, has been almost destroy'd'.[81] Historical examples were also invoked to advocate maritime war. It was asserted that the former monarchs of England, such as Henry VII, Henry VIII and Queen Elizabeth, seldom engaged in war on land. Even when Elizabeth assisted her allies on the continent, she sent only a limited number of troops and took care to recover the costs of doing so. By contrast, at sea, the queen 'engag'd in War with more Frankness' and conducted 'Pyratical Wars upon the *Spaniards*, in which the Prizes taken did infinitely more than make good the Charge'. According to the *Examiner*, wars at that time were the opposite of the modern wars, 'for by them we grew richer, instead of being impoverished and mortgaged'.[82] Again, in

77 Henry St John, *A Letter to the Examiner* ([London] 1710), pp. 6–7.
78 *Examiner*, II, no. 35, 31 July 1712.
79 Swift, *Conduct of the Allies*, pp. 20–4.
80 *Examiner*, II, no. 44, 2 October 1712.
81 *Ibid.*
82 *Examiner*, II, no. 35, 31 July 1712.

February 1713, the *Examiner* invoked the memory of the reign of Queen Elizabeth and praised the fact that she pursued naval war, made settlements in Americas and encouraged navigation, by which 'her Dominions were enlarg'd, her People enrich'd', while lending some troops to allies at their expense. Thus, it was claimed, 'every where the War was husbanded to the great Gain and Benefit of the Publick'.[83]

Also, Charles Davenant, who was working for the Harley ministry at that time, severely criticised English commitment to the continental war for the allies, which sacrificed the nation's own interests.[84] He maintained that, while expenses for the naval fleet contributed to the domestic economy, those for land forces caused an outflow of wealth and, consequently, impoverishment of the nation. Moreover, large subsidies tended to incline the allies to prolong the war, in the expectation of further income. Thus, claimed Davenant,

> By Land-Armies we enrich other Countries, by great Fleets we cherish and maintain our own People, and protect our Trade from the Insults of our Enemies, and from the Incroachments of our Allies and Friends.[85]

In another pamphlet written in the form of a dialogue, Davenant applauded the West Indian expeditions by quoting the example of the Elizabethan period:

> as to invading the *West-Indies*, the Reign of Queen *Elizabeth* shews how easie and profitable those Expeditions were, and what Masses of Gold and Silver were brought from thence. And considering how much weaker the *Spaniards* are now, than they were in that Age, 'tis more than probable, that an attempt there would have paid its own Charges.[86]

Likewise, in *The Conduct of the Allies*, Swift deplored that Britain had fought a disadvantageous continental war for ten years while neglecting such part which 'would have saved and gained us many Millions', and 'would have soonest weakened the Enemy, and must either have promoted a speedy-Peace, or enabled us to go on with the War'. The sphere of warfare that Britain should have chosen was at sea, 'a noble Field of Honour and Profit'. Swift claimed that, at half the cost that Britain had already spent, Britain might have maintained her quota for land forces in Flanders while, through her navy, Britain might have 'so distressed the Spaniards in the North and South Seas of *America*, as to prevent any Returns of money from thence, except in our own Bottoms'. He

[83] *Examiner*, V, no. 26, 26 February 1713/14.

[84] According to Waddell, Davenant, who had been working for Godolphin, made his peace with Harley, his former patron, when the Tory ministry took power in August 1710. D. Waddell, 'Charles Davenant (1656–1714) – A Biographical Sketch', *EcHR*, new ser, 11, no. 2 (1958), 287.

[85] Charles Davenant, *A Report to the Honourable the Commissioners for Putting in Execution the Act, intitled, An Act, for the Taking, Examining, and Stating the Publick Accounts of the Kingdom* (London, 1712), part II, pp. 60–1.

[86] Charles Davenant, *Sir Thomas Double at Court, and in High Preferments. In Two Dialogues, between Sir Thomas Double and Sir Richard Comover, alias Mr. Whiglove* ([London] 1710), pp. 73–4.

asserted, 'This is what best became us to do as a Maritime Power.'[87]

Even in this promising maritime war, however, Britain was hamstrung by her allies. Swift mentioned possible objections to such an expedition from the Netherlands and Austria, and he admitted that this actually happened in the Quebec expedition in May 1711. The two countries made complaints about the expedition, suspecting that the expedition was intended against Peru. He questioned the sincerity of the Dutch in particular, who expressed their anxiety over the British West Indian expedition, even though the two countries had already reached an agreement as to whom new conquests in Spanish America would belong to in accordance with the sixth article of the Treaty of the Grand Alliance. Swift claimed that this was the only article 'in all our Treaties or Stipulations, with any view of Interest to this Kingdom' and, for that very reason, had been 'altogether neglected'.[88]

Thus, the second argument advocated maritime war as the means of warfare that Britain should have adopted. While this argument stressed the economic advantages of maritime war, as in the first argument, it depicted the Dutch as a self-serving ally and criticised the continental war for creating Britain's financial problems and serving only the interests of the allies. In these respects, the second argument was clearly distinctive from the first argument, which emphasised unity with the Dutch and lacked the criticism of the continental land war.

What, then, was the purpose of this argument? Coombs has regarded *The Conduct of the Allies* as a part of an anti-Dutch campaign that was designed by the ministry at that time, especially Robert Harley, whose main policy was to proceed with peace negotiations with France. In this campaign, the Dutch were singled out as scapegoats and were criticised, in order to convince the public of the necessity of peace. This was especially needed at this juncture, because the revelation of the secret agreement between Britain and France, signed by the French diplomat Mesnager in September 1711, provoked a cool or hostile reaction in Britain and abroad.[89] Similarly, James A. Downie has explained the pamphlet as a culmination of the propaganda campaign to pave the way for announcing the signing of the agreement.[90] Although which of the two chief ministers, moderate Harley or the more extreme St John, had more influence on the production of this pamphlet is still debatable, there is little doubt that one of the chief purposes of these publications, including *The Conduct of the Allies*, was to smooth the way for Harley's peace negotiations.[91]

87 Swift, *Conduct of the Allies*, pp. 26, 30. However, according to Denman, Swift's personal opinion was not necessarily in favour of the West Indian expedition. Denman, 'Political Debate', p. 255.

88 Swift, *Conduct of the Allies*, pp. 32–3.

89 Coombs, *Conduct of the Dutch*, pp. 277–8.

90 James A. Downie, 'The Conduct of the Allies: The Question of Influence', *The Art of Jonathan Swift*, ed. Clive T. Probyn (London, 1978), p. 111.

91 Downie has pointed to Harley's role in the composition of the pamphlets, as well as that of St John, who is usually thought to have influenced content of the pamphlet. *Ibid.*, pp. 118–26.

However, a question still remains as to what role the support for maritime war and emphasis on its economic advantages played in this campaign for peace. First, the pro-maritime war argument was employed to make the criticisms against the previous ministry and the allies more effective. This second argument stressed the possible benefits that Britain could have reaped if war had been pursued at sea, instead of the lengthy and costly land war on the continent conducted by the former ministry. By demonstrating this contrast between maritime war and land war, the argument aimed to stir the anger of the people against the former ministers and dishonest allies who were believed to have dragged Britain into the war, as well as to help Harley to win more support for the peace talks.

In addition to the promotion of peace negotiations, this second argument seems to have had another purpose: to support the Tory ministry's policy of promoting Spanish-American trade, especially the trade of the South Sea Company. In the second argument, the Tories' criticism of the alleged mismanagement of the war by the Marlborough–Godolphin ministry was often connected with criticism of the neglect of Spanish-American trade, as well as the increase in the national debt, which the second argument inherited from the preceding 'Country' pro-maritime war argument. For example, in May 1711, in a letter to Lord Raby, Thomas Wentworth, St John complained that Britain was obliged to fight as a principal actor, while the dishonest allies, the Netherlands and Austria, put their private interests above the common cause. Consequently, he argued,

> our commerce has been neglected, while the French have engrossed the South Sea trade to themselves, and the Dutch encroach daily upon us, both in the East Indies, and on the coast of Africa.[92]

A similar claim was also present in Swift's *The Conduct of the Allies*. After lamenting the neglect of maritime war in America, Swift wrote,

> while We for Ten Years, have been squandring away our Mony upon the Continent, *France* hath been wisely engrossing all the Trade of Peru, going directly with their Ships to *Lima* and other Ports, and there receiving Ingots of Gold and Silver for *French* Goods of little value.

He expressed concern that this might divert the channels of Spanish-American trade in the future, from which Britain used to make a great profit by trading via Cadiz.[93] As we will see in Chapter 6, one of the original aims of the South Sea Company proposed by Harley in May 1711 was trade with the Spanish colonies on the Pacific coast. In order to support this company, the second argument criticised the former ministry's alleged neglect of British commercial interests in Spanish-American trade, as well as their neglect of maritime war.[94]

[92] *Bolingbroke Correspondence*, I, pp. 192–3, St John to Lord Raby, 6 May 1711.
[93] Swift, *Conduct of the Allies*, pp. 30–1.
[94] The debate over the South Sea Company and its connection with the second argument are dealt with in more detail in Chapter 6.

Defence of the Marlborough–Godolphin Ministry

Against these Tory arguments criticising the Marlborough–Godolphin ministry for allegedly neglecting maritime war and the Spanish-American trade, Whig writers tried to vindicate the Whigs and the former ministry. The *Observator*, a Whig periodical, refuted the *Examiner*'s accusation against the Whigs as unfair. In the issue of 20 June 1711, the *Observator* pointed out that the *Observator* himself had been complaining about neglect of the war in Spain, West Indian trade and trade protection, which the *Examiners* attributed to the Whigs, and that it was rather the Whigs who had been trying to make advances in these issues.[95]

In defending the past management of the war by the former ministry, some of the Whig writers pointed out problems with the colonial maritime war, which was now supported by the Tory writers. For example, John Oldmixon claimed that, if Britain had adopted what the author of *The Conduct of the Allies* proposed, 'we shou'd have bent all our Thoughts on Settlements in the S.S. [i.e. South Sea], and been at Two Millions a Year charge to carry on a Maritime War with a King that had no Fleet, and a Nation that has but a beggarly Trade, only to take a few Salt-Ships'. He believed that, in terms of geographical conditions, Britain was at a disadvantage in war on trade ('a Piratical War'), compared with France. He claimed that, 'considering the Length of his Coast, 'tis impossible for us so to prevent, as to hinder complaint'.[96]

Likewise, an author of *A Full Answer to the Conduct of the Allies* scoffed at the idea of active colonial maritime war advocated in *The Conduct of the Allies.* Referring to the disastrous expedition to Quebec in 1711, the author dismissed the idea of colonial expeditions as 'a Castle in the Air'. 'Experiment is over,' he pronounced, 'I hope we shall make no more of them at so dear a rate.' In a later part of the pamphlet, the author criticised the idea again by quoting the example of the Dutch, who seldom sent fleets to the colonies. The reason was, according to him, 'the *Dutch* are too Wise a People to be fond of Expeditions' that were risky, and quite often resulted in the loss of both vessels and troops. Moreover, in defending the Marlborough–Godolphin ministry, he disparaged such plans as the Quebec expedition in 1711 as 'Chymerical in themselves'. According to him, such schemes 'have only Specious outside to delude unthinking People, who look no further than the bare View of things, as they find them Represented'.[97] Thus, by the late stage of the war, a reversal of roles occurred. Although the Whigs supported the colonial maritime war at the beginning of the war, by this time some of them had come to criticise the pro-maritime war argument, while the Tories now embraced it as their ideal war policy.

As we have seen so far, in the debates over British policies in the War of the Spanish Succession, there were chiefly two different arguments supporting maritime war.

[95] *Observator*, no. 49, 20 June 1711.

[96] John Oldmixon, *Remarks on a False, Scandalous, and Seditious Libel, Intituled, The Conduct of the Allies* ... (London, 1711), p. 19.

[97] *A Full Answer to the Conduct of the Allies: To which is Added, Some Observations on the Remarks on the Barrier Treaty*... (London, 1712), pp. 24, 49, 86.

The first argument, which was Whiggish in tone, appeared just before the war, while the second Tory argument, which inherited several features from the 'Country' pro-maritime war argument in the early and middle stages of the war, became influential in the late stages of the war. They shared common features, such as emphasis on the economic advantages of war at sea and allusions to historical examples, especially the glorious memory of the Elizabethan maritime war.

There was, however, a stark contrast, in terms of their content, between the first and the second argument. While the first argument did not show antipathy towards continental land war and emphasised the necessity of maintaining land forces and cooperation with the Dutch, the second argument regarded war on the continent as costly and unnecessary, and it severely criticised the allies, in particular, the Dutch, for their treachery. Furthermore, the function of each pro-maritime war argument was different. In the first argument, the economic advantages of maritime war were emphasised to motivate the English to prepare for war. On the other hand, in the second argument, those advantages were stressed to make the criticism of the past war conduct of the Marlborough–Godolphin ministry and the allies more plausible by contrasting supposedly profitable maritime war, which Britain could have fought, with costly and lengthy land war on the continent.

These differences reflected the intentions of the backers of each argument. The first argument was probably claimed by the Court or Junto Whigs; it was aimed at encouraging the nation to enter into the war, in alliance with the Dutch and Austria. On the other hand, the second Tory argument was intended to smooth the way for the ongoing peace talks with France by Harley, as well as to promote trade for the newly established South Sea Company, by pointing out the alleged neglect by the former ministry of Spanish-American trade. As we shall see in Chapter 7, these two pro-maritime war arguments, with different functions, mobilisation of support for war and criticisms of the conduct of the government, reappeared in conflicts with Spain in the late 1710s and 1720s, albeit in different political contexts.

Thus, while the pro-maritime war arguments shared common features, their contents and functions were also influenced by the political struggles of the time. As N.A.M. Rodger has rightly pointed out,

> Only the Navy united the political world, and provided a common language of political rhetoric. It was a screen on which every party could project its own ideology – a blank screen, thanks to their ignorance of what it was really like.[98]

This would also apply to the pro-maritime war arguments during the War of the Spanish Succession. The argument was employed by different political groups for different purposes, which made its content varied, reflecting the political biases of the groups. However, this does not mean that the pro-maritime war argument was a mere tool for political manipulation. The supposed economic advantages of maritime war had a real appeal to some of the leading politicians, and the arguments had actual impact on the naval operations and legislation during the war, as we shall see in the following chapters.

98 Rodger, 'Queen Elizabeth and the Myth of Sea-Power', 165.

PART II

Impact on Reality

– 4 –

Impact on Reality: Naval Policy

This chapter examines the impact of the pro-maritime war argument upon the actual naval policy of the government during the War of the Spanish Succession, and reveals to the extent of the government attempts to implement the two major operations against Spanish America that we have seen in the previous chapter: interception of the Spanish silver fleets and colonial expeditions. Ian R. Mather, who studied activities of the Royal Navy in America and the West Indies in the period between 1660 and 1720, emphasised its defensive character and relatively modest success in territorial conquest in that period, while colonists were more enthusiastic and probably more successful in attacks on enemy territory.[1] If we look only at the outcome of the naval operations in that region, this remark seems to be adequate. In fact, enthusiasm in expeditions for colonial conquests was not lacking in the mother country. Moreover, those who showed interest in naval operations against Spanish America were not confined to opposition politicians. N.A.M. Rodger has pointed out that, irrespective of political allegiance, all English politicians were committed to the 'myths of English sea power'; the true distinction tended to be between those in opposition who were fully committed to it, and those in power who were obliged to make some compromises with reality.[2] However, this does not mean that the supporters of colonial maritime war gave up their policy when they came to power. This chapter will show that those upholders of pro-maritime war policy in the ministry tried to carry out naval operations against Spanish America that they believed to be an effective means to deprive the enemy of its financial resources. It also investigates why plans for colonial expeditions did not materialise or were unsuccessful, and despite the failures, why the belief in colonial expeditions continued to survive.[3]

[1] Ian R. Mather, 'The Role of the Royal Navy in the English Atlantic Empire, 1660–1720' (unpublished Ph.D. thesis, Oxford University, 1995), pp. 392–3.

[2] N.A.M. Rodger, *The Command of the Ocean: A Naval History of Britain, 1649–1815* (London, 2004, repr. London, 2005), p. 178.

[3] For the details of the operations in the West Indies, see Ruth Bourne, *Queen Anne's Navy in the West Indies* (New Haven, 1939), especially Chapter 5, and Rodger, *Command of the Ocean*, Chapter 11.

Operations in the Early Stage of the War

Capture of the Spanish Silver Fleet at Vigo

Spanish silver fleets had already attracted great attention in both France and England even before the war was declared. In April of 1701, Louis XIV dispatched the marquis de Coëtlogon to the Spanish colonies with the offer to escort the *flota*, the Spanish silver fleet, from New Spain (Mexico) back to Europe, and secure the bullion and effects on board the fleet. However, Coëtlogon failed to convince Moctezuma, viceroy of Mexico, and returned to France.

In the meantime, England watched the movement of the French in the West Indies with concern.[4] James Vernon, Secretary of State for the South, was alarmed by the French activity in the West Indies and emphasised the importance of West Indian operations to William III: 'I don't see that Wee can make the Spaniards feel our weight, unless it bee in the West Indies & here wee might make the best advantages both against France & Spain.'[5] The news of French naval preparations stirred anxiety among the allies too. Franciscus van Schonenberg, Dutch envoy at Lisbon, who was in charge of English interests in Spain at that time, strongly urged that the allies should take appropriate measure to prevent the French from securing the *flota*, for, he claimed, 'if the French Squadron happily meete the said Fleete, it will take, and Conduct it into France in somuch that the Most Christian King will render himselfe absolutely Master of it'. [6]

William also had a strong concern about the *flota*. Marlborough, who accompanied the king to The Hague, stated that William thought the interception of the *flota* was of 'the last consequence', and through him, William ordered the Lords Justices to dispatch Vice Admiral John Benbow to the West Indies again to secure the *flota*.[7] This was also significant for the protection of the English commercial interest. As explained in Chapter 2, the trade with Spanish America via Cadiz by the silver fleets was one of the two main channels of Spanish-American trade for England, and English as well as Dutch merchants invested in the goods on board the fleet. Therefore, in July 1701, the English merchants trading to Spain asked the Lord Justices to send a squadron to secure their goods on board the *flota*.[8] This concern for the merchants' cargoes was also reflected in an instruction to Benbow

4 TNA, SP 44/102, pp. 3–7, James Vernon to Admiralty, 4 March 1700/1; SP 44/102, pp. 44–8, Vernon to Admiralty, 4 April 1701; ADM 1/4087, fol. 197, Extract of a letter from Plymouth, 1 April 1701; BL, Add MS 34348, fols 124–124v, William Beeston to Vernon, 7 July 1701, and fol. 126, Beeston to Vernon, 11 July 1701.

5 BL, Add MS 40775, fol. 37v, Vernon to William III, 25 July 1701.

6 TNA, ADM 1/4087, fols 430–430v, Schonenberg to Vernon, 20 October 1701. For the French preparation to meet the *flota*, see also TNA, SP 44/102, pp. 255–6, Vernon to Admiralty, 8 November 1701.

7 *Marlborough–Godolphin Correspondence*, I, no. 17, p. 18, Marlborough to Godolphin, 6/17 August 1701; no. 17A, p. 19, Marlborough to the Lord Justices, 6/17 August 1701.

8 TNA, ADM 2/400, fol. 387, Josiah Burchett, secretary of the Board of Admiralty to Robert Yard, secretary to the Lord Justices, 16 July 1701; ADM 1/4087, fol. 386, Yard to Admiralty, 25 September 1701.

of August 1701, which ordered him to take care to prevent embezzlement, stating that it was king's intention that the properties aboard the *flota* 'be entirely and safely preserved for the use of those that have a just Title to the same'.[9]

In contrast to William and some of the ministers who were keen to dispatch a large squadron to the West Indies, the Lords of Admiralty were more cautious about the plan, mainly out of concern for the defence of the home waters and the protection of trade.[10] In December, the Admiralty proposed sending only Captain William Whetstone with several ships instead of a large squadron of twenty-seven ships originally designated for the West Indies.[11] Similarly in the Cabinet Council of February 1702, the Earl of Pembroke, the first Lord of the Admiralty, opposed sending a large fleet to reinforce Benbow in the Caribbean, a plan that had been proposed by two Whig magnates, the Duke of Somerset, Lord President of the Council, and the Duke of Devonshire, Lord Steward of the Household, unless the news of Château-Renault's dispatch to the West Indies was confirmed.[12]

News of Coëtlogon's failure to escort the *flota* raised William's hopes of winning over the Spanish colonists.[13] Consequently, in February 1702, Benbow was ordered to persuade them by promising protection of their colonies, and in return asked them to allow free trade to the English as sign of goodwill. He was also ordered to secure one of their ports, especially Havana, under the pretence of helping their defence, but if the Spanish colonists declined to come over to the allies' side, he was to put pressure on them and seize the *flota*.[14]

In March 1702, William died and Queen Anne succeeded him. Shortly after her accessio, in May, England formally declared war on France and Spain. Even after the war began, the attempt at persuasion continued. Benbow tried to win over the governor of Havana, mentioning that England had lent her fleet to the Archduke Charles to assist him, and would also offer ships and men to the Spanish governors who would support Charles 'to the rescue of his Country out of Bondage and Slavery' under French rule.[15] This attempt, however, did not bear fruit.

In contrast to England's failure, the Marquis de Château-Renault, who had been sent to Spanish America in September of 1701, succeeded in persuading the

[9] TNA, SP 44/206, p. 2, Instructions for Sir George Rooke, 12 August 1701. The instruction to Benbow was included in that to Rooke.

[10] TNA, ADM 3/16 [not foliated], Board's minutes, 7 August 1701.

[11] TNA, SP 42/6, fols 151–2, Memorial by the Lords Commissioners of Admiralty for the King, 3 December 1701. For this proposal, see also S.W. Singer, ed., *The Correspondence of Henry Hyde, Earl of Clarendon, and of his Brother Laurence Hyde, Earl of Rochester*, II (London, 1828), pp. 428–30, Vernon to the Earl of Rochester, 4, 9 December 1701.

[12] BL, Add MS 40775, fol. 367, Cabinet minutes, 18 February 1701/2.

[13] TNA, SP 42/67/10, no. 8 [not foliated], Benbow to Vernon, 9 December 1701; James, ed., *Letters Illustrative of the Reign of William III*, III, p. 181, Vernon to Stepney, 17 February 1701/2.

[14] BL, Add MS 33028, fols. 18–21v, Instructions for John Benbow, 19 February 1701/2.

[15] TNA, CO 137/45, no. 4, p. 16 [Benbow] to Vernon, 13 May 1702; TNA, SP 42/6/115A, fol. 333 [Benbow] to the Governor of Havana, 21 May 1702.

Spanish colonists to allow him to escort the silver fleet, and on 13 July 1702, he set sail for Europe with the fleet.[16] Upon hearing this news, Nottingham thought that this would be 'a strong inducement to the Dutch to send us their Ships' to intercept the fleet.[17] As is seen in this remark, at the beginning of Anne's reign, there was not open hostility towards the Dutch, and even Tories like Nottingham recognised the importance of cooperation with them. According to Coombs, the chief reason for this absence of outright hostility was that those involved in politics, such as the queen, chief ministers and most of the politically conscious subjects, accepted the necessity of the war with France, in which Dutch assistance was essential.[18]

To secure their assistance, the English government sent Sir David Mitchell to The Hague. One of his missions was to persuade the Dutch to send the warships that had been assigned to them by the treaty of Anglo-Dutch alliance signed in November 1701, by mentioning the advantage of intercepting Château-Renault's squadron.[19] However, the Dutch appeared uncooperative, and in a letter to Mitchell, Nottingham expressed his frustration that they did not understand the significance of the operation.[20] Yet, Nottingham and Godolphin still hoped for Dutch assistance, and tried to press them further to reinforce Shovel's squadron, which was off the French coast at Brest, waiting for the arrival of the silver fleet.[21]

In the meantime, owing to the presence of Sir George Rooke's squadron off Cadiz and at the Spanish admiral's insistence, Château-Renault changed his destination from Cadiz to Vigo in Galicia. When the English chief ministers received this news, they considered attacking the fleet there.[22] Nottingham hoped that the capture of the silver fleet might compensate for the disastrous failure at Cadiz and 'support the Spirit of ye Dutch', which would also make them more willing to meet their naval quota.[23]

16 In the meantime, in August, Benbow encountered the French squadron of Jean-Baptiste du Casse sailing for the West Indies to assist Château-Renault and to negotiate the Asiento at Cartagena. He could not win a victory because of the disobedience of his captains, and three months later, died of the wound he suffered during the battle. The accounts of this battle were given by Lieutenant Governor Beckford of Jamaica. TNA, CO 137/45, no. 15, pp. 62–4, Beckford to Nottingham, 4 September 1702. See also John B. Hattendorf, 'Benbow's Last Fight', *The Naval Miscellany*, vol. V, ed. N.A.M. Rodger (London, 1984), pp. 143–206.

17 FH MSS 275, p. 52, Nottingham to Rooke, 15 July 1702.

18 Coombs, *Conduct of the Dutch*, p. 381.

19 FH MSS 275, pp. 46–7, Instructions for Sir David Mitchell, 9 July 1702.

20 FH MSS 275, p. 69, Nottingham to Mitchell, 9 August 1702, and p. 77, Nottingham to Mitchell, 14 August 1702.

21 FH MSS 275, pp. 112–13, Nottingham to Godolphin, 10 September 1702; *Marlborough–Godolphin Correspondence*, I, no. 100, p. 114, Godolphin to Marlborough, 13 September 1702.

22 *Ibid.*, I, no. 106, p. 121, Marlborough to Godolphin, 5/16 October 1702; BL, Add MS 29588, fol. 318, Godolphin to Nottingham, 8 October 1702.

23 FH MS 275, pp. 161–2, Nottingham to Marlborough, 6 October 1702. Actually, on 19 October, Nottingham asked Philips van Almonde, the Dutch senior admiral, to send ships

On receiving the information of the arrival of Château-Renault's fleet at Vigo, Rooke resolved to sail there, and on 12 October, the Anglo-Dutch squadron under his command assaulted the port, destroying a large part of the French and Spanish ships.[24] Shortly after this attack, he hastily wrote to Prince George of Denmark, Lord High Admiral of England, congratulating him on this success, which, he hoped, would 'prove as gloriouse to her Majtie, and as advantagiouse to her Country, & subjects as any thinge that has beene perform'd in the time of her's & your Rll Highness predecessors'.[25]

The news of the capture of the silver fleet at Vigo was greeted with great enthusiasm in England. Sir Charles Hedges, Secretary of the State for the North, ordered the Lord Mayor of London that he should immediately prepare for the celebration of the victory in the City. [26] The *Observator* triumphantly wrote, 'Let'em boast of a Plate-Fleet from *New Spain*! What is that Purchase to their Loss at *Vigo*, and their Merchant Ships? What Havock has been made among their Bankers?', and claimed that this capture as well as their other losses at sea would 'make Statutes of Bankrupt in *France* as Numerous as Merchants'.[27]

From a financial viewpoint, however, the capture at Vigo was not a great victory of the allies over the enemy as was boasted at that time. As Henry Kamen has pointed out, before Rooke's attack, the fleet's bullion had already been unloaded and was secured by the Spanish authorities without being lost to Seville smugglers, as usually happened when the fleet sailed into Cadiz. It was rather English and Dutch merchants who suffered from this action, for they not only lost their merchandise on board the fleet that they had traded indirectly through agents in Seville, but also the silver belonging to them by confiscation by the Spanish crown in reprisal for the attack.[28]

It should be noted, however, that the ministers did not necessarily expect a direct economic gain from this capture. Before Rooke sailed to Vigo, Nottingham thought that Rooke would have enough time to destroy the French fleet, 'tho not to seize the Silver on the Galeons, which will probably be unloaden'.[29] Likewise, Godolphin hoped that, if the English fleet destroyed the enemy convoy, or at least forced them to unload and carry the silver into Spain, it would prevent the silver

to reinforce Shovel's fleet. FH MSS 275, p. 189, Nottingham to Admiral Almonde, 19 October 1702. By this time, however, the attack on the silver fleet at Vigo had already happened.

[24] Oscar Browning, ed., *The Journal of Sir George Rooke, Admiral of the Fleet, 1700–1702* (London, 1897), p. 228, 'At a Council of War of flag-officers held on board her Majesty's ship the *Royal Sovereign*, at sea, 7 September 1702'.

[25] Society of Antiquaries of London, SAL/MS/444/A, fol. 48, Rooke to Prince George of Denmark, 16 October 1702.

[26] TNA, SP 44/101, p. 251, Hedges to Lord Mayor, 31 October 1702.

[27] *Observator*, no. 56, 4 November 1702.

[28] Henry Kamen, 'The Destruction of the Spanish Silver Fleet at Vigo in 1702', *BIHR* 39 (1966), 171–2; Henry Kamen, *The War of Spanish Succession in Spain, 1700–15* (London, 1969), pp. 179–80.

[29] FH MSS 275, p. 178, Nottingham to Godolphin, 7 October 1702.

from going to France.[30] Thus, the ministers expected rather to destroy the French fleet or to prevent the silver from falling into French hands.[31] Moreover, this capture had a positive impact on English diplomatic efforts. As A.D. Francis has pointed out, the news of the capture at Vigo was one of the contributing factors that inclined Peter II of Portugal, who needed naval protection for the Brazilian trade, to join the Grand Alliance.[32]

The Plan for Peterborough's Expedition and its Cancellation, 1702–3

In parallel with the attempt to intercept the silver fleet, there was a plan to send an expeditionary force to the West Indies to seize a part of Spanish America in the early stage of the war. When the War of the Spanish Succession approached, some of the ministers showed a keen interest in war in the West Indies. In August 1701, in a letter to William III, James Vernon, Secretary of the State for the South, deplored delay in sending warships to the English West Indies for reinforcements, and claimed, 'if Wee are to have a war the operations at Sea in all probability will bee carried into those parts & the advantages or disadvantages there will have great Influence here'.[33] In another letter, Vernon supported naval operations in America, where, he thought, the allies could 'most perplex France', and again argued for immediate dispatch of more naval forces.[34]

It seems that plans for a Spanish-American expedition were proposed even before the war started. The author of 'Explanatory Observations on the South Sea Trade & Company' mentioned that a plan to establish a settlement on the Pacific coast of South America was submitted to William III twice before the war. The author claimed that this plan would have been pursued if the king had not died. But it is not certain to what extent William was actually committed to the project.[35]

After the declaration of war in May 1702, private individuals made several attempts on Spanish America. In August, Jamaican privateers made an attempt on Panama ('ye Store-house of all ye riches of Mexico & Peru'), probably encouraged by the sixth article of the Treaty of the Grand Alliance.[36] According

30 BL, Add MS 29588, fol. 324, Godolphin to Nottingham, 11 October 1702.

31 As to the latter point, Godolphin's expectation was not met. Out of the money the royal treasury of Spain obtained by the arrival of the fleet, nearly one-third (2,396,800 pesos) was dispatched directly to France as repayment of debts contracted by Louis for Spain. Kamen, *War of Spanish Succession*, pp. 180–1.

32 A.D. Francis, 'John Methuen and Anglo-Portuguese Treaties of 1703', *HJ* 3, no. 2 (1960), 116–17.

33 BL, Add MS 40775, fol. 47, Vernon to William III, 1 August 1701.

34 BL, Add MS 40775, fol. 55, Vernon to Marlborough, 5 August 1701. A similar view was seen among country Tory politicians. Anthony Hammond supported war in the West Indies as well as in Italy, which he thought were 'weak places' for France. BL, Add MS 69938, fol. 183v, Anthony Hammond to Thomas Coke, 11 October 1701.

35 BL, Add MS 70163, fol. 241v, 'Explanatory Observations on the South Sea Trade & Company', 1711. This manuscript was later published as *A True Account of the Design, and Advantages of the South-Sea Trade* (London, 1711).

36 TNA, CO 137/45, no. 20, pp. 105–6, Beckford to [Nottingham], 16 October 1702.

to a report by Lieutenant Governor Beckford of Jamaica, four hundred Jamaican privateers landed at the Isthmus of Darien, with the purpose of taking mines at St Mary. However, they failed to surprise the town, and after obtaining some gold in the mine, were obliged to retreat because of the unhealthy conditions of the place.[37] Privateering expeditions also set out from England. In April 1703, William Dampier set sail for the Spanish colonies on the Pacific coast, backed by London and Bristol investors, in the hope of taking Spanish silver fleets and sacking towns, though this ended up in complete failure.[38]

On the other hand, the government was also determined to take the offensive in the West Indies. In May 1702, the government ordered Governor Codrington of the Leeward Islands to seize the French part of St Kitts [St Christopher]. Codrington had already prepared for the attack and carried it out in mid-July.[39] Moreover, in June, Secretary of State Nottingham informed Benbow of a plan to send a large expeditionary force to the West Indies 'wth Prospect of making some very considerable attempts in those parts'.[40] This force was to be reinforced by a dispatch from the Anglo-Dutch forces engaged in the Cadiz expedition under the Duke of Ormonde and Rooke, with some persons of credit and priests to make the Spanish colonists believe that England and the Netherlands were fighting not for their own interests, but for the interests of the House of Habsburg.[41]

In the early stage of the war, Nottingham was one of the main proponents of West Indian expeditions. In a letter to Marlborough, he stated, 'nothing can be more for our interest and to the prejudice to France' than to support the emperor in Italy and 'to prevent France from the Fruits he expects from the W. Indies', where France made 'the greatest efforts to ye expence of vast sums and almost to the ruine of his fleet which he has been raising these 40 years'. However, he did not aim to make conquest there, but to secure a right to free trade, which would be more acceptable for the Dutch, England's partner in the expedition.[42]

As already mentioned, Nottingham thought that Dutch cooperation was essential for both defensive and offensive operations. Therefore, the government sent Sir David Mitchell to The Hague to secure their assistance for naval operations including West Indian expeditions.[43] The instruction to Mitchell stated that England would send twenty-five warships and five thousand troops under the command of able officers to some places in the Spanish colonies, especially Havana and Cartagena. In order to persuade the Dutch, the instruction advised Mitchell

37 TNA, CO 137/45, no. 29, pp. 149–50, Beckford to [Nottingham], 8 December 1702.

38 As for Dampier's voyage, see B.M.H. Rogers, 'Dampier's Voyage of 1703', *MM* 10, no. 4 (1924), 366–81.

39 BL, Add MS 29591, fol. 11, 'Minutes of the Secret Committee', 26 May 1702; Bourne, *Queen Anne's Navy*, pp. 189–90.

40 BL, Add MS 29595, fol. 214, Nottingham to Benbow, 1 June 1702.

41 FH MSS 275, pp. 11–12, Nottingham to Marlborough, 5 June 1702; p. 34, Nottingham to Marlborough, 26 June 1702; TNA, SP 44/208, p. 24, Hedges to Rooke, 22 June 1702.

42 FH MSS 275, pp. 33–4, Nottingham to Marlborough, 26 June 1702; Denman, 'Political Debate', p. 168.

43 FH MSS 275, pp. 43–4, Nottingham to Marlborough, 7 July 1702.

to mention the possibility of obtaining assistance from the emperor, such as emissaries and priests to negotiate with the Spanish colonists, and to imply that the Dutch failure to send the ships might lead to English reluctance to assist them.[44]

At first, Anthonie Heinsius, Grand Pensionary of Holland, seems to have shown interest in the project, and asked for more details.[45] However, the negotiation with the Dutch made little progress, and in a letter to Mitchell of August 1702, Nottingham lamented, ''tis impossible for us to carry on the Sea War, as it ought to be, without their [the Dutch] vigorous concurrence in it'.[46] He was irritated by the uncooperative attitude of the Dutch, but still hoped that they would give satisfactory answer, for 'the possibility of intercepting Chateau-Renaud's squadron is not to be despised, much lesse the matter of the West Indies'.[47]

At the beginning of that September, the Dutch still seemed reluctant to give assistance to England, either for the interception of the silver fleet or for the West Indian expedition.[48] Therefore, the English government was resolved to carry on the preparation on its own and appointed the Earl of Peterborough as the commander of the expedition.[49] However, within a few days, the situation took a dramatic turn and the Dutch expressed their willingness to join the expedition. Heinsius wrote to Marlborough, 'Nostre affaire secrette pour les Indes avance beaucoup.'[50] On 8 September, Mitchell reported that the Dutch agreed to send reinforcements for the West Indian expedition.[51] Godolphin, who was also a keen supporter for the plan, was delighted with this news, and in a letter to Nottingham, he stated, 'at least Wee shall have dutch ships & land men for ye W: Indies, next year'. He had believed that the Dutch 'wd [would] doe all that was possible for them to joyn wth us in that expedition, Both from a desire of having their share of ye booty & a jealousy of our getting any new Acquisition in those parts wthout them', though he was concerned that their demand for reimbursement by the emperor of expenses for the expedition and objections to the sixth article from Count Wratislaw, Imperial Ambassador Extraordinary, might hamper the plan.[52]

Although England finally succeeded in persuading the Dutch, too much time had already been lost, and the departure of the expeditionary force was severely delayed. The Earl of Rochester reported, 'ye whole expedition to ye West Indys, lyes as it

44 FH MSS 275, pp. 48–9, Instruction for Sir David Mitchell, 9 July 1702; p. 51, [Nottingham?] to [Mitchell] [9 July 1702].

45 Sir George Murray, ed., *The Letters and Dispatches of John Churchill, First Duke of Marlborough, from 1702 to 1712*, I (London, 1845), p. 8, Marlborough to Nottingham, 13 July 1702.

46 FH MSS 275, p. 77, Nottingham to Mitchell, 14 August 1702.

47 FH MSS 275, pp. 80–1, Nottingham to Mitchell, 21 August 1702.

48 FH MSS 275, p. 106, Nottingham to Hedges, 2 September 1702.

49 FH MSS 275, pp. 104–5, Nottingham to Godolphin, 2 September 1702.

50 *Marlborough–Heinsius Correspondence*, no. 53a, p. 30, Heinsius to Marlborough, 15 September 1702 [N.S.].

51 TNA, SP 84/225, no. 51, fol. 183, Mitchell to [Nottingham], 8 September 1702.

52 BL, Add MS 29588, fol. 233, Godolphin to Nottingham, 17 September 1702.

were quite asleep & much delayed at least'.[53] The delay created several problems. In Ireland, there were soldiers recruited by Major-General Thomas Erle waiting for departure for the West Indies, and there was a danger that further delay might cause more desertion and the spread of disease among them. Therefore, the government decided that the English fleet to convey them should sail directly from Ireland to the West Indies without waiting for other English warships or the Dutch fleet, while the Dutch fleet were asked to sail directly to Jamaica to join the English fleet there.[54] However, the arrival of these ships to transport the regiments was delayed too, and this increased the danger of desertion by the soldiers, who had a strong aversion to service in the epidemic-stricken West Indies.[55]

This delay of the departure could also cause another problem: exposure of the plan. Rochester was worried that the secrecy could 'not be kept so long except the squadron be hastened away'.[56] There was a sufficient reason for his concern. The rumour of the expedition started to spread and the Dutch were suspected of letting slip the secret. As early as the end of September, Nottingham remarked 'our designe on the W Indies is not a secret abroad'. Both the number of Dutch ships allocated to the West Indies and the plan itself were the subjects of gossip, and this made him 'very desponding of any success, if we cant find a way of transacting the matters with the Dutch with more secrecy'.[57] In another letter, he repeated the complaint about just such a leak of information in the Netherlands: 'how great soever our fleet are, and how probable soever our designs may be, yet if there can't be found a method of concerting them with secrecy, we must not expect much fruit of it'.[58]

Godolphin claimed that Peterborough should be sent to Jamaica without delay and without waiting for the Dutch or recruits from Ireland, because he was afraid that the expedition would 'bee so publick as to press France & Spain upon all the measures they are capable of Taking to disappoint it'. He proposed making some attempt on the enemy colonies in the West Indies before further reinforcement from England and the Netherlands arrived there.[59] Nottingham agreed to hasten Peterborough's departure, though he thought nothing could be attempted until the Dutch fleet arrived.[60]

53 BL, Add MS 29588, fol. 253, Rochester to Nottingham, 15 September 1702.

54 FH MSS 275, p. 117, Nottingham to Hedges, 24 September 1702; BL, Add MS 29587, fol. 101, Notes for Sir David Mitchell's instruction, 29 September 1702.

55 BL, Add MS 29588, fol. 316, Rochester to [Nottingham?], 8 October 1702; FH MSS 275, pp. 179–80, Nottingham to Major General Erle, 10 October 1702. Rochester also attributed the delay to the fact that Spanish governors had not yet declared for Charles III. BL, Add MS 29588, fol. 253, Rochester to Nottingham, 15 September 1702.

56 BL, Add MS 29588, fol. 253, Rochester to Nottingham, 15 September 1702.

57 FH MSS 275, p. 121, Nottingham to Godolphin, 24 September 1702.

58 FH MSS 275, p. 164, Nottingham to Marlborough, 6 October 1702.

59 BL, Add MS 29588, fols 304–5, Godolphin to Nottingham, 5 October 1702.

60 FH MSS 275, p. 168, Nottingham to Godolphin, 6 October 1702.

In the meantime, the preparation for the expedition continued. In a plan notified to Benbow in October, the expeditionary force was to consist of six warships and two thousand soldiers detached from Cadiz, four more men of war sailing from England with Peterborough and six hundred soldiers recruited in Ireland, to which the Dutch force of ten or twelve ships and three regiments of foot was to join at Jamaica.[61] On 15 October, the government ordered that three or four men of war should depart immediately to transport the six hundred soldiers recruited in Ireland to the West Indies.[62]

The plan for the expedition was finally put into practice, but severe delays in departure forced the government to modify the original plan. Accordingly, Governor Codrington of the Leeward Islands was permitted to attack Martinique and other French islands in the West Indies before the whole expeditionary force arrived, if he judged it feasible.[63] Codrington, who did not seem to have received this instruction yet, was frustrated with the delay in the arrival of Peterborough. In November, Codrington deplored that the opportunity for surprise attack had passed and the enemy was already well prepared for an attack from the allies. However, he did not give up hope, believing that 'Such a Fleet wth Such a Man at ye head of it must not come to ye Indys for nothing,' and that, 'He had better lose fifteen hundrd [sic] Men Sword in hand than twice as many wth feavers and fluxes.'[64]

In England, the preparation for the expedition carried on, and two instructions were drawn up for Peterborough.[65] They stipulated that, if he failed in persuasion, he should subdue the Spanish towns, especially Havana and Cartagena, by force and attack French colonies in cooperation with Benbow's naval force, the Dutch force and the English colonists. Speedy action was required because much of the good season for the operation had already passed. In addition, strong economic incentives were offered to the expeditionary force. The instruction declared that all the spoils that might be taken from the enemy should be divided among Peterborough and others who were engaged in the expedition, except such parts as were reserved for the queen, States General and the Lord High Admiral of England, while it strictly forbade arbitrary plunder in the captured towns.[66]

Although the plan was perfect on paper, the departure was still delayed by administrative problems. There was difficulty in obtaining medicine for soldiers, which was thought essential for operations in the West Indies where epidemics such as yellow fever and malaria often took a heavy toll in the lives of troops sent

61 FH MSS 275, p. 172, Nottingham to Benbow, 7 October 1702.

62 TNA, ADM 1/4088, p. 81, Nottingham to Prince's council, 15 October 1702.

63 FH MSS 275, pp. 197–8, Queen Anne [Nottingham] to Codrington, 31 October 1702; pp. 199–200, Nottingham to Codrington, 31 October 1702; p. 201, Nottingham to Codrington, 3 November 1702; p. 214, Queen Anne [Nottingham] to Codrington, 14 November 1702; and p. 215, Nottingham to Codrington, 14 November 1702.

64 TNA, CO 239/1, no. 3, fol. 10v, Codrington to [William Popple?], 30 November 1702.

65 FH MSS 275, pp. 250–4, Instructions for the Earl of Peterborough, 7 December 1702; pp. 254–8, Instructions for the Earl of Peterborough, 9 December 1702.

66 FH MSS 275, p. 257, Instructions for the Earl of Peterborough, 9 December 1702.

from Europe. Peterborough complained, 'in some short time I expect to find every body resolved not to goe, but those that must goe or hang'. It was also difficult to find officers for the expedition, probably because of their reluctance to go to the epidemic-stricken West Indies. Peterborough was despondent about the future of the expedition: 'it is enough to make mee loose all hopes of future seasonable supplies & support, when I find such dificulties when I am present', though he still hoped to have assistance from the queen and the ministry.[67]

On the other side of the Atlantic, Governor Codrington, who had been informed that Peterborough would arrive in the West Indies with the Dutch squadron in February, was busy preparing for the expected military operation.[68] In spite of the reluctance of the inhabitants to cooperate with Peterborough's expedition, he managed to prepare twelve companies of regiments and two independent companies to embark. He insisted on Martinique as the first place to attack, claiming that, if England seized the island, 'every thing else will follow of course' and its capture 'onely wo'd be A greater service to the Nation then to conquer the Dutch spice Islands'. Thus, 'my Lord Peterborough I am Sure did not come into the Indies to trifle'.[69] Nevertheless, he was unaware that the ministers in London had already reconsidered the plan. Following the discussion at the committee of the Privy Council, on 13 January, the Prince's council, an advisory body on naval affairs to the queen's consort, Prince George of Denmark, recommended that the forces sent to the West Indies should attempt the French colonies first.[70]

The Dutch started showing reluctance to press on with the expedition. In a letter to Marlborough of 12 January 1703, Heinsius wrote, 'on trouvera, que cet esquadre viendra trop tard pour exécuter l'expedition concertée', and 'les vaisseaus et troupes angloises sont assez forts pour exécuter les desseins projestés'. Instead, he proposed employing the Dutch force for operations in Portugal, with which Marlborough agreed.[71]

The plan for the expedition received a further blow when Peterborough refused to go to the West Indies in protest at the reduction of the force that was to accom-

[67] TNA, CO 137/45, no. 37, fols 110–110v, Peterborough to [Nottingham?], 3 January 1702/3.

[68] FH MSS 275, p. 237, Nottingham to Codrington, 15 December 1702.

[69] TNA, CO 239/1, no. 5, fols 14–14v, Codrington to [Nottingham?], 18 January 1702/3. From a strategic viewpoint, this proposal is an appropriate one. According to Michael Duffy, in the Caribbean of the age of sail, campaigns had to be conducted from windward to leeward, and if Martinique was left intact, there was a danger that France would launch an attack from there on the British islands and recapture any conquests made by the British force. Duffy, *Soldiers, Sugar, and Seapower*, p. 64.

[70] TNA, SP 42/7/8 [not foliated], Prince's council to [?], 13 January 1702/3.

[71] *Marlborough–Heinsius Correspondence*, no. 76, p. 45, Heinsius to Marlborough, 12 January 1703 [N.S.], and no. 78, p. 46, Marlborough to Heinsius, 5/16 January 1702/3. In the same month, Heinsius also asked the Earl of Portland, who was a Dutch confidant of William III, to support speedy dispatch of English troops to the continent, and to prevent the West Indian expedition. David Onnekink, *The Anglo-Dutch Favourite: The Career of Hans Willem Bentick, 1st Earl of Portland (1649–1709)* (Aldershot, 2007), p. 251.

pany him; this obliged the government to abandon the original plan.[72] Consequently, on 18 January, Nottingham informed Thomas Handasyde, the new deputy governor of Jamaica, that Peterborough was assigned to another service and would not come to Jamaica, though Nottingham also announced that 'a considerable Number of Troops' would come to Jamaica by the end of May.[73] The newly adopted plan was similar to the proposal made by the Prince's council. The government ordered Codrington to attack French islands, such as Martinique and Guadeloupe, with the forces already dispatched from England and with volunteers from the colonists.[74] Accordingly, an attack on Guadeloupe was carried out in the spring of 1703 under the command of Codrington and Rear Admiral Sir Hovenden Walker, though it could not achieve anything remarkable.[75] Thus Peterborough's expedition to Spanish America did not materialise, and for the next few years, the government did not consider plans for offensives in the West Indies.

Operations in the Middle Stage of the War

Attempts at Persuasion of the Spanish Colonists

After the capture of the Spanish silver fleet at Vigo and the cancellation of Peterborough's expedition, the next few years did not see vigorous naval operations in the West Indies. In February 1704, there was information of a Spanish fleet from Buenos Aires, and Nottingham ordered Rooke to watch and intercept it off Lisbon, though it was not the English but the Dutch fleet under Van Almonde that succeeded in driving one of the ships ashore in the Algarve in Portugal.[76] Also, in May 1705, Hedges, Secretary of the State for the South, received news of a rich fleet expected from the Indies, probably the French fleet coming back from Peru, though this did not lead to any capture.[77]

Attacks on the enemy colonies were also unsuccessful. Vice-Admiral John Graydon, who was sent in January 1703, failed in attacking the French colony at Placentia in Newfoundland, and in fighting du Casse's squadron, which was on the way to France. Without achieving any success, Graydon returned to England with Whetstone in October.[78] It seems that the destination of Graydon's fleet was an

72 E.S. De Beer, ed., *The Correspondence of John Locke*, VII (Oxford, 1982), pp. 740–1, Peterborough to John Locke, 27 January 1702/3.

73 FH MSS 275, p. 272, Nottingham to Handasyde, 18 January 1702/3.

74 FH MSS 275, pp. 265–6, Instructions for Codrington, 18 January 1702/3.

75 For details of this attempt, see Bourne, *Queen Anne's Navy*, pp. 195–200. However, Bourne has failed to recognise that the forces used in the attack were originally designated for Peterborough's expedition.

76 TNA, SP 44/209, p. 135, Nottingham to Rooke, 2 February 1703/4; SP 42/67/45, no. 43, fol. 38, Rooke to Nottingham, 6 February 1703/4; SP 42/67/50B, fol. 65v, Rooke to Nottingham, 29 February 1703/4; A.D. Francis, *The Methuens and Portugal, 1691–1708* (Cambridge, 1966), p. 234.

77 TNA, SP 63/365, no. 99, fol. 251, Edward Southwell, secretary to the lord lieutenant of Ireland, to Hedges, 24 May 1705.

78 Rodger, *Command of the Ocean*, p. 168; Bourne, *Queen Anne's Navy*, pp. 161–2.

open secret even before his departure. Gilbert Burnet commented, 'the secret of this was so ill kept, that it was commonly talked of before he sailed', which allowed the French to send a force to defend their colony.[79]

In contrast to the failure of the English operations, in 1706, the French went on the offensive against the English colonies in the West Indies. In February, the French captain Louis-Henri Comte de Chavagnac, attacked Nevis and St Kitts, and in March, the Canadian captain Iberville raided Nevis with Chavagnac and carried away most of the slaves.[80] Thus, after the cancellation of Peterborough's expedition and the failure of Graydon's expedition, England was generally on the defensive in the West Indies.

Plans to attack Spanish or French colonies were, however, continuously proposed by those versed in colonial affairs. In June 1705, one Theofille Allain suggested sending a squadron to the Spanish West Indies with Spanish officers and priests to subjugate the Spanish colonists to Charles III by persuasion, and if refused, by force.[81] Likewise, in April 1706, one Dr Moses Stringer proposed a plan to establish a settlement at Tobago to which the Duchy of Courland claimed title.[82] Colonial governors showed interest in expeditions against the enemy colonies, as well. In December 1704, Colonel Christian Lilly, chief engineer in the West Indies, submitted a detailed plan to take Havana at the request of Sir Bevil Granville, governor of Barbados.[83] Furthermore, in August 1706, Daniel Parke, newly appointed governor of the Leeward Islands, proposed attacking the French Islands such as Martinique, or Porto Rico, emphasising the low cost of the expedition and the profit which could be made by plunder.[84]

Nevertheless, the government did not adopt these proposals. The reason is not entirely clear, but it can be conjectured that the consideration of further expenses discouraged even these proponents of colonial expeditions in the ministry from embracing the plans, especially after the failure of Peterborough's expedition. Moreover, consideration for relations with the Spanish colonies was also a significant factor. The Spanish colonists were regarded as potential supporters of

[79] Gilbert Burnet, *Bishop Burnet's History of his Own Time*, ed. M.J. Routh, V (Oxford, 1833), p. 91.

[80] Bourne, *Queen Anne's Navy*, pp. 204–8.

[81] BL, Add MS 70164 [not foliated], Theofille Alain to Robert Harley [n.d.], 'Project of reducing ye Spanish West Indey', 22 June 1705; 'Mr Allain's proposal for ye Spanish West Indeys', 29 July 1705.

[82] BL, Add MS 22265, fols 94–9 [Dr] Moses Stringer to the Earl of Strafford, April 1706.

[83] BL, Add MS 70164 [not foliated], Christian Lilly to Sir Bevil Granville, 22 December 1704.

[84] TNA, CO 239/1, no. 12, fols 46–47v, Daniel Parke to Hedges, 28 August 1706. In January 1707, he again made a proposal to attack Martinique or Porto Rico by using ten thousand Scotsmen. However, his condescending remarks about the Scots infuriated the ministers, especially the Earl of Sunderland, Secretary of State for the South, who were engrossed in achieving the Union with Scotland at that time. TNA, CO 239/1, no. 19, fols 61v–62, Parke to Hedges, 19 January 1706/7; TNA, CO 152/42, no. 18, fol. 36, Parke to Sunderland, 11 May 1710.

Charles III, particularly during the first half stage of the war. Furthermore, as we shall see in Chapter 5, at the request of West Indian merchants and in the expectation of recovery of the Spanish-American trade, the English government allowed the English colonists to resume their trade with the Spanish colonies in February 1704. The regard for the reopened Spanish-American trade also put the brakes on a plan to establish a new colony in Spanish America. For example, in May 1703, Lieutenant Governor Handasyde of Jamaica proposed appointing one John Lewis as a governor for the Bay of Campeche, where English interlopers had been engaged in cutting logwood since the 1660s.[85] However, the Board of Trade disapproved of the plan because of a possibility of hampering ongoing negotiation with the Spanish colonies to reopen the trade as well as the issue of cost.[86] Probably arising from this regard for cost and relations with the Spanish colonists, after the cancellation of Peterborough's expedition, English naval policy in Spanish America shifted to a less costly and aggressive form: persuasion of the Spanish colonists.

After Peterborough's expedition was cancelled, in September 1703, Nottingham proposed a plan to persuade the Spanish colonists to declare for the House of Habsburg. According to his plan, if the Archduke was declared the king of Spain, the news was to be conveyed to the Spaniards in Hispaniola with the offer of good correspondence and assistance. He explained, 'For as wee are not likely this year to attempt any conquest of the Span[ish] Indies, & This, if accepted will secure our own plantations, and be very advantageous to our trade.' Even when the offer was rejected, he claimed, 'wee may the more reasonably insist on the clause in the additional Article to the grand Alliance wch preserves to Us ye right to what wee take from them who will own no duty to ye house of Austria'.[87]

In September 1705, an Anglo-Dutch force succeeded in taking Barcelona and the allies were gaining ground in Spain. Against this background, the English government made a further attempt at persuasion. In January 1706, the government instructed Governor Handasyde to publicise among the Spanish colonists the allies' success in Spain and the French designs on monopolising trade with the Spanish West Indies. Handasyde was directed to assure the colonists that sea and land forces would come 'for rescuing them from the yoake of France, and restoring their trade to the ancient Channel between Old and New Spain'.[88] Following this order, in March, Handasyde decided to send a Spanish captain employed by the English to Cartagena with the declarations of Charles III and a letter warning the governor about an alleged French plan to

85 TNA, CO 137/5, no. 107, fols 373v–374, Handasyde to Board of Trade, 30 May 1703; TNA, CO 137/6, no. 42, fol. 236, Handasyde to Board of Trade, 5 March 1703/4; fols 239–239v, enclosure i, John Lewis to [Handasyde?], 2 March 1703/4.

86 TNA, CO 138/11, p. 264, Board of Trade to Hedges 25 April 1704; TNA, CO 138/11, p. 266, Board of Trade to Handasyde, 4 May 1704.

87 FH MSS 277, p. 102, Nottingham to Hedges, 10 September 1703.

88 TNA, CO 324/30, p. 56, Hedges to Handasyde, 17 January 1705/6.

seize Cartagena and Havana and assuring him of help from the English. This attempt entailed a show of English naval force: Rear-Admiral William Whetstone was to accompany the ship. Whetstone was joined by Captain William Kerr's fleet in August, and Handasyde believed 'their Appearance there will have a very good Effect'.[89]

The allies' successes in Europe during the summer of 1706 encouraged the attempt further. To convince the Spanish colonists to support Charles III, Hedges asked English colonial governors to notify them of the news of the allies' achievements. These included lifting the siege of Barcelona, the temporary occupation of Madrid by the Earl of Galway in April and Marlborough's victory at Ramillies in May.[90]

Moreover, the attempt at persuasion became linked to a concern for a Spanish silver fleet that had recently arrived in the West Indies. This was a combined fleet of *galeones* and *flotas* under Santillán, which left for the West Indies in March 1706 without French escort, and, narrowly escaping an English squadron commanded by Sir John Leake, arrived at Cartagena in April. The movement of this fleet attracted the attention of the ministers in the mother country. In July, Godolphin expected that, if Spain declared for 'Charles III', England would be able to spare a part of the fleet in the Mediterranean to prevent the silver fleet from coming into France.[91] By contrast, Marlborough was not so optimistic, considering the many accidents that tended to happen in naval operations. However, he admitted, 'what is right aught to be attempted'.[92] Thus, to prevent the silver fleet from falling into French hands became important to the agenda again, and the attempt to publicise the news of the allies' success was intended not only to persuade the Spaniards to support the Archduke Charles, but also 'not to trust their Estates on the Galeons in the hands of the French'.[93]

The negotiations, however, made little progress. In September, Governor Handasyde reported that because the letter sent to the Spanish governor was wrongly interpreted by some Frenchmen, the governor did not give back a good answer.[94] In spite of this failure, Handasyde did not give up hope. He believed that, as most of the Spaniards were in favour of the House of Habsburg, there would be no opposition against the English force, which was to be sent at the

89 TNA, CO 137/45, no. 76, pp. 335–6, Handasyde to Hedges, 1 April 1706; TNA, CO 137/7, no. 23, fols 100–100v, Handasyde to Board of Trade, 1 April 1706; no. 31, fol. 138, Handasyde to Board of Trade, 6 August 1706. Kerr also tried to intercept Ducasse's fleet, which had arrived in the West Indies in April, and to take Santo Domingo, but both attempts were unsuccessful.

90 TNA, CO 324/30, pp. 84–6, Hedges to Edward Nott, governor of Virginia, 9 May 1706; pp. 96–7, Hedges to Handasyde, 30 June 1706, and pp. 99–100, Hedges to Sir Bevil Granville, governor of Barbados, 1 August 1706.

91 *Marlborough–Godolphin Correspondence*, II, no. 619, p. 611, Godolphin to Marlborough, 2 July 1706.

92 *Ibid.*, II, no. 629, p. 622, Marlborough to Godolphin, 11/22 July 1706.

93 TNA, CO 324/30, p. 97, Hedges to Handasyde, 30 June 1706.

94 TNA, CO 137/7, no. 32, fol. 142v, Handasyde to Hedges, 16 September 1706.

request of Charles to encourage the Spanish colonists and convoy back the silver fleet to Spain.[95] This was an English fleet under the command of Sir John Jennings, who was detached in September 1706 from the fleet under Sir John Leake operating in the Mediterranean.[96] The Dutch also seemed to have obtained information about Jennings' dispatch. In August, Godolphin reported that Marinus Dibbout van Vrijbergen, Dutch envoy in London, gave a memorial that proposed an Anglo-Dutch joint expedition to the West Indies.[97] Harley conjectured that this was because they heard the Queen's order for dispatching a squadron for the West Indies.[98]

In December 1706, Jennings reached the West Indies and subsequently sent three warships to Cartagena with a letter to its governor to persuade him to declare for 'Charles III'. However, knowing that Philip V had retaken Madrid, the governor flatly refused the proposal and stated that he and colonists would 'spill the last drop of our Blood' in the defence of Philip.[99]

The tide of war was turning against the allies. At that time, increasing French influence at the Spanish court caused changes in personnel of colonial governments, replacing supporters of Charles with pro-French governors, which was reported by Handasyde in March 1707.[100] For example, in May 1707, the marquis of Castelldosríus, a new pro-French viceroy, arrived in Peru, which entailed a change in personnel in the government office there in the interest of Castelldosríus and French traders.[101] The prospect of war looked bleak in Europe, too. In April, the Allied force under Galway suffered a crushing defeat by the Duke of Berwick, the commander of the French troops, at Almanza in Spain. These events put England at a great disadvantage in the attempt to persuade the Spanish colonists, and consequently the English government gave it up.

There was, however, at least one good piece of news for the allies: a delay in the departure of the silver fleet. In March 1707, Handasyde reported that the fleet was in such a poor condition that no more than six vessels were able to depart. Moreover, 'very few Spanish merchants will venture their mony in them, and the pretended king [Philip V] has not much to receive'.[102] By May, it had become clear that the silver fleet would not come back to Europe until the Spaniards had certain

95 TNA, CO 137/7, no. 34, fols 150–150v, Handasyde to Board of Trade, 25 October 1706.

96 Geoffrey Callender, ed., *The Life of Sir John Leake: Rear-Admiral of Great Britain by Stephen Martin-Leake*, II (London, 1920), pp. 122–4, 127.

97 *Marlborough–Godolphin Correspondence*, II, no. 658, p. 650, Godolphin to Marlborough, 13 August 1706.

98 Portland Papers, PO/VOL V, fol. 79, Harley to Marlborough, 19/27 August 1706.

99 TNA, CO 137/7, no. 37, fol. 171v, Handasyde to Board of Trade, 29 January 1706/7 and enclosure i, fol. 175, the Governor of Cartagena to Sir John Jennings, 5 January 1706/7.

100 Charles Frostin, 'Les Ponchartrain et la Pénétration Commercial en Amérique Espagnole (1690–1715)', *Revue Historique*, no. 498 (Avril–Juin 1971), 333; TNA, CO 137/7, no. 42, fol. 192, Handasyde to Board of Trade, 8 March 1706/7.

101 Walker, *Spanish Politics*, pp. 34–8.

102 TNA, CO 137/7, no. 42, fol. 192, Handasyde to Board of Trade, 8 March 1706/7.

news of peace.[103] Marlborough was delighted by the news, and hoped 'France can't continu the war', owing to lack of money.[104]

Revival of Interest in West Indian Expeditions

After the attempt to persuade the Spanish colonists failed, the government seems to have turned its attention again to an aggressive naval policy in the West Indies: the capture of the silver fleet and naval expeditions. In June 1707, one Captain Richard Jennings, a commander of a merchant ship trading in the West Indies, submitted a memorial to Prince George of Denmark, which proposed a means to intercept the silver fleet near Havana as well as suppressing the French privateers of Martinique and Guadeloupe.[105] In order to carry out this plan, Captain Jennings asked the Prince's council to employ him with some reward on board the ship of Sir Charles Wager, who was to set sail for the West Indies.[106]

Later in that year, there was talk about a naval operation in the West Indies among the chief ministers, though it is not clear whether this directly resulted from Jennings' proposal. In September, a new expedition to that region was discussed in the Privy Council. In the discussion, destroying the French colonies was proposed as an option preferable to occupying them as they were thought difficult to maintain. Among the Spanish colonies, Havana was particularly mentioned as an important hub of transport in the West Indies.[107] Interception of the silver fleet was also mooted in their talk. In November, in accordance with an order from the Privy Council, the Prince's council submitted a plan for the interception. Accordingly, Godolphin proposed laying the state of fleet before the queen, and it was also decided to ask the Dutch for their help.[108]

As we saw in Chapter 3, this period falls into the first boom in the trade by French merchants, especially those of St Malo, which began in May 1705 and continued until the summer of 1708. On the other hand, in July 1707, England concluded a commercial treaty with Archduke Charles that included a secret clause giving England privileges in Spanish-American trade. It is possible that, behind this revival of the interests in the West Indian expeditions in the government, there was a concern over the rapid French advance in the Spanish-American trade and

103 *Marlborough–Godolphin Correspondence*, II, no. 778, p. 767, Godolphin to Marlborough, 3 May 1707.

104 *Ibid.*, II, no. 787, p. 776, Marlborough to Godolphin, 12/23 May 1707.

105 TNA, CO 323/6, no. 36, fols 82–86v, Richard Jennings to the Lord High Admiral, [13 June] 1707.

106 TNA, CO 323/6, no. 37, fol. 88, R. Jennings to the Prince's council [June?] 1707. There is a table that contains the summary of his proposal with Sir David Mitchell's objections and Jennings' answer to them, which seems to have been also submitted to the Prince's council. TNA, CO 323/6, no. 38, and no. 39 [not foliated] [R. Jennings] to [the Prince's council] [30 June] 1707.

107 BL, Add MS 70338, bundle 48 [not foliated], Minutes of the Privy Council, 13 September 1707.

108 BL, Add MS 70338, bundle 48 [not foliated], Minutes of the Privy Council, 26 October 1707; bundle 49 [not foliated], Minutes of the Privy Council, 2 November 1707.

the expectation of establishing Spanish-American trade with better conditions on the basis of the commercial treaty.

The plan for an expedition, however, did not go unopposed. In a letter of January 1708 to Marlborough, Don Bernardo de Quiros, ambassador of the Archduke Charles at The Hague, argued that if the expeditionary force did not go there under the name of 'Charles III' and without the Spaniards who would help to win the support of the Spanish colonists, the expedition would serve only to reinforce the support for the Duke of Anjou in the Spanish colonies as well as in Spain, and also to confirm a wrong impression that the allies fought the war not to support Charles, but for their own interests and to establish Protestantism there. Instead, De Quiros claimed, 'en Conquerant l'Espagne les Indes le Seront en meme Temps, et qu'il ne faudroit point afaiblir les forces pour arriver a la Source'.[109] In the end, in spite of the revival of the interests in the Spanish-American expeditions, no expedition was carried out in 1708.

In contrast to the plans for colonial expeditions, interception of the silver fleet saw a great success. In June 1707, a fleet under Commodore Wager arrived in the West Indies.[110] At that time, there was information that some of the silver fleet would sail from Cartagena in a month or six weeks, and Wager set sail for the Spanish coast, accompanied by English merchant ships sent out in the hope of recovering the trade with the Spanish colonies.[111] Although the arrival of the French Admiral du Casse in the West Indies in December posed a risk for Wager's operation, in May of the following year, he successfully intercepted the Tierra Firme galleon under Count of Casa Alegre on its way to Havana, and captured the *Santa Cruz*, while the other ships took refuge in Cartagena.[112]

The news of Wager's success was greatly welcomed in England. Upon hearing the capture of the silver fleet, which was reported to be 'the richest that have for many years return'd to Europe', Sunderland wrote with excitement: 'This must in all probability prove a fatall blow to France, for I believe this was one of their last resources for carrying on the war.'[113] Similarly, Godolphin thought that this was a shattering blow to France and Spain. In France, 'it must quite compleat the ruine of their credit' and in Spain, it would make people more inclined to declare for

109 BL, Add MS 61196, fols 133v–134v, De Quiros to Marlborough, 17 January 1707/8 [N.S].

110 TNA, CO 137/7, no. 62, fol. 235, Handasyde to Board of Trade, 25 June 1707.

111 TNA, CO 137/7, no. 60, fol. 229, Handasyde to Board of Trade, 29 August 1707; CO 137/7, no. 72, fol. 261v, Handasyde to Board of Trade, 5 December 1707.

112 The account of this battle is given in BL, Add MS 61643, fol. 146, 'Accounts of Admrll Wager's proceeding on the Spanish Coast', 3 June 1708. For further details of the battle, see Daniel A. Baugh, 'Sir Charles Wager, 1666–1743', *Precursors of Nelson: British Admirals of the Eighteenth Century*, ed. Peter Le Fevre and Richard Harding (London and Mechanicsburg, PA, 2000), pp. 109–11; Carla R. Phillips, *The Treasure of the San Jose: Death at Sea in the War of the Spanish Succession* (Baltimore, 2007), Chapter 5.

113 BL, Add MS 61126, fols 130–130v, Sunderland to [Marlborough], 2 August 1708.

'Charles III'.[114] He also stated that this success gave 'great temptation and encouragement' to send further naval and land forces there, though he was afraid that most of the land officers were reluctant or incapable to take charge of such duty.[115] The news was also received with great joy by the allied force fighting in Flanders.[116]

In the meantime, the other silver fleet, the *flotas*, escorted by du Casse's squadron, slipped out of the Caribbean in July 1708 and safely arrived in Los Pasajes in the Bay of Biscay in August. Yet even this news seems to have stirred the imagination of the supporters of colonial maritime war about the immense wealth of Spanish America. In a letter to Marlborough, Godolphin wrote that the news of du Casse's return with the *flotas* and the expectation of another attack on the galleons that winter made 'a great ferment' among the English to send some regiments to the West Indies, though he lamented, 'I think the thing is right, but wee want proper persons for the execution of almost anything.'[117]

Another factor seems to have contributed to returning Godolphin's attention to the West Indies. Since the defeat in Almanza in April 1707, Portugal under her new king John V had showed reluctance to engage herself in a new operation in the Iberian Peninsula.[118] Therefore, it was uncertain whether Britain could dispose Portugal to launch the offensive there again even if she sent new troops and furnished greater subsidies, and Godolphin considered sending a part of those troops originally designed for Portugal to the West Indies.[119] Although it was later decided that the troops were to be employed in Flanders, in September 1708, he still proposed bringing regiments from Ireland for the West Indian expedition, and Sunderland, Secretary of State for the South, asked the Admiralty to prepare six warships for the intended expedition.[120] However, this plan was not put into execution.

The interest in the West India expedition among some of the chief ministers continued in 1709. At the beginning of that year, France, suffering from the poor harvest of 1708, showed an inclination to start peace negotiations, and Britain and the Netherlands proposed a preliminary peace treaty. However, Louis XIV was opposed to the preliminary treaty, especially to an article that required the removal

114 *Marlborough–Godolphin Correspondence*, II, no. 1061, p. 1057, Godolphin to Marlborough, 2 August 1708.

115 *Ibid.*, II, no. 1081, p. 1079, Godolphin to Marlborough, 20 August 1708.

116 Murray, ed., *Letters and Dispatches of John Churchill*, IV, p. 178, Marlborough to Henry Boyle, Secretary of the State for the North, 20 August 1708.

117 *Marlborough–Godolphin Correspondence*, II, no. 1092, p. 1093, Godolphin to Marlborough, 1 September 1708.

118 David Francis, *The First Peninsular War, 1702–1713* (London and Tonbridge, 1975), p. 331.

119 *Marlborough–Godolphin Correspondence*, II, no. 1094, p. 1094, Godolphin to Marlborough, 3 September 1708.

120 *Ibid.*, II, no. 1095, p. 1095, Godolphin to Marlborough, 6 September 1708; TNA, ADM 1/4092, fol. 33, Sunderland to Burchett, 7 September 1708.

of the Duke of Anjou from Spain, as he knew that Philip would not agree to it. This disagreement between the allies and France over this article suspended the peace talks. In the face of the suspension of the negotiations, the British government decided to renew offensives on several fronts, including America, believing military pressure on Louis would bring him back to the negotiation table and force him to agree to the evacuation of Philip from Spain.[121]

In early 1709, there was a plan for an expedition to French Canada, which was originally proposed and supported by British colonists in North America, such as Samuel Vetch and Governor Dudley of Massachusetts. To their dismay, the ministry had decided to cancel the plan by the end of May, probably in light of the progress in the peace negotiations with France, and the force designated for the expedition was diverted to the Iberian Peninsula.[122] After the peace negotiations were suspended, however, in August, Godolphin mentioned a new plan for an expedition to the Spanish West Indies that was to be launched from Jamaica.[123] This time, the project was supported not only by Godolphin, but also by the Junto Whigs, especially Halifax and Somers, who were, in the judgement of some merchants, 'made very fond of such expeditions'.[124] As we shall see in Chapter 5, they were also one of the main promoters of the American Act of 1708 intended to encourage colonial maritime war. Thus, at this time, it seems that Godolphin tried to implement a plan for a colonial expedition in cooperation with the Junto Whigs who were gaining ground in the ministry.

However, there was a difficulty in assembling the four thousand troops who were to be put under the command of Governor Handasyde of Jamaica. To solve this problem, it was proposed that New York and New England should be united into one colony and the new governor of that colony be made to raise 1,500 men. Godolphin claimed, 'the hopes of plunder will naturally enough incline them' to that service.[125] By contrast, Marlborough was quite negative about the expedition: 'I do not remember any that has hethertoo, ever served for anything but a pretext to plunder.' What concerned him was further growth of debt, which would give parties more power to control politics.[126]

121 Hattendorf, *England in the War of the Spanish Succession*, pp. 200–2.

122 William T. Morgan, 'Some Attempts at Imperial Co-operation during the Reign of Queen Anne', *TRHS*, 4th ser, 10 (1927), 181–5; Bodleian Library, MS Eng. Hist. d. 147, fol. 17, Henry Boyle to [Marlborough and Townshend], 27 May 1709; fol. 19v, Henry Boyle to Townshend, 31 May 1709. I would like to thank Professor Steven Pincus for drawing my attention to these sources. These letters mentioned the West Indies as the original destination of the expedition. However, judging from the date of the letters, it is likely that what is actually referred to here is the expedition against French Canada that was planned at the time. Similar confusion about the destination can be also seen in the talk of a Canadian expedition planned in the following year.

123 *Marlborough–Godolphin Correspondence*, III, no. 1379, p. 1346, Godolphin to Marlborough, 18 August 1709.

124 *Ibid.*, III, no. 1388, p. 1355, Marlborough to Godolphin, 27 August/7 September 1709.

125 *Ibid.*, III, no. 1381, pp. 1348–9, Godolphin to Marlborough, 19 August 1709.

126 *Ibid.*, III, no. 1388, p. 1355, Marlborough to Godolphin, 27 August/7 September 1709.

The destination of this expedition appears to have been later changed to the Spanish colonies on the Pacific coast, where the French merchants were starting to make huge inroads again at this time. In October 1709, in a letter to Lord High Admiral the Earl of Pembroke, Sunderland referred to the expedition as 'the secret Expedition to the South sea'.[127] However, this plan was abandoned, and the ships designated for this expedition were discharged.[128] This was probably because of the resumption of the peace talks with France at Gertruydenberg in September 1709, which continued until March 1710.

Thus, after the cancellation of Peterborough's expedition, the government switched to a more conciliatory policy and tried to persuade the Spanish colonists to come over to the allies' side. However, after this attempt failed, probably owing to the French growth in the Spanish-American market and the expectation of recovering the Spanish-American trade on the basis of the commercial treaty with Charles, the government returned to the idea of a colonial expedition, though none of the proposed expeditions materialised in the end.

Operations in the Later Stage of the War

Further Attempts: Interception of a Silver Fleet and Colonial Expeditions

After the capture of Spanish silver fleet in May 1708, Wager remained in the West Indies and tried to intercept French merchant ships coming to Hispaniola.[129] In September 1709, there was information from a Spanish prisoner that the vice-admiral of the Tierra Firme galleon that had escaped Wager's attack and stayed in Cartagena showed an inclination for 'Charles III'. Accordingly, Wager and Handasyde sent a letter to persuade him to come over to the allies' side with the cargoes on board the fleet, promising protection and reward, though Wager himself did not hold out much hope because the vice-admiral had already been suspected of betrayal.[130] As Wager had expected, the attempt failed, and he returned to England in December.

Another success was achieved not by a naval ship but by a privateer. In August 1708, backed and financed by Bristol merchants, Captain Woodes Rogers set sail on a privateering voyage with two armed ships, the *Duke* and the *Duchess*. It can be conjectured that this voyage was encouraged by the enactment of the American Act passed in April of the same year, which contained a clause to allow societies or private individuals to seize enemy ships, goods and territories in America and

[127] TNA, ADM 1/4093, fol. 192, Sunderland to the Lord High Admiral, 11 October 1709.

[128] BL, Add MS 61500, fol. 68, Sunderland's Minutes of the Cabinet Council, 13 November 1709. I am grateful to thank Professor Steven Pincus for drawing my attention to this document.

[129] TNA, CO 137/8, no. 33, fols 129, 130v, Handasyde to Board of Trade, 1 February 1708/9.

[130] BL, Add MS 61643, fols 199–199v, Handasyde to Sunderland, 18 September 1709; Add MS 61585, fols 65–6, Wager to Burchett, 21 November 1709.

retain them.[131] In December 1709, Rogers succeeded in capturing several ships including one of the Manila galleons, a fleet engaged in the trade between Manila and Acapulco, and came back to England with the prizes. The net profits of the prizes were estimated to be at about £170,000.[132]

These captures, however, could not completely stop the flow of bullion from America to Europe. In March 1709, a French fleet under Captain Michel Chabert came back from the voyage to the South Sea, with silver from Peru he collected by the order of Philip V. Furthermore, a *flota* comprised of Spanish and French ships under the command of Andrés de Pez, which had left for Spanish America in May 1708, returned to Cadiz in March 1710, and in March 1711, another *flota* commanded by Arriola reached Cadiz.[133]

On the other hand, the Tierra Firme galleons that Wager tried to secure by persuasion still stayed in Cartagena. This delay in departure was caused partly by a deteriorating relationship between Spain and France because of the illicit trade conducted by the latter, which made the Spaniards reluctant to allow the French to convoy the silver fleet.[134] In spite of this friction, the French attempts to bring the silver fleet back to Europe continued. In December 1710, Handasyde reported the arrival of a Franco-Spanish fleet that was suspected to have come to convoy the galleons back. The duty to intercept them fell on Commodore James Littleton, who had arrived in the West Indies in the previous month.[135]

In May, there was news that the French Admiral du Casse had sailed for Cartagena to convoy the galleons, while the English fleet was not in good condition.[136] In August 1711, du Casse secretly sailed out from Cartagena with treasure, including the money of French merchants and the French Asiento Company transferred from the *San Joaquín*, one of the galleons that survived Wager's attack in 1708. The *San Joaquín* and the other Spanish ship tried to follow suit and sailed out of Cartagena without escort. Their movement, however, did

131 With respect to this point, there is one interesting piece of information given by Robert Allen, a Scottish merchant who participated in the Jamaican privateers' expedition against Spanish America at the beginning of the war, and became a captive of the Spaniards. When Rear-Admiral Wager captured the *Santa Cruz*, one of the Spanish galleons in May 1708, Allen happened to be on board the vessel and reported that Wager referred to the American Act and one expedition intended from England to Spanish America at that time. It is possible that the expedition that Wager mentioned was Rogers' privateering expedition. BL, Add MS 61644A, fol. 99, Robert Allen to Sunderland [n.d., but 1710?]. For Robert Allen's early life in Spanish America, see J.D. Alsop, 'A Darien Epilogue: Robert Allen in Spanish America, 1698–1707', *Americas* 43, no. 2 (1986), 197–8.

132 For Rogers' voyage, see Woodes Rogers, *A Cruising Voyage Round the World, with Introduction and Notes by G.E. Mainwaring* (London, 1928), Introduction. For its aftermath, see also Donald Jones, *Captain Woodes Roger's Voyage round the World, 1708–1711* (Bristol, 1992).

133 Kamen, *War of Spanish Succession*, pp. 185–9.

134 Walker, *Spanish Politics*, p. 48.

135 TNA, CO 137/9, no. 31, fol. 72, Handasyde to Board of Trade, 4 December 1710.

136 TNA, CO 137/9, no. 42, fol. 111, Handasyde to Board of Trade, 27 May 1710/11.

not escape Littleton's notice and he captured those vessels.[137]

The value of the prizes turned out not so rich as expected. This disappointed Lord Archibald Hamilton, the new governor of Jamaica, though he still hoped to intercept du Casse's ships, into which a large part of the treasure had been moved.[138] To Hamilton's dismay, du Casse's fleet managed to escape the English fleet, and though separated on their way, arrived safely in Spain in November 1711 and February 1712.

Although it was a modest success compared with the precedent captures, Littleton's achievement encouraged the advocates of colonial maritime war. St John wished that this capture would make the English aware of the significance of the naval interest, which, he believed, had been almost completely neglected, and of the unfairness in reward and punishment in the naval service. He stated, 'I am hopeful that we shall at last see our error, and that the sea will, for the future, have a greater share of our attention applied to it.'[139] Littleton's capture was to prove the last successful capture during the War of the Spanish Succession, though attempts to intercept the silver fleets still continued.[140]

On the other hand, talk of a colonial expedition appeared again in Godolphin's letter to Marlborough at the beginning of May.[141] Commenting on this, Henry Snyder states that what actually was planned was the expedition to Canada, though Godolphin referred to it as intended for the West Indies.[142] It is true that there was a project to send a force under Viscount Shannon to Canada in 1710 at the request of the British colonists in North America.[143] Also, in April, Godolphin mentioned that the Cabinet Council was inclined to renew the expedition to North America planned the previous year, but this was aborted owing to the peace negotiations with France.[144] Yet, from the beginning of May, as already stated, he suddenly started to mention that the regiments were preparing for the West Indian expedition.

One explanation for this baffling change in Godolphin's statement is that Godolphin tried to conceal the true destination of the expedition by mentioning a false one, a ruse that St John used in the Quebec expedition of 1711. Another explanation is that this was simply a matter of the usage of words, and the ministers simply confused or did not distinguish between the West Indies and Canada.

137 Walker, *Spanish Politics*, p. 49; Kamen, *War of Spanish Succession*, pp. 189–90.

138 TNA, CO 137/9, no. 48, fol. 129, A. Hamilton to Board of Trade, 29 August 1711.

139 *Bolingbroke Correspondence*, I, p. 293, St John to Drummond, 3 August 1711.

140 TNA, CO 137/51, no. 61, fol. 107v, Hamilton to the Earl of Dartmouth, 15 May 1712.

141 *Marlborough–Godolphin Correspondence*, III, no. 1521, p. 1481, Godolphin to Marlborough, 2 May 1710.

142 *Ibid.*, III, no. 1504, p. 1467, Godolphin to Marlborough, 20 April 1710, note 9, and no. 1521, p. 1481, Godolphin to Marlborough, 2 May 1710, note 1.

143 Morgan, 'Some Attempts', 186–91; TNA: CO5/9, no. 64, fols 152–154v, Instructions for Richard Viscount Shannon, July 1710.

144 *Marlborough–Godolphin Correspondence*, III, no. 1504, pp. 1467–8, Godolphin to Marlborough, 20 April 1710; no. 1510, p. 1471, Godolphin to Marlborough, 25 April 1710.

According to Morgan, this confusion was not so unusual at that time, even among educated writers such as Abel Boyer and Narcissus Luttrell.[145] It is also probable that the words 'the West Indies' were used to refer to the Americas in general. An example of this can be seen in one memorandum for the expedition, in which the term 'W. India Expedition' was used in its heading, though what was described there is clearly a plan for a Canadian expedition.[146] In any case, the true destination seems to have been Canada. There is a piece of evidence that supports this hypothesis. In a letter to Marlborough, Godolphin mentioned seamen's opinion that if they could not sail by the tenth of July, it would be too late for the expedition.[147] Since the best season to sail for the West Indian expedition was normally regarded as late September, it would be more probable that the expedition was intended against Canada, not the West Indies.[148]

This plan for a colonial expedition met with strong opposition from Marlborough. As to the idea of sending several regiments for the expedition, he thought that the expedition could 'end in nothing but a great expence, and the ruining of those redgements'. He claimed that an operation in that region would not help to advance the peace, whereas 'if we can be so fortunate as to force them here, we may have by one dash of a pen, much more then any expeditions can gaine in many yeares'. He emphasised the uselessness of the expeditions, which he had learned from his past experience, and maintained, 'it is next to impossible that this can end in anything but an expence to make you uneasy, the ruining of the redgiments, and the encreasing the dept [i.e. debt] of the Ordenance'.[149]

While partly admitting Marlborough's argument, Godolphin still insisted on the expeditions, and emphasised that these things were, in their nature, 'contingent and uncertain'. He went on to say that if no peace was concluded in the present year, they would 'lose an opportunity of gaining a considerable advantage and satisfaction to England' by neglecting the expedition that was cancelled the previous year by preliminaries and which 'must infallibly have succeeded in case the first design had continued'. However, with the news that the enemy's army was approaching in Flanders, Godolphin backed down and accepted that Marlborough could keep the regiments if he needed them.[150]

In the meantime, the dispatch of the expeditionary force was severely delayed. In May, Godolphin reported, 'Our West Indies project is not layd aside, nor is

145 William T. Morgan, 'The South Sea Company and the Canadian Expedition in the Reign of Queen Anne', *HAHR* 8 (1928), 143–4.

146 TNA, CO 5/9, no. 24, fol. 95, 'Md [memorandum?], taken from Ld Sunderland's book of tres [letters?] & Instructions concerning ye W. India expedition' [n.d., but 1709].

147 *Marlborough–Godolphin Correspondence*, III, no. 1601, p. 1557, Godolphin to Marlborough, 4 July 1710.

148 Duffy, *Soldiers, Sugar, and Seapower*, p. 41.

149 *Marlborough–Godolphin Correspondence*, III, no. 1523, pp. 1484–5, Marlborough to Godolphin, 5/16 May 1710; no. 1524, p. 1485, Marlborough to Godolphin, 8/19 May 1710.

150 *Ibid.*, III, no. 1527, p. 1489, Godolphin to Marlborough, 9 May 1710; no. 1533, pp. 1496–7, Godolphin to Marlborough, 16 May 1710.

anybody here so fond of it.'[151] Faced with this delay, Samuel Vetch, who had experience of joining the Darien scheme, proposed using the provisions and other preparations for the Canadian expedition towards the operation in New Spain, in case the expedition was cancelled owing to the peace negotiation with France.[152] The force had not yet departed in July, and Godolphin mentioned the postponement of a decision regarding the expedition among ministers, which made it 'still more advisable in my opinion to lay it quite aside'.[153] In the end, the dispatch was cancelled in August, and the force was sent to Spain instead.[154] On the other hand, the New Englanders organised their own expedition, which mainly consisted of colonial forces, and captured Port Royal in Canada in October.

The Harley Ministry and Plans for Colonial Expeditions

In August 1710, a few days after the cancellation of the Canadian expedition, Godolphin resigned, and in his place, Harley came to power with St John, with the support of the Tories who had been dissatisfied with the management of war by the Marlborough–Godolphin ministry. As Denman has pointed out, many Tories were calling for a more vigorous effort in Spain and the West Indies, and the Tory victory in the general election in 1710 stimulated interest in the war in the Caribbean.[155] Also, in the Netherlands, John Drummond, Harley's agent in Amsterdam, urged him to give more support to the war in Spain and the West Indies, 'for peace or Warr must now be decided there and our second Victory is entire and glorious as ever any thing was'.[156]

Shortly after seizing power, it appears that Harley came to have an interest in West Indian expeditions again, though his intention at this point was not entirely clear. He collected information about the expeditions, asking the opinion of a wide range of people including William Paterson and Halifax.[157] Similarly, Henry St John, who rose to power with Harley, was keen on West Indian expeditions. In October 1710, in a letter to Drummond, after mentioning the French squadron that was believed to be intended for the West Indies, he stated that the French were 'wise enough to take care of that part'. He went on to say, ''tis from thence they

[151] *Ibid.*, III, no. 1539, p. 1503, Godolphin to Marlborough, 22 May 1710.

[152] TNA, CO 5/9, no. 54, fol. 142, Samuel Vetch to [Sunderland], 15 May 1710.

[153] *Marlborough–Godolphin Correspondence*, III, no. 1601, p. 1558, Godolphin to Marlborough, 4 July 1710.

[154] TNA, ADM 1/4094, fol. 97, Dartmouth to Admiralty, 7 August 1710; *Marlborough–Godolphin Correspondence*, III, no. 1504, p. 1467, Godolphin to Marlborough, 20 April 1710, note 9.

[155] Denman, 'Political Debate', pp. 237, 246–7.

[156] BL, Add MS 70026, fol. 129v, Drummond to Harley, 29 August/9 September 1710. As to Drummond, see Ragnhild Hatton, 'John Drummond in the War of the Spanish Succession: Merchant Turned Diplomatic Agent', *Studies in Diplomatic History: Essays in Memory of David Bayne Horn*, ed. Ragnhild Hatton and M.S. Anderson (London, 1970), pp. 69–96.

[157] Denman, 'Political Debate', p. 247; BL, Add MS 70026, fols 146–7, William Paterson to [Harley], 4 September 1710, and fols 166–167v, Halifax to Harley, 19 September 1710.

know that they may depend on a compensation for all the poverty and distress which the war has brought or can bring upon their nation', and wished that the same notion would be more prevalent among his acquaintances.[158]

In the Netherlands, at this time, some person of importance seems to have shown interest in the Anglo-Dutch joint expedition against Spanish America, which one Renaud, Harley's correspondent at Amsterdam, mentioned in his letter to Harley.[159] Accordingly, Harley asked Drummond to sound him out about the plan.[160] St John was also interested in the Dutch plan for the West Indian expedition. In a letter to Drummond, he claimed, 'nothing is more for the interest of the maritime powers, whether a war continues, or whether a peace succeeds; and, besides, there may be projects laid of this kind very well worth while, and not in the least chimerical'.[161] Thus, at this stage, the Tory ministry was still trying to obtain Dutch cooperation in the Spanish-American expeditions, in contrast to its later criticism against the Dutch.

In November, Drummond urged Harley to propose to Willem Buys, Pensioner of Amsterdam and a supporter of the West Indian expedition, sending a squadron to the West Indies. As a negotiator, Drummond recommended Sir James Wishart, who was one of the commissioners of the Admiralty and had an experience of serving in the Dutch Navy.[162] Consequently, in January 1711, Wishart was sent to The Hague to discuss naval affairs, including the Anglo-Dutch expedition to the West Indies.[163] St John expected that Woodes Rogers' success in his privateering voyage would invigorate the idea of Spanish-American expeditions both in Britain and the Netherlands. In a letter to Wishart, he suggested making use of private adventurers, as well as sending a government-sponsored expedition, as one option that Wishart should propose to the Pensioner for carrying out the expedition.[164] However, owing to the Dutch refusal to join the British plan, the project of a joint expedition did not bear fruit.[165]

At this time, there seems to have also been a plan to use a force originally prepared for Lord Shannon's expedition against Canada for an expedition against the French West Indian colonies. In late 1710, in a letter to Lord Raby, ambassador-extraordinary to Brandenburg-Prussia, the writer, probably his brother Peter

158 *Bolingbroke Correspondence*, I, p. 10, St John to Drummond, 27 October 1710.

159 BL, Add MS 70185, fols 60–61v, L. Renaud to Harley, 31 October 1710 [N.S.].

160 BL, Add MS 70026, fol. 253v [Harley] to Drummond, 7 November 1710.

161 *Bolingbroke Correspondence*, I, pp. 18–19, St John to Drummond, 14 November 1710.

162 BL, Add MS 70026, fols 276–276v, Drummond to Harley, 29 November /9 December 1710.

163 Coombs, *Conduct of the Dutch*, pp. 241–2.

164 TNA, SP 104/79, fol. 22, St John to Sir James Wishart, 16 February 1710/11.

165 It seems that the Dutch pursued the plan separately from Britain. In June 1711, there was talk of the West Indian expedition in the Netherlands. Drummond reported that Baron van Sommelsdijk, a Dutch Admiral, made several proposals including an attempt upon the coast of Mexico. H.M.C. *Portland*, V, pp. 9–10, Drummond to the Earl of Oxford [Harley], 15/26 June 1711. In July, this developed into a more concrete plan, in which six men of war with troops were to be sent to establish a colony, funded by the city of Amsterdam, the Surinam Company and subscription. However, this project seems to have come to naught.

Wentworth, reported that Peterborough was appointed as general of all the marines, and troops that were originally intended for Viscount Shannon's expedition were to be added to Peterborough's force to go to the West Indies. According to the writer, this project 'to possest themselves of all the Fren[ch] has there' was a revival of a plan that was proposed at the beginning of Anne's reign or the end of William's reign.[166] Indeed, in December 1710, the government seems to have been considering an attack on the French colony Guadeloupe, on the basis of the information from the island about the weak state of the government there and a recent slave rebellion. Nevertheless, this plan did not materialise either.[167]

Instead, by this time, St John had already come up with another plan for a colonial expedition to be carried out without the assistance of the Dutch: an expedition against Quebec. In January, in a letter to Harley, he mentioned a plan for an expedition, though initially he referred to it as the West Indian expedition.[168] In another letter, St John tried to convince Harley that he was 'not light nor whimsical' in that project, and emphasised the importance of secrecy for its success: 'It will certainly succeed, if ye secret is preserv'd and if it succeeds, you will have done more service to Brittain in half a year, than the ministers who went before you did in all their administration.'[169]

However, St John's project met with fierce opposition from other ministers. The Earl of Rochester, President of the Privy Council, objected to it on the grounds of the change in the political situation caused by the unexpected death of Emperor Joseph I.[170] Harley also strongly opposed the plan. Nevertheless, an attempted assassination of Harley and his temporary withdrawal from politics with an injury allowed St John to push ahead with the project. In May, the expeditionary force under Sir Hovenden Walker and Colonel John Hill left Plymouth. St John was confident of this project and boasted that he knew 'nothing of this kind, since Drake and Cavendish, performed by our nation'. [171] The expedition, however, ended in a catastrophic fiasco. In August, when navigating the St Lawrence, Walker's fleet ran aground and lost seven transport ships with more than eight hundred men. After this accident, the expedition was abandoned.

BL, Add MS 70028, fols 6–6v, 14 July 1711, Drummond to the Earl of Oxford.

166 BL, Add MS 31143, fol. 626v [Peter Wentworth?] to [Lord Raby] [n.d., but December 1710 or January 1711?]. There was no date on this letter. However, judging from the chronological order of the documents, it is likely that this letter was written in December 1710 or January 1711.

167 TNA, CO 152/39, no. 120, fol. 127, Board of Trade to Dartmouth, 8 December 1710, and no. 120, enclosure i, fol. 130, 'Abstract of a Letter, Dated at St. Christophers', 16 September 1710; TNA, ADM 1/4094, fol. 145, Dartmouth to Admiralty, 8 December 1710.

168 BL, Add MS 70027, fols 5–6, St John to Harley, 8 January 1710/11. The reason for this is not clear, but it is possible that he tried to conceal the true destination of the expedition.

169 BL, Add MS 70027, fols 21–21v, St John to Harley, 17 January 1710/11.

170 BL, Add MS 70027, fols 105–105v, Rochester to Harley, 18 April 1711, and fol. 107v, St John to Harley, 19 April 1711.

171 *Bolingbroke Correspondence*, I, p. 294, St John to Drummond, 3 August 1711.

Again there arose an idea to use a part of the forces in another operation in the West Indies when the attack of Canada was over, which was mentioned by St John.[172] After the failure of the Quebec expedition, Walker himself considered this one possible option.[173] Also, after the news of the failure arrived, there was a proposal in Britain to use part of the forces of the Canadian expedition for attempts on Hispaniola, Porto Bello and the Spanish colonies in the South Sea.[174] However, these plans were not adopted, and the last project for colonial expeditions during the war ended without success.

Frustration and Expectation: Analysis of Plans for Colonial Expeditions

Why did Plans for Colonial Expeditions not Materialise?

As we have seen so far, during the War of the Spanish Succession, the British government had explored several plans for naval expeditions to Spanish America. However, none of them was actually carried out, and the only colonial expedition on a large scale launched from the mother country was that against Quebec in 1711. What can account for this unimpressive record on Spanish-American expeditions in spite of recurrent demand for vigorous colonial maritime war against the Spanish colonies during the war?

One of the causes for the failure often mentioned was the negative attitudes of the Marlborough–Godolphin ministry towards colonial expeditions. This view was held by contemporaries, as well. In the *Memoirs of Queen Anne* published in 1729, one Gibson wrote that, though several proposals of making conquest in the Spanish West Indies were submitted to the Marlborough–Godolphin ministry, 'they looked upon all such Projects to be both expensive and impracticable, and such as might expose the common Cause to the greatest Hazards', and therefore were firmly resolved to pursue a war in Flanders as a feasible means to subdue France.[175] This is not entirely correct, for Godolphin continued to uphold the idea of colonial expeditions, as we have seen.

On the other hand, some historians attribute one of the reasons for the failure to considerations for operations in other regions, such as the Iberian Peninsula or the Mediterranean, which reputedly diverted the force away from the West Indian expedition. Denman has stated that the necessity of a cutback in the English effort, especially the need for sending troops to Portugal, persuaded Godolphin to abandon the plan for the West Indian operation of 1702–3.[176] On the other hand,

172 Gerald S. Graham, ed., *The Walker Expedition to Quebec, 1711* (London, 1953), p. 349, St John to General Hill, 7 August 1711; p. 356, St John to Admiral Walker, 7 August 1711.

173 *Ibid.*, p. 144, 'The Journal of Admiral Sir Hovenden Walker', 4 September 1711.

174 BL, Add MS 70164 [not foliated], 'Some thoughts concerning attempts on the WI', [n.d.]. Judging from the passage referring to the end of Walker's expedition, it seems that this proposal was written probably in October or November 1711, shortly after the news of the failure of the expedition reached England.

175 Gibson, *Memoirs of Queen Anne: being a Compleat Supplement to the History of her Reign* ... (London, 1729), p. 116.

J.H. Owen has mentioned a demand for the forces in the Mediterranean as one reason why the policy of West Indian expeditions was abandoned in the early stage of the war.[177]

To be sure, the Iberian Peninsula or the Mediterranean had a strong correlation with the colonial operations, though in a pamphlet war, what was often juxtaposed with maritime war was war in Flanders and Germany. For example, in October 1702, Godolphin stated that the operation in the West Indies would be less costly in 1703, and accepted that the money that England saved there might be applied to a new expense in Portugal, which Methuen was trying to win to the allies' side at that time.[178] It is also true that the Peninsula and the Mediterranean became one of the main theatres of the war, especially after the conclusion of the offensive and defensive treaties with Portugal in May 1703.[179] Under the circumstances, England had to choose the fields where she deployed her forces. In March 1703, writing to Harley, Godolphin stated, 'I doubt we have too many irons in the fire. We can't be in the Mediterranean, in Portugal, upon the coast of France, and in the West Indies all at once.'[180]

However, it is worth pointing out that, in the case of Peterborough's expedition, the departure of the expedition had been severely delayed by the end of 1702, and, by January 1703, the government had already decided to cancel it. Therefore, as far as Peterborough's expedition is concerned, it would be more appropriate to say that the need for the forces in the Iberian theatre and the Mediterranean was the last straw that obliged the government finally to abandon the long-delayed expedition, rather than a direct cause of the cancellation.[181] Thus, though the strategic considerations of war in the Iberian Peninsula or the Mediterranean constituted one factor that hindered West Indian expeditions, it was not always a decisive one.

A more important factor was the reluctance or opposition of the other allies to Spanish-American expeditions. William T. Morgan has mentioned objections from the Netherlands and Austria as one of the important reasons why little attention had been paid to the Caribbean area between 1703 and 1710.[182] In the case of Peterborough's expedition, the objection from Austria seems to have been indeed one of the direct causes for the cancellation. The account of this incident was given in a letter from the Earl of Halifax to Robert Harley in September 1710. According to Halifax, when the preparation for the expedition was nearly ready, Count Wratislaw, Imperial Ambassador Extraordinary in England, made new

176 Denman, 'Political Debate, p. 169.

177 Owen, *War at Sea under Queen Anne*, pp. 42–4.

178 BL, Add MS 29588, fols 325–325v, Godolphin to Nottingham, 11 October 1702.

179 Hattendorf, *England in the War of the Spanish Succession*, pp. 80–2, 107.

180 H.M.C. *Portland*, IV, p. 59, Godolphin to Harley, 28 March 1703.

181 It should also be noted that the large part of the forces originally intended for Peterborough's expedition was dispatched to the West Indies, though they were employed not in an attack on Spanish colonies as was originally planned, but in the attempt on Guadaloupe by Codrington and Walker.

182 Morgan, 'Canadian Expedition', 151–2.

demands regarding the expedition. What he particularly insisted on was that garrisons for the places occupied by the expeditionary forces should take an oath to the emperor, which, in the English ministers' eyes, was contrary to the sixth article of the Treaty of the Grand Alliance. However, Wratislaw would not compromise on this point, which hindered further prosecution of the expedition.[183]

Equally important was the relationship with the Netherlands. Although Dutch assistance was often thought essential for successful expeditions, the Dutch were reluctant to join, and in the case of Peterborough's expedition, lengthy negotiations to persuade them caused severe delay in preparation. Moreover, even after they decided to join, they were cautious about sparing large forces for the expedition. In the above letter to Harley, Halifax mentioned that a doubt cast by the Dutch ministers upon the prospect of Peterborough's expedition also contributed to the cancellation of the plan.[184] It might not be entirely fair to say that, as Morgan puts it, the Dutch checked the English plan in the Caribbean, for they agreed to join Peterborough's expedition in the end.[185] However, it can be claimed that their hesitation to join the expedition also contributed to the cancellation by causing a severe delay in the departure.

No less important a factor was the incapability and inexperience of the English naval administration in this period to dispatch a large-scale expedition without delay. According to Richard Harding, it was only during the Seven Years War that ideological belief regarding how war should be conducted was effectively aligned with the capability of carrying out such a war.[186] Christian Buchet has ascribed the British success in the West Indian expeditions during the Seven Years War to two reasons. The first is that Britain gradually formed a better overall geo-strategical view, such as the concept of relay stations and the supply of manpower and food from the North American colonies. The second is a better-structured organisation of the Navy, such as clearly defined duties and responsibilities between the navy and the army, improvement of naval ships in terms of firepower and sheathing, more regular and frequent supply of food and naval equipment by a convoy system, and development of naval bases in Jamaica and Antigua.[187]

In the War of the Spanish Succession, however, the British naval administration had not yet made these improvements. In West Indian expeditions, a particularly critical factor was the incapability of fitting out an expeditionary force without delay. In Peterborough's expedition, even after England succeeded in negotiation with the Dutch, there were still administrative problems, such as the delay of transports and difficulty in finding money or appropriate officers for the expedition. This led to a further delay in departure that could expose the

183 BL, Add MS 70026, fols 166–7, Halifax to Harley, 19 September 1710.

184 BL, Add MS 70026, fols 167–167v, Halifax to Harley, 19 September 1710.

185 Morgan, 'Canadian Expedition', 151.

186 Richard Harding, 'The Ideology and Organisation of Maritime War: An Expedition to Canada in 1746', XIV International Economic History Congress, Helsinki 2006, session 69, p. 3.

187 Christian Buchet, 'The Royal Navy and the Caribbean, 1689–1763', *MM* 80 (1994), 32–41.

expeditionary force to hurricanes and epidemics rampant in the summer season. Governor Codrington of the Leeward Islands, who knew the reality of the West Indies, was well aware of the danger caused by such delay:

> one false step ruins the whole Expedition, in Europe, there may be roome for a back game, but here the designe must be laid well & ffully at first, and then Vigorously Executed. For delays will cost more men then the warmest actions.[188]

Thus, the lack of administrative capability and experience was one of the significant factors that caused the delay in departure, and ultimately abandonment of the plan.

Why did the Support for Colonial Expeditions Survive?

In the end, the plans for colonial expeditions did not bring any tangible territorial gains to Britain during the War of the Spanish Succession. If we look only at the results of the attempts, they were almost nothing but continuous failures. Nevertheless, the support for the colonial expeditions survived even after the war ended. What were the reasons?

As far as expeditions to the West Indies were concerned, one obvious factor would be the lure of the wealth of Spanish America, the attraction of which was boosted by the occasional captures of Spanish silver fleets by the navy and privateers. The anxiety about the growing debts, which we have already seen in Chapter 3, also must have sustained the belief in expeditions as an easy solution to the Britain's financial problems. However, there seem to have been other reasons as well. Richard Harding has pointed out that, at that time, even when colonial expeditions were unsuccessful, questions of operational capability, underlying causes of the failure, were rarely discussed or examined seriously. Instead, investigations were usually focused on establishing the blame or innocence of those concerned with the operations, such as ministers, generals and admirals. This tendency helped the belief in Britain's capability for successful colonial expeditions to stay resilient.[189]

Although Harding mainly takes the Canadian expedition of 1746 as an example, similar attitudes can be seen for the expeditions during the War of the Spanish Succession. In this case, supporters of the expeditions tended to assume that there were some specific persons responsible for the abortion of the plans. For example, when Defoe enumerated various mismanagement of the war so far, he claimed, 'I must further here examine who Discourag'd early proposals, for Attempts upon the Spanish West Indies' by Peterborough as well as by private undertakers, which, Defoe believed, would have effectually taken over the trade by the French.[190] Likewise, Halifax firmly believed that John Methuen, English envoy at Lisbon, 'diverted the war from being made in the West Indies which would have enriched us, and touched Spain most sensibly', though, as A.D. Francis

188 TNA, CO 7/1, no. 3 [not foliated], Codrington to [Nottingham?], 24 February 1702/3.
189 Harding, 'Ideology and Organisation', pp. 4, 13–14.
190 *Review*, IV, p. 158, no. 40, 2 April 1706.

has stated, this would be an unfair view, for such a decision was clearly beyond his power.[191]

This tendency to look for persons responsible for abandonment of the plans was so strong that even Marlborough was afraid of being made a scapegoat. In May 1710, when he objected to sending several regiments for the intended colonial expeditions, he wrote, 'I had much rather venture my life with to[o] few troops, then to have villains insinuat that any other service is neglected in order to strenghen this army.'[192] Likewise, in July 1710, he asked Godolphin that any project of expedition might not be stopped on his account, 'for that might give a couller to my enemys to lay to my charge the failling of the expedition'.[193]

Mismanagement of naval affairs in the West Indies was also sometimes attributed to the alleged corruption and dishonesty of the naval administration. In reference to a lack of sufficient support for Admiral Wager when he took the Tierra Firme galleons in 1708, the *Observator* implied that the neglect of maritime war in the West Indies was related to the Prince's council's failure in their duty.[194] These tendencies, to a certain extent, seem to have helped shift the whole blame on to specific persons and to distract the attention of the supporters of the colonial expeditions who were not necessarily familiar with the practicalities of naval administration away from the actual problems. At the same time, it also allowed them to continue to believe that the expeditions would have succeeded if they had not been disturbed by evil advisers.

It would be unfair to say that those supporters were completely unaware of the practical problems. Some of them did recognise several actual difficulties, such as conflict between army and naval officers, and the danger of uncontrollable plunder.[195] However, it seems that these supporters tended to focus on only such issues as were not so hard to understand even for laymen, and did not necessarily pay enough attention to other more mundane and basic administrative problems such as supply of provisions and speedy transportation of soldiers. For example, one Thomas Ekines, an ex-naval officer who made a proposal for an expeditions to Spanish America and Newfoundland, mentioned that the failure of four West Indian expeditions in William's reign and one in Anne's reign was attributed to disagreement between naval and army officers.[196] It is true that this was one of the main obstacles to successful amphibious operations, but it would be too extreme to say that the failures were caused only by it.

One of the issues with which the planners of the expeditions were often

191 H.M.C. *Bath*, I, p. 155, Halifax to [Earl Rivers], 27 January 1706/7; Francis, *The Methuens and Portugal*, p. 330.

192 *Marlborough–Godolphin Correspondence*, III, no. 1534, p. 1499, Marlborough to Godolphin, 18/29 May 1710.

193 *Ibid.*, III, no. 1593, p. 1550, Marlborough to Godolphin, 29 June/10 July 1710.

194 *Observator*, no. 63, 22 September 1708.

195 As to the latter, this was still a problem at the end of the eighteenth century. See Joseph M. Fewster, 'Prize-Money and the British Expedition to the West Indies of 1793–94', *JICH* 12, no. 1 (1984), 1–28.

196 BL, Add MS 61644A, fol. 49v, Thomas Ekines to ?, 8 September 1708.

preoccupied was the secrecy of the projects. The anonymous author of 'Some considerations about forming a Descent in the Spanish West Indies' mentioned disclosure of plans as one of the two main causes of failures of colonial expeditions, together with the irresolution of the planners when they thought the plans were known to the enemy.[197] The government's care to keep the plans for expeditions secret can be seen in the negotiations with the Dutch for the naval force for Peterborough's expedition of 1702–3. In a letter to Heinsius, the queen stated that the matters that Mitchell was to discuss with him required speedy resolution and some of them 'should be transacted with the greatest secrecy too', and asked Heinsius to persuade the states to concur with England 'in Such manner as that the services may not suffer by any delay, or our Enemys discover our designes'.[198] In particular, the targets of the expedition, Havana and Cartagena, were top secret, and Mitchell was directed that he did not need to mention the specific places until he found it necessary in persuading the Dutch.[199]

The possibility of exposure of the plans often caused serious concern. In March 1704, in the examination of Graydon's conduct during his operation in America in 1703, the Lords committee pointed out the possible exposure of the destination of his fleet, Newfoundland, which allowed the enemy to make preparations for defence against the attack.[200] A similar concern was also shown regarding Jennings' expedition of 1706, which had already been made public before his arrival in the West Indies, and in October, Hedges ordered the Prince's council to investigate this matter.[201] When a plan for a West Indian expedition was discussed in the Privy Council in September 1707, this issue seems to have been raised again. The minutes of the council, probably written by Harley, mentioned that the design on the West Indies was 'knowne or suspected'.[202] Shortly afterward, investigation resumed, and subsequently Sir John Leake gave an account of the situation when Jennings was dispatched in 1706. According to Leake, when he received the order from Prince George of Denmark to dispatch Jennings, he discussed the matter with Sir George Byng and Jennings privately. Although he admitted that the destination of the fleet had been already talked of publicly before it sailed, he believed that it was simply

197 BL, Add MS 70049, fol. 182, 'Some considerations about forming a Descent in the Spanish West Indies' [n.d.].

198 FH MSS 275, p. 50, Queen Anne to the Pensioner of Holland, 9 July 1702.

199 FH MSS 275, pp. 50–1 [Nottingham?] to [Mitchell] [9 July 1702]. Heinsius was notified of this plan through Marlborough, who was Commander in Chief of the English forces in Holland and Ambassador Extraordinary to the United Province at that time, and the necessity of secrecy was again emphasised.

200 *L.J.*, XVII, p. 510, 23 March 1704.

201 TNA, ADM 1/4091, fol. 38, Hedges to the Prince's council, 15 October 1706. Accordingly, George Byng, who was engaged in the operation in the Mediterranean under the command of Leake at that time, was ordered to report the situation when Jennings was dispatched, though it is not certain whether Byng actually submitted this report. TNA, ADM 2/419, p. 68 [Burchett] to Byng, 17 October 1706.

202 BL, Add MS 70338, bundle 48 [not foliated], Minutes of the Privy Council, 13 September 1707.

based on conjecture.[203] These episodes demonstrate well the government's concern about the secrecy of the plans for the colonial expeditions.

Thus, politicians who supported colonial expeditions tended to focus on such problems as would be easy for them to understand. This seems to have kept their hope of successful expeditions alive by making them believe that the projects would have succeeded if these specific difficulties had been overcome. In the case of the Quebec expedition in 1711, St John regarded secrecy as one of the most important keys to its success. In a letter to Harley, he wrote, 'Morally Speaking, if we keep our secret, we shall succeed.'[204] To keep the true destination of the expedition secret, St John took as much care as possible. He asked Drummond to spread false information that some preparation was intended for the French or Spanish coast to distract people's attention from North America.[205] It seems that he even made use of the negotiations with the Dutch about the Anglo-Dutch expedition to the West Indies to conceal the true destination.[206] However, as Gerald S. Graham has pointed out, ironically St John's care for secrecy, which led him to avoid disclosing its destination even to the Board of Admiralty, hampered effective preparation for the expedition, because provisions were prepared for only three months to pretend that the force was intended for near home waters.[207]

The ignorance of the practicalities of naval expeditions also seems to have allowed pamphleteers to be over-optimistic about prospects and feasibility of the colonial expeditions. For instance, in September 1708, the *Observator* deplored the neglect of naval affairs in the West Indies. It referred to the abortive expedition under the command of the Earl of Peterborough at the beginning of the war, and claimed that, if Peterborough, who made a success in campaign in Catalonia and Valencia even without enough men or money, had been sent to the West Indies with a well-manned squadron and honest officers, it 'would probably by this Time have put the *Spanish West Indies* into the Hands of King *Charles* III'.[208] Likewise, in October 1713, the *Examiner* lamented that the navy was neglected in the late war, and emphasised the necessity of rebuilding the naval force and reforming the naval administration. If Britain carried it out, the *Examiner* argued, she would soon find able commanders like Blake and John Narborough, and 'They who have done Wonders in *Privateering* with our *Ships of War*, for their own particular Advantage' would perform well 'when they come to act upon Principles of Honour and Advantage to the Publick'.[209]

Thus, in this period, the ambition of the advocates of colonial expeditions was

203 BL, Add MS 61581, fol. 182, Extract of a letter from Leake to Burchett, 26 September 1707.

204 BL, Add MS 70027, fol. 6, St John to Harley, 8 January 1710/11.

205 *Bolingbroke Correspondence*, I, pp. 111–12, St John to Drummond, 20 March 1710/11. Even Drummond himself was kept in the dark about the destination of the expedition. H.M.C. *Portland*, V, p. 10, Drummond to the Earl of Oxford [Harley], 15/26 June 1711.

206 BL, Add MS 70300 [not foliated], St John to Drummond, 26 June 1711.

207 Graham, ed., *Walker Expedition to Quebec*, Introduction, pp. 19–21.

208 *Observator*, no. 63, 22 September 1708.

209 *Examiner*, IV, no. 39, 19 October 1713.

not yet matched to the capability and experience of the British naval administration to carry out successful expeditions. Paradoxically, however, the very fact that colonial expeditions were not carried out seems to have enabled their supporters to continue to claim that such expeditions could be an effective and profitable means to subdue the enemy, if only given a full chance to prove themselves.

As we have seen so far, throughout the War of the Spanish Succession, there were always politicians of importance who regarded maritime war in the Americas as an effective means to subdue the enemy by depriving him of its financial resources. They were not confined to opposition politicians. They included some of the politicians in the ministry such as Vernon, Nottingham, Rochester, Godolphin and St John.

Of the two means for that purpose, interception of the Spanish silver fleet was a relatively more acceptable policy, and several successful captures boosted the enthusiasm for colonial maritime war. On the other hand, opinions about colonial expeditions were more divided, and while the government included keen supporters of colonial expeditions, there was also opposition from some politicians such as Marlborough and, in the case of the Quebec expedition of 1711, Harley. In addition to these two operations, the government also attempted to persuade the Spanish colonists in expectation of opening direct trade with the Spanish colonies.

In the end, the plans for a large-scale West Indian expedition did not materialise during the war. Several factors contributed to this failure. The necessity of sending forces to the Iberian Peninsula or the Mediterranean occasionally diverted the force from the colonial expeditions, though this was not always a direct cause of the cancellation of the plans. A more important factor was rather a diplomatic one. In particular, negotiations with the Dutch, who were regarded as an essential partner in West Indian expeditions but were hesitant about the project, often caused a delay in departure of the expeditionary forces. In addition, the capability of British naval administration had not yet developed enough to carry out the expeditions speedily, compared with the middle of the century when Britain saw several successes in colonial expeditions. These two factors tended to delay departure of an expeditionary force, which ultimately led to cancellation of the plans. Thus, as far as the period of the War of the Spanish Succession was concerned, what was lacking was not the will of the government to launch naval expeditions, but the experience and administrative capability to implement them, without relying on the assistance of the reluctant partner, the Dutch.

In spite of these failures, however, support for colonial expeditions continued to survive. This was partly made possible by the tendency to attribute the reason for the failure to specific persons or several simple reasons, such as secrecy and the timing of departure. While these tendencies distracted the attention of the supporters of colonial maritime war from more mundane and practical difficulties of naval operations, they also helped the supporters to continue to believe that, if only these obstacles were removed, colonial expeditions would easily succeed.

– 5 –

Impact on Reality: Legislation

The pro-maritime war argument has an impact not only on naval policy but also on legislation in Parliament. During the War of the Spanish Succession, there were several attempts to promote colonial privateering and private expeditions to conquer enemy territory by legislation. The 'Act for the Encouragement of Trade to America' (hereafter, the 'American Act'), enacted in 1708, together with the 'Act for the better securing the Trade of this Kingdom, by Cruisers and Convoys' (hereafter, the 'Cruisers and Convoy Act'), can be regarded as the culmination of these attempts.[1]

This American Act has been referred to by several historians who study maritime or American colonial history of the eighteenth century in different contexts. Those who study privateering, such as David J. Starkey and Carl E. Swanson, have regarded the American Act, as well as the Cruisers and Convoy Act, as momentous because the legislation granted the whole value of prizes to captors and established a legal procedure for the condemnation of prizes and distribution of profits.[2] Likewise, according to historians who look at the issue of naval impressments, such as Richard Pares and Nicholas Rogers, the act was significant in that it exempted seamen from impressment in America.[3] On the other hand, Curtis Nettels has mentioned the act in the context of Spanish-American trade and English privateers' attacks on it.[4]

However, when it comes to the question of what political and economic interests

1 'An Act for the Encouragement of Trade to America', 6 Anne C. 37, 64 (Common printed editions); 'An Act for the better securing the Trade of this Kingdom, by Cruisers and Convoys', 6 Anne C. 13, 65 (Common printed editions).

2 David J. Starkey, *British Privateering Enterprise in the Eighteenth Century* (Exeter, 1990), pp. 86–7; Carl E. Swanson, *Predators and Prizes: American Privateering and Imperial Warfare, 1739–1748* (Columbia, SC, 1991), pp. 34–6. From the viewpoint of legal history, these two acts are also important in that they gave Parliamentary recognition and some measure of Parliamentary regulation to the Prize Court. Edward S. Roscoe, *A History of the English Prize Court* (London, 1924), p. 38.

3 Richard Pares, 'The Manning of the Navy in the West Indies, 1702–63', *TRHS*, 4th ser, 20 (1937), 51; Nicholas Rogers, *The Press Gang: Naval Impressment and its Opponents in Georgian Britain* (London and New York, 2007), pp. 85–6. See also Dora Mae Clark, 'The Impressment of Seamen in the American Colonies', *Essays in Colonial History: Presented to Charles McLean Andrews by his Students* (Free Port, NY, 1966), pp. 206–7.

4 Nettels, 'England and Spanish-American Trade', 23–4.

were behind this act, there has not been a detailed examination. Political historians have placed a debate in Parliament in November 1707, the starting point of the enactment of the American Act and the Cruisers and Convoy Act, in the context of the Junto Whigs' attack on the Admiralty to win an Admiralty post for one of their members, the Earl of Orford.[5] Likewise, Denman has explained that the act was 'chiefly the work of a group of parliamentary Whig merchants', with support from Lord Halifax, one of the Junto.[6] It is true that the Junto Whigs were among the main promoters of the American Act. Nevertheless, the question whether other political groups also supported the act should be examined.

As to the vested interests involved in the act, Starkey states that the enactment of the American Act and the Cruisers and Convoy Act was a response of Parliament to merchants' complaints about French attacks on British seaborne trade and to a certain extent an attempt to provide regular trade protection for home trade and to encourage commerce-raiding activities by both the navy and privateers to counter the French *guerre de course*.[7] On the other hand, some historians have emphasised the role of privateering interests. For example, Swanson claims that the American Act represented the increasing political strength of the privateering interests as well as serious attempts by Parliament to regulate privateers.[8] Likewise, Pares regards the act as a triumph of privateering interests in their long-running fight against naval impressment.[9] Thus, it is not yet clear which of the two groups – merchants, who demanded better protection of trade, or privateers, who asked for the encouragement of commerce-raiding activities – was the main promoter of this act and what the relation between them was.

To reveal what political and vested interests were behind the American Act, this chapter examines the process of its enactment, taking into consideration the preceding attempts to encourage colonial maritime war. In particular, it focuses on the issue of Spanish-American trade, where the relations between merchants and privateers can be seen most clearly.

Through the analysis of the political interests involved in the act, this chapter will show that the policy favouring colonial maritime war drew support from a much wider range of politicians than is commonly understood. Moreover, it will reveal that the pro-maritime war policy was affected not only by party politics but also by conflicting interests concerned in colonial maritime affairs, especially the tension between Whig West Indian merchants and Jamaican privateers regarding Spanish-American trade.[10]

5 Henry L. Snyder, 'Queen Anne versus the Junto: The Effort to Place Orford at the Head of the Admiralty in 1709', *HLQ* 35 (August 1972), 324–6; Holmes, *British Politics*, pp. 111–12.

6 Denman, 'Political Debate', p. 275.

7 Starkey, *British Privateering Enterprise*, p. 86.

8 Swanson, *Predators and Prizes*, p. 36.

9 Pares, 'Manning of the Navy', 51.

10 Biographical information in this article is from *ODNB*, and *House of Commons 1690–1715*, III–V.

The Context of the American Act

The Privateering Bill of 1702

The American Act of 1708 was not an isolated attempt to promote maritime war during the War of the Spanish Succession. There were several preceding bills and instructions, some of whose contents were later incorporated into the American Act. At the end of William's reign, in anticipation of a new war, a bill to encourage privateering was considered in Parliament. On 10 January 1702, a committee was appointed to bring in a 'Bill for the encouragement of Privateers' (hereafter, the 'Privateering Bill'), with Francis Scobell as its chairman.[11] However, this bill did not pass owing to the Commons' opposition to the Lords' amendments on the grounds that the amendments would cause alterations in several duties and in the manner of disposing public money, which was regarded as 'the undoubted Right of the Commons alone, and an essential Part of their Constitution'.[12]

There are several clauses in this bill that were relevant to the American Act. One of them concerns the custody and sale of prizes. The clause was intended to transfer those tasks from the prize office, which was often accused of alleged irregularities and inefficiency, to the commissioners of the customs, though the latter were reluctant to accept it, claiming that it would overload them.[13] Another important clause in relation to the American Act is one 'for incorporating Persons to make Acquisitions', which was offered as a rider and agreed to by the Commons.[14] It is not entirely clear exactly what this clause meant because of the brevity of the description. However, judging from the fact that in their address the Commons later asked the Queen for further encouragement of conquests in the East and West Indies, it is possible that this clause was intended to facilitate the formation of corporations for the purpose of launching privateering expeditions to seize enemy territory.

Who was involved in this bill? An analysis of the membership of several committees in the Commons involved in the development of this bill does not indicate a clear dominance of either Whigs or Tories.[15] It does not seem that the

11 *C.J.*, XIII, p. 665, 10 January 1701/2.

12 *C.J.*, XIII, p. 899, 19 May 1702. The contents of this bill and the Lords' amendments can be gleaned from the following sources: PA, HL/PO/JO/5/1/37, Minutes of Proceedings, 11 and 13 May 1702; HL/PO/JO/10/6/32/1795, Main Papers, 'Provisoes & Clauses added to Privateers Bill', fols 19–22v, 15 May 1702.

13 PA, HL/PO/JO/5/1/37, Minutes of Proceedings, 11 April [May] and 13 May 1702; TNA, T1/79, fol. 253, Commissioners of the Customs to Lords of the Treasury, 29 April 1702. For the criticism against the prize office, see John S. Bromley, 'Prize Office and Prize Agency at Portsmouth, 1689–1748', *Corsairs and Navies, 1660–1760*, ed. John S. Bromley (London and Ronceverte, 1987), pp. 466–9.

14 *C.J.*, XIII, p. 872, 5 May 1702.

15 The proportion of the Whig and Tory MPs in the committees concerned with the Privateering Bill in the Commons was as follows: the committee to prepare the bill, Whigs 18, Tories 13; the committee to receive proposals for the better encouragement of privateers in the West Indies, Whigs 23, Tories 22. *C.J.*, XIII, pp. 665, 776, 10 January, 4 March 1701/2.

Privateering Bill was legislation with a partisan character. What ultimately ruined the bill was the question of control over the monetary supply, which had been a sore point between the two houses rather than a political conflict between the Tories and Whigs or objections to the aims of the bill itself: the encouragement of privateers for trade protection and the capture of enemy colonies.

That there was consensus on the promotion of maritime war at this point is shown in the fact that both houses immediately prepared addresses requesting the encouragement of privateering and colonial conquest. On 23 May, the Commons resolved to present an address to the Queen, asking her to encourage the capture of enemy assets, especially by issuing commissions and charters to those who would attempt to conquer some part of the East or West Indies. Similarly, the Lords prepared an address to the Queen on 23 May that asked first for the encouragement of privateers to protect English seaborne trade from French attacks and second for the granting of commissions or charters to those who would venture to seize enemy territories in the Indies. According to the address, the latter demand was intended such that the English could have 'a real and effectual Advantage' of the sixth article of the second Treaty of the Grand Alliance concluded between Austria, England and the Netherlands in September 1701, which allowed England to 'take and seize Lands and Cities belonging to the *Spanish* dominions in *the Indies*, and retain the same as Your own'. In answer to these two addresses, the Queen promised to address the issue.[16]

The demand for more vigorous maritime war from both Houses was, to a certain extent, answered by the royal proclamation of 1 June 1702, which aimed at motivating crews of men of war and privateers to capture enemy ships by granting them gun money, the right to retain pillage (i.e. goods found upon or above the gun deck of captured ships), and a better share of prizes. [17] At the same time, the government tried to tighten its grip on privateers by giving instructions forbidding them from committing transgressions such as embezzlement, torture and attacks on English or allies' subjects, as well as detailed instructions about the procedure for the condemnation, custody and sale of prizes.[18]

Thus, though the Privateering Bill of 1702, which seems to have been supported by both the Whigs and Tories, failed to pass, both Houses demanded the encouragement of privateering and colonial conquest in the addresses of May 1702, which the government partly answered with the proclamation and instructions to privateers. Moreover, as we have seen in Chapter 4, at the same time, the government started to plan a large-scale naval expedition against Spanish America under the command of the Earl of Peterborough. However, this plan was cancelled

16 *C.J.*, XIII, p. 907, 23, 25 May 1702; *L.J.*, XVII, pp. 147–8, 23, 25 May 1702.

17 *Her Majesties Most Gracious Declaration, for the Incouragement of Her Ships of War and Privateers*, 1 June 1702.

18 BL, Add MS 70044, 'Instructions for such Merchants and others, who shall have Commissions or Letter of Marque, or Commissions for Private Men of War…', fols 193–5, 1 June 1702.

in January 1703, and instead, an attack on Guadeloupe, a French colony in the Caribbean, was carried out, though it ended in failure.

The West Indies Bill of 1703

It was not long before another legislative attempt was made to encourage colonial privateering and colonial conquest. On 18 November, in the Commons, William Clayton, 'Mr Johnson' (probably Thomas Johnson) – both of whom were tobacco and sugar merchants from Liverpool – along with Solicitor General Simon Harcourt, were ordered to bring in a 'bill for the better encouragement of privateers'. Although this bill seems to have been lost after the first reading in January 1703, there was soon another attempt to bring in a bill to promote colonial maritime war. On 9 February 1703, 'an Act for the better carrying on the War, by Sea and Land, in *The Indies*' [hereafter, the 'West Indies Bill'] was brought into the Lords. As its title shows, this bill was focused more on the encouragement of colonial maritime war than the Privateering Bill of 1702 had been.

The West Indies Bill included three clauses. The first was intended to exploit the right of conquest granted by the sixth article of the Treaty of the Grand Alliance, which the House of Lords had demanded in the address of May 1702. 'For the more effectual prosecution and Carrying on that part of the present war with France and Spain which relates to the sea, And more Especially to the Indies', it was to give powers and privileges to those who were willing to take any ships, properties or territories belonging to the French or the Spaniards at sea or in their American colonies. The next two clauses were intended to alleviate the manning problem, which was 'a great obstruction to the Effectuall carrying on the warrs by sea' as well as the trade of England, by allowing English ships the use of foreign seamen without limitation and by admitting the naturalisation of foreign seamen after service of one year in the Indies.[19]

With some amendments, the bill was sent to the Commons on 15 February, where it met with resistance. After the division, it was decided the debate should be postponed, and while the Parliament itself was prorogued again and again until November, the bill was dropped.[20]

[19] PA, HL/PO/JO/10/6/43/1901, Main Papers, 'An Act for the better carrying on the prsent Warr by Sea & Land in the West Indies', fols 40–3. The original title of the bill was 'An Act for the better carrying on the prsent Warr by Sea & Land in the Indies'. However, in the Lords' committee, the word 'West' was inserted before 'Indies', probably in order to exempt the East Indies from its scope. HL/PO/JO/5/1/38 [not foliated], 12 February 1703. As we shall see later, the East India Company also showed an interest in bills to encourage maritime war in America as it could violate their privileges if the Pacific Ocean was included within the scope of the bills.

[20] *L.J.*, XVII, pp. 277–8, 12, 15 February 1702/3; *C.J.*, XIV, pp. 205–6, 19 February 1702/3. Soon after the debate was postponed, the Queen announced to Parliament in her speech at the close of the session on 27 February 1703 that all her share in prizes taken during the war was to be applied to the public service in order to show the crown's keenness for the pursuit of the war and to call for the unity of the nation. *Cobbett*, VI, cols 145–6.

Although the cause of this disagreement in the Commons is not clear, if we look at the tellers for the division over the adjournment of the debate, we can perceive one interesting point. The tellers for the adjournment of the debate, whose intention seems to have been to drop the bill by postponing the debate, were Tories Edward Nicholas and Edward Knatchbull.[21] On the other hand, the tellers for the noes, Hugh Boscawen and James Stanhope, who seem to have intended to proceed with the bill without further ado, were both Whigs.[22] Moreover, Baron Herbert of Cherbury, who chaired the select committee to consider the bill in the Lords, was also a Whig.

Judging from this, it can be conjectured that this bill, which was focused more on the encouragement of private expeditions to the West Indies, was supported mainly by the Whigs, in contrast to the Privateering Bill of 1702, which was supported by both parties and whose content was not necessarily confined to the promotion of colonial maritime war. What, then, was the reason for their support? Whose interests was this bill expected to serve?

There are some clues to this question. In reference to the bill, the Whig periodical *Observator* of 24 February 1703 wrote that the Commons 'could have done nothing better for the common good of their People, especially the Trading part of the Nation' because new colonies that England might obtain in the West Indies during the war and keep in peace time would increase the exportation of manufactured products, which could provide more employment for the poor.[23] This suggested that the colonial conquests that the bill was aimed to encourage were expected to serve English commercial and industrial interests.

In particular, behind this bill, there seems to have been support from Whig magnates in the City who had interests in the West Indian trade.[24] They were represented by Sir Gilbert Heathcote and Sir Bartholomew Gracedieu, both of whom were leading West Indian merchants and agents of Jamaica, as well as

[21] Edward Nicholas (1662–1726) was Court Tory MP for Shaftesbury and the treasurer to Prince George of Denmark (1702–7). Edward Knatchbull (c. 1674–1730) was Tory MP for Rochester, who had a connection with Nottingham, and was a sub-commissioner of prizes at Portsmouth in 1702 and then Dover (1702?–8).

[22] Hugh Boscawen (c. 1680–1734) was MP for Tregony and had strong political influence in Cornwall. He was a nephew of Godolphin and one of the 'Lord Treasurer's Whigs'. James Stanhope (c. 1673–1721) was Whig MP for Cockermouth. He was an army officer and diplomat who played an important role in Spain later in the war.

[23] *Observator*, no. 88, 24 February 1702/3.

[24] De Krey points out that many of the colonial merchants during William's reign, including some of the wealthiest City leaders such as Sir Gilbert Heathcote, were politically inclined towards the Whigs, religiously to Dissent, and unsympathetic to the privileged monopolistic corporations established before the Glorious Revolution, such as the Royal African Company, while they had a strong connection with the Bank of England and the New East India Company through investment. The Iberian merchants, who were growing rapidly under William's reign, had similar Whig preferences and strong links with the Bank and the New East India Company. Gary S. De Krey, *A Fractured Society: The Politics of London in the First Age of Party, 1688–1715* (Oxford, 1985), pp. 136–9, 149–50.

politically affiliated with the Whigs.[25] Before the war started, Heathcote had already showed concern about the security of Jamaica, which was under the threat of attack from the French and Spaniards because of its strategic importance, and he asked James Vernon, Secretary of State for the South, to send a naval force to protect the island.[26] After war was declared, Heathcote came to demand active maritime war in the West Indies. On 16 January 1703, when the government finally decided to cancel the plan for Peterborough's expedition, Heathcote and Gracedieu urged the Admiralty to make an immediate attempt on Spanish America, submitting a document entitled 'Reasons why the united Forces of England and Holland should sail without delay to the West Indies'. In this document, they claimed that this was the most proper time for England and the Netherlands to send a fleet, as the enemy naval force had not yet recovered from the damage it had suffered at Vigo in October 1702.

The main purpose of the proposed expedition was to take some ports in Spanish America, such as Havana. This would be useful not only for the safety of the English West India colonies but also for the Spanish-American trade, which, they claimed, could bring bullion in return for English products and was the only possible means to compensate merchants for the interruption of trade in Spain, the Mediterranean and other regions. Heathcote and Gracedieu further maintained that such an acquisition of new colonies in America would oblige the Spaniards to come over to the allies' side in the hope of securing the safety of their colonies and trade against 'powerfull and publick Calamitys, by ye Arms of the Allys, and eternall attempts of Privateers Buckaneers and other particular undertakers'.[27]

Thus, at the beginning of 1703, leading Whig West Indian merchants such as Heathcote and Gracedieu tried to promote a more active colonial maritime war, particularly an expedition to Spanish America to secure a trading base there.[28] Considering these facts, it is probable that the West Indies Bill, which focused more on colonial expeditions than on prize business, reflected the interest of these Whig tycoons. However, it should be emphasised that their primary aim was not to make a profit from plundering the Spanish colonies but to regain access to the Spanish-American market. Therefore, when trade resumed, depredation by Jamaican privateers became an obstacle to the Spanish-American trade, and this

25 Sir Gilbert Heathcote (1652–1733), Whig MP for London, was one of the most successful merchants in the City, with a wide range of commercial interests, including the West and East India Trade, the Baltic trade and the Mediterranean trade. He also contributed greatly to the establishment of the Bank of England and the New East India Company. Sir Bartholomew Gracedieu (c. 1657–1715), later Whig MP for St Ives, was a prominent West India merchant, though from about 1708, he got into financial difficulty. Both were the agents for Jamaica between 1693 and 1704.

26 TNA, SP32/12, fols 159–60; Heathcote to Vernon, 10 May 1701.

27 TNA, CO318/3, no. 7, fols 51–2, Heathcote & Gracedieu to [Admiralty], 16 January 1703.

28 Zahedieh points out that Heathcote also profited from war by obtaining supply contracts for English military forces stationed in Jamaica, as in the case of the West Indian expedition of 1695. Zahedieh, *Capital and the Colonies*, p. 135.

led to changes in attitude of those merchants regarding the encouragement of colonial maritime war, as we shall see next.

Trade with the Spanish Colonies

Even after the cancellation of Peterborough's expedition in January 1703 and the dropping of the West Indies bill, the support for colonial maritime war did not die down. The supporters of pro-maritime war policy in the opposition in Parliament continued to emphasise the importance of the West Indies as a theatre of war. However, their tone slightly changed and emphasis was laid more on the protection of the West Indian colonies, which were useful as bases for Spanish-American trade, than on colonial expeditions and the acquisition of new territories.

On 29 March 1704, the Lords committee chaired by the Earl of Rochester, a staunch supporter of maritime war, who joined the opposition after resigning his position as the Lord Lieutenant of Ireland in February 1703, made an address concerning naval affairs, such as irregularities in victualling of the navy and complaints of the misconduct of Vice-Admiral John Graydon. In the address, the Lords committee stressed the economic and strategic importance of Jamaica, especially its role as a centre for trade with the Spanish colonies. Then it proposed the recruitment of a sufficient number of soldiers for regiments in Jamaica and the maintenance of a certain number of warships stationed there to defend the colony and attack the enemy. It also stressed the necessity of due care in pressing seamen for naval ships in order to prevent their desertion from the island in fear of impressments, which would weaken the island.[29]

On the other hand, as we saw in Chapter 4, after the cancellation of Peterborough's expedition, the government put aside the policy of active maritime war against the Spanish colonies and temporarily adopted a more conciliatory approach, with attempts to win over the Spanish colonists to the allies' side. The government's attitude towards Spanish-American trade also changed. After the declaration of war on France and Spain, trade with Spanish America was formally forbidden, though it seems that direct trade with the Spanish colonies through the English West Indian colonies did not stop completely. In early 1703, the government tried to tighten control on trade with the Spanish colonies as well as the French colonies.[30] As the year progressed, however, it gradually shifted its attitude to lifting the ban.

One of the backgrounds of this change was pressure from the West Indian merchants. After the failure to promote colonial expeditions, Heathcote seems to

[29] *L.J.*, XVII, pp. 551–2, 29 March 1704. In the same year, Parliament actually tried to strengthen colonial defence by increasing five-fold the fund provided to the army for the defence of the West Indian colonies. However, this increase was not reflected in the actual employment of troops by the government. Hattendorf, *England in the War of the Spanish Succession*, pp. 172–4.

[30] TNA, CO323/5 no. 10, enclosure i, Nottingham to the Governors of all the Plantations, 25 February 1702/3, and enclosure ii, Nottingham to the Governors of all the Plantations, 20 March 1702/3.

have realised that the chance of gaining a new trading base in Spanish America by force was slim, and became more inclined to the idea of making use of the existing trade channel. In August 1703, probably in a meeting with the members of the Board of Trade, he brought up the issue of Spanish-American trade and asked for the connivance of illicit trade between Jamaica and the Spanish colonies. One of the probable factors that drove Heathcote to make this request was an alarming rise of the Dutch, a trading rival of England, in the Spanish-American trade. While English subjects were prohibited from engaging in trade with the enemy, after the war began, the Netherlands continued to trade with the Spanish colonies through Curaçao, which put England at a huge disadvantage.[31] Heathcote referred to this issue in his request to reopen Spanish-American trade: 'This [Spanish-American trade] is done by ye Hollanders from Curasoa, & we have as good an Appetite for Gold and Silver as they have, & much better conveniencys from Jamaica to Gratify it.'[32]

The Board of Trade also recognised this danger of losing the Spanish-American market to the Dutch and supported the resumption of trade with the Spanish colonies, emphasising the necessity to distinguish between the French and Spaniards in America in terms of trade.[33] On the other hand, the Dutch had a cause for complaint, for their ships trading with the Spanish colonies were suffering from attacks by English privateers. Marinus Dibbout van Vrijbergen, Dutch envoy in London, asked the Queen to forbid such attacks on the Dutch vessels, claiming that the Spanish-American trade was beneficial for both England and the Netherlands in that it could deprive the French of the chance to monopolise trade and bring bullion to both countries.[34]

In answer to these requests, the English government decided to alter its policy towards the Spanish-American trade. In February 1704, the government sent circular letters to colonial governors that allowed the English to trade with the Spanish colonists as the Dutch were doing while forbidding attacks on Dutch ships engaged in trade unless they carried naval stores or munitions of war.[35] Thus, at the request of the West India merchants who were alarmed by competition with the Dutch, the government steered away from the prohibition of Spanish-American trade and towards its promotion.[36]

31 Nettels, 'Spanish-American Trade', 19–20; Cornelis Ch. Goslinga, *The Dutch in the Caribbean and in the Guianas, 1680–1791*, ed. Maria J.L. van Yperen (Assen, Netherlands, Dover, NH, 1985), pp. 190–1.

32 TNA, CO137/45, no. 51, pp. 236–7, Heathcote to [Board of Trade], 28 August 1703.

33 TNA, CO324/8, pp. 264–6, Board of Trade to the Queen, 29 October 1703; pp. 270–1: Board of Trade to Nottingham, 9 November 1703.

34 TNA, CO323/5, no. 41, enclosure i, fols 142–4, 'Memor[ia]ll from M. Van Vryberge, Envoy Extraordinary from the States Gener[a]l to Her Maty, relating to Trade wth ye Spaniards', 13/24 February 1703/4.

35 TNA, CO323/5, no. 40, fols 131–131v, Nottingham to Board of Trade, 24 February 1703/4, and enclosure i, fols 133–133v [A copy of the circular letter to the several governors in America about trade with the Spaniards] [n.d.].

36 George N. Clark has explained that there was a shift in 1705 in English trade policy from prohibition of trade with the enemy to promotion of the Spanish colonial trade. Early on in

There was, however, still a great obstacle to this new policy: attacks on the Spanish vessels and territories by Jamaican privateers. While the Dutch granted immunity to the Spaniards who were willing to trade with them, these English privateers attacked not only French vessels but also those of friendly Spanish colonists, which, Governor Handasyde of Jamaica feared, would 'Ruine our Correspondence with the Spaniards'.[37] Furthermore, their attempts on the Spanish colonies, such as the private expedition in August 1702, were thought to be harmful to trade. In a report to the House of Lords submitted on 21 December 1703, the Board of Trade explained that such an attempt had 'only tended to the Loss of a considerable trade without any real advantage to her Majesty's Subjects', and was 'the present cause of turning that Trade into the hands of our Neighbours'.[38]

To restrain their activities, an additional instruction was issued in May 1704 that forbade the privateers from committing any violent action on land within the Spanish colonies or attacking English or Dutch ships engaged in trade with the Spanish-American colonies unless they were found to be carrying French goods or contraband.[39] However, this was not intended to prohibit raids on enemy commerce completely, and attacks on Spanish ships at sea or in ports by privateers and men of war remained lawful. This was necessary from a strategic viewpoint. As the Board of Trade worried, if the instruction permitted the Spanish ships free passage and forbade English privateers from attacking them, it would 'indeed amount to a Cessation from all Hostilities with the Spaniards in America', and 'they, or the French under their Names may have an opportunity of bringing such Galleons and Treasure unmolested to Europe'.[40] As a result, a compromise was

the war, England tried to prohibit all trade with France, which created an adverse trade balance with England. In 1703, in return for an offer of additional troops, England asked the Dutch to stop nearly all trade and correspondence with the enemy for one year, including bills of exchange – which France could make use of for payment of her armies. This prohibition, however, was not renewed after its expiration, in recognition of its ineffectiveness to exclude French goods from England and because of a diminution of English exports. Therefore, England shifted her focus from the prevention of French trade to the enhancement of Spanish-American trade. After this shift, Clark claims, the Spanish empire became the focus of rivalry between the English and Dutch. George N. Clark, 'War Trade and Trade War, 1701–1713', *EcHR* 1 (1928), 267–73. To be sure, there was a change in policy as to the Spanish-American trade. However, Clark seems to overlook the fact that the rivalry between the English and Dutch and the fear of losing trade to the Dutch was one of the main reasons why the English government permitted the resumption of trade. Moreover, this resumption had already been ordered by February 1704, earlier than Clark thinks.

[37] Nettels, 'Spanish-American Trade', 23; TNA, CO137/51, no. 3, fol. 31, Handasyde to Hedges, 17 December 1704.

[38] PA, HL/PO/JO/10/6/52/1951, Main Papers, 'Report from the Commissioners of Trade and Plantations, of the 16th of December 1703', p. 54.

[39] TNA, CO324/8, pp. 437–9, enclosure iii, 4 May 1704. These restrictions were repeated in the instructions to privateers issued in January 1705. TNA, ADM1/4090, fols 61–8v, 2 February 1704/5.

[40] TNA, CO5/3, no. 13, fols 29–29v, William Popple Jr, secretary to the Board of Trade, to Richard Warre, under-secretary of state, 11 April 1704.

reached, and only private attempts on the Spanish colonies by land were forbidden, which means that England partly gave up the right of conquest on the grounds of the sixth article, though the option of colonial expeditions by the navy was not ruled out.

Nevertheless, this compromise made the control of privateers' activities incomplete, and Jamaican privateers continued to harass Spanish-American trade. In July 1707, the Board of Trade reported privateers' attacks on Spanish ships trading with the English and warned that such practices would be 'tending to the Ruin of Our Present Trade' with the Spanish colonists.[41] Thus, after the resumption of trade with Spanish colonies, there emerged a divergence of interests between those engaged in Spanish-American trade, such as Heathcote and Gracedieu, and those involved in colonial privateering, especially in Jamaica. As we will see next, this clash of interests had an influence on the content of the American Act.

The Process of Enactment

The enthusiasm for colonial maritime war revived in parliamentary debates in late 1707, which eventually led to the enactment of the American Act and the Cruisers and Convoy Act. As mentioned in Chapter 3, 1707 saw a sequence of disheartening losses at sea to the French fleet. These losses triggered severe criticism of the government management of naval affairs in the parliamentary session of 1707–8. On 12 November, 1707, the House of Lords was dominated by a heated debate over naval affairs. Instead of the customary address of thanks for the Queen's speech, several peers levelled a storm of criticism at the government. It was the Earl of Wharton, a Junto lord, who took the lead, pointing out the decay of trade and scarcity of money. He was soon seconded by Somers, another Junto lord, and joined by High Tories such as the Duke of Buckingham, the Earl of Rochester and Baron Guernsey. Accordingly, the house was ordered to be put into a committee of the whole house to consider the state of the navy and trade, chaired by Lord Herbert of Cherbury.[42]

On 19 November, this committee received a petition from several merchants of the City complaining about the losses caused by inadequate convoys and cruisers.[43] After the reading of the petition, Wharton resumed the debate, stressing the miserable condition of Britain and the decay of her trade. He was followed by several peers, including Baron Haversham, who made a long speech concerning the fleet and trade, criticising the ministry severely.

As the debate went on, it became more acrimonious and, according to Cobbett, 'some lords endeavour to allay it, by proposing ways and means to retrieve our losses at sea'. Among them was Halifax's motion to appoint a committee to receive proposals to encourage trade and privateers in the West Indies, which was seconded

[41] TNA, CO138/12, pp. 141–2, Board of Trade to Handasyde, 31 July 1707.

[42] *Cobbett*, VI, col. 597; *L.J.*, XVIII, p. 338, 12 November 1707.

[43] *L.J.*, XVIII, p. 341, 19 November 1707.

by Lord Treasurer Godolphin.[44] Consequently, two committees were appointed: 'the committee to consider the merchants' petition', chaired by the Duke of Bolton, and 'the committee to receive proposals for setting out and encouraging privateers in the West Indies' (hereafter, the privateers committee), chaired by Halifax.[45] It was the latter committee that discussed the American Act.[46]

There are two points to be emphasised here. The first is that the encouragement of privateering in the West Indies was put forward by Halifax, one of the Junto lords, as a means to appease the anger caused by losses at sea. Of course, this does not mean that he tried to mitigate the effect of the attacks on the government launched by his fellow Junto Whigs. A more plausible explanation was that he did a favour to the Marlborough–Godolphin ministry in expectation of their returning it in the form of the coveted Admiralty post for Orford, in which they ultimately succeeded in November 1709. At the same time, Halifax made use of this opportunity, the furore over naval affairs stirred up by his colleagues, to promote the pro-maritime war policy that he endorsed.

The second point to note is that his proposal was also supported by Lord Treasurer Godolphin, who was at the very centre of the government. Godolphin was also appointed as one of the members of the privateers committee. As we shall see later, together with the Junto Whigs, Godolphin and his 'Lord Treasurer's Whigs' played an important role in the enactment of the American Act.

After the privateers committee was appointed, on 21 November, John Dolben, who had connections with Godolphin, was called into the committee with another unnamed person to give an account of colonial privateering. Dolben explained the difficulties faced by those concerned in colonial privateering, and offered to propose a scheme relating to privateers and trade, which was, accordingly, submitted on 25 November.[47]

The direct background of Dolben's proposal was the desertion of seamen from Jamaica, which was allegedly caused by several problems, such as mismanagement of the distribution of prize money and the impressment of inhabitants by the navy. This desertion had a serious effect on Jamaica, which was suffering from a shortage

[44] *Cobbett*, VI, col. 600.

[45] *L.J.*, XVIII, pp. 342–3, 19 November 1707.

[46] As for the process of the enactment of the Cruisers and Convoy Act of 1708, see Johnston, 'Parliament and the Navy', pp. 291–300.

[47] PA, HL/PO/CO/1/7, Minutes of Committees, pp. 245, 248–9, 21, 25, and 26 November 1707. Dolben, MP for Liskeard, seems to have had some links with the West Indies as well as the East Indies. After squandering his fortune gambling, Dolben went to a West Indian colony in 1686 and got married there. In terms of political affiliation, he seems to have had a connection with Godolphin and Halifax. Holmes counts him among the 'Lord Treasurer's Whigs'. See W.P. Courtney, 'Dolben, John (*bap.* 1662, *d.* 1710)', rev. Anne Pimlott Baker, *ODNB*; *House of Commons, 1690–1715*, III, pp. 896–9; Holmes, *British Politics*, p. 258. It is possible that the reason he presented the proposal was his connections with Godolphin and Halifax, two main figures who backed the American Act, as well as his possible links with the West Indian colonies.

of whites in the population, the essential defence force for the island.[48] After emphasising the strategic importance of the island, Dolben argued that due encouragement should be given to bring back the deserters and to invite reinforcement from other parts.[49] For this purpose, he made several proposals, which later became the basis of the American Act.

The first proposal was to abolish the prize office in America. Irregularities in the distribution of prize money by the colonial authority were a great discouragement to colonial privateering, and this was regarded as one of the causes of desertion. One solution to this problem was to remove the interference of middlemen, such as colonial governors and agents of the prize office, in the distribution of prize money, and to leave it entirely in the hands of the privateers themselves. Likewise, giving sole property of prizes to captors was proposed to encourage colonial privateers.

Another significant proposal was to give protection from impressment to registered seamen on board privateers and merchantmen. The harmful effect of impressment on Jamaican privateers had already been recognised both in the colonies and the mother country before the war started, and this was also mentioned as a cause of seamen's desertion from Jamaica in Dolben's proposal.[50] As a solution to this problem, Dolben proposed the complete protection of seamen from impressment.

It should be noted that the two proposals described above had already been attempted in the West Indian colonies. Colonial assemblies in Barbados and Jamaica seem to have passed colonial legislation that included several clauses for that purpose.[51] However, the government in the mother country regarded these laws as a violation of the royal prerogative, and consequently they were

[48] The gap in ratio between the white male population and the black slave population in the West Indian colonies, which occurred as their economy was shifting towards sugar monoculture, was a serious problem for the colonies, which needed a defence force against both the external threat of the French and Spaniards and the internal threat of slave rebellions and maroons (groups of runaway slaves). Richard B. Sheridan, *Sugar and Slavery: An Economic History of the British West Indies, 1623–1775* (Baltimore, 1974), pp. 220–1; 'The Formation of Caribbean Plantation Society, 1689–1748', *The Oxford History of the British Empire, Volume 2: The Eighteenth Century*, ed. Peter J. Marshall (Oxford, 1998), pp. 399–402. Richard Pares states that the distinction between seamen and landmen was probably less noticeable in America than in Europe. Pares, 'The Manning of the Navy in the West Indies', 44–5.

[49] Dolben's proposals are in HL/PO/JO/10/6/128, Main Papers 2402 [Proposal for Encouragement of Privateers in the West Indies], fols 1–1v, 25 November 1707. All quotes from his proposals are taken from here, unless specifically stated otherwise.

[50] TNA, ADM1/4087, pp. 590–1, William Selwyn to [Nottingham?] [n.d., but 1702?]; TNA, SP42/67/35, no. 34 [not foliated], 19 January 1702/3.

[51] National Maritime Museum, SOU/10, p. 209, Charles Thomas to [?], 13 November 1702; TNA, CO31/6, p. 273, 'Minutes of Council in Assembly of Barbados', 8 September 1702; *Journals of Assembly of Jamaica* [microfilm] (St Jago de la Vega, 1811–1829, repr. Wilmington, DE., n.d.), I, pp. 288, 295–7, 304, 306.

repealed.[52] Dolben's proposals were, in a sense, an attempt to revive these clauses in the colonial laws that had been revoked, and to obtain parliamentary sanction for them. When called to the privateers committee for the first time, he stated that those who had been concerned with fitting out privateers 'mett with discouragemts that coud not be remedyed but by authority of Parlt'.[53]

Finally, there was a proposal to encourage private expeditions against the enemy by allowing those who were engaged in such expeditions to keep what they seized. This proposal reopened the way for private expeditions against the Spanish colonies by land, which had once been forbidden by the additional instructions to privateers of 1704 and 1705 to prevent them from offending the Spanish colonists. The fact that this clause was included in Dolben's proposal seems to suggest a revival of interest in active colonial maritime war and territorial conquest in Spanish America on the basis of the sixth article of the Treaty of the Grand Alliance, which was present in the addresses from both Houses in May 1702 and the West Indies Bill of 1703.

One aspect of its background seems to have been concern about the French advance in the South Sea trade, whose first boom started from May 1705 (see Chapter 3). In his proposal, Dolben specifically referred to the South Sea, in which 'the French have this year twenty two Trading Ships and are endeavouring to fix themselves', as a place where private expeditions should be attempted.

Thus, there was continuity between Dolben's proposal and the pro-colonial maritime war policy that appeared at the beginning of the war. Nevertheless, Dolben's proposal focused more on the local interest of the Jamaican colonists, especially those concerned with privateering. Its principal aim was to stop the outflow of the seafaring population from the colony by encouraging privateering and removing problems that caused desertion. These interests of the colonists concerning privateering clashed with the interests of other concerned groups in the American colonies, and this conflict became clear in the committee hearing.

The privateers committee considered each clause in Dolben's proposal and sought the advice of experts regarding issues of naval impressments and Spanish-American trade, who accordingly made several proposals concerning them. All these proposals by Dolben and the others were incorporated in a report by Halifax from the privateers committee on 15 December, with minor alterations. However, the bill was not submitted to the Lords. Instead, the 'Bill for the better Security and Encouragement of the *American* Trade', based on Halifax's report, was presented by Sir Richard Onslow to the Commons on 19 December. The reason is not clear. One possibility is that the Commons was considered more appropriate to deal with the bill as it contained several clauses regarding prizes and customs, which had

52 TNA, CO28/7, no. 1 and 3, 20 and 23 October 1703, fols 500v–501, 504, Attorney General Edward Northey to Board of Trade; CO29/10, pp. 67–8, Board of Trade to the Queen, 7 June 1706; TNA, CO138/11, pp. 59–61, Board of Trade to the Queen, 22 October 1703; TNA, CO138/11, pp. 139–41, Board of Trade to Handasyde, 16 February 1704.

53 PA, HL/PO/CO/1/7, Minutes of Committees, p. 245, 21 November 1707.

a direct bearing on the revenue.[54] The bill was considered in the committee of the whole house chaired by Onslow.[55]

Although James Vernon imagined that the bill might 'miscarry for want of time', after three divisions, it passed in the Commons on 17 March and passed in the Lords with amendments on 24 March. After the conference of the houses upon the Lords' amendments, the bill received the royal assent on 1 April.[56] Thus, the American Act was passed. Behind this process of enactment were cooperation, clashes and compromises between several political and vested interests, which we examine in detail in the next section.

The Politics behind the Act

Party Politics

In analysing the people involved in the passage of the American Act, we need to examine two different aspects: the political affiliation of the MPs and the vested interests involved in the act. As to political affiliation, the Whiggish tendency of the act can be clearly perceived by analysis of the MPs in the Commons who were involved in the 'Bill for the better Security and Encouragement of the *American* Trade', the original title of the American Act. Of the ten MPs who were ordered to bring in the bill, all except Robert Heysham were Whigs, including Sir James Montagu, Sir George Byng, Sir John Jennings and Matthew Aylmer, who were all followers of the Junto, and Sir Gilbert Heathcote, a Whig tycoon with strong commercial interests in the Spanish-American trade.[57] On the other hand, the committee for disagreeing with the Lords' amendments chaired by Onslow on 29 March 1708 was also dominated by the Whigs. All fifteen members of the committee were Whigs including three MPs affiliated with the Junto: Sir James Montagu, Sir Walter Yonge and Richard Hampden.[58]

If we look at the tellers of divisions concerning the bill, here again, we can see

54 I owe this point to Professor Shin Matsuzono.

55 *L.J.*, XVIII, pp. 361–2, 15 December 1707; *C.J.*, XV, pp. 476, 544–5, 584, 19 December 1707, 14 February 1707/8, 2 March 1707/8.

56 *Letters from James Vernon to the Duke of Shrewsbury, 1696–1708, from the Shrewsbury Papers in Boughton House, Northamptonshire*, ed. Dennis Rubini (East Ardsley, 1980) [microfilm], no. 197, fol. 196, Vernon to the Duke of Shrewsbury, 2 March 1707/8; *C.J.*, XV, p. 614, 17 March 1707/8; *L.J.*, XVIII, pp. 545, 550, 562–3, 566, 20, 24 March 1707/8, 31 March 1708, 1 April 1708.

57 *C.J.*, XV, p. 454, 8 December 1707. The ten members were Sir Richard Onslow, Sir James Montagu (Solicitor General), Sir Gilbert Heathcote, John Dolben, Sir George Byng Sir John Jennings, Robert Heysham, William Lowndes, Matthew Aylmer and Henry Boyle (Chancellor of the Exchequer).

58 *C.J.*, XV, p. 640, 29 March 1708. The fifteen members were Sir Richard Onslow, Henry Boyle (Secretary of State for the North), Craven Peyton, Thomas Coningsby, Sir James Montagu, Mr Neville (Richard or Grey Neville), Spencer Cowper, Sir John Swinton, Lord William Powlett, James Vernon, Sir Walter Yonge, Thomas Bere, John Dolben, Richard Hampden and John Cockburn.

clear evidence of Whig support for the bill and Tory objection to it. In the division on 14 February 1708 on whether the Speaker should leave the chair, this tendency was not yet evident. While the tellers for the yeas, John Dolben and 'Mr Neville', were both Whigs, one of the tellers for the noes, Thomas Bere, was also a Whig.[59] However, in the division on 17 March on whether the bill should be read a third time, the Whigs' support became clearer. While the tellers for the yeas, Lord William Powlett and Roger Gale, were Whigs, the tellers for the noes, John Ward and Charles Fox, were both Tories.[60]

In the next division upon an additional clause that ordered the owners of privateers to make compensation if British subjects suffered from their attacks, a clause aimed at restraining privateers' activities, the tellers for the yeas were Sir Robert Davers, a High Church Tory, and John Manley, a Tory affiliated with Robert Harley. On the other hand, those for the noes were Bennett William, one of the 'Squadrone', a group of Scottish MPs allied with the Junto, and Onslow, a staunch Country Whig. In the last crucial division on the passage of the bill, the tellers for the yeas were Spencer Compton, one of the Lord Treasurer's Whigs, and 'Mr Wortley', also a Whig.[61] On the other hand, the tellers for the noes, 'Mr Pitts' and 'Mr Jeffreys', were both Tories.[62] Judging from this, it is obvious that the American Act was predominantly promoted by the Whigs.

Among the Whigs, the central figures who promoted the act were the Junto Whigs, as Denman has pointed out. Their involvement can be seen from the very beginning of the process of enactment. It was Halifax, one of the core members of the Junto, who moved for the appointment of the privateers committee, and the

[59] *C.J.*, XV, pp. 544–5, 14 February 1708. 'Mr Neville' could be either Richard Neville (1655–1717), MP for Berkshire, or his son, Grey Neville (1681–1723), MP for Abington. Both were politicians with a Country Whig proclivity.

[60] *C.J.*, XV, pp. 544–5, 614, 14 February 1707/8, 17 March 1707/8. There were two 'John Wards' who were both MPs at this time. It is likely that this teller was John Ward (1650–1726), MP for Bletchingley. He was one of the leading City merchants, with strong commercial interest in the Mediterranean cloth trade and the East India trade, and was temporarily allied with the Tories at this time. It was he who offered a clause for 'head money', a system adopted by the Dutch to encourage their privateers, as well as gun money. James (ed.), *Letters Illustrative of the Reign of William III*, III, p. 326, James Vernon to the Duke of Shrewsbury, 27 January 1707/8. The other John Ward (1670–1749), MP for Newton and one of the leading politicians in the north-west, was also a Tory.

[61] 'Mr Wortley' could be the Honourable Sidney Wortley Montagu (1650–1727), Whig MP for Peterborough, or his son, Edward Wortley Montagu, one of the leading Country Whigs and MP for Huntingdon.

[62] It is difficult to discern which of the Pitt family this teller was. There were at least three Pitts in the Commons at this time, Thomas ('Diamond Pitt'), George and Robert. All of them were Tories. 'Mr Jeffreys' was identified as John Jeffreys (c. 1659–1715) in *House of Commons, 1690–1715*. However, it is also possible that this was his brother Jeffrey Jeffreys (c. 1652–1709), who was MP for Brecon and had commercial interests in a wide area, including the Leeward Islands, for which he was an agent, Virginia, Spain and the African slave trade.

chairmen of the two committees appointed as a result of the debate were Halifax and Bolton, a follower of the Junto.

Halifax's strong involvement was also evidenced by a remark of Joseph Addison, protégé of Halifax and Somers and Under-Secretary of State in the Southern Department. In a letter to the Earl of Manchester, Addison mentioned that Halifax was looked upon as 'the chief promoter' of the American Bill, now discussed in the Commons. Addison wrote, 'His Lordship and his friends form'd it with the advice and assistance of most of the Admirals and chief Citizens of London.'[63] It is quite likely that the 'Admirals' referred to those flag officers affiliated with the Junto such as Byng, Jennings and Aylmer.[64] It is also probable that Heathcote, one of the City's magnates who had a strong commercial interest in Jamaica, was included among the 'chief Citizens of London'.

However, it should be noted that other Whigs were also involved in the passage of the act. Among them were the Country Whigs. It was Sir Richard Onslow, a leading Country Whig with a connection with the City and knowledge of naval affairs, who submitted the bill to the Commons and chaired the committee of the whole house to consider it. It can be conjectured that the American Act, aimed at encouraging colonial maritime war, was also welcomed by these Country politicians, who believed that maritime war was more effective and suitable for England than an expensive and lengthy land war on the continent conducted by a corrupt ministry that would lead to the further growth of national debt and taxes.

More importantly, Godolphin and his Whig supporters, the 'Lord Treasurer's Whigs', were also deeply involved in the passage of the American Act. The latter group included politicians such as Chancellor of the Exchequer Henry Boyle, Thomas Lord Coningsby, John Smith and Spencer Compton.[65] In addition, several politicians or administrators who had a close connection with Godolphin, such as John Dolben and William Lowndes, Secretary of the Treasury, were also involved.

Godolphin and his supporters played an active role in the enactment of the American Act. As we have seen, Godolphin seconded Halifax's motion to appoint the privateers committee and became one of its members. Moreover, Compton, one of the 'Lord Treasurer's Whigs', was a teller for the yeas in the division over the passage of the act, and it was Dolben, who was close to Godolphin, who

63 Walter Graham, ed., *The Letters of Joseph Addison* (Oxford, 1941), no. 104, p. 93, Addison to Charles Montagu, the Earl of Manchester, 20 February 1707/8.

64 Byng and Jennings were also involved in an abortive attempt of 'bill for the Encouragement and Increase of Seamen, and better manning Her Majesty's Fleet', which was presented by Viscount Townshend, another follower of the Junto, on 15 January 1708 in the same session as the American Act. Johnston also regards this bill as a part of the Whig attack on the government. Johnston, 'Parliament and the Navy', pp. 406–12.

65 Henry Boyle (1669–1725, created Baron Carleton in 1714) was the Chancellor of the Exchequer, and from February 1708, the Secretary of State for the North. He was one of the leaders of the 'Lord Treasurer's Whigs' and played an important role as a ministerial manager and spokesman. Thomas Lord Coningsby (1657–1729) was a typical Court Whig, and long-term friends with Godolphin and Marlborough. Henry Boyle was his cousin.

submitted the proposals that became the basis of the American Act.

What, then, was the reason for their support? One possible explanation is that Godolphin thought that the encouragement of privateering could help to alleviate merchants' anger towards the government over naval affairs. However, Godolphin himself was a keen supporter of colonial maritime war and often endorsed or proposed colonial expeditions until the summer of 1710, when he was ousted from power. In particular, as we saw in the previous chapter, in August 1709, he supported a plan for an expedition against Spanish America with some of the Junto Whigs such as Halifax and Somers. In addition, there was one advantage for him in the encouragement of colonial privateering under the American Act, namely that a privateering war in America was not likely to divert land forces from the continent, unlike the large-scale amphibious expeditions to the Americas to which his political partner, Marlborough, who was commanding the army in Flanders and Germany, was strongly opposed. Thus, though the American Act was originally promoted by the Junto Whigs, it also had support from other political groups, such as Country Whigs and, more importantly, Godolphin and his 'Lord Treasurer's Whigs'.

Vested Interests

Next, we examine the vested interests involved in the American Act, the relations between them, and how they influenced the content of the act. As for the issue of naval impressment, one of the main problems that the act addressed, three different groups were involved: privateer owners, the navy, and merchants trading with the West India colonies. Whereas Dolben, who represented the privateering interests, proposed complete protection from impressment, the navy and the West Indian merchants were concerned that the protection might encourage further desertion of seamen from their vessels to privateers.

The rivalry between privateers, the navy and merchants over manpower in the American colonies was present from the early stage of the war. In December 1702, Rear-Admiral Whetstone reported that the government in Jamaica was unable to supply men to warships because of colonial privateering, 'which has not yet been so successful, but carryes of the men'.[66] The encouragement of privateers could have exacerbated this problem of the desertion of seamen from naval ships to privateers. Therefore, in the hearing of the committee, it was proposed that, 'the Islands have an inviolable Protection for their Seamen, so as a sufficient provision be made to prevent desertion from her Mastyes Ships'.[67]

Furthermore, on 28 November, the experts who attended the committee expressed their opinions.[68] One Captain Jones, probably a captain of a West India packet boat, insisted that the protection for privateers ought to be general. Otherwise, 'the Privateers will give no credit to it'. Rear-Admiral Sir John Jennings, a

[66] TNA, CO137/45, no. 34, fol. 161, Rear Admiral Whetstone to the Principal Secretaries of State, 28 December 1702.

[67] PA, HL/PO/CO/1/7, Minutes of Committees, p. 249, 26 November 1707.

[68] PA, HL/PO/CO/1/7, Minutes of Committees, p. 250, 28 November 1707.

naval officer and MP affiliated with the Junto, also admitted the necessity of the encouragement to bring back seamen who had fled from the British West Indian colonies.[69] However, as a naval officer, he also had to consider the manning problem of the navy, and suggested that packet boats and merchantmen sailing to the West Indies should carry supernumerary men for the navy. It was also proposed that privateers who would take in any deserters from naval ships should be penalised. On the other hand, in two papers submitted to the committee on 4 December, several merchants proposed measures to prevent the desertion of seamen to privateers, such as the submission of a crew list and a penalty for harbouring deserters from merchant ships, while they also demanded exemption of their seamen from impressment.[70]

These proposals were incorporated into the final form of the American Act. As a consequence, whereas the act protected registered seamen on board privateers and merchantmen from naval impressments, it also included several clauses to prevent the desertion of seamen from men of war to privateers and merchantmen.

On the other hand, the aforementioned conflict between West Indian merchants and colonial privateers regarding Spanish-American trade also had an impact on the content of the American Act. A dispute over Spanish-American trade had already existed in the West Indian colonies in an earlier period. As Zahedieh explains, in the 1680s, there was a confrontation in Jamaica between a small number of Whig asiento traders who monopolised the lucrative trade with the Spanish-American colonies, especially the slave trade, and its opponents, such as small planters, merchants and sloop masters, who suffered from a shortage and rising price of slaves resulting from the trade. Encouraged by the attempts of Charles II and James II to tighten their grip on the colonies, and in cooperation with new colonial governors appointed by those kings, the latter group took several measures to suppress the trade conducted by the Whig asiento traders. The promotion of privateering and the seizure of Spanish goods were among these measures. The ambition of the Stuart kings was thwarted by the Glorious Revolution, and the Whig traders recovered their dominance over local government and Spanish-American trade. Heathcote was one of their associates in London.[71]

69 Jennings was also MP for Queenborough. He was sent to the Mediterranean with Sir George Byng in 1706, and served under him in the intended French invasion in March 1708. He was a staunch supporter of the Junto Whigs, together with Byng, and refused an offer of a place on the Prince's council in April 1708, which outraged Queen Anne.

70 PA, HL/PO/CO/1/7, Minutes of Committees, p. 253, 4 December 1707; HL/PO/JO/10/6/129, Main Papers, 'Merchants Papers Relating to Privateers in the West Indies', fol. 112, and 'Merchants Papers Relating to trade in the West Indies', fol. 113, 4 December 1707.

71 Zahedieh, 'Regulation, Rent-seeking, and the Glorious Revolution', 877–86. Heathcote was also one of the major separate traders in the English slave trade in the 1690s. William A. Pettigrew, 'Free to Enslave: Politics and the Escalation of Britain's Transatlantic Slave Trade, 1688–1714', *WMQ*, 3rd ser, 64, no. 1 (2007), 18. Moreover, his three brothers in Jamaica were members of a small group that controlled the Asiento trade. Zahedieh, *Capital and the Colonies*, p. 132.

The clash over the reopened Spanish-American trade during the War of the Spanish Succession was, in a sense, a continuation of the disputes of the 1680s in a different political situation. As in the 1680s, those involved in colonial privateering during this period seem to have included some of the local Jamaican merchants who could not participate in Spanish-American trade and small planters. In July 1707, in the case of an attack launched by some Jamaican privateers on Spanish canoes trading with the English, the Board of Trade received information that 'Several of the Principal Traders of Jamaica' were concerned as owners of the privateers.[72] It can be conjectured that, for these local merchants who were faced with the economic predicament caused by the war, such as the destruction of property and the rise in freight rates, and who were excluded from the lucrative Spanish-American trade, privateering was one of the few options available to utilise their financial resources.[73]

On the other hand, those who were engaged in the reopened Spanish-American trade and who suffered from attacks by Jamaican privateers seem to have consisted mainly of the Whig West India merchants in the mother country and some Jamaican merchants cooperating with them. In a letter to Handasyde concerning complaints about the privateers' attacks on Spanish vessels, the Board of Trade mentioned that they 'received the like Complaint from some Eminent Merchants here, who were concerned in that Trade'.[74] Similarly, it was 'several Merchants, trading to, and of, the Island of *Jamaica*' who submitted a petition in February 1708 for further protection of the Jamaican trade with the Spanish colonies that suffered from the misconduct of Commodore Kerr.[75]

In addition, English woollen traders, for whom Spain and her American colonies had been one of the important markets until the war began, seem to have been on the side of these West Indian merchants, and they also showed an interest in the American Act. On 19 February 1708, 'the principal Traders and Dealers in the Woollen Manufactures in the Borough of *Sudbury*' in Suffolk, whose chief market had been Spain and Portugal, submitted a petition to the Commons.[76] In the petition, they explained the economic difficulties caused by the loss of the Spanish trade and the resultant scarcity of coins. Then they stressed the necessity to expand Spanish trade as a solution to these problems and asked for encouragement in the American Act to increase exports of woollen products to a region within the limits of the East India Company's charter, where the company did not actually conduct trade at that time.[77] The interests of these woollen traders also

[72] TNA, CO138/12, p. 142, Board of Trade to Handasyde, 31 July 1707.

[73] As for the economic difficulties that small planters and traders in the colonies experienced in war time after the Glorious Revolution, see Zahedieh, 'Regulation', 884.

[74] TNA, CO138/12, p. 321, Board of Trade to Handasyde, 23 August 1708.

[75] *C.J.*, XV, p. 527, 4 February 1707/8.

[76] *House of Commons, 1690–1715*, II, p. 568. The MPs for Sudbury at that time were Sir Hervey Elwes (1683–1763) and Philip Skippon (1675–1716). Both were Whigs.

[77] The region that the petitioners had in mind was probably the west coast of South America, where French traders were making a rapid advance. *C.J.*, XV, p. 554, 19 February 1707/8. However, a petition like this seems to have caused concern for the East India

clashed with the activities of the Jamaican privateers. In 1709, Jamaican trader William Bignall reported that one Gandy and several others bought slaves 'for the Trade to help of the Woollens which are now run downe in price so much by the Privateering that we expect no Profit'.[78]

Thus, the opponents of colonial privateering comprised the British West India merchants, some merchants in Jamaica who had connections with them, and other groups who had interests in the Spanish-American trade, such as the woollen traders. For them, it was necessary to mitigate the harmful effects of colonial privateering on Spanish-American trade to protect their commercial interests and, for that purpose, some merchants attended the hearing of the privateers committee and made several proposals.

In the hearing, it was proposed that the coast of New Spain (modern Mexico) should be exempted from their attacks because, 'If our Privateers should land in New Spain, they [the Spaniards] woud not trade with us at all.' Likewise, in the papers presented to the committee on 4 December, several merchants proposed that the Spaniards trading with the English should be exempted from attacks by privateers and men of war within an area on the coast of Spanish America extending from the river de la Hacha (Rio de la Hacha) to the river Chagres, though attacks on all Spanish ships sailing to and from Europe were still to be permitted. However, it should also be noted that these merchants were not opposed to the exertion of force to expel the French traders, whose advance in the Spanish-American market was a serious threat to them. In fact, the merchants requested escorts of two or three warships to protect their trade with the Spanish colonies and to deter the French from trade.[79]

These merchants' proposal to set a limit on the activities of the privateers was adopted, and a clause to forbid attacks on the Spaniards and British trading with each other was added to the act. Thus, the clash of interests between several groups involved in colonial maritime war and the Spanish-American trade resulted in the addition of several clauses to restrict the colonial privateering and colonial conquest that Dolben's proposal, the basis of the American Act, was intended to encourage.

The American Act was a culmination of legislative attempts to promote colonial maritime war, as well as attempts to improve the protection of trade during the War of the Spanish Succession. The demand for the encouragement of privateering

Company regarding the American Act. On 20 and 22 March 1708, the East India Company as well as the Hudson's Bay Company petitioned the Lords to protect their privileges from possible violations caused by some clauses in the American Act, though the Commons did not recognise the necessity to add a new clause proposed by the Lords to protect the privilege of the East India Company. PA, HL/PO/JO/10/6/149/2482, Main Papers [Trade to America Encouragement Act] [not foliated], 20 March 1707/8; *L.J.*, XVIII, pp. 545, 547, 20, 22 March 1707/8; *C.J.*, XV, p. 630, 24 March 1707/8; p. 640, 29 March 1708.

78 TNA, CO137/8, no. 35, enclosure i, fol. 136, William Bignall to [Edmund Dummer?], 17 January 1708/9.

79 PA, HL/PO/CO/1/7, p. 250, Minutes of Committees, 28 November 1707; p. 253, 4 December 1707; HL/PO/JO/10/6/129, fols 112–13.

and colonial conquest on the basis of the sixth article of the treaty of the Grand Alliance was already present in the address of both Houses in May 1702 and the abortive West Indies Bill of 1703. In 1707, against the backdrop of the grim prospects of war, heavy losses at sea and the French advance in the Spanish-American market, this demand reappeared in Dolben's proposal in the process of the enactment of the American Act.

In terms of political interests, the act was promoted mainly by the Junto Whigs, as Denman has pointed out. However, other political groups supported the act, as well. In particular, Godolphin, a proponent of colonial maritime war, also gave his support to this act with his 'Lord Treasurer's Whigs'. This demonstrates that the policy of promoting colonial maritime war had a wider range of support than usually thought.

The West Indian merchants in London such as Heathcote also supported colonial expeditions in the early stage of the war. However, their aim was different from those of the supporters of pro-maritime war argument among the politicians. For those merchants, colonial expeditions were just one of the means to recover the Spanish-American market, and they did not persist in it as long as they could secure access to the market by other means. Especially after 1704, when they regained access to the Spanish-American market, their interests were at odds with those of the Jamaican privateers whose occasional attacks on Spanish vessels were a major hindrance to trade.

The clash of interests between Jamaican privateers and the West Indian merchants, as well as that between privateers and the navy, had a great impact on the content of the act. As a consequence, while the act contained several clauses to encourage colonial privateering and private expeditions against enemy territories, it also came to include several clauses setting limits on privateers' activities, which took the edge off Dolben's original proposal to promote colonial maritime war. Thus, we cannot regard the American Act only as either the achievement of the mercantile community, which wanted better trade protection, or as a triumph of privateering interests, who demanded encouragement for their activities. Rather, the act was a qualified attempt to promote colonial maritime war, which resulted from the conflicting interests between several groups concerned with naval impressments and Spanish-American trade.

The idea of encouraging colonial privateering and colonial conquest was held by the Whigs as well as the Tories, and its proponents were not confined to the opposition politicians; leading politicians in the government, such as Godolphin, favoured the policy, as well. However, this somewhat optimistic policy of active colonial maritime war endorsed by these politicians in the mother country faced a strong headwind in the complex realities of the colonies. The pro-maritime war policy was affected not only by party politics but also by the conflict between vested interests when it was translated into reality.

1. *The Battle of Vigo Bay, 12 October 1702*, circa 1702

2. Medal commemorating the Expedition to Vigo Bay, 1702

The legend on its obverse reads: 'SPES ET VIRES HOSTIUM FRACTAE.' (The hope and forces of the enemy broken.) The exergue reads: 'INCENSA GALLOR CLASSE. HISPAN. OPES AMERIC. INTERCEPT.' (The French fleet being burnt, the American treasure of Spain intercepted.)

3. Stern of a Spanish galleon filled with prizes, early eighteenth century

This is part of the painting of the lower hall of the Painted Hall at the Old Royal Naval College, Greenwich, which was originally built as the Royal Hospital for Seamen. James Thornhill, who won a commission to decorate the interior of the hall, embarked on the work in 1708. Given that this was a year when Commodore Wager successfully intercepted a Spanish Tierra Firme galleon in the West Indies, it is possible that this capture by Wager, as well as that by Rooke at Vigo in 1702, inspired Thornhill to include the motif of the Spanish galleons in the paintings. I am grateful to the Old Royal Naval College for allowing me to reproduce this image. I am also grateful to Professor Barnaby Ralph for letting me see a transcription from a facsimile of the original edition of James Thornhill, *An Explanation of the Painting in the Royal-Hospital at Greenwich* (London, 1726)

4. A Map of the Americas from Herman Moll, *A New & Exact Map of the Coast, Countries and Islands within ye Limits of ye South Sea Company …* (London, 1711, repr. 1720?)

5. Admiral Hosier's Ghost, C. Mosley, July 1740

In the period of the War of Jenkins' Ear, opposition writers picked up the episode of the failure of Admiral Hosier's blockade of Porto Bello and Cartagena in 1727 in order to attack the government. In 1739, Richard Glover (1712–85), a writer and politician allied with the 'Patriot' Whigs and the Prince of Wales, composed a rhyme entitled 'Admiral Hosier's Ghost', which criticised the Walpole ministry's alleged inaction against the Spaniards, invoking the memory of the tragic death of Hosier and his men during the blockade. National Maritime Museum, Greenwich, London

– 6 –

The South Sea Company and its Plan for a Naval Expedition in 1712

As we saw in Chapter 4, expeditions to Spanish America did not materialise during the War of the Spanish Succession, and the only large-scale colonial expedition that was actually undertaken was destined for Quebec. At that time, however, there was another attempt to gain access to the wealth of Spanish America: the plan for establishing the South Sea Company, proposed by Robert Harley.[1]

It is well known that the South Sea Company, which later triggered a famous financial crisis in 1720, was originally established to resolve the government's floating debts contracted during the War of the Spanish Succession. It is also known that the company was awarded the Asiento, that is, the exclusive right to trade slaves to the Spanish-American colonies, and was also granted the right to send annual ships with cargoes in return for undertaking the government's debts. However, it is far less known that the company was planning to send a naval expedition to the Pacific in 1712.

Economic or financial historians who look at the history of the South Sea Company tend to discard this expedition as a mere bluff contrived by Harley to assist his peace negotiations with France. John G. Sperling views the proposed expedition as a 'farce' and offers the ministry's need to cover up the peace negotiations as the only plausible explanation.[2] Likewise, P.G.M. Dickson, following Sperling's interpretation, sees this expedition as 'no more than a flight of fancy'.[3] On the other hand, Glyndwr Williams, who studies the history of English exploration into the Pacific, does not necessarily deny the fact that the company was preparing the expedition in 1712. However, he calls it 'one of the most baffling aspects of the convoluted early years of the Company's existence' and does not give a plausible explanation for why the expedition was planned.[4]

1 Robert Harley was ennobled as the first Earl of Oxford and Mortimer in May 1711. However, for the sake of convenience, in this chapter, he will be referred to as 'Harley' also for the period after receiving his peerage.

2 John G. Sperling, *The South Sea Company: An Historical Essay and Bibliographical Finding List* (Boston, MA, 1962), pp. 16, 18.

3 Dickson, *Financial Revolution in England*, p. 66.

4 Glyndwr Williams, *The Great South Sea: English Voyages and Encounters, 1570–1750* (New Haven, CT, and London, 1997), pp. 173–4. Williams guesses that this expedition was intended to remind France and Spain of the likely consequences of a breakdown of peace negotiations, which had begun at Utrecht in January 1712.

One of the few historians who recognised the company's military purpose was William T. Morgan. He claimed that the South Sea Company was more than 'a political gesture' and 'a pawn in peace negotiations', and regarded it as a 'war measure which, should peace fail, might make the war pay for itself from the profits of the Caribbean trade'.[5] His argument has been severely criticised by Sperling as being based on insufficient evidence and stretching the facts too far.[6] However, Morgan's speculation is still worthy of note, because he placed the South Sea Company's project in the context of England's attempt to gain the wealth of Spanish America, an endeavour that can be traced back to voyages by Elizabethan seamen, such as John Hawkins and Francis Drake. Morgan also placed the company in the context of rivalry over the Spanish-American trade with France.[7] Nevertheless, he did not examine the plan for the South Sea expedition of 1712. Thus, historians have generally neglected the proposed 1712 expedition, and even those who rightly recognise that the company was actually considering the military expedition, such as Williams and Morgan, have not given convincing interpretation of its intention.

These divergent interpretations of the South Sea expedition of 1712 are partly caused by historians' tendency to focus on the financial aspect of the company's business that resulted in the famous financial crisis in 1720 while undervaluing its trading role. For example, John Carswell, who studied the South Sea Bubble in 1720, refers to the company's 'indifference to the proven unprofitability of the South American trade', and claims that the company was a finance corporation from the outset.[8] This view is also seen in more recent literature on the South Sea Bubble that debates whether the investors were driven by speculative mania, or whether at least some of them behaved rationally.[9] For example, Julian Hoppit, who takes the latter view, dismisses the role of the company's trade as of minor importance.[10]

Conversely, Helen Paul presents the prospects of the company's slave trade as an example of evidence that investors' behaviour during the South Sea Bubble was in fact rational.[11] Although this chapter is not concerned with the debate over the

[5] Morgan, 'South Sea Company and the Canadian Expedition', 157–8. He employed a similar argument in 'The Origins of the South Sea Company', *Political Science Quarterly* 44, no. 1 (1929), 16–38.

[6] Sperling, *South Sea Company*, pp. 9–10, note 9.

[7] Morgan, 'Origins of the South Sea Company', 16–20. However, he failed to recognise the important distinction between South Sea trade and trade in the Caribbean.

[8] John P. Carswell, *The South Sea Bubble* (London, 1960, repr. Stroud, Gloucestershire, 1993), p. 74.

[9] For this debate, see Helen J. Paul, *The South Sea Bubble: An Economic History of its Origins and Consequences* (Abington and New York, 2011), pp. 4–6, 86–7.

[10] Julian Hoppit, 'The Myths of the South Sea Bubble', *Transactions of the Royal Historical Society*, 6th ser, 12 (2002), 142.

[11] Paul, *South Sea Bubble*, pp. 56–65. She has mentioned the expectation that the South Sea Company would acquire a new colony in Spanish America with the assistance of the navy as one of the inducements to invest in the company during the Bubble. Nevertheless, it is

causes of the Bubble, and the situation between 1711 and 1712 with which this chapter deals was not the same as that in 1720, Paul's work is significant in that it calls attention to the importance of the company's trade and its impact on the company's share price. However, like those historians who study the company's trading activities, Paul focuses chiefly on the Asiento trade that the company actually carried out, and does not examine its earliest trade plans.[12]

This tendency to focus on a financial aspect of the South Sea Company's business or on its later trade activities has made it difficult to comprehend the original aim of the company's trading business and, consequently, the purpose of the South Sea expedition of 1712. However, in order better to understand why it had to plan the South Sea expedition, it is important to see the company's trade in its contemporary context. For this purpose, it is necessary to consider three factors that influenced the company's trading policy in its infancy: its initial focus on the Pacific, rather than the Caribbean, as its trading area; debate over the feasibility of the company's trade; and uncertainty as to what kind of trading privileges the company could obtain from the peace negotiations.

This chapter will investigate these three factors, and particularly the second, by examining contemporary pamphlets and periodicals that discussed the prospects of the company's trading activities, written both by opposition Whig pamphleteers such as Arthur Maynwaring and government pamphleteers such as Daniel Defoe. These pamphlets were, to a certain extent, part of the propaganda campaign to criticise or defend Harley's ministry, which came to power in August 1710. However, the impact of the debate in these pamphlets was not confined to the political arena, but had economic implications as well.

In the late seventeenth century, there was an intense debate about whether the emerging financial market was useful for the English economy, and both stock-jobbers and joint-stock companies such as the East India Company were criticised as detrimental to the process of funding trade and industry. As Anne Murphy has shown, this debate was an important source of information for potential investors and affected their decision-making.[13]

It is likely that the debate over the prospects of the South Sea Company had a similar impact on investors, for whom it was an important source of information. As we shall see, in the contemporary discussions about the company in its early years, the prospects of the South Sea trade were closely connected with those of the company as a whole, with obvious potential to affect investors' decisions and the company's share price. In addition, this debate could influence the company's directors. They were not able to ignore criticisms of the company's trade prospects

important to note that, after the South Sea expedition of 1712 failed, until the late 1730s, the British government did not seriously plan a colonial expedition for conquest in Spanish America out of consideration for the security of the company's trade and properties in Spanish America, as Chapter 8 will show.

12 For the company's trading business, for example, see Elizabeth Donnan, 'The Early Days of the South Sea Company, 1711–1718', *JEBH* 2 (1930), 419–50.

13 Anne L. Murphy, *The Origins of English Financial Markets: Investment and Speculation before the South Sea Bubble* (Cambridge, 2009), Chapter 3.

because they had to maintain credibility of its business in order to attract investors. Moreover, government pamphleteers like Defoe presented a blueprint for the company's trade to counter the criticisms against it; this blueprint provided theoretical options that the directors could adopt for the South Sea trade.

In its final section, this chapter will also discuss why the expedition failed to materialise, in spite of the intention of the directors – albeit not Harley – to carry it out. Examination of the company's official documents (such as court minutes) in a new light will offer a more plausible account of why the scheme for the expedition was ultimately abandoned. Thus, by placing this seemingly farcical plan for the South Sea expedition in its contemporary context, this chapter reveals the logic behind it and the reason why it was not put into action.

The French Success in the South Sea Trade and the Establishment of the South Sea Company

One point about the South Sea Company that historians have taken for granted, and consequently have overlooked, is the meaning of its name. In the geographical terminology of early eighteenth-century England, the words 'South Sea[s]' usually meant the Pacific Ocean, as opposed to the 'North Sea' (i.e. the Caribbean).[14] There was a reason why 'South Sea' was chosen as the company's name rather than, for example, 'West India'. The company was originally designed chiefly to trade with the Spanish colonies on the Pacific Ocean, not in the Caribbean. However, this fact is often overlooked, because the company was later involved with the slave and annual ships trades, which were chiefly conducted with the Spanish colonies in the Caribbean.

During the War of the Spanish Succession, the South Sea trade came to assume special significance for England. As we saw in Chapter 2, at the turn of the eighteenth century, France began participating in direct trade with the Spanish-American colonies.[15] They made rapid advances in trade with the Spanish colonies, not only on the coast of the 'North Sea' (i.e. the Atlantic) but also on the coast of the

[14] In the contemporary English-language sources, the words were often used in the plural, that is, 'South Seas'.

[15] Attempts by the English to intrude into this region began earlier than those by the French. After the voyages by Elizabethan seamen, such as Drake and Cavendish, in the late sixteenth century, English interests in the South Sea revived in the latter half of the seventeenth century. John Narborough's voyage to the South Sea of 1669–71 was followed by a series of attempts by buccaneers, such as Bartholomew Sharp, William Dampier and Lionel Wafer, in the 1670s and 1680s. In 1689, John Strong launched a trading and privateering voyage to that region, though this was commercially unsuccessful. For these voyages, see Peter T. Bradley, *The Lure of Peru: Maritime Intrusion into the South Sea, 1598–1701* (Basingstoke and London, 1989); Williams, *The Great South Sea*; and Florence E. Dyer, 'Captain John Strong, Privateer and Treasure Hunter', *MM* 13, no. 2 (1927), 145–58. After the War of the Spanish Succession began, the attempts resumed, and as mentioned in Chapter 4, during the war, Dampier and Woodes Rogers made privateering voyages into the South Sea.

'South Sea'. These French advances in South Sea trade were regarded as a primary factor that hampered Spanish-American trade via the West Indian colonies, which was resumed in 1704. In July 1708, in a letter to the Board of Trade, Governor Handasyde of Jamaica remarked: 'If there can be a method found out to prevent the French Trading to Lima, and the South Seas, Trade here will soon be in a Flourishing Condition.'[16] In the later stages of the war, the French trade in the South Sea was still thriving, and it was reported in 1711 that 'Some merchants of St Malo have very considerable Adventures in this Trade and preferr it before all the advantages allow'd by the King for Privateering.'[17]

It was also believed that this trade was a great support to the French war effort. In a pamphlet published in 1712, Robert Allen, a Scottish merchant who had lived in Spanish America for about six years, claimed that the French had continued to send ships with merchandise to the South Sea after 1700, and, as a result, 'the immense Treasures they have brought from thence has [*sic*] not a little contributed to the support of the present War against us'.[18]

A French presence in the Spanish-American trade was also a serious concern for the Harley ministry, which came to power in August 1710. Their anxiety about the South Sea trade can clearly be seen in the secret instructions to Sir James Wishart, who was sent to The Hague in January 1711 to discuss naval affairs with the Dutch. Wishart was ordered to mention the prodigious profits that the French obtained from the South Sea trade, and to ask the Dutch to join an expedition to destroy the French trade in the South Sea. He was also ordered to gather information about how the French carried on their trading activity, which might be useful for the expedition or for any other future undertaking in that region.[19] Thus, at that time, there was serious concern about French success in the South Sea trade.

In the plan for the South Sea Company, this concern for the French South Sea trade was combined with the problem of the government debt, which was growing rapidly because of the cost of military engagement with France.

The original plan to establish a new joint-stock company was proposed to Robert Harley in October 1710 by three men who had a strong connection with the Sword Blade Company: John Blunt, a London merchant; George Caswell, a

16 TNA, CO 137/8, no. 23 fol. 76, Handasyde to Board of Trade, 20 July 1708.

17 BL, Add MS 70163, fol. 175, Edmund Dummer to [Robert Harley?], 20 June 1711. Despite several bans imposed by the French government on the South Sea trade, the trade prospered until 1716, when it received a serious blow from a Spanish punitive expedition under J.N. Martinez. However, even after this disaster, the trade still continued, and it was not until the renewal of the ban of 1716 in 1724 that the French merchants abandoned the direct trade and returned to trading via Cadiz. Dunmore, *French Explorers*, pp. 22–3; Malamud Rikles, *Cádiz y Saint Malo*, p. 78.

18 Robert Allen, *An Essay on the Nature and Methods of Carrying on a Trade to the South-Sea* (London, 1712), p. 24.

19 *Bolingbroke Correspondence*, I, pp. 36–7, 'The Secret Instructions for Sir James Wishart', 14 January 1710/11.

stock-jobber; and Ambrose Crowley, an iron master and Navy contractor. This joint-stock company was designed to solve the problem of the floating debts contracted by several departments within the government, such as the Navy Board and the Victualling Board, by converting them into the company's stock. This was a standard means for dealing with government debt at that time, and had already been practised by the Bank of England and the New East India Company.[20]

The novelty of Harley's idea was that he combined this notion of converting government debts with a plan for the South Sea trade.[21] How he devised this idea is not clear. The proposal to establish the South Sea Company has been attributed to several persons, such as Hugh Chamberlain and Daniel Defoe.[22] However, there is no evidence that their proposals contained both elements, that is, conversion of debt and the South Sea trade.[23] As far as the scheme for the South Sea trade is concerned, we can find its origin in earlier plans with similar content. As we saw in Chapter 3, after the secret commercial treaty with Archduke Charles was concluded in July 1707, several proposals to establish a company for Spanish-American trade appeared in the press. It seems that similar plans were actually

[20] Sperling, *South Sea Company*, pp. 4–5.

[21] This idea of granting a company trading privileges in return for the company taking over government debts was adopted in 1717 by John Law in his plan for the 'Compagnie d'Occident' (the Company of the West), which was granted an exclusive trading right to French Louisiana. Merging with other trading companies, by 1719, this company had grown into the 'Compagnie des Indes' (the Company of the Indies). Interestingly, in its early stages, Law's plan included a project of colonial expedition to found a settlement in America, as in the case of the South Sea Company. For this purpose, in November 1718, Law established another company together with Richard Cantillon and Joseph Gage to found a colony in Mississippi and to dispatch an expedition under the command of Cantillon's younger brother Bernard in March 1719. However, the settlement established near New Orleans was not economically successful, and Bernard returned to France in 1723. Antoin E. Murphy, *Richard Cantillon, Entrepreneur and Economist* (Oxford, 1986), pp. 71–3, 76–7, 92–101.

[22] Gibson attributed this proposal to Dr Paul Chamberlain, a person well known for his skill in midwifery. Gibson, *Memoirs of Queen Anne*, p. 115. Morgan has claimed that Gibson confused him with his brother, Dr Hugh Chamberlain, a proposer for a land bank. Morgan, 'The South Sea Company and the Canadian Expedition', 158, note 50. Likewise, Daniel Defoe was often mentioned as a progenitor of the scheme, although this possibility has been denied by J.R. Moore, who has established that Defoe was not consulted in advance by Harley about the South Sea Act. J.R. Moore, 'Defoe and the South Sea Company', *Boston Public Library Quarterly* 5 (1953), 177. William Paterson, who had proposed the ill-fated Darien scheme, is mentioned by Morgan as one of those who influenced Harley's plan for the South Sea Company, in addition to Chamberlain and Defoe. Morgan, 'Origins of the South Sea Company', 32–3, 38.

[23] John Carswell has attributed the idea to John Blunt, a member of the Sword Blade syndicate, relying on Sperling's research. Carswell, *South Sea Bubble*, p. 35. It is true that Blunt was one of the first proposers of the plan to establish a new joint-stock company to solve the problems of floating debts. However, this proposal does not seem to have included the idea of trade to the South Sea. BL, Add MS 70296, fols 39–39v, George Caswell to Harley, 6 October 1710.

submitted to the government several times. In a pamphlet explaining the area where the company was given a monopoly, Herman Moll, a cartographer, mentioned that plans to establish a company for the South Sea trade were proposed by some London merchants during the reign of William III and also in the winter of 1710.[24] Furthermore, according to the author of 'Explanatory Observations on the South Sea Trade & Company', there was a similar plan submitted to William, and he would have pursued it, 'had he not been diverted either by the short and self interested Views of some Persons about him, or by ye Contradictions wch that Prince met in most of his Publick-Spirited Designs'.[25]

Also, Harley himself received a similar proposal in November 1707, which suggested establishing the 'South Sea Company' to encourage Spanish trade, which would make up for the loss of silver exported in the East Indian trade and stimulate the woollen industry. The anonymous author of the proposal postulated that if the company founded a settlement in the South Sea, it would deal 'a fatal blow' to France, and the author explained that there was a possibility that England might be able to secure a right to the settlement from 'Charles III', who was at that time in a disadvantageous position in Spain after the allies' defeat at Almanza in April 1707. Although there was the possibility of a similar attempt by the Dutch, the author claimed, 'First come first served, is an ould Proverb. Therefore now or Never.'[26]

There was also another proposal to establish a private company, which was possibly submitted to Harley in May 1711. This company was to attack the enemy territory in the Caribbean and in the Pacific with the company's armed vessels, as well as with warships provided by the government, and also to trade with the Spanish colonists if they were inclined to do so. Furthermore, the author of the proposal mentioned the possibility of the company's capturing a part of the enemy territory and establishing a colony there. This new colony could be used as a trading base, as well as a naval base, from which the company could launch attacks on Spanish colonies and on Spain's silver fleet. The author claimed that, either by gaining bullion in return for British products or by forcing the Spanish colonies to increase their defence costs, the activities of the company would contribute to preventing bullion from going to France, which had supported her war efforts in Europe and in America.[27]

Thus, Harley was already familiar with the idea of establishing a joint-stock company to trade in the South Sea and to make a settlement there. He combined

24 Herman Moll, *A View of the Coasts, Countries and Islands within the Limits of the South-Sea-Company* ... (London, 1711), p. 212.

25 BL, Add MS 70163, fol. 241v, 'Explanatory Observations on the South Sea Trade & Company', 1711.

26 BL, Add MS 70277 [not foliated] [no title], 20 November 1707. As far as I am aware, this is the earliest usage of the words 'South Sea Company', although the conversion of government debts was not included in this proposal.

27 BL, Add MS 70163, fols 163–8, D.P., 'Proposal about the South Sea', May 1711. As the exact date of this proposal is not clear, it is also possible that it was submitted after the introduction of the bill in the House of Commons to create the South Sea Company.

a trade scheme with the plan for the conversion of government debt in the bill to establish the South Sea Company, which was introduced in the House of Commons on 17 May 1711 and was given the royal assent on 12 June.[28]

There are three points to note about the earliest trading activities of this newly established South Sea Company. First, the Spanish colonies in the Caribbean, especially those on the coast of Tierra Firme (the north coast of South America), where Britain had been conducting illicit trade mainly through Jamaica, were excluded from the areas where the company was given a monopoly. On the eastern coast of the continent, the company was allowed to trade exclusively 'from the River *Aranoco* [Orinoco] to the Southermost [*sic*] Part of the *Terra del Fuego*'. Although at first sight this seems to have included the majority of the eastern side of South America, in reality, the area in which the company had a monopoly was more limited – Brazil, a Portuguese colony, and Dutch Surinam were exempted. By contrast, on the western coast, a vast area ranging from 'the said Southermost [*sic*] Part of *Terra del Fuego*, through the South Seas, to the Northermost [*sic*] Part of America' was granted to the company.[29] Thus, during its earliest stage, the company's trading activity was focused on those areas beyond the scope of the existing trade with the Spanish colonies in the Caribbean. In particular, its main target was the South Sea, where the French merchants were enjoying much success. As one anonymous author ironically remarked, 'it was undertook in imitation of what Riches *France* got from thence since the War begun'.[30]

This South Sea trade, however, posed a new challenge to British merchants. The Spanish colonies on the Pacific coast were very far away from the British colonies in the West Indies, the only place from which traders could expect supplies and assistance with any certainty. The company might be able to conduct the trade with the connivance of Spanish colonists who were willing to exchange goods with the British, and receive assistance from native tribes who were not under Spanish control. However, unless the company obtained official permission from the Spanish government to trade in Spanish America, there was always a danger of being attacked by the Spaniards, as happened with the Scottish Darien Company, which attempted to establish a new colony on the Isthmus of Panama between 1698 and 1700.[31] Moreover, if such an attack actually happened, there was no colony in the South Sea where the British merchants could take refuge.

The problem of remoteness was further compounded by the interference of the

[28] *C.J.*, XVI, pp. 678–9, 25 May 1711; *L.J.*, XIX, p. 322, 12 June 1711.

[29] *Statutes at Large*, IV, p. 483. It should be also noted that according to clauses XLIX and LI, British ships other than the company's ships were forbidden to sail into and to trade in the above-mentioned area, and they became liable to seizure by the company. *Ibid.*, IV, p. 484. These clauses made even voyages into the Pacific Ocean the company's monopoly, at least on paper.

[30] *A Letter from a Merchant in Amsterdam to a Friend in London, about the South Sea Trade* (London, 1712), p. 13.

[31] For a detailed account of this Scottish Darien venture, see Prebble, *Darien Disaster* and Watt, *Price of Scotland*.

East India Company, which managed to insert one clause into the South Sea Act to protect its privileges.[32] This clause allowed the South Sea Company to travel to the Pacific only through the Straits of Magellan or around Tierra del Fuego. The company was also forbidden to sail from the Pacific to the East Indies or other parts of the world other than via these two routes. This made it virtually impossible for the company's ships to return to Britain by a westbound route, which would have allowed them to cross the north Pacific in about two months with the help of trade winds, then call at Canton, and come back to Europe round the Cape of Good Hope. Instead, they were forced to retrace a more hazardous route round Cape Horn.[33] One pamphleteer later claimed that this clause alone was enough to prevent the company from gaining any advantage from the South Sea trade, though this may be a slight exaggeration.[34]

The second point to note is that almost none of the company's directors had any knowledge or experience of the Spanish-American trade, and particularly of the South Sea trade. The leading merchants who were engaged in West Indian trade at that time were both Whigs and Tories, such as Sir Gilbert Heathcote and William and Robert Heysham respectively. Oddly, none of these merchants was included in the first directorate of the company.[35] Sperling has regarded this as an indication of the directors' indifference to trading activities,[36] but, as we will see later, at least in the early days of the company, the directors were keen to carry on the South Sea trade. There must be other explanations for the exclusion of the West Indian merchants.

The failure to include such men might be partly explained by political struggles in the City. The South Sea Company has been often regarded by historians as a

32 *C.J.*, XVI, p. 671, 18 May 1711.

33 Actually, in the circumnavigation of 1740–44, Commodore George Anson chose a westbound route as safer than the eastbound route round Cape Horn. Glyn Williams, *The Prize of all the Ocean: The Triumph and Tragedy of Anson's Voyage Round the World* (London, 1999, repr., London, 2000), p. 128.

34 *Some Observations upon a Late Pamphlet, Intitled, A Modest Representation of the Past and Present State of Great Britain, Occasion'd by the Late Change in the Admistration …* (London, 1711), pp. 13–14.

35 The directors included those who did not have any knowledge of West Indian trade but had an interest in navy bills, such as Sir Ambrose Crowley, who was one of the major suppliers of ironware to the navy. Michael W. Flinn, 'Sir Ambrose Crowley and the South Sea Scheme of 1711', *Journal of Economic History* 20, no. 1 (March 1960), 51–66. The only director who had some connection with West Indian trade was Samuel Shepheard Senior, a leading City Whig who had headed a group of Leeward Islands merchants petitioning the House of Lords to open the East India trade in 1695. However, judging from his later career, the focus of his business interests in the 1700s seems to have been more on the East India trade and banking. See Philip Carter, 'Shepheard, Samuel (c. 1648–1719)', *ODNB*, and the entry in *House of Commons, 1690–1715*. De Krey mentions Shepheard, together with Sir James Bateman, as a leading Iberian Whig City merchant in the 1690s who was also an opponent of the Old East India Company and who had a close connection to the New East India Company. De Krey, *A Fractured Society*, pp. 150–1.

36 Sperling, *South Sea Company*, p. 7.

Tory-dominated corporation.[37] However, as Gary de Krey has pointed out, although the company was supported by the Tory government, its directorate was not necessarily dominated by the Tories. In reality, the directorate mainly consisted of Harley's supporters in the City, who included both Tory financiers and merchants, such as Sir Richard Hoare, and those with Whig affiliations, such as Sir James Bateman, sub-governor of the company, and Samuel Shepheard Senior. The real conflict in the City at that time was between those leading men of the City, Whigs as well as Tories, who quickly accommodated to the new Harley ministry, and those who hesitated to turn their coats because of their strong connections with the former government. In the election of directors of the Bank of England and the East India Company in April 1711, a group loyal to and encouraged by Harley tried to defeat the resistant faction, which dominated both directorates as well as the City magistracy. Although their attempt was unsuccessful, many of the group were appointed directorates in the South Sea Company instead.[38] Heathcote was one of the directors of the Bank challenged by Harley's supporters, which probably explains why he was not given a directorship of the South Sea Company.

Another probable reason for the exclusion of the West Indian merchants is a conflict of interest between the South Sea trade, conducted with the Spanish colonies through the Pacific, and trade with Spanish America via British colonies in the Caribbean, such as Jamaica. The existence of this conflict can be inferred from a debate about whether the existing Spanish-American trade via the British West Indian colonies was more advantageous than that in the South Sea. For example, a Whig writer, Arthur Maynwaring, claimed that the trade with the Spanish West Indian colonies through Jamaica would be more beneficial and safer than the intended South Sea trade, which was entirely dependent on the good faith of the Spaniards.[39] Similarly, one pamphleteer claimed that the planned settlements in the South Sea would secure for England no produce that could not already be found in its West Indian colonies, and that the settlements might even cause harm to the West Indian colonies by leading to overstocking.[40]

The harmful effects of the South Sea trade on the existing trade through the West Indian colonies were, to an extent, demonstrated by the success of French South Sea trading activity. Robert Allen remarked in 1712 that France's direct South Sea trade changed the course of the Spanish-American trade because the French supplied the goods at a lower price than those brought from Spain and Jamaica into Peru via Porto Bello.[41] It was possible that if the company traded

[37] Sperling has adopted this view and has interpreted the division on 25 May as a struggle over control of the South Sea Company, between the Tory financial interests, backed by Harley, and the Whig financial interests dominant in the Bank of England and the East India Company, which resulted in the victory of the former. *Ibid.*

[38] De Krey, *Fractured Society*, pp. 239–42.

[39] Arthur Maynwaring, *A Letter to a High-Churchman, in Answer to a Pamphlet, Intitled, Reasons Why this Nation should Put a Speedy End to this Expensive War* (London, 1711), pp. 26–7.

[40] *A Letter from a Merchant in Amsterdam to a Friend in London*, pp. 5–6.

[41] Allen, *Essay on the Nature and Methods*, p. 32.

in the South Sea, similar problems might arise.[42]

Moreover, there was another reason the West Indian merchants were reluctant to open a new trade route. As we saw in Chapter 5, in 1704, at the request of leading West Indian merchants, such as Heathcote and Sir Bartholomew Gracedieu, English traders were allowed to reopen direct trade with the Spanish colonies through Jamaica, which had been forbidden after the war began. For the West Indian merchants who could take advantage of this reopened channel, it was probably unnecessary, or even harmful, to start a new trade through the South Sea. It is likely that this conflict between the two trades contributed to the exclusion of most of the West Indian merchants from the company's directorate.[43]

In any case, the directorate of the company consisted mainly of persons who lacked experience and knowledge about the direct Spanish-American trade. They were not those City magnates who had been engaged in direct trade with the Spanish-American colonies via Jamaica, such as Heathcote and Gracedieu, but rather they were novices at trade who were trying to open up a new trading channel.

As we shall see later, one important consequence of this difference was the directors' complete dependence in the planning of the South Sea trade and expedition on information from a few explorers. However, at the same time, the company was given power that could counterbalance these difficulties. In particular, to help its trade, the company was equipped with the legal authority to seize enemy territory and establish settlements, which is the third point to note. The fiftieth clause of the South Sea Act gave to the company sole property in the places where the company or its employees would 'discover or find out, seize or possess, in any manner whatsoever', within the areas where the company had a monopoly.[44] This privilege virtually guaranteed the company's power to claim conquests in those areas. This right to establish settlements was reinforced by the company's charter, granted on 8 September 1711, which gave the company the power to control all of its forts, factories and settlements within the area, as well as the power to appoint

42 Ironically, this success of the new direct trade by French merchants, especially those of St Malo, with the Spanish colonies via the Pacific caused a similar conflict of interest among the French. Not only did it turn Pontchartrain, French secretary of state for the marine, into an opponent of the South Sea trade out of consideration for its negative impact on the French Asiento Company and the diplomatic relations with Spanish, but it also provoked anger among the French colonists in Saint-Domingue, who lost opportunities to resell French products to the Spanish colonies. Frostin, 'Les Ponchartrain et la Pénétration Commercial Française', 322–3.

43 As we shall see later, the focus of the company's trading activities shifted from the South Sea into the Caribbean after the plan for the expedition was dropped. This turned the potential tension between the two trades into a more direct conflict. The company's Asiento trade threatened the interests of various groups in Jamaica, such as planters and traders, who tried to counter the intrusion by imposing duties on exported slaves and continuing their illicit trade with Spanish America, paying little regard to the company's monopoly. Donnan, 'Early Days of the South Sea Company', 440–3; Sperling, *South Sea Company*, pp. 21–2.

44 *Statutes at Large*, IV, p. 484.

governors and officers there who might 'Raise, Train and Muster Military Forces, not only for the Defence of the Company's Forts and Factories, &c, but for taking and recovering others within their Limits'.[45] Thus, the newly established South Sea Company had to launch in an unfamiliar trade environment under inexperienced directors, but with great powers to conduct trade, at least on paper.

Controversy over the South Sea Company: Free Trade and Settlements

The uncertainties about the projected South Sea trade drew harsh criticism from the opponents of the ministry. While such men tried to discredit the South Sea Company by pointing out expected trading difficulties, ministerial writers attempted to defend it by writing pamphlets that demonstrated the practicability of the trade to their readership, which probably included shareholders and investors. Early in the debate, ministerial writers proposed two principal methods that could make the South Sea trade viable: obtaining a settlement in Spanish America; and securing 'free trade' (or 'liberty of trade'), that is, the right to trade with the Spanish colonies as freely as Spanish subjects. However, as the debates progressed, and especially after the ministry's failure to obtain security ports in peace negotiations, the establishment of settlements through a military expedition eventually came to be regarded by the company's directors as the only remaining option for making the South Sea trade feasible.

As soon as the South Sea Bill was submitted to the Commons, the ministerial writers supported the project by extolling the expected benefits of the South Sea trade.[46] Conversely, opposition writers cast doubt on the practicability of the trade and raised concerns about the company's financial manipulation. One anonymous author satirised the prospect of the South Sea trade (which had to be conducted in the middle of the enemy territory) as follows:

> Whether Erecting a Company, and Appointing a Stock to Trade to a Place actually in Possession of Our Enemies, and of which we see no Prospect of Dispossessing them, does not Encorporate the Proprietors into the Spectator's Worthy Society of *Castle-Builders* ? … Whether a Voyage to the *South-Seas* (where neither Friends or Enemies will Trade with us either now or hereafter) and a Voyage to the *World in the Moon*, are not founded upon the same *Phenomena* of Probabilities?[47]

One Richard Martyn, a ministerial writer, replied that this difficulty could be overcome by using Portuguese ports in Brazil or by establishing a settlement as a

[45] South Sea Company, *Abstract of the Charter of the Governour and Company of Merchants of Great Britain, Trading to the South-Seas, and Other Parts of America, and …* ([London] [1711]), p. 6. The company's right to ships and goods taken as prizes within the limits was also confirmed by this charter. *Ibid.*, p. 5.

[46] For example, *A Letter to a Member of Parliament*, pp. 4–5; *Examiner*, no. 45, 7 June 1711.

[47] *Some Queries, which being Nicely Answered may Tend very much to the Encouragement of the South-Sea Company* … ([n.p.] 1711), p. 1.

trading base, with military assistance from the government.[48] However, this was soon countered by another opposition writer, who claimed that there would be strong resistance from France and Spain against any attempt by other European countries to establish a settlement in the South Sea.[49] Thus, whether Britain would be able to obtain a settlement for trade in Spanish America became one of the cruxes of the debate about the feasibility of the South Sea trade.

An equally important option for the South Sea trade was securing the right to free trade with the Spanish colonies. As we saw in Chapter 2, at the beginning of the War of the Spanish Succession, this right to free trade had already been proposed by Austria and the Netherlands as a quid pro quo for the conquests that England and the Netherlands might make in Spanish America. The idea of obtaining such a right was revived in the late stages of the war. In June 1711, Harley seems to have been considering insisting on free trade with Spanish America, as well as with several places in the Mediterranean and the Americas, in the peace negotiations with France, which he had began through the Earl of Jersey in July 1710, although he dropped the demand later.[50]

The expectation of gaining free trade, as well as new settlements, can also be seen in the debate over the South Sea trade. The anonymous author of a pamphlet entitled *The Considerable Advantages of a South-Sea Trade to our English Nation*, which was probably published just before the South Sea Act passed in June 1711, claimed that if England secured free trade with the Spanish colonies on the Pacific coast, she might be able to dispose of all her manufactures, especially woollen goods, and increase employment. The author also emphasised the necessity of having two or three colonies with fortifications, so that the English could control the area, defend themselves and force a trade if they were refused.[51]

However, this expectation of obtaining both free trade and fortified settlements was criticised by opponents as being unrealistic. Ministerial writers defended the company by drawing up a revised, more realistic blueprint for the trade. Primary responsibility for this task fell to Daniel Defoe, who was working for Harley as a propagandist at the time and had been a staunch supporter of a plan to establish a new colony in Spanish America, especially in Chile.[52] In June 1711, he

48 Richard Martyn, *A Modest Representation of the Past and Present State of Great Britain, Occasion'd by the Late Change in the Administration* (London, 1711), p. 13.

49 *Some Observations upon a Late Pamphlet*, p. 12.

50 BL, Add MS 70332, bundle 17 [not foliated] '[no title (memorandum about peace negotiations written by Harley)]', 16 June 1711.

51 *The Considerable Advantages of a South-Sea Trade to our English Nation* (London [1711?]), p. 7. As there is no reference to the name of the 'South Sea Company' in the pamphlet, it is possible that it was published before the South Sea Act was passed in June, probably to promote its passage by publicising the advantages of the trade.

52 Defoe was a member of a cultural circle in London, which included eminent intellectuals, such as Herman Moll, Robert Hook, Jonathan Swift and William Stukeley, an antiquarian, as well as famous explorers, such as William Dampier and Woodes Rogers. Of these, Moll and Rogers were also supporters of the idea of establishing colonies in Spanish America

launched a series of articles on the Spanish-American trade in the *Review*. He explained French influence in the Spanish-American colonies, and claimed that the English could imitate France's success if they could obtain a similar footing in the region.[53]

In his article published on 12 July, however, Defoe noted an important reservation. He expressed doubt that any plan could be successful if it was based on the principle of free trade with all of the Spanish colonies following the seizure of some South Sea settlements – it was unlikely that Spain or France would allow such a trade either during or after the war.[54] Nevertheless, it should be noted that what Defoe criticised was not the trade itself but rather people's unrealistic expectations for it. Indeed, in the next issue of the *Review*, he explained that he was not opposed to a South Sea trade, but was against 'our Entertaining a Whymsical Notion, and building Castles in the Air'. He believed that excessive expectations for the trade tended to lead people to disappointment and then to discontent with the project, and eventually to cast scorn and blame on the plan and its originators.[55]

Defoe believed that this notion of 'free trade' afforded opponents of the company an easy opportunity to criticise the entire trade as impracticable. Therefore, in a document submitted to Harley in July 1711, he proposed to stop using this problematic term. He claimed that, even if England did not obtain free trade, some settlements in Spanish America would 'be of Sufficient Consequence to justifye The prudence of ye wholl Undertakeing, Give a Credit to ye Design and Answer all the Ends of a South-Sea Company'.[56] Thus, as a feasible option for the South Sea trade, Defoe proposed the establishment of settlements in the South Sea and trading from there without a right to free trade.[57]

Another aspect of the South Sea project that the ministerial writers had to defend was the legitimacy of establishing a new settlement in the middle of the

and were involved in the company's plan for the South Sea expedition, as we will see later. For this circle, see Dennis Reinhartz, *The Cartographer and the Literati: Herman Moll and His Intellectual Circle* (Lewiston, NY, 1997), Chapters 5 and 6.

53 *Review*, VIII, pp. 178–9, no. 44, 5 July 1711; p. 181, no. 45, 7 July 1711.

54 *Review*, VIII, p. 190, no. 47, 12 July 1711.

55 *Review*, VIII, pp. 202–3, no. 50, 19 July 1711.

56 BL, Add MS 70291, fols 9v–10, Defoe to Harley [c. 17 July 1711]. He repeated a similar argument in another document submitted to Harley. BL, Add MS 70291, fols 23–4, Defoe to Harley, July 1711.

57 Defoe continued to be a staunch supporter of the South Sea trade and colonial conquest, even to the point of defying the original idea of his patron Harley. In one pamphlet, he proposed separating the trading and financial aspects of the company's business in order to protect the credibility of the South Sea trade in the face of criticism from debt-holders, who were ignorant of trading affairs and tended to be sceptical of the company's prospects in this area. This pamphlet shows that his support for the idea of the South Sea trade and colonial expeditions was not mere political expediency but indicated his own personal commitment. Daniel Defoe, *An Essay on the South-Sea Trade. With an Inqury into the Ground and Reasons of the Present Dislike and Complaint against the Settlement of a South Sea Company* ... (London, 1712 [1711]), p. 47.

Spanish territories in America. For this purpose, Defoe invoked the sixth article of the Treaty of the Grand Alliance and the notion of colonial conquest as compensation for the British war effort, which we saw in Chapter 2. In the *Review* of 7 August 1711, he claimed that this sixth article was 'the Legal Foundation of our new Undertaking to the South-Seas'. Conquests based on this article were thought to be just reward for the British war effort. In answer to a criticism that such an attempt might tarnish the British fight for the liberty of Europe, Defoe argued that Britain, which had been fighting for the interest of Austria, deserved some compensation for her war effort and that the sixth article gave Britain full title to such lands as she would obtain in Spanish dominions. Therefore, 'this Undertaking is not as one call'd it, a Piracy upon the *Spaniards*' under pretence of helping them, but rather it was 'a fair Capitulation'. Defoe dismissed the slander that the new company 'ought to be call'd the *Buccanier Company*', as an excessively harsh view, as this transaction was 'a free Convention, or Agreement, on both Sides'.[58]

Government pamphleteers proposed Chile, in particular, as a suitable place for a new settlement. Defoe was a keen supporter of this idea. In July 1711, he submitted to Harley a proposal for a new settlement in southern Chile for the company's trade. Similarly, Herman Moll, who was one of the members of the intellectual circle that also included Defoe and Jonathan Swift, advocated this idea in a little book entitled *A View of the Coasts, Countries and Islands within the Limits of the South-Sea-Company*, which was published in 1711 with the intention of supporting the trade of the South Sea Company. Defoe and Moll emphasised the existence of friendly Native Americans who maintained independence from the Spaniards as one of the advantages of Chile. These natives were also believed to have control over rich goldmines.[59] Defoe and Moll anticipated that England could receive assistance from the native inhabitants and obtain gold in exchange for European goods, such as textiles and arms.[60]

A True Account of the Design, and Advantages of the South-Sea Trade was, in a sense, a culmination of the various arguments presented by ministerial writers for defending the South Sea Company. Its content also shows that the argument in favour of the South Sea Company overlapped with the pro-maritime war

58 *Review*, VIII, pp. 233–4, no. 58, 7 August 1711.

59 In southern Chile, there were Araucanian Indians who were not under Spanish rule at that time. In addition, in the eighteenth century, Chile, together with Brazil and Colombia, was one of the main gold producers in South America. Linda A. Newson, 'The Demographic Impact of Colonization', *The Cambridge Economic History of Latin America*, ed. Victor Bulmer-Thomas et al., I (Cambridge, 2006), p. 178; Carlos Marichal, 'Money, Taxes, and Finance', *Cambridge Economic History of Latin America*, ed. Bulmer-Thomas et al., I, p. 429.

60 BL, Add MS 70291, fols 19–20, Daniel Defoe, 'Proposall for a Settlement Upon The Coast of America', 23 July 1711. Moll, *A View of the Coasts*, pp. 43, 51, 209–12. Gillian Hutchinson has pointed out a strong anti-Spanish Catholic feeling in Moll's works. Gillian Hutchinson, 'Herman Moll's View of the South Sea Company', *Journal for Maritime Research* 6, no. 1 (2004), 109.

argument, especially the second argument, to a large extent.[61] The author began the pamphlet by describing the concern over Britain's financial situation burdened by debts and proposing a solution to this problem, that is, incorporating all of the debts into the stock of the South Sea Company. He lamented that Britain had 'been Fighting, like *Knight-Errants*, for *Honour's Sake*, and to redress Publick Grievances without any Regard to our private Interest', and, unlike the allies, Britain had 'ever neglected the Pursuit of those advantageous Conditions on which we enter'd into the Grand Alliance': the alleged right of conquest in Spanish America, based on the sixth article.[62]

After expressing this discontent with the allies, a typical element in the second pro-maritime war argument, the author contrasted Britain's situation with that of the French, who were increasingly taking control of the Spanish-American trade, and the author claimed that the French removal from Spanish America was the most effectual means to obtain a lasting peace and regain a balance of trade and wealth in Europe. However, as the Spaniards did not have sufficient power to perform this act, the duty had to fall to Britain, not least to the South Sea Company, which would have 'the Largest stock of any Trading Company in the whole world' and therefore would be the most suitable party to remove the French, or at least to establish colonies in Spanish America and conduct beneficial trade, with a small contribution from each proprietor, military assistance from the government, and other advantages granted by its charter.[63]

The author also countered several criticisms of the trading aspect of the company, as well as its financial aspects, among which was the question of the practicability of the South Sea trade. He argued that Britain should not expect free trade, as the French would strongly oppose it during the war, and after a peace, Spain would not consent to such a '*Partition of their Direct American* Trade'. Instead, the author insisted that trade by the South Sea Company from a new British settlement would be more acceptable to the Spaniards because there was sufficient land on the western coast of South America, where Britain could establish a settlement without invading Spanish property and damaging Spanish commerce and from where Britain could assist the Spaniards by supplying slaves. The author claimed, 'By this it appears, That the *Spaniards* have no Reason to be alarm'd, but rather to rejoice at, and favour our Undertaking.'[64] Thus, ministerial writers made it clear that, although Spain was unlikely to grant Britain the right to free trade, the South Sea trade would be still practicable as long as settlements could be established in Spanish America, notably in Chile.

[61] The original manuscript draft of this pamphlet is in BL, Add MS 70163, fols 239–246v, 'Explanatory Observations on the South Sea Trade & Company', which implies Harley's strong involvement in producing this pamphlet. The content of this draft is essentially the same as that of the published pamphlet, apart from some additional quotations from other documents. Donnan states that this pamphlet appeared in September. Donnan, 'Early Days of the South Sea Company', 424, note 9.

[62] *A True Account of the Design*, pp. 3–5.

[63] *Ibid.*, pp. 6–10.

[64] *Ibid.*, pp. 28–30.

Controversy over the South Sea Company: Peace Negotiations

Towards the end of 1711, the controversy over the South Sea Company became tied up with the issue of peace negotiations with France. One of the central issues in these negotiations was the interpretation of the phrase 'sûretés réelles' (real securities), which France had promised to Britain in April 1711. In July, in response to the proposal for peace from the French government, Mathew Prior was sent to Paris to discuss the British preliminaries with the Marquis de Torcy, the French foreign minister. By this time, it had been decided to demand these real securities in the form of four fortified ports in North and South America, in addition to Gibraltar and Port Mahon. This demand was, in a sense, a revival of the demand made by William III in the negotiations for the first partition treaty, which we saw in Chapter 2. Prior had several interviews with Torcy and tried to pin him down to conceding to the British demand for these security ports, which was, however, refused. After Prior's return, the negotiations were continued with Nicholas Mesnager, envoy extraordinary of France, who came to Britain with Prior. In the negotiations, the Harley ministry finally abandoned the demand for the security ports on 3 September, in return for several privileges, such as a reduction in duties on British goods at Cadiz, a Swiss garrison at Cadiz under British control, and extension of the period of the Asiento. At the end of September, the parties reached an agreement, and two articles were signed: the 'seven preliminaries', the basis for the general peace; and secret agreements about the privileges to be given to Britain including the Asiento.[65]

On 13 October, a summary of the seven preliminaries was leaked by the *Daily Courant*, a periodical aligned with the Whigs, who were critical of the peace proposals. In order to counter this leak and justify the peace negotiations, the pro-government *Post Boy* revealed several privileges that had secretly been promised to Britain by France. As far as the Spanish-American trade was concerned, however, the *Post Boy*'s description was ambiguous: '*full Liberty to the* South-Sea-Company to *establish themselves on the Continent of that Country, according to the Act of Parliament of last Sessions*'.[66] This revelation triggered a pamphlet war over the peace negotiations, into which the issue of the South Sea Company soon intruded.

Even before the *Daily Courant* leaked the content of the agreement with France, Defoe had started to defend the peace negotiations. In one pamphlet, he claimed that if Britain could recover the Spanish-American trade by gaining some settlement in Chile or Peru and securing a favourable duty in Spanish and Spanish-American trade, it would not be necessary to continue the war to restore Spain to the House of Habsburg. Then, Defoe proposed two plans for a partition of the

65 Sperling, *South Sea Company*, pp. 12–13; B.W. Hill, 'Oxford, Bolingbroke, and the Peace of Utrecht', *HJ* 16, no. 2 (June 1973), 247–51.

66 *Daily Courant*, no. 3121, 13 October 1711; *Post Boy*, no. 2562, 13 October 1711; Coombs, *Conduct of the Dutch*, pp. 260–1.

Spanish dominions that would give part of Spanish America to Britain.[67] After the revelation, the ministerial press continued its defence of the peace negotiations. The *Post Boy* argued that the privileges concerning the Spanish and Spanish-American trade promised in the secret agreements with France might be sufficient reason for making a peace, as they would guarantee England great wealth in the future and would justify the English war effort of the previous ten years.[68]

By contrast, Whig opposition writers argued that the aims of the war, including the recovery of the Spanish-American market, would never be achieved if Britain left Spain and its dominion in the hands of the Duke of Anjou, the French candidate for the Spanish crown in the war. One pamphleteer argued that giving Spain to the duke was almost tantamount to giving it to Louis XIV, and would enable the French king to increase his wealth and power and to take control of Portugal, Brazil, Peru and Mexico.[69] Although not necessarily denying the prospects of the South Sea trade, the author insisted that England should try to set Archduke Charles, the Habsburg candidate, on the Spanish throne and thus recover the profitable Spanish trade, which could bring a vast amount of income, whereas the South Sea trade had several problems, such as possible opposition from the French and Spanish and uncertain profitability.[70] Similarly, one opposition writer argued that British interests would be best protected when the Spanish crown was in the hands of 'Charles III', with whom Stanhope had made a secret treaty, including a clause regarding commercial privileges in the Spanish-American trade, and who would be dependent on the naval power of Britain and the Netherlands.[71]

Arthur Maynwaring, a Whig writer and one of the main opponents of the Tory pamphleteers, criticised the 'seven preliminaries' for failing to restore Spain and the West Indies to the House of Habsburg. He claimed that this failure would eventually lead to a French monopoly of all the Spanish and Spanish-American trade and, ultimately, the destruction of the British colonies in America.[72] As for the South Sea trade, Maynwaring argued that the agreement in the peace treaty to give the British privileges in the South Sea trade was not sufficient reason for

[67] Daniel Defoe, *Reasons Why this Nation Ought to Put a Speedy End to this Expensive War* ... 2nd edn ([London], 1711), pp. 42–8.

[68] *Post Boy*, no. 2563, 16 October 1711. Defoe had also defended the peace negotiations after the leak. See Daniel Defoe, *Armageddon: or, the Necessity of Carrying on the War, If such a Peace cannot be Obtained as may Render Europe Safe, and Trade Secure* (London, [1711]).

[69] *A Letter to a Member of the October-Club: Shewing, that to Yield Spain to the Duke of Anjou by a Peace, Wou'd be the Ruin of Great Britain* (London, 1711), pp. 6–7. Coombs has attributed the authorship to Francis Hare, chaplain-general to Marlborough's army. Coombs, *Conduct of the Dutch*, p. 262.

[70] *A Letter to a Member of the October-Club*, pp. 39–40.

[71] *A Letter from an Exchange Broker to a Country Gentleman, concerning Peace and South-Sea Stock* (London, 1711), pp. 6–7. Sperling states that this pamphlet was published on 20 November 1711. Sperling, *South Sea Company*, p. 15. Coombs has dated it to the end of November. Coombs, *Conduct of the Dutch*, p. 271.

[72] Arthur Maynwaring, *Remarks upon the Present Negotiations of Peace Begun between Britain and France* (London, 1711), pp. 13–15.

giving up Spain, for this was completely based on the assumption that Louis XIV would keep his promise. He also dismissed the prospects of a South Sea expedition to establish a permanent settlement, arguing that there would be strong opposition from the Spaniards, the French and the native population. He suggested that even if Britain could obtain the silver or gold mines through a peace treaty or an expedition, this would only serve to destroy British industry, making the British as lazy as the Spaniards and overturning a free government. Instead, he claimed that Britain should obtain liberty of trade.[73]

Thus, in the debate over the peace negotiations, ministerial writers argued that one of the original aims of the war, the recovery of the Spanish-American trade, could be achieved through the trading privileges that would be given to Britain and the South Sea Company by the peace treaty, while the opposition Whig writers maintained that these privileges were not sufficient guarantee.

This debate demonstrates that the trade scheduled to be conducted by the South Sea Company was closely connected to the question of who would have control over Spanish-American trade after the war. Moreover, through the debate, the South Sea trade came to assume not only economic importance but also political significance, for the Harley ministry could be exposed to severe criticism if the trade did not turn out to be profitable enough to compensate for giving up the Spanish throne to the Duke of Anjou.

It was not until 1712 that the directors of the company started to plan a military expedition to the South Sea. During the latter half of 1711, there was still hope that Britain might be able to obtain security ports through negotiations with France, an expectation perhaps encouraged by the *Post Boy*'s revelation of the secret agreements between the two countries. Nevertheless, the directors were not reassured that the peace would deliver a trading base for the company in Spanish America, which was an essential condition for successful trade to the South Sea. Even if the agreements with France included cession of some territories in Spanish America to Britain, fulfilment of this cession completely depended on Louis XIV keeping his promise, as Maynwaring pointed out. In any case, as we have seen, the ministry had in fact given up the demand for security ports by September in return for several trading privileges, though it is not clear whether the company was informed of this decision. Unable to count on obtaining some trading bases as a result of the peace treaty, the directors had to seek other means to secure them. It was under these circumstances that the South Sea Company began to plan an expedition to the South Sea to establish a settlement there.

[73] *Ibid.*, pp. 24–6. Maynwaring repeated his objections to the South Sea trade in another pamphlet, criticising the proponents of the South Sea trade, including Defoe, for underestimating the Castilian's reluctance to allow foreigners to participate in the trade, and warning that those new settlements would certainly be bones of contention between England and Spain and would destroy the trade itself. Maynwaring, *A Letter to a High-Churchman*, pp. 27–8.

Plan for the South Sea Expedition in 1712

At the end of January 1712, the directors of the South Sea Company first mentioned a scheme for a colonial expedition to establish settlements. An examination of the planning process for this expedition offers the historian three insights. First, it was the company's directors who took the initiative in proposing and planning the expedition. Sperling implies that the first court of directors, who had been personally chosen by Harley, followed his lead in this issue (his agents on the board certainly made his thoughts known).[74] However, in reality, it was the company's directors, not Harley, who were keen on the expedition. It is important to distinguish between the intention of the directors, who were actually running the company, and that of the ministry, especially Harley.

On 31 January 1712, Sir James Bateman, sub-governor, and Samuel Ongley, deputy-governor, submitted a petition to Harley. The petition stated that, to carry on the South Sea trade, 'it is necessary that some settlements be obtained in America, within ye limitts of their Charter' and requested naval and land forces, which were to consist of twenty men-of-war, a land force of four hundred men and forty transport ships. The deadline for the departure was set for 15 June.[75] The destination of the expedition was the South Sea. This fact can be confirmed by a petition to the queen, which the company submitted on May 1712, when the departure of the expedition was delayed. The petitioners desired speedy preparation of the expeditionary forces, as it was 'very difficult and hazardous for a fleet to Attempt to pass ye Cape [i.e. Cape Horn] into ye South Seas' unless the fleet departed by the end of June.[76] From this statement, it is clear that the directors' intention was to establish settlements in the South Sea for the trade there, which the directors had resolved to pursue according to the power given to the company by the South Sea Act and its charter.[77] The company's plan was accepted, and on 13 March, Bateman was notified by Henry St John, Secretary of State for the North, that sufficient force would be provided.[78] Thus, it should be emphasised that the directors acted on their own initiative in the plan for the South Sea expedition.

Second, the advice that the directors obtained for judging the feasibility of establishing a settlement by force was generally over-optimistic. They collected information about problems that they might encounter on an expedition to the South Sea from those who were familiar with the region.[79] Among them were

[74] Sperling, *South Sea Company*, p. 18.

[75] BL, Add MS 25559, fols 8v–9, Bateman and Ongley to Harley, 31 January 1711/12.

[76] BL, Add MS 25559, fol. 9v, 'The Humble Petition of ye Governor & Compy of Merchants of Great Britain Trading to the South Seas & other Parts of America & for Encouraging the Fishery', 23 May 1712.

[77] BL, Add MS 25494, fol. 58v, The South Sea Company, Court Minutes, 20 February 1711/12.

[78] BL, Add MS 25562, fol. 3, St John to Bateman, 13 March 1711/12; BL, Add MS 25494, fols 65v–66. The South Sea Company, Court Minutes, 14 March 1711/12.

[79] On 5 March 1712, the court of directors resolved that the committee of the affairs of the company should take charge of considering 'any Proposals that may from time to time be

Woodes Rogers, a Bristol privateer, who had just come back from a privateering circumnavigation, and Edward Cooke, who sailed with him. Rogers recommended that the company should 'make first one good settlement & not … distribute your men in small numbers but carry a great force at once'. He also reported on the Spanish antipathy towards the French and their inclination to trade with the English.[80] Likewise, Cooke was optimistic about taking Valdivia in southern Chile, claiming that 'wth a sufficient force Baldivia may be taken & garrison'd so secure as to keep it'. He also expected assistance from the Native Americans there, and hoped that the Spaniards would allow the company to trade in their ports or settle a factory after the peace.[81]

On 28 February 1712, one of the directors received a letter from Thomas Bowrey, a merchant with experience of the East Indies, who in September 1711 had submitted to Harley a proposal to establish a settlement at Valdivia for the South Sea trade. Bowrey wrote that some places in the South Sea might be ceded to Britain by the peace with France. However, he claimed, 'whether we gain such Places by Peace or Wars or whether such advantage be gaind this year, or hereafter, yet ye Port for Refreshment by ye way is absolutely neadfull & ye more earnestly to be attempted', in the hope of trade with the natives for gold and with the Spaniards at Buenos Aires in peace time.[82] Thus, much of the information that the company received from those experts pointed to the necessity and feasibility of establishing a settlement by force, ideally at Valdivia, for the South Sea trade.

The excessive size of the expeditionary force requested by the company is cited by Sperling as evidence that the plan for the expedition was not a serious one.[83] However, it should be noted that, for men who had little knowledge of the South Sea, the advice of the experts, such as Rogers and Cooke, was their only reliable source of information. Although the latter were seasoned sailors and had first-hand knowledge of the region, they did not have experience of a large-scale

offered by Persons Experienced in the Trade to the South Seas' and any other issues concerning the region. BL, Add MS 25494, fol. 62, The South Sea Company, Court Minutes, 5 March 1711/12.

80 BL, Add MS 28140, fols 30–30v, 'Acct how a Trade may be carried on to ye South Sea' [n.d., but c. late 1711 or early 1712].

81 BL, Add MS 28140, fols 29–30, 'An Account of ye Places which ye Duke and Dutchess anchor'd at in ye South Seas wrote by Edw: Cook, Commander of ye Marquess Prize' [n.d., but c. late 1711 or early 1712].

82 BL, Add MS 28140, fol. 33, 'Copy of a Letter Wrote by Capt Thos Bowrey', 28 February 1711/12. Moreover, on 19 March, it was ordered that a letter from one Alexander White and a paper from one Allen should be referred to the committee, which was to discuss the issue of the South Sea trade with the authors of the documents, one Major Pullen, probably John Pullen, ex-governor of Bermuda, and Woodes Rogers. BL, Add MS 25494, fol. 69v, The South Sea Company, Court Minutes, 19 March 1711/12. It is possible that this paper was 'An Essay on the Nature and Methods of Carrying on a Trade to the South Sea', written by Robert Allen, which explained the history and nature of the South Sea trade and extolled its advantages and was later published as a pamphlet in 1712. BL, Add MS 28140, fols 20–8, 'An Essay on the Nature and Methods of Carrying on a Trade to the South Sea [n.d.]'.

amphibious operation to the South Sea. Rather, it was they who enthusiastically pointed to the necessity and practicability of establishing a settlement at Valdivia. The combination of this lack of experience and optimistic advice from experts probably resulted in too ambitious a plan for the exhibition.

Third, in contrast to the eagerness of the South Sea Company's directors, the ministry was not responsive to the plan, and preparations for the promised fleet were severely delayed. In April and May, the directors repeatedly beseeched the ministry to prepare for the expeditionary force, emphasising that it was necessary to depart at the right time for a successful voyage.[84] On 23 May, they submitted a petition to the queen through Harley, with a copy of the original proposal for the expedition from 31 January. In the petition, they explained that, based on the government's promise of military support, the company had started preparations for the South Sea trade and had raised capital of £200,000, the largest part of which had already been spent on merchandise for the trade. They then asked that the force should be raised promptly, stressing the danger of passing Cape Horn too late in the season.[85]

On the same day, Bateman and Ongley sent a letter to Harley outlining the difficult situation in which the company found itself. They emphasised the need to depart before July, referring to the French traders who minimised their loss of ships in the South Sea by leaving at the right time of the year. A speedy departure was also important from a financial standpoint, as any delay could lead to further expense in relation to freightage and the loss of cargo. Moreover, they were worried that if the cargo did not leave on time 'they [the General Court of the company] may not without difficulty be again induced to believe that any Trade is intended & it cannot fail of being attended with many ill Consequences'. In the face of delay, the huge expenditure on cargo could result in accusations being levelled against the court of directors and might also have a negative impact on the company's share price. Bateman and Ongley concluded the letter by asking for swift advice and assistance so that the company could 'Prosecute the great Ends proposed by this Proffitable Trade'.[86]

Clearly, at this stage, the directors believed that they had to launch the expedition as quickly as possible not only to ensure that the voyage was safe but also to convince shareholders that the company was actually going to carry out the South Sea trade. Of course, this could not be a mere pretext to reassure the shareholders. The directors had already spent a large amount of money on preparations, and if the shareholders realised that there was no prospect of the company's making a profit from its trading business, they might start selling its

83 Sperling, *South Sea Company*, p. 18.

84 BL, Add MS 25559, fol. 7v, Bateman to St John, 3 April 1712; fol. 8, Bateman and Ongley to St John, 7 May 1712; fols 8–8v, Bateman and Ongley to Harley, 7 May 1712.

85 BL, Add MS 70163, fol. 24, 'The Humble Petition of ye Governor & Compy of Merchants of Great Britain Trading to the South Seas & other Parts of America & for Encouraging the Fishery', 23 May 1712.

86 BL, Add MS 25559, fols 10v–11, Bateman and Ongley to Harley, 23 May 1712.

shares. Sperling claims that the financial community judged the value of the company's stock based on the security of the 6 per cent annuity paid by the Treasury, and that profits from the trade had been discounted to zero.[87] However, this is a somewhat extreme opinion. Helen Paul suggests that the prospect of the Asiento trade was an important inducement to invest in the South Sea Company during the Bubble.[88] Similarly, the lure of profit from the South Sea trade may have had a significant impact on investment in the company's share in the earlier period. As Hutchinson points out, the share price and the attractiveness of the company to investors depended on whether they believed in the practicability and profitability of the company's South Sea trade, an area in which the French were making a huge profit at that time.[89] Thus, the company's directors had good reason to implement the plan for the South Sea expedition as soon as possible.

Frequent requests from the company finally pushed the government to take action. On 23 May, the Board of Admiralty was ordered to produce a report about available ships and victualling for the voyage, which was sent to the Earl of Dartmouth, Secretary of the State for the South.[90] The overall tone of the report was not necessarily unfavourable to the voyage. However, it did suggest that it would take about six weeks for the fleet to be prepared and provisioned.[91] From an administrative perspective, it was possible for the Admiralty to provide a fleet of a certain scale. What was almost impossible, however, was to prepare the excessively large fleet originally requested by the company to the proposed deadline.

When Bateman and some other members of the company visited the Board of Admiralty to ask about the progress of the naval preparation, they were informed that so far it had only received the direction from Dartmouth on 23 May about available ships and provisions for the West Indian voyage.[92] However, Bateman seems to have taken this as a sign that preparation for the departure had begun. On 30 May, he reported to the court of directors that the Board of Admiralty 'gave them good hopes to believe they would be ready in good time', and recommended to the company's committee of buying that they should prepare the cargo as soon as possible.[93]

The directors finally knew that the preparation of the fleet was at least being considered by the Board of Admiralty. However, it had also become evident by this time that the best time for the departure of the South Sea expedition had nearly passed, a fact that seems to have caused a change in the directors' policy regarding the plan for the expedition. On 4 June, at a meeting of the court of directors, Bateman proposed a clause to be added to a bill for continuing the South Sea

87 Sperling, *South Sea Company*, p. 16.
88 Paul, *South Sea Bubble*, p. 73.
89 Hutchinson, 'Herman Moll's View', 10.
90 TNA, ADM 1/4096, fol. 259, Dartmouth to Admiralty, 23 May 1712.
91 TNA, SP42/11, fols 171–2, Admiralty to Dartmouth, 30 May 1712.
92 TNA, ADM 3/26, fols 293v–294, Minutes of the Board of Admiralty, 28 May 1712.
93 BL, Add MS 25494, fols 95v–96, The South Sea Company, Court Minutes, 30 May 1712.

Act, which he had presented to the Commons on 14 May.[94] This clause, drawn up by Francis Annesley, aimed to give the company ownership of the places that the company or its agents would 'take seize or Possess and not within the Limits of the Companys Charter but at present Possession of the Crowns of Spain or France and that exclusive of all others'. The court of directors agreed to offer this clause to the Commons after sounding out its disposition.[95] It should be noted that this clause theoretically afforded the company the right to seize Spanish or French colonies, not only in the South Sea but also in the Caribbean. Judging from this, it can be conjectured that Bateman and other directors tried to make the plan for the company's expedition more flexible by inserting this clause, considering the possibility that the fleet would not be provided by 15 June, the deadline for the South Sea voyage, to save the plan in which the company had already invested money. In any case, the clause was not offered to the Commons, because Bateman found that they were not disposed to receiving it.[96]

Although the deadline had passed, there was as yet no sign of the departure of the promised fleet. Probably frustrated with this slow progress, on 20 June, Bateman and three other directors – Robert Benson, the Chancellor of the Exchequer, Edward Harley and Arthur Moore – visited St John, who informed them that the queen would lend three warships to carry goods and sufficient force for the convoy and that 'all other Care should be taken to assist them in their First Onsett'. On the same day, following St John's recommendation, the company appointed a committee to confer with St John or other persons 'in Relation to the extraordinary Affairs of the Company'. Presumably, this committee was expected to serve as an intermediary between the government and the company over the issue of naval support.[97] Although the government promised the company that it would lend three warships, this was far from the company's original request, and it was evident by this time that it was too late to send an expedition to the South Sea that year. It was probably the general suspension of arms agreed by Britain and France in late July, and declared by the queen on 18 August, that put the final nail in the coffin of the company's plan for a military expedition. Thus, the South Sea expedition that the company originally planned did not materialise in the end.

As we have seen, in contrast to the eagerness of the directors, ministers were not responsive to the plan. How can we explain this lukewarm response, especially on

94 *C.J.*, XVII, p. 224, 14 May 1712. This bill was enacted as an 'Act for Continuing the Trade to The South-Seas, granted by an Act of the last Session of Parliament, although the Capital Stock of the said Corporation should be redeemed' (10 Anne c. 30).

95 BL, Add MS 25494, fols 96–96v, The South Sea Company, Court Minutes, 4 June 1712. Francis Annesley was a Tory MP of Irish origin, who was also involved in the preparation of the South Sea bill.

96 BL, Add MS 25494, fols 97v–98, The South Sea Company, Court Minutes, 13 June 1712.

97 BL, Add MS 25494, fols 99–99v, The South Sea Company, Court Minutes, 20 June 1712.

the part of Harley? Sperling claims that, although there were three plans for expeditions between 1710 and 1711 – an Anglo-Dutch expedition to the West Indies, the Quebec expedition and the expedition planned by the South Sea Company – Harley had no real desire for overseas military action.[98] It is true that he was strongly against the Quebec expedition promoted by St John. However, it would be an exaggeration to say that Harley ruled out any possibility of a naval expedition from the beginning.

The fact that Harley collected information about trade and expeditions to Spanish America, including the South Sea, shows that he had a continued interest in that region.[99] He had already started to gather opinion before the submission of the South Sea bills. As we saw in Chapter 4, in September 1710, Harley asked the opinion of the Earl of Halifax, one of the Junto Whigs, about the West Indian expedition, possibly to gather information for the Anglo-Dutch joint expedition, which was being considered at that time. After he proposed the South Sea bill to the Commons, Harley consulted regional experts about trade and expeditions to the South Sea. For instance, in July 1711, Admiral George Byng submitted to Harley a document giving professional advice about just such an expedition.[100]

At this point, it seems that Harley was still trying to find out whether military expeditions were a feasible option. This was not necessarily incompatible with the ongoing peace negotiations. As MacLachlan has pointed out, when Harley started the peace negotiations in July 1710, they were regarded as an insurance policy. Even when the discussion became more serious after the defeat in Spain in December 1710, possibilities other than peace had not been ruled out.[101] Moreover, Harley could not neglect the trade of the South Sea Company for political reasons: as a result of the controversy over the peace negotiations, the trade came to be regarded as one of the touchstones of the validity of the 'peace without Spain and West Indies'.

However, it seems that Harley gradually moved away from the idea of the South Sea expedition as a means to assist the South Sea trade, and he appears to have abandoned it completely by October 1711 when Britain finally reached an agreement with France, accepting the reduction of duties and a twenty-year extension of the Asiento in place of the coveted security ports. As T J. Denman has pointed out, it was probably the value that Harley placed upon diplomatic relations with the Netherlands, as well as opposition from France, that discouraged him

98 Sperling, *South Sea Company*, pp. 9–10.

99 The documents that Harley collected are found in BL, Add MS 70163, 70164, 70310.

100 BL, Add MS 70164 [not foliated], 'Some propositions relating to the fitting ships for the South Sea', George Byng to Harley, 20 July 1711. The other people who provided Harley with information included Thomas Bowrey, an East India merchant, John Pullen, ex-governor of Bermuda, Mitford Crowe, ex-governor of Barbados and Edmund Dummer, a civil engineer and the former Surveyor of the Navy (1692–99), who also started a packet service between Britain and her colonies in the West Indies.

101 A.D. MacLachlan, 'The Road to Peace, 1710–13', *Britain after the Glorious Revolution, 1689–1714*, ed. G. Holmes (London and New York, 1969), pp. 206–7.

from the idea.[102] He could not ignore relations with the Dutch, who were envious of and suspicious about the South Sea Company project and plan to establish a settlement in the region.[103] As MacLachlan says, unlike Jersey and St John, who did not scruple to obtain favourable terms for Britain at the expense of its allies, Harley was less willing to affront them.[104] The South Sea expedition could have been a bone of contention with the Dutch, so Harley had to consider the ramifications of securing settlements in Spanish America.

Instead, it seems that Harley was toying with the idea of conducting the South Sea trade without resorting to a naval expedition to the South Sea. In a letter sent to Harley, probably in 1711 or 1712, John Pullen mentioned that he was asked by Harley for his opinion of 'Our ensuing Trade to the So Sea, under the restrictions you [Harley] have it Conceded to you by the Spaniards'. In answer to this enquiry, Pullen proposed founding a settlement in the River Plate, which the Spaniards did not actually possess and which was close to recently discovered Portuguese gold mines, not by force, but with the consent of the Spaniards.[105] In the end, Harley abandoned the idea of a South Sea expedition and trade to the South Sea, settling instead on the Asiento and annual ships trades as more realistic options for the South Sea Company's mercantile activity.[106]

The cession of the Asiento to Britain had already been mentioned in July 1711 in the peace negotiations with France. However, it was initially brought up as a minor issue, not in connection with the South Sea Company but rather with the two African companies whose affairs were in great disorder.[107] As we have already

102 Denman, 'Political Debate', pp. 250–1.

103 BL, Add MS 70027, fols 205–205v, John Drummond to Oxford, 1/12 June 1711.

104 MacLachlan, 'The Road to Peace', 208.

105 BL, Add MS 70163, fols 233–233v [John Pullen], 'Paper on making settlements on the River Plate' [n.d., but 1711 or 1712?]. This manuscript was included in a pamphlet published in 1732, together with memoirs written by Pullen. Its preface mentioned that this letter was of a later date than the memoirs, which were composed in roughly 1711, and it appears to have been written 'when that Affairs was not thoroughly settled'. John Pullen, *Memoirs of the Maritime Affairs of Great Britain, Especially in relation to Our Concerns in the West-Indies* ... (London, 1732), pp. i–ii. As it was in March 1713 that the Asiento Treaty was signed, it can be conjectured that this letter was sent to Harley at some point in 1711 or 1712.

106 Although the plan to establish a British settlement at Buenos Aires did not materialise, after the war ended, the port gradually became an important base for the South Sea Company's contraband trade by land with Peru. In 1716, based on a new Asiento Treaty, the company was allowed to have storage there for goods left from bartering for slaves in Africa, which made the port more useful for the company. Walker, *Spanish Politics and Imperial Trade*, p. 139; George H. Nelson, 'Contraband Trade under the Asiento, 1730–1739', *AHR* 51, no. 1 (1945), 60.

107 Sperling, *South Sea Company*, p. 12; L.G.W. Legg, 'Torcy's Account of Matthew Prior's Negotiations at Fontainebleau in July 1711', *EHR* 29, no. 115 (1914), 531. In May 1711, Harley was informed about the Asiento by Edmund Dummer, who sent Harley a proposal that he had received in the middle stage of the war from Jewish merchants, when there was still hope that Charles III might be able to take control of Spain. BL, Add MS 70163, fols 171–2, 'Asientos' [n.d.], and fols 173–173v, Edmund Dummer to Harley, 19 May 1711.

seen, a more important issue in the early stages of the peace negotiations was whether Britain could obtain security ports in North and South America. It was this point with which the British government persisted, and to which the French government was vehemently opposed.[108] Presumably, it was not until September 1711, when the ministry surrendered the demand for security ports, that Harley came to regard the Asiento as a key privilege that the government could offer to the South Sea Company for its trade.

Thus, the company failed to obtain sufficient support for the South Sea expedition from the government. The ambitious plan for the South Sea expedition devised by the directors, who were driven by the need to secure settlements for successful trade, foundered on diplomatic considerations and on the practical difficulties faced by the naval administration. After the cessation of arms, the company planned a trading voyage without large-scale military forces. At the end of September 1712, it was lent two warships, the *Anglesey* and *Warwick*, which it had been soliciting to transport their cargoes.[109] Initially, the destination of the cargoes was still referred to as the 'South Seas', though it was soon replaced with 'Spanish West Indies'.[110] However, this plan for a trading voyage in 1712 was not carried out either. It was not until 1714 that the company started slave trading on the basis of the Asiento.

The plan for the South Sea expedition was not a mere bluff to assist Harley's peace negotiation. At least for the directors of the South Sea Company, it was a serious attempt to secure a trading base for the South Sea trade. With the benefit of hindsight, this grandiose plan for the expedition might look a farce. However, if we consider three factors that exercised great influence upon the company's trading policy at its embryonic stage, we can perceive the logic behind the plan. First, in terms of its trading business, the company was originally set up to launch a trade with the Spanish colonies on the Pacific coast, where French merchants were making rapid advances. It should be noted that this South Sea trade was a new channel of trade for Britain, and one that might collide with the interests of West Indian merchants who had traded with the Spanish colonies through the existing Caribbean route. Together with the issue of the political affiliation, these conflicting interests were probably what led to the exclusion of prominent West Indian merchants, such as Heathcote, from the directorates of the company, thus depriving the company of high-quality leadership.

Second, when the plan for the South Sea Company was first mooted, there was harsh criticism from the opposition, especially the Whigs, who pointed out the difficulties of the South Sea trade. This forced the government to defend the company's prospects by presenting a feasible blueprint for the trade. Through the

108 H.M.C. *Portland*, V, pp. 35–9, 'Prior's Negotiations in France', 12/23 July 1711.

109 BL, Add MS 25559, fol. 12v, Thomas Vernon, John Blunt, John Fellows and Henry Durley to Harley, 25 September 1712.

110 BL, Add MS 25495, fols 11, 15v, The South Sea Company, Court Minutes, II, 24 September, 15 October 1712.

controversy, it became clear to the directors and investors that the trade was practicable as long as the company possessed some settlements in Spanish America as trading bases, even if a right to free trade was not given.

Finally, however, at this stage, the directors were still uncertain as to what kind of privileges, including trading bases in Spanish America, would actually be granted by the peace treaty. Although there was an expectation of obtaining some security ports, the directors could not really count on this, as there was no guarantee that France would keep its promise. In fact, in September, the Harley ministry had given up the demand for the security ports in the peace negotiations. Thus, a military expedition to the South Sea was left to the directors as the only means to secure settlements. The success of this expedition was significant for the company, not only for the South Sea trade, but also to maintain its credibility and share price.

It should be emphasised that it was the directors, not Harley, who took the initiative in planning the South Sea expedition in January 1712. However, few of them had knowledge of either military expeditions or the South Sea trade, and the advice from the experts such as Rogers and Cooke enthusiastically pointed to the necessity and practicability of establishing a settlement at Valdivia. It seems that these factors made the directors push forward with their excessively ambitious plan.

Although the government initially promised to offer assistance for the expedition, the required force was not provided quickly enough. Harley was not necessarily dismissive of the Spanish-American expedition in 1710 and for most of 1711, as the success of the South Sea Company trade was politically important to him. However, the military expedition was too risky an option from a diplomatic standpoint, and it is possible that by late 1711 he had withdrawn his support. As a result, the company failed to obtain sufficient naval backing for its planned South Sea expedition, although several men of war, without any land force, were later lent to the company to help its trade. It was as a result of these diplomatic considerations and administrative difficulties that the plan for the South Sea expedition was shelved.

The ministry's abandonment of the plan and the government's acceptance of the Asiento treaty were watersheds in the rivalry for the Spanish-American market and the British policy towards it. Britain obtained a direct and legal channel to the Spanish-American market for the first time in her history, which gave Britain a great advantage, at least in theory, over her trading rivals, such as France and the Netherlands. As we shall see in Chapter 8, from this point on, the British government's policy in Spanish America focused on improving the conditions of the Asiento trade for the South Sea Company, as well as tacitly supporting the existing illicit trade via the West Indian colonies, such as Jamaica, although conflict between the company and private traders continued after the war.[111] On the other hand, the idea of naval expeditions to establish new colonies was set aside as too high risk an option, as such expedition might have ruined Britain's newly acquired privilege in the Spanish-American trade. As a result, the British government refrained from taking an aggressive policy towards the Spanish colonies until the late 1730s.

[111] Scammell, 'A Very Profitable and Advantageous Trade', 166.

PART III

Pro-maritime War Arguments after 1714

– 7 –

Pro-maritime War Arguments during the War of the Quadruple Alliance and Anglo-Spanish Conflict of 1726–29

This chapter analyses debates in the press and in Parliament over two conflicts with Spain in which Britain was involved from the 1710s to 1720s: the War of the Quadruple Alliance of 1718–20 and the Anglo-Spanish conflict of 1726–29. In particular, it reveals what role a pro-maritime war argument played in these debates, who supported the argument, and how their positions shifted as the conflict went on.

In the late 1730s, the pro-maritime war argument was basically used by the opposition to criticise the government. It is true that, as Philip Woodfine states, there were some sympathisers of the colonial maritime war within the Walpole ministry as well, but, at least in political debates in the press, it was one of the main weapons of the opposition.[1] However, as was shown in Chapter 3, the pro-maritime argument during the War of the Spanish Succession was employed by several different political groups for different purposes: to dispose the nation towards the war or to criticise the former government's war policy. In that period, the pro-maritime war argument was not necessarily a tool of the opposition to criticise the government. How and when did this change happen?

Kathleen Wilson has pointed out that the opposition after 1725, composed of the Tories and dissident Whigs, deliberately incorporated commercial and expansionist grievances into their propaganda.[2] The exploitation of the pro-maritime argument by the opposition can be regarded as a part of this process. However, because the focus of Wilson's study is the late 1730s, the process of change in the period between the end of the War of the Spanish Succession and the outbreak of the Anglo-Spanish War of 1739 is not made clear. She also ignores the clash of interests between two groups that were both concerned with Spanish-American trade: the South Sea Company and private merchants. This chapter traces the process by which the pro-maritime war argument became the opposition's weapon in the press, and reveals what kind of conflict of interests affected this process. First, we examine the pro-maritime war argument during the War of the Quadruple Alliance.

1 Woodfine, 'Ideas of Naval Power', pp. 72–4.
2 Wilson, 'Empire, Trade and Popular Politics', 96–9.

Pro-maritime War Arguments during the War of the Quadruple Alliance

European and Domestic Context

The main cause of the War of the Quadruple Alliance was a dispute between Spain and Austria over Italian territories.[3] Although the War of the Spanish Succession ended with the treaties of Utrecht, Rastadt and Baden, some issues remained unsettled. Among them was the conflict between Philip V of Spain and Emperor Charles VI over former Spanish territories in Italy, such as Milan, Sardinia and the Two Sicilies (Naples and the island of Sicily), which were ceded to Charles VI and Victor Amadeus II of Savoy after the war. Dissatisfied with these cessions, Philip V refused to conclude a peace treaty with Charles VI and waited for an opportunity to recover the territories. This dispute was also compounded by the desire of Elizabeth Farnese, the new queen of Spain, to secure the succession to the Italian duchies of Parma, Piacenza and Tuscany for her son, Don Carlos.

An Italian priest, Cardinal Alberoni, who had virtually taken charge of Spanish foreign policy by 1716, was slaving away at fulfilling his master's desire. Urged by Philip V of Spain and Elizabeth, Alberoni took the first step towards recovering the Italian territories in the summer of 1717, when Charles VI was still occupied with a war with the Turks. Alberoni dispatched a naval squadron, the fruit of his rebuilding of the Spanish navy, to Sardinia and captured it by force.

This expedition posed a serious threat to the safety of Britain and to equilibrium in Europe, which James Stanhope, a leading figure in British foreign policy in this period, was trying to preserve by a collective security system: alliances with major European powers such as France, Austria and the Netherlands to guarantee each other's title and territory. Britain had already concluded the Treaty of Westminster with Austria in May 1716 and the Treaty of the Triple Alliance with France and the Netherlands in January 1717. In the face of the Spanish expedition to Sardinia, Stanhope, along with the Abbé Dubois, who was in charge of French foreign policy, planned an additional alliance to put pressure on Spain. This resulted in the Treaty of Quadruple Alliance, which was initially concluded between Britain and France in July 1718 and later joined by Austria in August and by Savoy in November.

While the attempts to seek a diplomatic solution continued, Alberoni took further action and sent a force to Sicily in June 1718. In response, Britain dispatched a naval squadron under Admiral Sir George Byng to prevent the seizure of the island by Spain. Stanhope still believed that Spain would be deterred from her attempt by the presence of Byng's squadron.[4] To his dismay, however, the Spaniards did not stop their operations, which obliged Byng to attack the Spanish

[3] For the diplomatic and political background of the War of the Quadruple Alliance, see Williams, *Stanhope*, Chapters 11 and 12; Wolfgang Michael, *England under George I, Vol. 2: The Quadruple Alliance*, trans. Annemarie MacGregor and George E. MacGregor (London, 1939), Chapters 5–7.

[4] Williams, *Stanhope*, pp. 302–4.

squadron at Cape Passaro on 31 July, destroying and capturing many of their vessels.

Even this defeat did not force Spain to come to terms with Britain and her allies, mainly due to objections from Queen Elizabeth of Spain.[5] Therefore, in December 1718, Britain formally declared war on Spain, followed by France's declaration of war in January 1719. Now Spain was put on the defensive. A Jacobite expedition to Scotland under the Duke of Ormonde with the assistance of Spain ended in a fiasco in June 1719. Conversely, French troops commanded by the Duke of Berwick invaded Spain in April, which resulted in the capture of Fuentarabia and San Sebastian. These events finally made Philip V despair of winning the war, and he dismissed Alberoni in December. In January 1720, Philip V agreed to accede to the Treaty of Quadruple Alliance, by which Charles VI and Philip V formally recognised each other's title, sanctioning the succession of Queen Elizabeth's son to the Italian duchies. Thus the War of the Quadruple Alliance ended.

The British involvement in this conflict between Austria and Spain became the subject of a heated controversy both in the press and Parliament. For a better understanding of the controversy, we also have to look at the political situation in Britain in this period, which is known as the 'Whig schism'.[6] The succession of George I led to a purge of the Tories who were in power in the last years of Queen Anne's reign, because the new king held a grudge against them for their neglect of Hanoverian interests in the peace negotiations of the last war. The Whigs thus came to power in place of the Tories, but, in April 1717, mainly owing to differences over the Baltic policy, the Whigs split into two factions: one led by Stanhope and the Earl of Sunderland, who supported Britain's active commitment to European politics in order to secure the Utrecht settlement, and the other led by Viscount Townshend and Sir Robert Walpole, who were more hesitant about European commitment.

It was Stanhope and Sunderland who remained in power by winning favour with the new king, who wanted to use British resources to protect Hanoverian interests, while Walpole and Townshend moved into opposition and became fierce critics of the government. This conflict within the Whigs was further compounded by a bitter feud between the king and George Augustus, Prince of Wales, who joined the opposition with his entourage, which included Earl Cowper, Spencer Compton and the Duke of Argyll. Thus, the Stanhope–Sunderland ministry faced an opposition composed of several political groups: the Walpole–Townshend Whigs, the Prince and his supporters and Tories ranging from Hanoverian Tories, such as Sir Thomas Hanmer, to Jacobites, such as William Shippen. This was how matters stood when the debate over the War of the Quadruple Alliance took place.

[5] *Ibid.*, p. 319.

[6] On the 'Whig schisms' (or Whig split) of 1717, see William A. Speck, 'The Whig Schism under George I', *HLQ* 40, no. 2 (1977), 171–9. For the British commitment in the Baltic, the background of the schism, see John J. Murray, *George I, the Baltic and the Whig Split of 1717: A Study in Diplomacy and Propaganda* (London and Chicago, 1969).

Controversy over the War of the Quadruple Alliance and Pro-maritime War Arguments

As the prospects of war with Spain loomed large, controversy over the British commitment to a war emerged both in the press and Parliament.[7] The first point to be emphasised in the controversy in connection with the pro-maritime war argument is that it was the ministerial side that advocated the use of naval power in the conflict. The ministerial writers defended the preventative measures taken by the government: the dispatch of a fleet to the Mediterranean and later Byng's action against the Spaniards in the battle of Cape Passaro. For example, one ministerial pamphleteer called the navy, 'the first and best Means, either to prevent a War, or bring it to a successful Period', and supported the idea of sending a fleet to the Mediterranean.[8]

This exertion of naval force was defended on the grounds of securing British trade, which should be understood in the context of the anxiety of the British mercantile and financial community about the impact of the approaching war on trade. The possibility of war with Spain alarmed some Whigs and British merchants who had interests in the Spanish and Mediterranean trade, which was reported by several Jacobite correspondents in Britain; however, the extent of the panic they reported should be taken with a grain of salt, because it is possible that they overstated the vulnerability of the British economy. In June 1718, John Menzies, a Jacobite agent in Britain, reported that, while German ministers hoped Byng would act vigorously, 'the body of even our Whigs are mad to think of a war with Spain, by which our South Sea, Africa and Turkey trade must all sink'.[9] It was also feared that this damage to trade could trigger a financial crisis. In September, one Hugh Thomas reported that, because of the dire financial situation in Britain, which had huge debts and most of whose taxes had been mortgaged,

> all the people are almost mad and say that, if the King of Spain seizes our merchants' effects and proclaims war against us, our South Sea Company is undone and all our trade ruined. This will cause such a run on the Bank, South Sea, East India Company and Exchequer as must infallibly ruin the kingdom.[10]

In order to win the support of the mercantile community that was averse to war, the ministerial writers emphasised the necessity of curbing Spanish naval power to protect British commercial interests in the Spanish and Mediterranean trades. In a supposed letter from a reader, the *Whitehall Evening Post* of 29 November 1718 stressed that it was necessary for Britain to exert herself to prevent the growing power of Spain. Otherwise, it claimed, Britain would have to 'give up from this

[7] On the debate in Parliament over the war and the Treaty of Quadruple Alliance in general, see G.C. Gibbs, 'Parliament and the Treaty of Quadruple Alliance', *William III and Louis XIV*, ed. Hatton and Bromley, pp. 287–305.

[8] *A Letter to a Friend at the Hague, concerning the Danger of Europe, and particularly of Great-Britain* .. .(London, 1718), p. 32.

[9] H.M.C. *Stuart*, VI, p. 558, John Menzies to Lieutenant-General Arthur Dillon, 9/20 June 1718. Dillon was ambassador in Paris for 'James III' (James Francis Edward Stuart).

[10] H.M.C. *Stuart*, VII, p. 276, Hugh Thomas to the Duke of Mar, 1/12 September 1718.

Moment all her Pretences to the Trade either of the Mediterranean or Mexican Seas'.[11] Likewise, one Reeve Williams defended Byng's action at Cape Passaro by pointing out the danger of growing Spanish naval power, which would eventually allow Spain to take control of the trade and navigation to the Mediterranean as well as the Portuguese trade.[12] Moreover, to assuage people's anxiety over the war, the *Whitehall Evening Post* pointed out the foolishness of the Spaniards, who were trying to fight against the other three major European powers: Britain, France and Austria.[13]

At the same time, ministerial writers had to dismiss the opposition's claim that the allies were taking advantage of Britain and stressed that the measures against Spain would serve British interests. The *Whitehall Evening Post* argued that the war was not undertaken to aggrandise Austria and make the emperor the terror of Europe, but to prevent Spain from becoming 'the Terror of Great Britain, by ruining our Trade, overthrowing our Colonies, and destroying the Liberty of that Commerce'.[14] France, Britain's new ally, had to be defended as well. One ministerial pamphleteer praised France, who used to be 'our Terror and Aversion', as 'one of the Bulwarks of Europe's Liberties, a fast Friend to just Councils'.[15]

It should be noted that, although the ministerial writers defended the government's precautionary military measures in the press campaign, in reality, the ministers did not unanimously support the British commitment at the beginning of the conflict. In October, a dispute between Stanhope and Sunderland over Byng's action was reported, and Stanhope objected to Britain's entering into the war.[16] When a new parliamentary session opened in November, however, he supported the war in the House of Lords, together with other peers in the ministry such as the Earl of Sunderland and Baron Carteret.[17] In the House of Commons, the government's policy was defended by MPs such as James Craggs the younger, the Secretary of State for the South, Martin Bladen, a new leader of the Board of Trade, William Stanhope, diplomat and cousin of the Earl of Stanhope and Nicholas Lechmere, attorney general.[18]

11 *Whitehall Evening Post*, no. 33, 29 November to 2 December 1718.

12 Reeve Williams, *A Letter from a Merchant to a Member of Parliament, relating to the Danger Great Britain is in of Losing her Trade, by the Great Increase of the Naval Power of Spain* (London, 1718), p. 5.

13 *Whitehall Evening Post*, no. 53, 15 January to 17 January 1719.

14 *Whitehall Evening Post*, no. 33, 29 November to 2 December 1718.

15 *Observations and Remarks upon the Declaration of War against Spain …* (London, 1719), p. 16.

16 H.M.C. *Stuart*, VII, p. 417, H. Thomas to Mar, 20 October 1718. One informant for the Duke of Mar, a Jacobite peer, mentioned Sunderland, the Duke of Roxburghe and the German ministers of the king as persons who were suspected of abetting a rupture with Spain. H.M.C. *Stuart*, VII, p. 542, G. Home of Whitfield to the Duke of Mar, 3/14 November 1718.

17 H.M.C. *Stuart*, VII, p. 568, H. Thomas to the Duke of Mar, 13/24 November 1718.

18 H.M.C. *Stuart*, VII, p. 570, J. Menzies to Dillon, 13/24 November 1718.

The government's endorsement of the exertion of naval power was well represented in the king's speech on 11 November 1718. After referring to the obstinacy of the king of Spain and the reduction of the land force, it expressed trust in British naval power as a means to settle the dispute.

> Our Naval Force imploy'd in Concert with our Allies, will, I trust in God, soon put a happy End to the Troubles which the ambitious Views of that Court have begun, and secure to my Subjects the Execution of the many Treaties in Force relating to our Commerce.[19]

Thus, in this period, it was the government that advocated commitment to the conflict between Austria and Spain and the use of naval power as a deterrent.

By contrast, the opposition, both Whig and Tory, was averse to a commitment to the conflict, and criticised the use of British naval power in the Mediterranean. As we have seen, concern over the security of trade was used by the ministerial press as a reason for war, but the same security of trade was put forward by the opposition writers as a reason against war. One pseudonymous writer emphasised the importance of trade with Spain and Spanish America, including the Asiento trade, and deplored that England was committed to hostilities against 'their natural Ally and best Friend'. Then, the author warned that, by this war, Britain would lose not only Spanish trade but also trade to other parts of the world, especially Italy and Turkey, and fisheries to its rivals in trade such as the Netherlands and France.[20]

The objection against the war with Spain on economic grounds also can be seen in a petition from Norwich that highlighted the city's economic predicament caused by the loss of markets for woollen manufacture, the main industry of the city. The petitioners claimed that Spain, one of the chief markets for woollens, was 'torn once more from us by a seemingly unavoidable new War'. They also feared that it could lead to an interruption of the Levant trade, another large market for woollens, by the Spanish fleet in the Mediterranean and the confiscation of the goods of British merchants.[21]

Furthermore, to underscore the risk created by war with Spain, the opposition writers warned of the Spanish capability to fight a war, in contrast to the ministerial writers, who tried to play down Spain's power. The *Weekly Journal or Saturday's Post* of 11 January 1718 reported that a vast amount of money had recently been shipped from New Spain, which enjoyed better management than before, and claimed that the Spaniards were well provided with money for military preparation.[22]

19 *Chandler*, VI, p. 183.

20 *A Letter from a Merchant at Amsterdam, to His Correspondent in London* ([London] [1718]), pp. 1–2.

21 *The Humble Petition of the Mayor, Sheriffs, Justices, Aldermen and Common-Council of the City of Norwich; to His Majesty King George* ([Norwich?] [1718?]), p. 1. Given that one of the MPs for Norwich at that time was Robert Britiffe, a Whig who had a strong connection with Townshend and Walpole as their legal adviser, it is possible that the content of the petition partly reflected the view of the Townshend–Walpole Whigs as well as the general interest of the city of Norwich.

22 *Weekly Journal or Saturday's Post*, no. 57, 11 January 1718.

This opposition argument against commitment to war was closely connected with reluctance to supply British resources to the allies, especially to the emperor. The above petitioners deplored that Britain had to fight on behalf of the emperor, with whom Britain had no important commercial relations and who was 'a biggoted Papist, a Bloody Prosecutor of poor Protestants, and an implacable Enemy' to Britain, while they praised Spain as a country which 'generously gave us the Liberty of the South-Seas for the advantage of our Trade'.[23] Likewise, in *The Character of an Independent Whig*, Thomas Gordon, an active independent Whig writer working with John Trenchard, wrote with irony that it was 'a very uncommon, though perhaps a necessary Kindness' to use naval ships at great expense for the emperor and insinuated that there was a hidden reason for the government to do so.[24] He was implying that the government was trying to win the emperor's support in the question of the cession of Bremen and Verden, former Swedish duchies in Germany that George I coveted, in return for British naval assistance. This government policy of using British naval force for Hanoverian interests was another target of criticism by the opposition. After explaining the danger of losing trade because of the British involvement in the war, the author of *A Letter from a Merchant at Amsterdam* asked. 'Is not this done to gratify the Emperor, that he may secure *Bremen* and *Verden* for____ [Hanover]?'[25] Moreover, there was distrust of the French. In October 1718, in a fictitious letter from a reader, the *Weekly Journal or Saturday's Post*, edited by a Jacobite writer Nathaniel Mist, expressed suspicion that France might take control of the trade with Spain, by pretending to fight against Spain, but virtually leaving the war to Britain.[26]

Thus, the opposition was generally opposed to British involvement in the war, which, they believed, would only benefit untrustworthy allies. They also criticised the dispatch of Byng's fleet and his fight off Cape Passaro. This, however, does not mean that the argument for the exertion of naval power was completely absent on the opposition's side. Even among the opposition, there was support for naval force based on antipathy towards the standing army, a typical characteristic of the 'Country' pro-maritime war argument. For example, one ministerial writer referred to those who over-emphasised British naval power just to underplay the necessity of land force, without having any practical plan to strengthen the navy in an emergency. According to the writer, in an argument against the land force in the parliamentary session that started in November 1717, they contended that 'the chief Security of this Island consisted in a powerful Navy, such as may enable us to defend our own Coasts from Invasions, to protect our foreign Trade and to annoy a Public Enemy either in their own Country, or foreign Plantations on Occasion'.[27]

23 *Ibid.*

24 Thomas Gordon, *The Character of an Independent Whig*, 2nd edn (London, 1719), p. 15.

25 *Letter from a Merchant at Amsterdam*, p. 2.

26 *Weekly Journal or Saturday's Post*, no. 98, 25 October 1718.

27 *Letter to a Friend at the Hague*, pp. 28, 33. In this parliamentary session, Sir Thomas Hanmer, the leader of the Hanoverian Tories, used this argument. In his speech criticising the maintenance of the land force in peace time, he claimed, 'Our Situation is our natural Protection; our Fleet is our Protection', *Chandler*, VI, p. 169.

It seems that it was mainly the Tories who made this opposition pro-maritime war argument tinged with a 'Country' ethos. As Jeremy Black has pointed out, after the exile of Bolingbroke, who played a leading role in Tory foreign policy, the Tories reverted to a 'Country' policy that was against commitment in European politics, and many of them came to oppose a Hanoverian foreign policy. They also objected to the policy of George I and Stanhope of using British naval force for Baltic and Mediterranean affairs, which might lead to higher taxation and a larger army.[28] Some features of the above-mentioned opposition pro-maritime war argument corresponded closely to this political stance of the Tories.

In contrast, among the opposition, there was an argument supporting colonial maritime war on different grounds. In the *Weekly Journal or Saturday's Post* of 25 October 1718, when the possibility of war with Spain loomed larger after the battle of Cape Passaro, one fictitious writer by the name of 'Sir Andrew Politick' presented an argument against the British commitment to the conflict, which he called 'the Emperor's Quarrel'. Expressing distrust of allies such as Austria, France and the Netherlands, Sir Andrew claimed that embroilment in the conflict was not in Britain's interests, enumerating its possible negative consequences, such as a loss of Spanish trade, an increase in debts and the confiscation of British merchants' goods in Spain. In answer to this, Mist pointed out the profitability of maritime war against Spain in Spanish America: 'Jack Spaniard may be made to pay for the Supper, whoever pays for the Breakfast.' Mist, who had served in war ships in the West Indies, claimed that he was not 'so out of Love with a War at Sea' as Sir Andrew thought and that the Spaniards could 'never be brought by any new Measures, or new Management in the World to be a Match at Sea for the British Nation'.[29]

It is difficult to know Mist's intention in this article, especially given that he had been unfavourable to the British commitment to the conflict in February.[30] However, it should be remembered that Mist was a firm Jacobite and that Spain supported the exiled Stuart court at that time.[31] As Daniel Szechi has pointed out, support from major European powers gave the Jacobites various strategic advantages and, as far as the naval aspect is concerned, conflicts with European powers would have obliged the British navy to concentrate its forces on defence, which would prevent the navy from effectually blockading other parts of the British isles and consequently help the rebellion in those parts.[32] Mist might have had as similar idea in mind: by encouraging colonial maritime war, British naval forces could be diverted from home waters, which would facilitate Jacobite rebellion in Britain

[28] Jeremy Black, 'Parliament and the Political and Diplomatic Crisis of 1717–1718', *Parliamentary History* 3 (1984), 93.

[29] *Weekly Journal or Saturday's Post*, no. 98, 25 October 1718.

[30] *Weekly Journal or Saturday's Post*, no. 60, 1 February 1718, and no. 62, 15 February 1718.

[31] I am grateful to Professor Harry Dickinson for drawing my attention to the possible connection between the pro-maritime war argument and Jacobite strategy.

[32] Daniel Szechi, *The Jacobites: Britain and Europe, 1688–1788* (Manchester and New York, 1994), p. 86.

and a planned Spanish invasion under the Duke of Ormonde.[33]

Thus, it seems that there were some supporters of maritime war among the opposition in this period, although the reasons for their support varied. It should be noted, however, that they did not represent the mainstream opposition. In the parliamentary session of the winter of 1718, the opposition's argument in the debate over naval policy was dominated by criticism of the government's measures. In particular, they criticised Byng's attack on the Spanish fleet before the declaration of war as being contrary to the law of nations and as a cause that dragged Britain into an unnecessary war. In the House of Commons, this view was expressed vehemently by Robert Walpole, who claimed that giving sanction to the measures could have no other view than 'to skreen Ministers, who were conscious of having done something amiss, and, who having begun a War against Spain, would now make it the Parliament's War'.[34] Similarly, in the House of Lords, the Earl of Orford, Walpole's old patron, and Earl Cowper strongly criticised the British involvement in the war.[35] Thus, in Parliament, the government came under fierce attack from the opposition for its involvement in the conflict with Spain.

We can summarise two important points in the debate over the War of the Quadruple Alliance that we have seen thus far. First, it was the government that defended Britain's active engagement in the war in cooperation with the allies and the use of British naval force as a deterrent, whereas the opposition was averse to the commitment to war, expressing distrust of the allies. Second, however, both the government and opposition invoked the security of trade as a justification for their respective arguments. The government stressed the need to protect British trade in the Mediterranean and the West Indies by nipping Spanish naval power in the bud, whereas the opposition emphasised the danger of losing the Spanish and Mediterranean trade by embroilment in the war. As we shall see next, a similar argument was repeated in the debate in the beginning of the Anglo-Spanish conflict of 1726–29. However, in this case, it was Walpole and Townshend who were bombarded by a barrage of criticisms from the opposition.

Pro-maritime War Argument during the Anglo-Spanish Conflict of 1726–29

European and Domestic Context

The pro-maritime war argument appeared again during the period between 1726 and 1729, which saw an undeclared war between Britain and Spain. In 1725, the

[33] There is another possible interpretation. The author of this article could have been Defoe, who was a keen supporter of colonial expeditions. In this period, he was secretly employed by the government and contributed to Mist's paper from August 1717 until October 1724 to moderate its anti-Hanoverian and anti-Whig tone. Paul Chapman, 'Mist, Nathaniel (*d.* 1737)', *ODNB*. Therefore, it is possible that he wrote this article in order to lead the reader subtly to support the maritime war.

[34] *Chandler*, VI, p. 185.

[35] H.M.C. *Stuart*, VII, p. 568, Hugh Thomas to the Duke of Mar, 13/24 November 1718.

diplomatic situation in Europe took a dramatic turn.[36] Frustrated with the failure of the Congress of Cambrai, Spain approached Austria, which had increasingly become estranged from Britain over several issues including the establishment of the Ostend Company. This resulted in the First Treaty of Vienna between Austria and Spain in April and May 1725, an agreement joined by Prussia and Russia in 1726. According to this treaty, each monarch's possessions and successions were mutually recognised. Moreover, the emperor acknowledged Don Carlos' succession to the Italian duchies and promised to support Spain in recovering Gibraltar from Britain. In return, Philip gave to the emperor's ships not only most-favoured nation treatment but also permission to provision in any port in the Spanish dominions, which could open the door for the emperor's subjects to trade directly with the Spanish colonies.[37]

Alarmed by this rapprochement between Austria and Spain, in September 1725, Britain formed a new alliance with France and Prussia through the Treaty of Hanover, which guaranteed the possessions and commercial rights of each country inside and outside Europe. This treaty was joined by the Netherlands, Sweden and Denmark, although later Prussia dropped out of it. This treaty also provoked Austria and Spain to enter into another treaty in November, by which Philip V promised to subsidise Austria and, in return, Charles agreed to the marriage of his daughters to the sons of Philip and Elizabeth.

With tensions increasing between the two sides, Britain decided to dispatch three fleets as a deterrent: one to the Baltic to win the support of Sweden and Denmark and to contain the Russian fleet, one to Spanish waters to put pressure on Spain and to prevent the blockade of Gibraltar, and one to the West Indies. The main task of the West Indian fleet under the command of Admiral Hosier was to prevent the return of the Spanish silver fleets from America in cooperation with the fleet off the Spanish coast. This was a significant operation for Britain, because bullion and merchandise on board the fleets, some of which belonged to British merchants and those of her allies, was to be appropriated for the use of Spain and Austria. On the other hand, Spain opened hostilities by laying siege to Gibraltar in December 1726.

While the hostilities on both sides continued, a settlement of the dispute by diplomatic negotiations was sought. In May 1727, disappointed with the delay in the arrival of the promised Spanish subsidies, the emperor agreed to the preliminaries proposed by Britain and France to arrange for a new peace congress. However, because Spain refused to agree to terms, Britain continued to put pressure on Spain with a fleet under the command of Sir Charles Wager in Spanish waters.

With assistance from France, Britain finally persuaded Spain to accept the terms

36 For the diplomatic context of this period, see Jeremy Black, *British Foreign Policy in the Age of Walpole* (Edinburgh, 1985) and *The Collapse of the Anglo-French Alliance, 1727–1731* (Gloucester, 1987); G.C. Gibbs, 'Britain and the Alliance of Hanover, April 1725–February 1726', *EHR* 73 (1958), 404–30; Arthur M. Wilson, *French Foreign Policy during the Administration of Cardinal Fleury, 1726–1743* (Cambridge, MA, and London, 1936), Chapters 3–6.

37 Gibbs, 'Britain and the Alliance of Hanover', 409.

of the preliminaries. Consequently, the Convention of the Pardo was signed in March 1728, by which Spain promised to lift the siege of Gibraltar, to deliver up the *Prince Frederick*, a ship of the South Sea Company seized by Spain, and to restore the import duties to their usual rate, in return for Britain's promise to withdraw her fleets from Spanish waters and the West Indies. It was decided that other issues such as contraband trade with the Spanish colonies were to be discussed in the forthcoming congress, which opened in Soissons in June 1728.

However, this Congress of Soissons soon faced difficulties, and the provisional treaty proposed by the Hanover allies in August 1728 was spurned by Spain and Austria. There were still several thorny questions that hindered both parties from reaching an agreement, such as the suppression of the Ostend Company, the introduction of Spanish garrisons into the Italian duchies and the 'Spanish depredations', attacks on British merchantmen by the Spaniards in European and American waters on the grounds of searching for smugglers. In order to put further pressure on Spain, Britain assembled a large fleet in cooperation with the Netherlands in the summer of 1729.

The efforts of the Hanover allies finally bore fruit in November 1729. Disappointed with the emperor's resistance to the introduction of the Spanish garrisons in Italy, Spain agreed to conclude the Treaty of Seville with Britain and France, which stipulated the restoration of the commercial status of Britain and France to their pre-1727 conditions, the return of the *Prince Frederick* and the introduction of Spanish garrisons into several towns in Italy. Thus, the conflict between Britain and Spain saw a temporary settlement, although the issue of the Spanish depredations remained a bone of contention between the two countries.

Next, we turn to the domestic political context in Britain in this period.[38] As in European politics, a significant change occurred in British politics after the end of the War of the Quadruple Alliance. Many of the leading political figures in the late 1710s had gone by this time. Stanhope and the two Craggs died in the middle of the financial crisis caused by the collapse of the South Sea Company in 1720, which was soon followed by the death of Sunderland in 1722. The Stanhope–Sunderland faction, which had lost its leaders, was gradually replaced by Townshend and Walpole, who handled the crisis skilfully. Even after George II's succession in 1727, contrary to expectations, Walpole continued to hold power along with Townshend and the Duke of Newcastle.

[38] The political conflict of this period, especially the opposition's attack on the Walpole ministry, has been studied by several historians. See Howard F. McMains, 'The Parliamentary Opposition to Sir Robert Walpole, 1727–1731' (unpublished Ph.D. thesis, Indiana University, 1970); and Andrew A. Hanham, 'Whig Opposition to Sir Robert Walpole in the House of Commons, 1727–1734' (unpublished Ph.D. thesis, University of Leicester, 1992). On Bolingbroke's attempt to form a new coalition between the Whigs and Tories, see Isaac Kramnick, *Bolingbroke and his Circle: The Politics of Nostalgia in the Age of Walpole* (Cambridge, 1968); and Harry T. Dickinson, *Bolingbroke* (London 1970). Goldgar has dealt with this issue from a literary perspective. Bertrand A. Goldgar, *Walpole and the Wits: The Relation of Politics to Literature, 1722–42* (Lincoln, NE, and London, 1976).

There was a new movement in the opposition as well. Bolingbroke, who returned to Britain in 1725 after spending ten years in France in exile, planned to form a new coalition between the opposition Whigs and the Tories to subvert the Townshend–Walpole ministry. As a platform for this coalition, Bolingbroke set up an opposition newspaper, the *Craftsman*, with William and Daniel Pulteney and launched an active press campaign against the ministry. Although this coalition was not as successful as Bolingbroke expected owing to the differences in policy between the opposition Whigs and the Tories, it still posed a serious threat to the ministry. Thus, Walpole had to face a formidable challenge from the opposition, which adopted tactics similar to those used by Walpole himself in the late 1710s. It was under these circumstances that debate over the British commitment to the war took place.[39]

Controversy in the Early Stage of the Conflict: Threats to British Commerce and Naval Action against Spain

The formation of the Vienna alliance posed a serious threat to British commercial interests as well as to the Protestant succession and the security of British acquisitions such as Gibraltar and Minorca. In particular, Spanish support for the Ostend Company was a major concern for Britain and provoked an outcry against Austria. This issue was exploited by some of the opposition, such as Charles Forman, a Jacobite writer, to criticise the government for its inaction.[40] However, from about 1726 on, the issue was increasingly taken up by ministerial writers. As Gibbs has stated, although the supposed Austro-Spanish marriage alliance was more serious for the British government, it had to emphasise the threat from the Ostend Company in order to win the support of Parliament, as well as that of the Dutch, for the Treaty of Hanover.[41]

In the early stages of the controversy, the Ostend Company was regarded as a threat not only to British East Indian but also to West Indian interests, because it was feared that the permission given to the company to provision ships in any port in the Spanish dominion might open the way to direct Spanish-American trade by the company.[42] Moreover, the Ostend Company was also represented as a menace to British and Dutch naval power, because the company's trade could help to train seamen for the Austrian Netherlands.[43]

[39] On the overall picture of the debates, see McMains, 'Parliamentary Opposition'.

[40] Charles Forman, *Mr. Forman's Letter to the Right Honourable William Pulteney …* (London, 1725). William Pulteney, who was named in the title as the addressee of this letter, was a leader of the opposition Whigs and one of the main opponents of Walpole.

[41] Gibbs, 'Britain and the Alliance of Hanover', 409–10.

[42] *Ibid.*, 409. It was also reported by Dr William Stratford that, in the company's meeting at Brussels, the West Indian trade was included among the businesses that the company was resolved to start. H.M.C. *Portland*, VII, p. 407, Dr William Stratford to Edward Harley, second Earl of Oxford, 4 December 1725.

[43] *The Importance of the Ostend-Company Consider'd* (London, 1726), p. 31. This argument was repeated in 1730 by one ministerial pamphleteer who claimed that the greater concern to England than the threat to the British trade was that the company was 'setting up a new

The year 1727 began with a further increase in tensions between Britain and Spain. On 19 January, Viscount Percival reported from London frenzied shouts by the 'Mob', who gathered around the king when he went and returned from Parliament and 'were above 3000 crying out God save King George who protects our trade, down with the Jack Spaniards, No Pretenders &c'.[44] As diplomatic relations with Spain and Austria deteriorated, the issue of the Ostend Company came to be more closely connected to the government's argument against the Vienna Alliance. Ministerial writers such as Benjamin Hoadly, a Whig bishop with a strong connection to the government, emphasised that the company posed a serious threat to East and West Indian trade and to the naval power of Britain and the Netherlands.[45]

The menace of the Ostend Company was also invoked by ministerial writers to defend the dispatch of the fleets to Spanish waters and the West Indies, along with other issues such as Spanish claims to Gibraltar and Port Mahon and the Spanish depredations. The author of *The Tallies of War and Peace* maintained that, if any nation attempted to interfere with British trade, deprive Britain of her possession or force the Pretender upon Britain, 'we must have a War'. In answer to the accusation that it was Britain that had commenced hostilities by sending those fleets, the author claimed that they were sent not only to protect British trade but also to prevent military action planned by Austria and Spain, who were the real aggressors.[46]

Spanish military preparations for the siege of Gibraltar alarmed Britain further, and some ministerial writers tried to dispose the nation towards further action against the Vienna Alliance by using a pro-maritime war argument. Among them was Daniel Defoe. In a pamphlet entitled *The Evident Approach of a War*, Defoe repeated the official argument that Austria and Spain were the aggressors and claimed, 'War is begun already', because the invasion of British commercial interests by the Vienna Alliance was equivalent to an act of hostility. He defended the blockade by the British fleets in Spanish America to contain the silver fleet as well as that in the Baltic as a necessary and justifiable action to prevent war preparations by the Vienna allies, 'for Money appropriated for War, is War in Embrio'.[47]

To assuage people's anxiety over the impact of war on commerce and stock prices, Defoe argued that there was no need to fear Spain, which had neither silver

Naval Power in *Europe*, and that at our door, as it were, and in our Channel'. A.B., *The Treaty of Seville, and the Measures that have been Taken for the Four Last Years, Impartially Considered* (London, 1730), p. 6.

44 BL, Add MS 47032, fol. 2, Lord Percival to Philip Percival, 19 January 1726/7.

45 Benjamin Hoadly, *An Enquiry into the Reasons of the Conduct of Great Britain …* (London, 1727), pp. 71–4, 78; *Weekly Journal or British Gazetteer*, no. 90, 28 January 1727.

46 *The Tallies of War and Peace: or, What may be Expected from the Present Situation of Affairs in Europe* (London, 1727), pp. 21–3.

47 Daniel Defoe, *The Evident Approach of a War; and Something of the Necessity of It, in order to Establish Peace, and Preserve Trade* (London, 1727), pp. 15–17.

from the American colonies and the naval assistance from Russia that she had initially expected, nor an ally upon which she could depend for land and naval forces.[48] Instead, he encouraged the reader by emphasising the profitability of war against Spain, as in the first pro-maritime war argument during the War of the Spanish Succession:

> where is the Nation of the World that we can get more by, and are likely to lose less, by in case of a War? In how many Places in the World are they exposed even to our Adventurers and Letters-of-Mart Men, where they cannot defend themselves against five hundred Men, and yet have immense Riches to lose? How easie is it, not only to insult their *West-India* Colonies, but even to dispossess them; and to take from them the immense Riches of Mexico and Peru?[49]

One of the expected sources of profit was the capture of the Spanish silver fleet. Defoe claimed that one or two galleons that would fall into British hands might 'make us Amends for a whole Expedition'.[50]

He repeated this emphasis on the profitability of Spanish war in another pamphlet. Defoe admitted that it was difficult to prevent the silver fleets from returning to Spain completely. However, he claimed, even the occasional interception of a galleon 'would make the Fortune of the War go smilingly forward on our Side' and 'might make good a Summer's Service, and help the Government to carry on the War', which was a better method of raising money than land taxes, and at the same time, would certainly demoralise Spain and her allies. Then, Defoe quoted the saying, '*England* may Gain by a War with *France*, but never Loses by a War with Spain.'[51]

Another possible economic advantage of Spanish war was the opportunity for free trade with the Spanish colonies, which he once mentioned in the argument regarding the South Sea Company. If a war was started by Spain, Defoe argued, the belligerent countries would be freed from the obligations of the former treaties regulating the trade with the Spanish colonies. Consequently, this would open the way for Britain and her allies to conduct trade without breaching those treaties.[52]

Thus, in 1727, the ministerial writers defended the government's naval policy of sending fleets as a deterrent by emphasising the threat to British commercial interests as well as to British territorial security and to the Protestant succession posed by the Vienna Alliance. This argument was made along the same lines as the king's speech in the House of Commons on 17 January 1727.[53] Moreover, some writers such as Defoe went further and stressed the economic advantages of maritime war against Spain to dispose the nation towards a more active participation in the conflict, which bears a striking resemblance to the first pro-maritime war argument at the beginning of the War of the Spanish Succession.

48 *Ibid.*, pp. 3–7.

49 *Ibid.*, p. 9.

50 *Ibid.*, p. 53.

51 Daniel Defoe, *The Evident Advantages to Great Britain and its Allies from the Approaching War* (London, 1727), pp. 12–13.

52 *Ibid.*, p. 23.

53 The King's speech of January 1727 is in *Chandler*, VI, pp. 372–6.

By contrast, the opposition was against commitment to a war. We can see an objection out of 'Country' concern in a pamphlet entitled *Reasons against a War*, published in 1727. The pseudonymous author, 'Old Whig', opposed entering into a war against Spain unless it was absolutely necessary, pointing out several inconveniences that could be caused by the war, such as the cost of sea and land forces, the increase in land taxes and public debts, and the loss of several branches of trade.[54] The author deplored that Britain had to bear all these burdens for untrustworthy allies, especially the Netherlands and France: 'Without doubt we shall pay the Piper at last, as we have hitherto done, and they will parcel out the contended Advantages among themselves.'[55]

There was good reason for their concern. In 1727, owing to the increased expenditures caused by the conflict with the Vienna Alliance, the government was obliged to increase the land tax to its wartime level of four shillings, a measure that Walpole had tried to avoid. This would undoubtedly have deepened the anxiety of the landed interest about the effects of war.[56] Moreover, the mercantile community was alarmed by the possibility of military action against Spain. The pro-Tory *Farley's Exeter Journal* of 6 January 1727 reported that there was dissatisfaction among some traders who claimed that Hosier's blockade 'put an intire Stop to all Trade'.[57]

This concern over the possibility of war was seen in a debate in the House of Commons as well. In the parliamentary session that began in January 1727, a motion for an address of thanks for the king's speech asking for supplies for sea and land forces was opposed by both Tories, such as William Shippen, Sir William Wyndham, John Hungerford and Sir Thomas Hanmer, and by opposition Whigs, such as William Pulteney. They criticised the address for using some expressions that they believed were tantamount to a declaration of war.[58] Furthermore, they tried to refute the necessity for British commitment in the conflict by playing down the gravity of the threat from the Vienna Alliance. On the other hand, Wyndham criticised the inconsistency in the government's recent foreign policy of switching allegiance from Austria to France, which, he argued, would lead to the growth of the latter and consequently would drag Britain into continual wars under the pretence of maintaining the balance of power in Europe.[59] Nevertheless, in spite

[54] *Reasons against a War. In a Letter to a Member of Parliament* (London, 1727), pp. 11–12. There are many similarities between the content of this pamphlet and that of an article in the *London Journal* of 21 July 1722, which was one of the main opposition Whig papers at that time and was famous for 'Cato's Letters' by John Trenchard and Thomas Gordon. It can be conjectured that this pamphlet was based on that article.

[55] *Reasons against a War*, p. 21.

[56] Michael Jubb, 'Economic Policy and Economic Development', *Britain in the Age of Walpole*, ed. Jeremy Black (London, 1984), p. 135.

[57] *Farley's Exeter Journal*, 6 January 1727. Judging from the fact that this article also mentioned that these people were referred to as 'Enemies to our *Happy Constitution*', they might be merchants of Tory affiliation.

[58] *Knatchbull Diary*, p. 59, 17 January 1726/7.

[59] *Chandler*, VI, pp. 377–8.

of their vigorous attack, they could not win enough support in the House of Commons, and the motion for the address of thanks was carried by a majority of 251 against 81.[60]

Thus, at this stage, the opposition was generally opposed to the war owing to financial and commercial considerations. However, it seems that some of the writers with a 'Country' inclination accepted that war was necessary, on the condition that it was fought chiefly at sea, especially in the West Indies. The author of *Great Britain's Speediest Sinking Fund is a Powerful Maritime War* supported a colonial maritime war as a means to win a war more speedily and easily than a land campaign. In particular, the author advocated maritime war in the Spanish West Indies, the wealth of which had been a 'continual Source of all the Miseries of *Europe*' for the last hundred and fifty years and had also become one of the causes of the current conflict by providing subsidies to the emperor.[61] Although Britain had already amassed a huge amount of debt in the previous two wars, the author maintained that further financial problems could be avoided by fighting a maritime war in the West Indies:

> By sending such a well proportion'd Naval Force thither, as would tear the Power of *Spain* to pieces there, oblige them to pay the Expences of this necessary War, to which their Injustice has forced us, nay and perhaps compel them to be the Quickest sinking fund for the Debt of fifty Millions … or excite the *Mexicans*, the *Chilians* and the *Peruvians*, with the *Creolian Spaniards* to tear asunder the feeble Yoke of their impotent Master, to set up for themselves, and open a free trade to us.[62]

The author emphasised that this was practicable because of the 'contemptible Weakness' of the Spaniards in Spanish America and enumerated past examples of raids against the Spanish colonies or shipping, such as the expedition by Jamaican privateers in 1702 and Woodes Rogers' privateering voyage of 1708–11.

For a vigorous maritime war, he proposed giving privateers several encouragements such as head and bounty money, protection of their crews from impressment and speedy condemnation of prizes, for which purpose the Cruisers and Convoy Act and American Act of 1708 would serve as models.[63] Thus, also among the opposition, there was an argument that admitted the necessity of war

60 Although the opposition was against the war, they took a tougher attitude towards Spain on another important issue. This was the Spanish claim to Gibraltar, which was besieged by the Spaniards from February 1727 and was on the negotiation table for the preliminaries. The *Craftsman* was strongly opposed to giving it up to Spain, emphasising its importance in controlling navigation in the Mediterranean. *Country Journal or The Craftsman* [hereafter, *Craftsman*], no. 35, 3 April 1727, and no. 36, 10 April 1727.

61 *Great Britain's Speediest Sinking Fund is a Powerful Maritime War, Rightly Manag'd, and Especially in the West Indies* (London, 1727), pp. 2–4, 11–13.

62 *Ibid.*, pp. 14–15.

63 *Ibid.*, pp. 15, 18–19.

on the condition that Britain confined her war effort to a colonial maritime war.[64] This, however, seems to have been rather an isolated opinion.

As we have seen, in the controversy in the early stage of the Anglo-Spanish conflict of 1726–29, the government defended its policy of using naval force as a deterrent by emphasising the threat posed by the Vienna Alliance to British commercial interests. Moreover, when tensions with Spain further increased, some of the ministerial pamphleteers such as Defoe used the pro-maritime war argument to dispose the nation towards further action against the Vienna Alliance. On the other side, apart from an opinion in favour of maritime war in the West Indies from the 'Country' viewpoint, the opposition was generally against Britain's involvement in a war, expressing concern over its costs, mistrust of the allies and its impact on trade. Thus, at this stage, the argument on each side was strikingly similar to that of the War of the Quadruple Alliance. However, as we shall see next, the positions of both sides gradually interchanged.

Controversy in the Middle Stage of the Conflict: Peace Negotiations with Spain and Criticism of the Naval Policy

In the first half of 1728, the ministerial press continued their defence of the government's measure of using the fleets as a deterrent and extolled its success.[65] The focus of the argument, however, gradually shifted after the hostilities ceased with Spain's accession to the Convention of the Pardo in March and the opening of the Congress of Soissons in June 1728.

While the negotiations with Spain were ongoing, the ministerial writers switched their focus to a defence of the peace talks, although they continued to emphasise that Britain could exert her naval power to subdue Spain whenever she wanted. For example, in answer to the argument of 'the sanguine Part of this nation' that the British navy should have taken more aggressive measures against the Ostend Company and the Spanish fleets, the *London Journal* of 3 August 1728 claimed that Britain intentionally chose a peaceful solution. However, even if these negotiations should fail, the *London Journal* said, Britain could do herself justice: 'the *British* Fleet has that undoubted Strength and Sufficiency, that should we proceed to any vigorous Resentment, we might soon destroy all the Naval Power and Commerce of *Spain*'.[66]

Conversely, by 1728, the opposition had shifted the focus of its criticism from embroilment in the conflict to the measures taken by the government during the

64 The possibility that the above pamphlet was written by a ministerial pamphleteer in order to appease those who opposed the war out of 'Country' concerns cannot be denied.

65 For example, see *Weekly Journal or British Gazetteer*, no. 140, 27 January 1728, and no. 151, 13 April 1728.

66 *London Journal*, no. 470, 3 August 1728. A similar claim was repeated in a later issue to refute the *Craftsman*'s ironical remark that Britain chose to suffer herself 'out of good Nature' instead of punishing the enemy. *London Journal*, no. 473, 24 August 1728; *Craftsman*, no. 111, 17 August 1728.

conflict. One of their main criticisms was the government's alleged timidity during the period of hostilities. In the debate in the House of Commons over the address of thanks to the king's speech of 23 January 1728, William Shippen reproached the government for using Hosier's squadron as a mere deterrent and blamed the squadron for 'not having rifled the galleons at Carthagena, and plundered Porto Bello'. This was soon supported by Sir William Wyndham, who argued that the measures adopted by the government had only led to the renewal of lengthy negotiations in a different place, instead of removing the difficulties.[67]

Although their arguments did not win enough support in Parliament, this issue became a stick with which the opposition press beat the government. The *Craftsman* of 23 November 1728 claimed that the negotiations were unlikely to bring Britain's demand into the preliminaries and that the government could have forced Spain to come to terms with the Hanover Alliance more speedily and effectively, if it had allowed Admiral Hosier to seize the galleons and had used them as a trump card in the negotiations with Spain.[68]

In answer to these criticisms, ministerial writers stressed that the blockade had successfully prevented the enemies' design by depriving them of their financial resources and had compelled Spain to ratify the preliminaries. They also pointed out that the seizure of the galleons could have caused possible friction with other countries, especially the allied countries, because some of the galleons' cargoes belonged to merchants of those countries.[69] Another argument used by the ministerial writers was that the treasure on board the galleons had already been unloaded when Hosier arrived in the West Indies. The *British Journal* of 11 January 1729 referred to this possibility.[70] Likewise, one pamphleteer argued that Hosier would have taken nothing but the empty hulks of the ships, quoting a letter from Hosier, which mentioned the possibility of the Spaniards sending money secretly by other routes.[71]

67 William Coxe, *Memoirs of the Life and Administration of Sir Robert Walpole*, II (London 1798, repr. London, 1800), pp. 38–9.

68 *Craftsman*, no. 125, 23 November 1728.

69 *London Journal*, no. 492, 21 December 1728; Benjamin Hoadly, *A Defence of the Enquiry into the Reasons of the Conduct of Great-Britain …* (London, 1729), pp. 30–2.

70 *British Journal or The Censor* [hereafter, *British Journal*], no. 52, 11 January 1729. See also *British Journal*, no. 83, 2 August 1729.

71 *Observations on the Conduct of Great Britain, with regard to the Negociations and Other Transactions Abroad* (Edinburgh, 1729), pp. 17–18. Hosier mentioned a rumour about the Spaniards' sending money on board the galleons from Panama around Cape Horn, although he doubted that they would actually attempt it. TNA, SP 42/80, fol. 55, 'An Account of my proceeding since my last from Tibrun [Tiberon] Bay to your Grace' [n.d., but about June 1726]. This possibility was reported also to Walpole. BL, Add MS 32687, fol. 202v [the Duke of Newcastle] to Sir Robert Walpole, 5 November 1726. Likewise, Woodes Rogers was highly sceptical about the possibility, although he thought it possible that they might transfer the money from Panama to Vera Cruz and then send it to Spain via Havana with the *flota*. BL, Add MS 32748, fols 317–318v, Woodes Rogers and Jonath[an] Dennys to Townshend, 10 November 1726. As we shall see in the next chapter, it was the latter plan that the Spaniards actually adopted.

These arguments provoked further criticisms from the opposition writers. The *Craftsman* of 4 January 1729 expressed doubt as to whether the blockade really achieved its end, by pointing out that Spain had not yet formally given up the claim to Gibraltar. By contrast, the *Craftsman* claimed, taking the galleons would have been a more effective, quicker and far less costly means of subduing Spain than the blockade, and it would have given Hosier time to take the *flota*, too. Moreover, the treasure on board could have been kept as a security for indemnifying the British merchants for their losses.[72] Likewise, Bolingbroke claimed that Britain had not yet received anything to make up for her expenses and loss during the period of hostilities or reached a final settlement on several issues, such as the Spanish claim to Gibraltar and the confiscated properties of the South Sea Company.[73]

As to the cargoes of the merchants of other countries, the *Craftsman* argued that Britain could have cleared her name by restoring them immediately and could not have been blamed by Spain, because Spain herself had started hostilities, a similar logic to that used by ministerial writers to defend the dispatch of Hosier.[74] Likewise, Bolingbroke maintained that the French and Dutch would have believed that their properties were as secure in Britain's hand as in Spain's.[75] In response to the claim that the cargo had already been unloaded before Hosier's arrival, Bolingbroke argued that, even if that had been the case, it could not have justified the government's instruction for not seizing the galleons, because the government could not have known that the galleons' cargo holds were empty when it drew up the instruction.[76]

Thus, Hosier's blockade became one of the central issues in the debate between the government and opposition. In this debate, while the ministerial writers continued to defend the policy of the blockade, the opposition came to agitate for a more aggressive naval policy against Spain and criticised the government for not having allowed Hosier to seize the galleons.

There was another important maritime issue that was exploited by the opposition in the pamphlet war to stir up anger against Spain and the government: the protection of British trade in the West Indies. This issue was discussed as two different, but closely connected problems: the Spanish depredations, and the government's alleged refusal to issue letters of marque and reprisal to the British merchants who had suffered from the Spanish depredations.

72 *Craftsman*, no. 131, 4 January 1729.

73 Viscount Bolingbroke, *The Craftsman Extraordinary; containing an Answer to the Defence of the Enquiry into the Reasons of the Conduct of Great-Britain* (London, 1729), p. 62.

74 *Craftsman*, no. 131, 4 January 1729.

75 Bolingbroke, *The Craftsman Extraordinary; containing an Answer to the Defence of the Enquiry*, p. 60.

76 *Ibid.*, pp. 58–9. Bolingbroke carried on his criticism in another pamphlet, pointing out some unrealistic parts in Hosier's instruction. Viscount Bolingbroke, *The Craftsman Extraordinary. Being Remarks on a Late Pamphlet, Intitled, Observations on the Conduct of Great Britain* (London, 1729), pp. 2–4.

The 'Spanish depredations', the capture of British merchant vessels by Spanish 'Guarda-Costas' (coast guards) on the grounds of illicit trade with the Spanish colonies, became a problem after the conclusion of the Treaty of Utrecht and continued to be a bugbear for the British merchants trading in the West Indies.[77] One of the criticisms of the opposition regarding this issue was that the naval ships stationed there did not provide sufficient protection from the depredations for British merchants. Bolingbroke maintained that the protection of trade was regarded as a secondary consideration in the instructions to Hosier, while the interception of the galleons was given first priority. Rather, he claimed, the trade was disturbed by the impressment to supply war ships with manpower, which was diminishing during the blockade.[78] Likewise, the *Craftsman* of 21 December 1728 deplored that Hosier's squadron had not been used to prevent or retaliate against the Spanish depredations.[79] However, as the next chapter will reveal, in this respect, the opposition's criticism was unfair, because Hosier had tried to protect the interests of merchants trading there.

The opposition also attacked the government for its alleged refusal to issue 'letters of marque and reprisal', official permission to recoup losses by taking vessels and effects belonging to the country whose ships had attacked British ships in peace time.[80] In the early stage of the conflict, these letters of reprisal had already been mentioned in one pamphlet as the 'most effectual Method' to redress the losses caused by the Spanish depredations, given the difficulties and delays commonly entailed in the process of obtaining satisfaction by soliciting Spanish

77 Not only illicit traders but also lawful traders were sometimes taken by the Guarda-Costas, being suspected of smuggling. In particular, those British ships that returned to Britain either through the Windward Passage or the Gulf of Florida had to sail near the Cuban coast and often became their victims. Richard Pares, *War and Trade in the West Indies, 1739–1763* (Oxford, 1936, repr. London, 1963), pp. 22–4.

78 Bolingbroke, *The Craftsman Extraordinary. Being Remarks on a Late Pamphlet, intitled, Observations on the Conduct of Great Britain*, pp. 4–5.

79 *Craftsman*, no. 129, 21 December 1728.

80 There was originally a legal distinction between commissions given to privateers in war time and letters of marque and reprisal (or letters of reprisal) given in peace time to permit those who had been attacked by foreign ships to recoup their losses by force. Nevertheless, by the seventeenth century, this distinction had become blurred, and the words 'letters of marque and reprisal' came to be applied also to commissions to privateers and armed merchantmen. Francis R. Stark, *The Abolition of Privateering and the Declaration of Paris* (New York, 1897, repr. Honolulu, HI, 2002), pp. 53–5; and Starkey, *British Privateering Enterprise*, pp. 20–1. There was similar confusion about the terminology in the controversy examined here, and several variations, such as 'letters of marque and reprisal', 'letters of marque' and 'letters of reprisal', were used. It seems that what they referred to were generally 'letters of marque and reprisal' in the original sense: permission for retaliation in peace time. However, one opposition pamphleteer pointed out this confusion and claimed that the British government should have issued 'letters of marque' (i.e. privateering commission), because the Spanish government had already issued them as in war time. *A Letter to Caleb D'Anvers, Esq; Occasioned by the Depredations Committed by the Spaniards in the West-Indies* (London, 1729), pp. 13–16.

colonial governors.[81] The *Craftsman* blamed the government for neglecting trade protection, insinuating that it refused to issue these letters of reprisal to the British merchants.[82] The motif of the glorious reign of Queen Elizabeth was employed to support the argument as during the War of the Spanish Succession. The *Craftsman* compared the current lamentable situation with the reign of Queen Elizabeth, who was believed to have actively fought against Philip II of Spain, seized his effects and applied them to the service of her government, issued letters of reprisal, destroyed the Spanish fleet and assisted fellow Protestants in France and the Netherlands without neglecting the interests of her own subjects.[83]

In response to these criticisms, the author of *Observations on the Conduct of Great Britain* maintained that the government had taken sufficient care to protect British merchants' properties in the instructions to Hosier. As for the letters of marque and reprisal, the author mentioned the commencement of the peace negotiations with Spain as the reason that the government had deferred their issue.[84] Moreover, the *British Journal* pointed out the ineffectiveness of the letters of marque and reprisal as a means to recover losses from Spain, because she had only a small mercantile marine.[85] These arguments, however, could not silence the opposition writers, and they continued to attack the government on this point.[86]

These questions of Spanish depredations and the alleged neglect of trade protection were connected with another controversy over the Spanish-American trade. This reflected the clash of interests between the South Sea Company and private traders engaged in trade with the Spanish colonies via Cadiz or Jamaica, which was mentioned in Chapter 6.[87] In this dispute, the opposition advocated private traders and criticised the South Sea Company for its monopoly and unprofitability. In a fictitious letter to the editor, the *Craftsman* of 11 November 1727 claimed that the company had failed to carry out its original plan, trade to the South Sea, and instead accepted the unprofitable annual ship trade while

[81] Person Who Resided Several Years at Jamaica, *The State of the Island of Jamaica* (London, 1726), pp. 24–5.

[82] *Craftsman*, no. 125, 23 November 1728, and no. 133, 18 January 1729.

[83] *Craftsman*, no. 137, 15 February 1729.

[84] *Observations on the Conduct of Great Britain*, pp. 19–20, 34–7.

[85] *British Journal*, no. 63, 8 March 1729.

[86] For further criticism from the opposition writers on this issue, see, for example, Nicholas Amhurst, *Some Farther Remarks on a Late Pamphlet, Intitled, Observations on the Conduct of Great-Britain* (London, 1729); and Bolingbroke, *The Craftsman Extraordinary. Being Remarks on a Late Pamphlet, Intitled, Observations on the Conduct of Great Britain.* Bolingbroke even wrote a pamphlet anonymously that seemingly defended the government's policy but was actually intended to fuel controversy, insinuating that letters of marque and reprisal were requested by the West Indian merchants to cover up their illicit trade with the Spanish colonies. This argument was soon countered by Nicholas Amhurst in his *Some Farther Remarks*. Viscount Bolingbroke, *One word with the Craftsman Extraordinary* (London, 1729), pp. 16, 19.

[87] A similar conflict between a chartered company and private traders was seen in the case of African slave trade. See, for example, Pettigrew, 'Free to Enslave'.

excluding other British subjects from the trade within the area where the company was given a monopoly. The *Craftsman* argued that this damaged the Spanish-American trade formerly conducted by private traders, in which Britain could make a profit without causing the jealousy of other countries, and advocated freedom of trade, which was 'the Spring of Riches, and the Animal Spirits of any Nation'.[88] The *Craftsman* also blamed the directors of the company for their involvement in the illicit trade, which, it was claimed, was not only harmful to private traders but also gave the Spaniards an excuse for their misconduct, such as the detention of the *Prince Frederick*, an annual ship of the company, the seizure of British ships and the refusal of the preliminaries.[89] Moreover, using the allegory of the Portuguese Asiento Company, the *Craftsman* satirised the corrupt directors of the South Sea Company and their influence on ministers who had overlooked insults to the nation by the Spaniards, lest the company's properties should suffer.[90]

By contrast, the government defended the South Sea Company, which still played an important role in the British economy even after the South Sea Bubble, not only as a financial institution but also as a trading company.[91] In reply to an accusation that the private trade with Spanish colonies via Jamaica was ruined by the company's trade, which started after the War of the Spanish Succession, one pamphleteer defended the company, attributing the decline of the Jamaican trade to other causes, such as the over-supply of commodities resulting from the resumption of the regular dispatch of the silver fleets, attacks by the Jamaican privateers on Spaniards trading with the British merchants, and the South Sea trade by the French.[92] Likewise, one ministerial pamphleteer criticised the opposition for providing the king of Spain with an argument against the restitution of the *Prince Frederick* by their complaining about the company's illicit trade.[93] Thus, the conflict between the South Sea Company and private traders over the Spanish-American trade was closely intertwined with the opposition's criticism of the alleged neglect of trade protection by the government.

Controversy in the Middle Stage of the Conflict: Debates in the Parliamentary Session of 1729

The controversy between the government and the opposition over the issue of maritime affairs in the West Indies also arose in Parliament. As in the pamphlet war, the issue of instructions to Hosier provided the opposition with a strong

88 *Craftsman*, no. 71, 11 November 1727.

89 *Craftsman*, no. 61, 2 September 1727; no. 68, 21 October 1727; and no. 96, 4 May 1728.

90 *Craftsman*, no. 65, 30 September 1727.

91 Sorsby estimates that the company controlled more than 25 per cent of all British exports to Spain and her American colonies in the period between 1715 and 1732. Victoria G. Sorsby, 'British Trade with Spanish America under the Asiento 1713–1740' (unpublished Ph.D. thesis, University of London, 1975), pp. 425–6.

92 *An Answer to a Calumny: with Some Remarks upon an Anonimous Pamphlet … entitled, Some Observations on the Asseinto trade … by the Factor to the South-Sea Company …* (London, 1728), pp. 8–9, 71–2.

93 *Observations on the Conduct of Great Britain*, pp. 56–7.

weapon to attack the government. On 21 January 1729, in the debate over the address for thanks in the House of Commons, William Pulteney referred to a ministerial pamphlet, *Observations on the Conduct of Great Britain*, which defended the government's policy of blockade by quoting from the instructions to Hosier. He claimed with irony that this pamphlet must be based on imperfect copies of the instructions, because it was full of inconsistency and mistakes. Also, Captain Edward Vernon, an opposition naval officer who would become famous for an attack on Porto Bello about ten years later, supported Pulteney's argument, pointing out the inconsistency and impracticability of those instructions.[94]

On 31 January, Vernon launched an attack again, claiming that the station to which Hosier was appointed was wrong. In answer to this, Sir Charles Wager, the first Lord of the Admiralty, argued that the station was appropriate for taking both the *galeones* and *flotas*, if they emerged from the ports. At the same time, Wager claimed that it would not have greatly damaged the king of Spain even if Hosier had actually taken the silver fleets, because a large part of the money on board belonged to private persons and some of the king's money was usually used for the service of the Spanish colonial government.

A remark on Wager's explanation made by Sir John Barnard, a London merchant and one of the MPs for the City, shows that the interests of the merchants who supported the opposition were not always in accord with those of opposition politicians. While refuting Wager's argument that the treasure on board the silver fleets was not so important for the king of Spain as people imagined, he admitted that blockading was the best way to keep the merchants' cargoes safe and that the government's decision not to rush into war was right.[95] As seen in this statement, there seems to have been a strong aversion to war, especially with Spain, even among those merchants affiliated with the opposition. This objection to war out of concern over its impact on trade can be seen in a letter from a reader that appeared in the opposition Tory press *Fog's Weekly Journal* of 9 August 1729. The supposed author of the letter introduced an English proverb, '*Peace with Spain, and War with all the World besides*', and wished for 'a firm and lasting Peace with Spain' in fear of losing the Spanish-American market to France, which was believed to be encroaching on the market while British relations with Spain soured.[96] However, even though the mercantile community might be sympathetic to the government's policy of avoiding war, when it came to the issue of trade protection, they often became fierce critics of the government. Actually, Barnard concluded the above-mentioned remark by blaming Wager for neglecting the protection of trade.[97]

94 *Chandler*, VII, p. 35.

95 H.M.C. *Egmont Diary*, III, pp. 339–40, 31 January 1728/9.

96 *Fog's Weekly Journal*, no. 46, 9 August 1729. A similar saying, '*Give* Spain *peace with* England *and War with all the World*', was mentioned as an old Spanish proverb in a paper that supported the Treaty of Seville. *Political State*, January 1730, p. 48.

97 H.M.C. *Egmont Diary*, III, p. 340, 31 January 1728/9.

Barnard, along with Micajah Perry, a prominent tobacco merchant, and William Pulteney, played a leading role in the attack on the government on this issue in the Commons. On 21 January 1729, a motion for an address of thanks to the king's speech was proposed by Sir George Oxenden, a commissioner of the Board of Admiralty. To this address, Barnard proposed adding a promise to support the king to 'restore the commerce of the kingdom', in order to draw attention to the issue of Spanish depredations and the government's alleged neglect of trade protection. Walpole did not oppose this motion outright, probably because he was well aware of discontent in the City with him, caused by a slump in trade and unfavourable exchange rates, which was reported by Lady Irwin.[98] However, Walpole tried to soften the effects of this motion and suggested using the word 'secure' instead of 'restore', claiming that 'restore' implied that the trade had been lost and that there were already measures to address this issue in the preliminaries. In the end, Walpole's argument carried the day and the word 'restore' was left out.[99]

Undeterred by this defeat, the opposition soon resumed their attack on the government. On 21 February 1729, Sir John Barnard submitted to the House of Commons a petition from the merchants trading with the American colonies that complained about the Spanish depredations, the lack of means to recover their losses and the cruel treatment by the Spaniards of British captives.[100] Likewise, on 13 March 1729, a petition was proposed by Portuguese, Spanish and Italian merchants, asking for help in recovering their properties seized and confiscated by the Spaniards.[101]

In the committee of the whole house chaired by Thomas Winnington to examine the merchants' petitions, two points became the centre of debate.[102] The first was the alleged unhelpfulness of the government in the merchants' attempt to recover their losses caused by Spanish depredations. One merchant who was called in by the committee stated that, when he demanded letters of reprisal from Townshend, Secretary of State for the North, he was told to apply first for restitution through the diplomatic negotiations at the Congress of Soissons. However, another merchant explained that an account of the losses that he submitted to the congress was not accepted by the Board of Trade, which Martin Bladen, a leading member of the Board, strenuously denied.[103]

The other point was about convoys. The merchants complained that there was not a sufficient number of naval ships to protect them in the West Indies and the Mediterranean, and, although they had made applications for convoys, they were

98 H.M.C. *Carlisle*, p. 57, Lady A. Irwin to Lord Carlisle, 6 February 1729.

99 H.M.C. *Egmont Diary*, III, p. 330, 21 January 1728/9; *Chandler*, VII, pp. 34–5.

100 *Chandler*, VII, p. 43; *Knatchbull Diary*, pp. 86–7, 21 February 1729.

101 *Cobbett*, VIII, col. 683.

102 There was a division over who should be the chairman of this committee on 6 March 1729. Winnington, an opposition Tory turned one of the leading government spokesmen in the House of Commons, defeated Barnard, the opposition candidate, and was chosen as the chairman by a majority of 252 against 133, which shows the dominance of the government party in the Commons. *Knatchbull Diary*, p. 89, 6 March 1729.

103 *Knatchbull Diary*, p. 90, 11 March 1729.

refused or delayed. Barnard and Perry pushed ahead with this issue and proposed a motion to accuse the government of the neglect of trade protection. Yet this was countered by Walpole, and their motion was not carried.[104]

The opposition's last attack on the government over naval affairs in this session was also unsuccessful. On 2 April 1729, Daniel Pulteney, the brother of William Pulteney, proposed a motion that the instructions to Hosier were 'impracticable, insufficient, and restraining him from doing justice to his nation and from protecting the trade'. This was rejected by a large majority.[105]

All in all, in these debates in the House of Commons over Hosier's instruction and the Spanish depredations the government managed to defend itself. This can be seen in the content of the resolution adopted on 2 April 1729 by the committee to examine the merchants' petitions. Although the resolution did refer to the damage caused by the Spanish depredations, the government's responsibility for it was not mentioned at all. Instead, it praised the instructions to Hosier, claiming that it had protected the interests of the subjects of Britain and her allies who had their cargoes on board the fleets, hindered the enemy from appropriating the treasure for their use and prevented war from breaking out.[106]

The opposition's attack on maritime affairs was not confined to the House of Commons. There was a similar attack launched in the House of Lords. Abel Boyer reported that, on 18 April 1729, it was proposed to resolve that the expense of Hosier's dispatch, which had been born by Britain alone, was an unreasonable burden. Although this resolution was not passed, several peers protested against this rejection.[107] The main thrust of the protest signed by these lords can be reduced to two points. First, the protest expressed the dissatisfaction with the allies, especially France, which was an undertone of the opposition's criticism of the government. The protest complained that only Britain bore the burden of the expense for military operations, drawing the entire resentment of Spain upon her, while France would not share the burden, even though she allegedly had larger cargoes on board the fleet, but rather took this opportunity to enlarge her trade with Spain by reconciling with her. Second, the protest pointed out the failure of the operations in terms of cost-effectiveness, which not only had cost Britain an immense amount of money but also failed to settle the dispute between the two countries and to obtain satisfaction for the losses caused by the Spanish depredations.[108] However, these protesters seem to have been in the minority in the House of Lords, and their argument was countered by peers on the government

[104] *Knatchbull Diary*, pp. 93–4, 27 March 1729.

[105] H.M.C. *Portland*, VI, p. 24, Thomas Bacon to E. Harley, 2 April 1729.

[106] *Chandler*, VII, pp. 46–7.

[107] *Political State*, May 1729, pp. 481–2; *L.J.*, XXIII, pp. 395–6, 18 April 1729.

[108] *Political State*, May 1729, pp. 482–3. Although it is hard to know the political allegiance of all fourteen lords who signed these protestations, many of them were High Tory or Jacobite lords, such as the Duke of Beaufort, the Earl of Scarsdale, the Earl of Strafford, Earl Gower, the Earl of Oxford (Edward Harley), Baron Foley, the Earl of Litchfield and Earl Bathurst. They also included at least one opposition Whig, the Earl of Coventry.

side who claimed that it had been in Britain's interest at that time to take action irrespective of the allies' inaction and that the operation had been effective because it had led Spain to sign the preliminaries, which had secured for Britain most of her demands.[109]

On balance, the opposition's attack in both Houses failed to achieve the desired result. Nevertheless, it should be noted that, through the debates, some of the opposition MPs came to associate themselves with the interests of a commercial sector, especially those private merchants trading with the West Indies and Mediterranean. Boyer reported that Pulteney, Barnard and others, 'who warmly espoused, and strenuously asserted the Cause of the Merchants, gain'd thereby great Applause, and endeared themselves to all the Trading Part of the Nation'.[110]

Thus, as we have seen thus far, in the latter half of the year 1728, there occurred a significant change in the content of the arguments on both sides. While the government came to advocate settlement of the conflict by negotiation, the opposition started to take a more aggressive stance and severely criticised the government's timidity on the issue of Hosier's instructions.[111] From that point on, this belligerent attitude towards Spain became a basic stance of the opposition in place of aversion to the war with Spain.

Furthermore, through the criticism regarding trade protection and the South Sea Company, the opposition emerged as a defender of the cause of the private traders, whose interests were allegedly neglected by the government and threatened by the South Sea Company. This later became one of the most important aspects of the opposition's argument in the late 1730s.

Controversy in the Late Stage of the Anglo-Spanish Conflict: The Treaty of Seville

In the second half of 1729, the issue of the Spanish depredations and trade

109 *Political State*, June 1729, pp. 602–5.

110 *Political State*, May 1729, p. 481.

111 In addition to these arguments, there was a pro-maritime war argument connected with aversion to a land war on the continent. In January 1729, William Pulteney argued in the House of Commons that, if the allies were loyal to Britain, she could concentrate her efforts on war at sea, while the allies fought on land and British and German troops took charge of the defence of Britain. H.M.C. *Egmont Diary*, III, pp. 337–8, 31 January 1728/9. This argument was close to the argument presented by the Country Whig writers at the beginning of the War of the Spanish Succession. There was also a pro-maritime war argument of a more defensive character. One opposition pamphleteer argued that the navy was the natural defence of Britain and that she should avoid unnecessary alliances, which could drag her into conflicts on the continent. This seems to have been a descendent of the Tory pro-maritime war argument at the beginning of the War of the Spanish Succession. *Reasons Shewing the Necessity of Reducing the Army, and, Proving that the Navy of England is her Only, and Natural Strength and Security* (London, 1728). By contrast, the ministerial writers stressed the necessity of maintaining the army until peace was concluded. *British Journal*, no. 27, 20 July 1728.

protection still continued to be a strong weapon for the opposition.[112] Towards the end of 1729, however, the issue of peace with Spain emerged as one of the new focal points of the controversy between the government and the opposition.[113] Even after the Treaty of Seville was concluded in November 1729, this remained one of the central issues.

In this controversy, the government tried to prove that this treaty satisfied British demands in commercial affairs as well as territorial issues such as the security of Gibraltar and Minorca. To defend the treaty, Walpole himself penned a pamphlet and emphasised that the treaty was beneficial for Britain's commercial interests, because all the privileges and advantages in the Spanish trade were restored on the basis of the former treaties and the vessels and goods of British merchants that had been taken by Spain during the conflict were to be returned.[114] Similarly, one ministerial writer stressed that this treaty would settle all grievances with regard to British commerce as well as her foreign territories and that great care was being taken of the merchants who suffered from the Spanish depredations.[115] By contrast, the opposition press was sceptical about the Treaty of Seville. In a supposed letter from a reader, the *Craftsman* of 13 December 1729 claimed that, if the treaty failed to satisfy British demands and dragged Britain into conflict over Italy on behalf of the sons of the king of Spain, the British should do their country justice.[116]

A similar controversy was repeated in a debate over the address of thanks for the king's speech in the House of Commons on 13 January 1730. William Pulteney and Sir John Barnard on the opposition side severely criticised the treaty as being dangerous and ineffective in obtaining compensation for the merchants' losses, whereas the government enumerated the advantages of the treaty, such as the dissolution of the Vienna Treaty, the recovery of trade and the reduction of taxes and forces.[117] In this debate, the government's decision to choose Spain, rather

[112] For criticism concerning Hosier's instruction, see, for example, William Pulteney, *A Short View of the State of Affairs, with relation to Great Britain, for Four Years Past* (London, 1730), pp. 7–9. The government's defence in this issue can be seen in A.B., *Treaty of Seville*, pp. 12–13. For criticism regarding the issue of the Spanish depredations, see *A View of the Depredations and Ravages Committed by the Spaniards on the British Trade and Navigation* (Dubln [Dublin], 1730), pp. iii–iv; *Political State*, August 1730, pp. 174–80.

[113] In their attacks on the government, the opposition also exploited the issue of the Anglo-Dutch fleet gathering at Spithead in the summer of 1729. The main purpose of this fleet was to put pressure on Spain to help the negotiations at the Congress of Soissons. Because this fleet did not even sail out of the port and launched no offensive, it was criticised for being useless and derided as a 'pacific armada' or 'pacific fleet' by the opposition press. Pulteney, *Short View*, pp. 12–13; *The Pacifick Fleet: a New Ballad* (London, 1729); *Craftsman*, no. 171, 11 October 1729, and no. 174, 1 November 1729.

[114] Robert Walpole, *Observations upon the Treaty between the Crowns of Great-Britain, France, and Spain, Concluded at Seville on the Ninth of November, 1729, N.S.* (London, 1729), pp. 14–15.

[115] A.B., *Treaty of Seville*, pp. 20–3.

[116] *Craftsman*, no. 180, 13 December 1729.

[117] *Knatchbull Diary*, pp. 97–8, 13 January 1729/30.

than Austria, as a partner in the peace treaty was also discussed. There was indeed an element of risk involved in this decision. The emperor was strongly opposed to an article in the treaty that stipulated the introduction of Spanish garrisons into the Italian territories to which Don Carlos was to succeed. If the emperor tried to resist this by force, Britain, bound by the treaty to help this introduction, might get entangled in a new war with the emperor. Therefore, the ministerial writers had to defend this decision by emphasising the economic advantages of the amity with Spain, which would surpass the disadvantages to the possible enmity with the emperor.

Walpole defended the government's decision and dismissed the opposition's claim of George II's preference for Hanoverian interests over those of Britain by pointing out that the king chose reconciliation with the king of Spain instead of the emperor, from whom he might have derived a lot of benefit for Hanover. He wrote that commercial advantages 'were too obvious for Him to hesitate a Moment in closing with *Spain*'.[118] Similarly, the anonymous author of a paper on the Treaty of Seville stressed that reconciliation with Spain was more economically advantageous than that with Austria. The author wrote, '*Spain* is not a formidable Enemy, but *Spain* is a valuable Friend.' Although Britain had the power to subdue Spain whenever she wanted and could trade with her by force, it was preferable for Britain to reconcile with Spain in a more amicable way and carry on trade peacefully, which was mutually beneficial. With respect to the emperor, the author claimed, 'the Emperor is a formidable Enemy, but is not the most valuable Friend'. Although the emperor had a good army, without subsidies from Spain, there was nothing to fear from him. The author went on to say,

> In a Word no Peace cold have been more welcome to us than this with *Spain*, because it restores Trade, settles the Peace of the Marines, spreads an universal Calm over the whole navigating World; puts an end to the famous *Ostend* Project (viz.) of a Trade to the *Indies*, leaves us an open Door to the *Spanish West-Indies*, and shuts every-Body else out...[119]

One ministerial writer expressed doubts as to whether the emperor would actually go to war over the issue of the introduction of the Spanish garrisons. Even if he chose to fight, the author claimed, the war would be easy if Britain had made peace with Spain, because, in that case, Britain had France, the Netherlands and Spain with her money on her side and the battlefield would be confined to Italy. Conversely, if Britain did not reconcile with Spain, she would have to fight against the emperor who was financially supported by Spain, and 'the War would be so extensive, as to take in both Worlds, and put us to an infinite Expence in the *West-Indies*'.[120] Thus, ministerial writers advocated amity with Spain by emphasising its economic advantages.

[118] Walpole, *Observations upon the Treaty*, pp. 23–4.
[119] This paper was circulated in manuscript and printed in the Abel Boyer's *Political State of Great Britain* [hereafter, *Political State*], January 1730, pp. 45–7.
[120] A.B., *Treaty of Seville*, p. 27.

The opposition writers refuted this argument by comparing the disadvantages of a war against the emperor with the advantages of a Spanish war, employing the pro-maritime war argument and the idea of self-financing war. William Pulteney claimed that, although peace with Spain might be more economically advantageous than peace with the emperor, 'yet a *War* with the *Emperor* would be, for the same Reason, more burthensome and impracticable to a *Maritime Power*, than a War with *Spain*'.[121] This argument was elaborated in *The Observations on the Treaty of Seville Examined*. Its author claimed that, if Britain could employ her maritime force freely, unlike in the case of the blockade by Hosier, a war with Spain could be neither burdensome nor difficult, because, in such a war, 'It will always be in our Power to make the *Enemy* do more than pay the *Charges* of it; to revenge our *Wrongs*, and to assert our *Rights*.' Britain should employ her '*natural Strength*' and '*natural born Subjects*' and the 'very Progress of the War would increase our own Strength, and the Expences of it would enrich our own People'. Thus, Britain could expect great advantages for herself, without apprehending the success of her allies. By contrast, in a war with the emperor, Britain would have to employ 'an *unnatural Strength* and *foreign Troops*' and conduct an expensive land war on the continent, where her maritime force was not useful and success would only profit the allies.[122]

Likewise, the author of a pamphlet entitled *Reasons for a War, in Order to Establish the Tranquillity and Commerce of Europe* strongly advocated a Spanish war. He deplored the immense cost that Britain had had to bear in the past four years just to maintain a fighting posture and claimed that war was preferable because, although it might be expensive, it could end the conflict sooner. There was an economic advantage as well. In a war with Spain, Britain might capture a prize that might 'largely contribute towards, if not fully supply the Expence of a whole Campaign'. The author claimed, 'One *well-freighted* Galleon would pay for equipping a whole Fleet.'[123] For him, 'War is a Game full of Hazards' and 'a Lottery in which many Blanks rise up to one Prize'. Although there were always cost and danger involved in war, Britain should not hesitate if there was a good prospect for victory, just as in this case, in which Britain had to deal only with Spain, whose commerce and colonies were at Britain's mercy and whom Britain could easily beat at sea. Furthermore, the war was necessary to protect British trade in the West Indies, which was being harassed by the Spaniards in the same manner as in war time.[124]

As we have seen thus far, in the late stages of the war, while the government defended the peace treaty with Spain by emphasising its economic advantages, the opposition criticised the peace by stressing the disadvantages of a possible war with the emperor and the advantages of a Spanish war. In this criticism of the peace, the opposition writers employed the pro-maritime war argument and stressed the

121 Pulteney, *Short View*, p. 26.

122 *The Observations on the Treaty of Seville Examined* (London, 1730), pp. 19–20.

123 *Reasons for a War, in Order to Establish the Tranquillity and Commerce of Europe* (London, 1729), pp. 6–8.

124 *Ibid.*, pp. 23–7.

economic advantages of a maritime war against Spain. Thus, in marked contrast to the early stages of the conflict, it was the opposition who came to embrace the idea of a vigorous maritime war with Spain.

In the controversy during the late 1710s and 1720s that this chapter has examined, there are three important points to note in connection with the pro-maritime war argument. First, in the War of the Quadruple Alliance and in the early stages of the Anglo-Spanish conflict of 1726–29, it was the government side that used the pro-maritime war argument to win the support of the nation for military mobilisation against Spain, while the opposition was generally reluctant to commit to the conflict, apart from some isolated voices of support for a maritime war from a 'Country' viewpoint.

Second, however, the positions of both sides regarding naval policy against Spain interchanged in 1728. The government, which had initially advocated active naval measures against the Vienna Alliance by emphasising the threats it posed to Britain's interest, gradually toned down its support and, by the second half of 1728, had come to defend a peace with Spain. Conversely, the opposition, which had originally argued against involvement in the conflict, had come to blame the government for its timidity and to agitate for tougher action against Spain by 1728. From the ministerial viewpoint, this was unreasonable and inconsistent criticism. One pamphleteer complained, 'The Government has been accused, on one hand, of insolently provoking the *Spaniards* to injure us, and, on the other, of tamely submitting to those Injuries.'[125] The opposition justified this seemingly contradictory change by claiming that the government's measure was indecisive. As William Pulteney put it, 'we had the Misfortunes to do enough to provoke the *Spaniards* to *Hostilities*, but not enough to bring them to a *Compliance with our Terms*'.[126]

Lastly, the controversy of this period added another feature to the opposition's argument, which came to play an important role in the late 1730s. Even though the opposition could not win a majority in Parliament in spite of their vigorous pamphleteering, through the controversy, they came to champion the cause of the private merchants, especially those trading with Spain and her colonies. They represented the Walpole ministry as being subservient to Spain out of considerations for the interests of the South Sea Company and unable to protect those of private merchants from the Spanish depredations.

The opposition's advocacy of a more vigorous maritime war gained momentum in the period before the War of Jenkins' Ear, when the opposition press launched a propaganda campaign calling for tougher action against Spain, including interception of the Spanish silver fleet and expeditions against Spanish America for colonial conquest.[127] However, it was the debate in the Anglo-Spanish conflict of 1726–29 that determined the political stance of the government and opposition

[125] *Observations on the Conduct of Great Britain*, p. 5.

[126] Pulteney, *Short View*, p. 9.

[127] Woodfine, *Britannia's Glories*, p. 170.

on the issue of Spanish war in the late 1730s, at least at the level of political debate: the Walpole ministry, which was reluctant to begin a war, and the opposition, which demanded an active maritime war against Spain and her colonies.

– 8 –

Changes in Naval Policy after 1714:
From Conquest to Security of Trade

As we saw in Chapter 4, during the War of the Spanish Succession, two types of naval operations in Spanish America were planned by Britain to deprive Spain and her ally France of their financial resources: seizure of the silver fleets, and colonial expeditions to establish a new colony. In the period between 1714 and 1729, however, neither type of operation was actually attempted by the government, and naval operations in this period were confined to those of a precautionary character, such as the blockade of Porto Bello and Cartagena of 1726–29.

This chapter investigates the reasons behind this change in British naval policy in Spanish America in this period. In particular, it sheds light on one important factor in naval operations in Spanish America, the significance of which has not been fully recognised by historians: the British government's consideration for the interests of the South Sea Company, which emerged as a new factor in Spanish-American trade after the Treaty of Utrecht. This chapter reveals how this consideration for the company's interests affected and limited British naval operations in Spanish America.

Naval Operations: Blockade

Background of the Blockade: The South Sea Company and the Government

We first examine naval operations regarding the Spanish silver fleets, especially the blockade by Admiral Hosier to contain the silver fleets during the Anglo-Spanish conflict of 1726–29. In March 1726, Hosier was ordered to sail with a squadron for the West Indies. His main task was to prevent the Spanish silver fleet from returning to Spain with the money and goods on board, which were going to be appropriated for the use of the Vienna Alliance. Hosier continued to blockade Porto Bello and Cartagena until he died in August 1727. After his death, the blockade was continued by his successors, Commodore Edward St Lo and Vice-Admiral Edward Hopson, who both succumbed to disease during their missions.

All in all, their attempts to prevent the return of the silver fleet do not seem to have been as successful as the British government claimed later. It was true that Hosier and his successors contained the galleons in America by blockading Porto Bello and Cartagena until the Convention of the Pardo was signed in March 1728 and withdrawal of the British squadron from the West Indies was decided. Nevertheless, the cargoes of the galleons were sent to Vera Cruz via Panama and transferred to the *flota*, which managed to slip back to Spain in the spring of 1727.[1] The price Britain paid for this operation was high. In addition to the damage to its ships, the lives of four thousand men and three commanders were lost.

As we have seen in the previous chapter, this blockade by the British fleet in Spanish America became one of the main issues in the debate over the Anglo-Spanish conflict of 1726–29. The opposition pointed out the great sacrifice that Britain was obliged to make for the blockade, and criticised the government for not having allowed Hosier to seize the galleons when he arrived in the West Indies, which might have saved the lives of seamen and reduced the financial burden on the British government. One of the defences by the government against this criticism was that such a capture could anger British allies who had interests in the silver fleets and would thus result in the loss of British merchants' goods on board the fleets. This was not mere rhetoric. The security of the cargoes of the merchants of Britain and her allies on board the silver fleets was a matter of grave concern for the government. This was reflected in the first instruction given to Hosier in March 1726, in which he was ordered not to commit any hostility, unless he was obliged to do it in order to ensure the safety of the property of the British and allies' merchants on board the silver fleets.[2]

Moreover, as Jeremy Black has stated, the allies, France and the Netherlands, expressed concern over British naval action against Spain, especially the possibility of the capture of the silver fleets.[3] The detention of the fleet in the Caribbean could cause financial damage to the French merchants engaged in the Spanish-American trade through the silver fleet, and this concern made the French first minister Cardinal Fleury hesitant to approve the dispatch of Hosier.[4] This consideration for relations with the allies was undoubtedly one important factor that influenced the government's naval policy in Spanish America.[5] The opposition seems to have obtained information about this French objection to the seizure. In the parliamentary session of January 1729, expressing a mistrust of France, William Pulteney mentioned 'the great familiarity of that Court and Spain' as the private reason why Hosier did not take the galleons.[6] In this respect, Pulteney's guess was not wide of the mark.

There was, however, one point that was not raised by the government in the

[1] Cesáreo Fernández Duro, *Armada Española desde la Unión de los Reinos de Castilla y de Aragón*, VI (Madrid, 1900), p. 189.

[2] TNA, SP 42/80, fols 6v–7v, 'Instructions for Francis Hosier', 28 March 1726.

[3] Black, *The Collapse of the Anglo-French Alliance*, p. 86.

[4] Wilson, *French Foreign Policy*, pp. 57–8.

[5] In the earliest stage of the conflict, this French apprehension that Britain might be aiming to seize galleons and support the independence of Peru from Spain was reported by Viscount Percival (later, first Earl of Egmont), MP for Harwich and a supporter of Walpole. BL, Add MS 47031, fols 121v–122, Lord Perceval to Daniel Dering, 15 March 1725/6.

[6] H.M.C. *Egmont Diary*, III, p. 338, 31 January 1728/9.

defence of its instructions to Hosier, namely its consideration for the interests of the South Sea Company. Sperling briefly mentioned the effect of this consideration on the government's diplomatic policy.[7] Nevertheless, its impact on British naval operations in Spanish America has not been fully examined. This section, therefore, investigates how it influenced actual naval operations, by focusing on the blockade by Admiral Hosier.

In order to understand the government's care for the South Sea Company's interests, we must first look at the special relationship between the British government and the company. The South Sea Company had had a close connection with the government since its foundation. One of the chief reasons was the idiosyncratic character of the Asiento trade conducted by the company. The trade was distinct from other Spanish-American trade conducted by private merchants in that it was based on an international treaty between Britain and Spain. As Georges Scelle pointed out, before gaining independence in 1640, Portugal had been the chief supplier of slaves to Spanish America. Thus, after 1640, Spain had to turn to foreign merchants for its supply. The Asiento contract, which was originally a contract between the Spanish crown and private individuals, increasingly became a tool of political bargaining, and it came to assume a more international character as a contract between Spain and other countries that was eventually solidified in the Asiento treaty between Spain and Britain of March 1713, by which the Spanish crown made the contract, at least in legal terms, not with private individuals but with the British crown.[8]

Even after the fall of the Harley ministry, the original promoter of the South Sea Company, the company continued to retain its special connection with the government. In February 1718, in place of the Prince of Wales who had joined the opposition, the company elected King George I as its new governor. Moreover, a purge of directors affiliated with the opposition, such as Sir Richard Hoare, Horatio Townshend and the Duke of Argyll, further strengthened the company's bond with the king and the Stanhope–Sunderland ministry.[9] This special relationship between the company and the government can also be perceived in the company's cooperation with the ministry to win the support of the City for the government's measures against Spain in the War of the Quadruple Alliance. In September 1718, on the advice of the Stanhope–Sunderland ministry, the company submitted to the king a representation accusing the king of Spain of breaching the treaties concerning the Asiento trade, which was made public in the *Daily Courant*, a ministerial newspaper.[10] According to Hugh Thomas, the Stanhope–Sunderland

7 Sperling, *South Sea Company*, p. 20.

8 Scelle, 'The Slave-Trade in Spanish Colonies of America', 626, 654–5.

9 Carswell, *South Sea Bubble*, pp. 61–2.

10 *Daily Courant*, 26 September 1718, Issue 5283. This representation was also included in *The Conduct of the Courts of Great-Britain and Spain, as to the Present Posture of Affairs, Briefly Set forth and Consider'd* (London, 1718), with other documents concerning the issue of the breach of the Asiento treaties by Spain.

ministry aimed at engaging the City 'to have addressed his Majesty for the glorious success of his fleet', though it did not have the desired effect because of the hesitation of the Common Council.[11]

The South Sea Bubble and the reconstruction of the company under Walpole's guidance did not sever this connection. One point that should be borne in mind is that even after the South Sea Bubble, the company continued to be one of the biggest joint-stock companies in Britain and the only organisation allowed to trade legally and directly with the Spanish colonies, though its profitability had been disappointing. Thus, the company still had political significance and economic potential, and irrespective of its real contribution to the British economy, the government could not neglect its interests.

The government's regard for the interest of the South Sea Company was shown in the first instruction given to Hosier in March 1726. In the thirteenth article of the instruction, Hosier was ordered to assist the company or other British subjects to recover their goods if they were seized by the Spaniards, or assist them to withdraw such goods out of the ports in Spanish America to prevent their seizure, as long as it did not hinder Hosier's main service – prevention of the return of the silver fleets.[12] On the other hand, the South Sea Company had a good reason to rely on the government's help. As the tension with Spain heightened after the formation of the Vienna Alliance, ships and cargoes of the company languished unprotected in the ports in Spanish America, including the *Prince Frederick*, one of the company's annual ships, which had reached Vera Cruz in October 1725. The seizure of the company's ships and goods by the Spaniards during the War of the Quadruple Alliance was still fresh in the company directors' minds, and they were worried that the same thing might happen again. Their concern was reflected in instructions given in February 1726 to a captain of one of the company's ships bound for Buenos Aires, which mentioned the diplomatic tension between Britain and Spain, and asked him to be careful of a surprise attack by the Spaniards when he came to the river of Buenos Aires.[13] Thus, both the government and the company were concerned about the company's goods in Spanish America, in the face of increasing tension with Spain.

Blockade by Admiral Hosier: May 1726–January 1727

After his arrival in the West Indies, Hosier immediately set about to protect the interests of the South Sea Company. In May 1726, he arrived off the west end of

[11] H.M.C. *Stuart*, VII, p. 374, H. Thomas to Mar, 29 September/10 October 1718.
[12] TNA, SP 42/80, fol. 11, 'Instructions for Francis Hosier', 28 March 1726.
[13] BL, Add MS 25567, fol. 121, 'Instructions to Captain Mathew Kent, Comdr [Commander] of the Bristol Galley', 17 February 1725/6. Likewise, in June 1724 and July 1726, the captain of another South Sea Company ship bound for Madagascar and Buenos Aires was given instructions that warned of possible danger of war and told the measures to take in case of war. BL, Add MS 25567, fol. 127v, 'Instructions to Captain Moor White of the ship Sea Horse', 16 June 1724, and fols 128–9, 'Additional instructions to Captain Moor White of the ship Sea Horse', 1 July 1726.

Hispaniola (modern Haiti) and then headed to Cartagena. At Cartagena, he learned that the galleons had sailed for Porto Bello, where the annual ship of the company was anchored. In fear of interrupting the sale of the cargo of the company's annual ship in Porto Bello, Hosier did not inform the governor of Cartagena about the conclusion of the offensive alliance and Hosier's intention of blockade.[14]

At Porto Bello, one Bumpsted, chief supercargo of the annual ship, informed Hosier that the money sent by the Spanish colonial merchants for the fair at Porto Bello had been sent back to Panama for its security before Hosier's arrival. Hosier refrained from announcing the offensive alliance and the blockade to Don Francisco Cornejo, general of the galleons, and Don Manuel de Alderete, president of Panama, until the South Sea Company had carried its property out of the port. At the same time, Hosier dispatched two ships under his command to prevent the Spaniards from carrying the money of the galleons secretly to Havana by small vessels.[15]

Hosier stayed in the Bay of Bastimientos near Porto Bello and continued to blockade the port lest the galleons or other Spanish ships tried to leave, and he occasionally captured small Spanish vessels.[16] In the meantime, he did not neglect the trade of the private merchants or that of the South Sea Company. As Howard McMains pointed out, the government did try to provide protection to merchants, and in this respect, the opposition's criticism was rather unfair.[17] It is true that containment of the silver fleets, not least the galleons, was listed as the top priority in the instructions given to Hosier, but he also arranged a convoy when one was requested by the private merchants there.[18] Hosier's presence offered security to the British merchants in that region, which seems to have encouraged their trade, and for which Newcastle expressed satisfaction in September 1726.[19]

The interests of the private merchants, however, were sometimes in conflict with the strategic considerations of the metropolis, and in such a case, Hosier refused to meet their demands. In June 1727, when some merchants asked him for a convoy to carry stores and provisions to the Spanish Main, he refused it, and

14 TNA, SP 42/80, fols 53–53v, 'An Account of my proceeding since my last from Tibrun [Tiberon] Bay to your Grace' [n.d., but about June 1726].

15 TNA, SP 42/80, fols 53v–55.

16 TNA, SP 42/80, fols 63–63v, Hosier to Newcastle, 29 July 1726.

17 McMains, 'The Parliamentary Opposition to Sir Robert Walpole', pp. 141–4. McMains mentioned the government's care of the interests of the South Sea Company, which distressed the private merchants. *Ibid.*, pp. 147–8. However, he overlooked the fact that it was partly this consideration for the company's ships and goods taken hostage by the Spaniards that discouraged the government from adopting an aggressive naval policy.

18 TNA, ADM 1/230 [not foliated], Hosier to Burchett, 9 June 1727.

19 TNA, SP 42/80, fol. 76v, Newcastle to Hosier, 29 September 1726. Ironically, Hosier's presence in these waters was welcomed by Lima merchants, as they benefited from the revival of the trade with the British smugglers, who had been kept away by the vigilance of the galleons and Guarda-Costas, but came back when the arrival of Hosier's fleet nullified attempts by the Spanish colonial authority to prevent the illicit trade. Walker, *Spanish Politics and Imperial Trade*, p. 155.

tried to dissuade them from the trade, saying that these cargoes were contraband and that there was news of an approaching war in the newspaper.[20] This trade with the Spanish colonies had been a thorn in the side of the British naval commanders in the Caribbean, because, as St Lo later reported in September 1727, through that trade, the Spanish colonies obtained not only contraband but also intelligence. Preventing this trade proved difficult. St Lo lamented, 'Admll Hosier was Inclinable to have put a stop to those transactions, as I cou'd willingly myselfe, but the Clamours of the Merchants deters me.'[21]

On the other hand, in the face of Hosier's blockade, the Spaniards took retaliatory action. In September 1726, the Spanish authorities at Porto Bello placed the South Sea Company's factory there under armed guard and stopped the company's ships. Hosier protested this action by the Spanish authorities and threatened to starve them, but in vain.[22]

With their properties under threat of confiscation, the directors of the South Sea Company sought assistance from the government. In November 1726, the directors reported that several ships belonging to them had been detained with money and goods in Porto Bello and Cartagena, and they asked the king for help to secure the properties and carry them away to a safe place.[23] Accordingly, the Duke of Newcastle, Secretary of State for the South, ordered Hosier to assist the company, as long as it did not interrupt the main service: the prevention of the return of the galleons.[24]

Even before receiving this instruction, Hosier had already started negotiations with Cornejo and Alderete to secure the ships and goods of the company as well as those of other British merchants in Porto Bello. He proposed that the Spanish authority should allow the South Sea Company's factory the same liberty as before and release the British ships in Porto Bello and all other ports in Spanish America. In return, Hosier would allow the Spaniards to trade with Chagre and free their ships, which he had detained near Porto Bello, though he insisted that treasure on board the galleons should be kept in Porto Bello.[25] Cornejo agreed to the exchange

20 TNA, SP 42/80, fols 186v–187, Hosier to Newcastle, 9 June 1727.

21 TNA, SP 42/80, fols 209v–210, St Lo to Newcastle, 24 September 1727. On the other hand, British naval ships themselves were suspected of being engaged in the illicit trade with the Spanish colonies. When a naval ship was dispatched to the West Indies with an order for the execution of the preliminaries after the conclusion of the Convention of the Pardo in March 1728, Newcastle had to make sure that the ship carried no merchandise on board lest it would offend the Spanish government. TNA, SP 42/80, fols 308v–309, Newcastle to Hopson, 25 March 1728; BL, Add MS 32755, fols 79–79v, Newcastle to Benjamin Keene, British envoy in Spain, 25 March 1728.

22 TNA, SP 42/80, fol. 69, Hosier to Newcastle, 23 September 1726, and fols 71–71v, Hosier to [Francis Cornejo?], 23 September 1726.

23 TNA, SP 42/80, fols 95–95v, D. Wescomb, secretary of the South Sea Company, to the king, 17 November 1726.

24 TNA, SP 42/80, fol. 93v, Newcastle to Hosier, 21 November 1726.

25 TNA, SP 42/80, fols 118–118v, 'Articles agreed with the President of Panama & the Genll of the Galleons at Porto Bello, upon the delivery of their Vessels I stopt at the Bastimientos', 9 October 1726.

of the vessels detained by both sides, but he refused to restore the factory's privileges as long as Britain contained the galleons.[26]

After a short stay in Jamaica, Hosier resumed his duties in January. This time, he sailed to Cartagena, where the galleons had moved while he was in Jamaica. There he found that money taken out of the company's ship was still detained despite the above agreement. At the request of the company's agents at Cartagena, who asked Hosier to put pressure on the governor of Cartagena with an implication of the exertion of force, Hosier made a strong protest against the detention, invoking an article in the Asiento treaty that gave the company a period of one and half years to transfer its properties if war was proclaimed.[27] Yet, the governor of Cartagena defended his action, pointing out the inequality of the agreement, which forbade them to trade freely and to use the money of the galleons while the British were allowed a liberty of trade.[28] The negotiations broke up. In accordance with an order from the king, Hosier left Cartagena in January 1727, and, after short stay in Jamaica, sailed to the Bay of Matanzas on the north coast of Cuba.

Blockade after February 1727

After Spain laid siege to Gibraltar in February 1727, the tension between the two countries heightened, and Hosier was ordered to 'take, sink, Burn or otherwise destroy' any Spanish ships that he encountered.[29] In May 1727, the emperor agreed to sign a preliminary treaty, but Spain still refused to join the treaty and continued the siege. As tensions increased, the danger faced by the company in Spanish America became more serious. On 27 March 1727, the Spanish authorities issued an order to seize all properties of the South Sea Company and other British merchants in the Spanish colonies.[30] Accordingly, in May, the company's properties at Cartagena were placed under a strict embargo, and it was feared that properties in other parts of Spanish America would suffer the same fate.[31]

With their ships and goods detained, in July, the South Sea Company pleaded for the government's help again. They asked the government to send a document to the West Indies to prove that the Spaniards had an obligation to return the company's ships and cargoes immediately according to the articles in Asiento treaty, and suggested that Hosier and his squadron should attend the negotiations.[32] Accordingly, Newcastle ordered that Hosier should continue the blockade until the Spaniards released those detained ships and goods, especially the *Prince Frederick* at

26 TNA, SP 42/80, fols 120–120v, Francis Cornejo to [Hosier], 18 October 1726 (N.S.).

27 TNA, SP 42/80, fols 133–133v, John Thompson, Thomas Butcher, John Burnet and Edward Garthwaite to [Hosier], 20 January 1726/7 (N.S.); SP 42/80, fols 130–130v, [Hosier] to Don Lewis de Aponte, Governor of Cartagena, 11 January 1726/7.

28 TNA, SP 42/80, fols 131–131v, Don Lewis de Aponte to [Hosier] [n.d.].

29 TNA, SP 42/80, fol. 140, Admiralty to Hosier, 4 March 1726/7.

30 Sorsby, 'British Trade with Spanish America under the Asiento', p. 136.

31 BL, Add MS 25560, fol. 64v, D. Wescomb to Newcastle, 14 September 1727.

32 BL, Add MS 25560, fols 61v–62, D. Wescomb to Newcastle, 4 July 1727.

Vera Cruz, in accordance with the preliminaries. If there was any opportunity to force the Spaniards to release the ship, Hosier was to make use of it as long as it did not divert him from his main service.[33] However, the negotiations made little progress, and in September, it was reported that the viceroy of Mexico would not release the company's ships as long as Hosier contained the galleons or until the viceroy received news that an agreement had been reached in Europe.[34]

Thus, just as Britain contained the silver fleets in the Spanish American ports to put pressure on Spain, the company's ships and cargoes were taken hostage by the Spaniards.[35] In May 1727, Hosier noted, 'if we make any Reprisalls on the Spaniards, they can always make it good on the South Sea Company'.[36] As long as the Spaniards held this trump card, the British government was obliged to be cautious about taking aggressive action.

As the blockade continued, other factors that restrained Hosier's action came into play, namely humidity and mosquitoes, two common problems that had harassed the navy in the West Indies.[37] As in other naval operations in the West Indies, Hosier's fleet could not escape the harmful consequences of long-term operations in that humid region, including yellow fever and malaria, deteriorating condition of the ships, shortage of seamen because of the high mortality rate and desertion, and want of provisions. Faced by these problems, Hosier was forced to sail back to Jamaica several times to careen his ships and to supply them with manpower and provisions. For example, in November 1726, the council of war resolved to return to Jamaica because of shortage of manpower and provisions.[38]

These considerations restricted the capability of Hosier's fleet, as well. As previously discussed, in October 1726, Hosier proposed to the president of Panama

[33] TNA, SP 42/80, fols 192v–194v, Newcastle to Hosier, 18 July 1727. More aggressive measures seem to have been considered as a last resort if Spain continued to refuse to execute the preliminaries. In an instruction written for Hosier in September, it was suggested that a detachment should be sent to Vera Cruz to bring back the *Prince Frederick* by force, if Hosier judged it compatible with the blockade. However, this part of the draft of the instruction was crossed out, and it does not seem to have been sent to Hosier, who had already died by this time. TNA, SP 42/80, fols 199–199v, [?] to Hosier, 12 September 1727.

[34] BL, Add MS 25560, fol. 64v, D. Wescomb to Newcastle, 14 September 1727.

[35] This situation was not necessarily confined to Spanish America. Sir Charles Wager, cruising off Cadiz, faced a similar difficulty and had to refrain from taking an aggressive action out of consideration of the security of ships and effects belonging to British merchants in the Spanish ports. Vernon–Wager MSS [not foliated], Newcastle to Wager, 20 October 1727; Vernon–Wager MSS, Newcastle to Wager, 25 December 1727.

[36] TNA, SP 42/80, fols 148–148v, Hosier to Newcastle, 12 May 1727.

[37] Duncan Crewe has examined in detail the British fleet's difficulties in the manning, provision and maintenance of ships in the West Indies during the period 1739–48. Duncan G. Crewe, *Yellow Jack and the Worm: British Naval Administration in the West Indies, 1739–1748* (Liverpool, 1993). The problems that Hosier faced in our period were basically the same, though he had fewer conflicts with the Jamaican local authority.

[38] TNA, SP 42/80, fols 122–122v, 'At a Council of War held on board of his Majs Ship *Bredah*...', 9 November 1726.

and the general of the galleons to exchange the ships detained by both sides, excluding the silver fleet. It was partly his concern over the safety and deteriorating conditions of his fleet that prompted Hosier to execute this exchange. The minutes of the council of war of 3 October 1726 mentioned the difficulty of keeping those Spanish vessels detained by Hosier because of hard winds and spread of disease among the British seamen, which made the council decide to release the vessels and leave the place to obtain provisions.[39]

There was no effective solution to these problems in those days. In particular, the manning of ships in the West Indies was a formidable task. In November 1726, Hosier complained of the Jamaican colonial government's recruiting measures and expressed concern about 'the great Misfortune' that might attend if he was not supplied with men.[40] In fact, the Jamaican local government at that time was relatively well disposed to help Hosier and allowed him to impress half of the sailors belonging to each vessel in the harbour of Kingston. Yet, this met with a complaint from inhabitants of Jamaica and merchants trading with the island who blamed the colonial government for breaching the American act of 1708.[41] Hosier was also hamstrung by the rapidly deteriorating condition of his ships. In May 1727, in a letter to Josiah Burchett, secretary of the Board of Admiralty, he complained that, 'all the ships are in so bad condition that it is impossible to do any other service, than block up a port unless they are careened'. However, Hosier wrote, this could not be done in any out-port, and if he attempted it, there would be a danger of the seamen deserting to the Spanish service.[42]

This combination of damage to the ships and shortage of seamen by sickness and desertion can be seen in the case of the *Berwick*, which was severely damaged when it ran aground on her way to Jamaica. Although the damage itself could be repaired in a fortnight, Hosier was at a loss how to man the ship again, as a great part of the seamen had deserted and one third of those who stayed were sick.[43]

Thus, as the blockade dragged on, the deteriorating condition of ships and the shortage of seamen and provisions increasingly deprived his fleet of the capability to carry out more active operations. In October 1726, in a letter to Newcastle, Hosier lamented as follows:

> I could have wish'd my orders had been to hae [have] distroy'd them in Port at our first comeing, instead of Blocking them up, it might have been done with

39 TNA, SP 42/80, fols 119–119v, 'Councell of Warr held on board his Majs Ship *Bredah*...', 3 October 1726.

40 TNA, SP 42/80, fol. 99, Hosier to Newcastle, 11 December 1726.

41 TNA, SP 42/80, fols 101–101v, Copy of the minutes of the Council of Jamaica, 14 December 1726; fol. 125, John Ayscough, et al. to [Hosier], 14 December 1726; and fol. 109v, Hosier to Newcastle, 15 February 1726/7. In May 1727, the merchants trading to Jamaica sent a petition to the Privy Council about the impressment by Hosier. William L. Grant and James Munro, eds, *Acts of the Privy Council of England, Colonial Series*, III 1720–45 (London, 1910, repr. Nendeln, Leichtenstein, 1966), p. 157, 31 May 1727.

42 TNA, ADM 1/230 [not foliated], Hosier to Burchett, 12 May 1727.

43 TNA, ADM 1/230 [not foliated], Hosier to Burchett, 9 June 1727; TNA, SP 42/80, fol. 186, Hosier to Newcastle, 9 June 1727.

> ease. but now we have buried 360 men and Nine hundred sick and considering the Long stay here, and no refreshments for the poor men since we left England, but a little Turtle now and then, which is all this place will afoard.[44]

Seemingly, these facts give credence to the opposition's criticism that Hosier should have attacked the galleons immediately. Nevertheless, it was uncertain whether he could really have captured the galleons even had he attempted it upon his arrival in the West Indies. Sir Charles Wager, one of the Lords of the Admiralty, expressed doubts about the prospect of such a capture. In one document, referring to his own encounter with the galleons, he explained that it was almost impossible to take ships in enemy ports, except by stealing them out under cover of night, for the Spaniards could easily prevent it by setting fire to the ships before they were taken. In addition, he was sceptical about the prospect of booty in taking Spanish towns, for the Spaniards would have time to run away and hide their money.[45]

It is difficult to say whether Wager's comment was accurate or not, and whether Hosier would have been able to take the silver fleet if he had attempted it. However, even if he had succeeded, such a capture would have caused confiscation of the properties of the South Sea Company and other British merchants in Spanish America in retaliation, just as the properties of the British merchants suffered after the capture of the silver fleet at Vigo in 1702. It is possible that the memory of this capture at Vigo and its aftermath was one factor that held back the Walpole ministry from giving orders to Hosier to take the galleons.

Hosier died in August 1727 without seeing a settlement of the conflict. After his death, his successor, Commodore Edward St Lo, inherited this difficult task of making the Spaniards release the company's ships (not least, the *Prince Frederick*), goods and personnel, as well as blockading of the galleons.[46] However, Spain would

44 TNA, SP 42/80, fol. 79v, Hosier to Newcastle, 22 October 1726.

45 BL, Add MS 19034, fols 66–66v [Wager?] to ? [n.d.]. This document was included in a collection of drafts and copies of papers relating to the Navy and Wager's service. Given that the siege of Gibraltar was mentioned, this was probably written after February 1727. The author was almost certainly Wager, because the description of the encounter with the galleons corresponds precisely to the circumstances of his capture of the galleons in 1708, and because James Littleton, another naval officer who succeeded in taking galleons in 1711, had already died in 1723. Unfortunately, the later part of the document is missing, and it is not clear to whom this document was addressed. However, judging from the content of other parts that explained the sensibleness of the naval policy regarding Hosier's operations and trade protection, it is possible that this was written in order to give professional advice to some of the ministers, who probably needed it for the debates in Parliament or in writing pamphlets.

46 For St Lo's effort to make the Spaniards release the ships, cargoes and personnel of the South Sea Company as well as those of other British merchants, for example, see, TNA, SP 42/80, fol. 217v, St Lo to Newcastle, 26 October 1727, and fol. 221, St Lo to Don Lewis de Aponte, 19 October 1727. However, the Spanish officials refused St Lo's demand on the ground that there had not been any order for the release from the king. TNA, SP 42/80, fol. 225, Don Lewis de Aponte, to [St Lo], 31 October 1727 (N.S.), and fol. 227, Francisco Cornejo to [St Lo], 31 October 1727 (N.S.).

not agree until Britain freed the galleons, and the return of the *Prince Frederick* became one of the main issues in the diplomatic negotiations with Spain in the Congress of Soissons that opened in June 1728.

As we have seen so far, in addition to the diplomatic considerations and the concern over security of goods on board the silver fleets, concern for the properties of the South Sea Company as well as those of the other British merchants in Spanish American ports constrained Hosier's freedom of action. Moreover, as the blockade wore on, the deteriorating condition of his ships and men also severely limited the capability of his fleet. These difficulties faced by Hosier show the British government's dilemma in the conflict with Spain. Britain obtained direct and legal access to the Spanish-American market by the Asiento trade conducted by the South Sea Company. Nevertheless, this also meant that she would put the company's properties in the Spanish colonies at risk in case of a rupture with Spain. Although the danger of confiscation of the British merchants' goods in a war with Spain was neither a new problem nor confined to Spanish America, the presence of the factories and ships of the South Sea Company in Spanish-American ports compounded this problem further, because they provided a suitable hostage for Spain. As Sperling has pointed out, British politicians always had to consider this predicament in their diplomatic decisions.[47] At the same time, it also caused some difficulties at the level of actual naval operations in Spanish America.

A similar dilemma continued even after the conflict ceased. In September 1730, when Rear Admiral Stewart was ordered to send men of war to take Spanish vessels in reprisal for the capture of a British merchant ship by a Guarda-Costa fitted out from Porto Rico, the agents of the South Sea Company opposed this measure, referring to previous seizures of their properties by the Spanish colonial authorities. In the representation of March 1731, the agents expressed their concern that capture of any Spanish merchant vessels by the men of war would lead to the retaliatory confiscation of the *Prince William*, one of the company's annual ships, which had been at Porto Bello for the fair, and its cargo. Even when the ship and cargo were returned later, they argued, financial loss owing to the disruption of the trade at the fair was inevitable. Furthermore, it would trigger a similar seizure in other ports in Spanish America, which 'must put a full stop to the Assiento Trade', and would lead Spanish governors to issue a commission to take British ships to Guarda-Costas, which would make it difficult for British merchant men to sail without a convoy. They argued that Spanish traders of the cities where the company had factories were not involved in such a practice conducted by a Porto Rican privateer and asked them not to send the men of war, or at least confine the target to Guarda-Costas.[48] Accordingly, the order to Rear Admiral

47 Sperling, *South Sea Company*, p. 20.

48 Ch (H) MSS, Political Papers 16/4 [not foliated], 'The Humble Representation of Edward Pratter & Jams Riggby, Agents and Factors for the Royal British Assiento Company', 4 March 1730/31; Political Papers 16/5 [not foliated], Edward Pratter to Rear Admiral Stewart, 4 March 1730/31.

Stewart was partly suspended.[49] As Pares states, this was an instance in which the government's effort to protect English shipping against Spanish depredations was hindered by a consideration for the company's interests, including their properties in the Spanish colonies.[50]

The British government had a reason to take special care of the company's interests, because the Asiento trade was not trade by private merchants, but trade based on an international treaty between Spain and Britain, as already mentioned. This point was emphasised by the directors of the company when they asked for the government's assistance. In April 1728, in a letter to Newcastle, they asked the government to obtain better security from the Spaniards for the company's trade, stressing that the Asiento contract was 'a National Treaty wherein the Honr & Interest of Great Britain is no less concerned than the company'.[51]

In their defence of the government's instructions to Hosier, the ministerial writers did mention the security of the goods of the British and allies' merchants on board the silver fleets. However, when it came to the security of the properties of the South Sea Company, the ministerial writers stayed silent. This is understandable given the opposition's criticism of the company and their defence of the interests of private merchants, which we discussed in Chapter 7. Reference to the protection of the company's interests could attract further criticisms from the opposition, a situation that the ministry wanted to avoid as much as possible. Thus, although consideration for the interest of the South Sea Company was one of the important factors that made the government hesitate to adopt an aggressive naval policy in Spanish America, it was an issue that the government wanted to keep low-key.

Naval Operations: Colonial Expeditions

Plans for Colonial Expeditions during the War of Quadruple Alliance

Next, we examine plans for colonial expeditions between 1714 and 1729. As we have seen in the previous chapter, in this period, the pro-maritime war argument was employed both by the government and the opposition as during the War of the Spanish Succession. However, there is a marked feature in the pro-maritime war argument after the peace of Utrecht: the relative scarcity of arguments supporting Spanish-American expeditions, compared with the preceding period.

As was shown in Parts I and II, during the War of the Spanish Succession, plans for a Spanish-American expedition to establish a new colony were often proposed by pamphleteers, colonial governors and projectors. There was also interest in such expeditions among some of the ministers who tried to put them into practice (as in the case of Peterborough's expedition in 1702–3), though they were not actually carried out owing to diplomatic and administrative difficulties. By contrast, in the pro-maritime war argument that appeared in the period 1714–29, proposals for colonial expeditions were scarce. More importantly, there was hardly any sign of

49 TNA, ADM 1/4107, fols 52–52v, Newcastle to Admiralty, 3 June 1731.

50 Pares, *War and Trade in the West Indies*, pp. 15, 19.

51 BL, Add MS 25557, fol. 7, D. Wescomb to Newcastle, 3 April 1728.

the government's commitment to these plans. What could account for this? This section attempts to show this change in the pro-maritime war argument and tries to explain the reasons behind it.

During the period of the War of the Quadruple Alliance, there were fewer proposals for colonial conquest than in the period of the War of the Spanish Succession. As far as the opposition of this period were concerned, this is not difficult to understand. The aim of the mainstream of the opposition, especially the dissident Whigs led by Townshend and Walpole, who was by no means a supporter of colonial expeditions, was to attack the government's tough measure against Spain which, they claimed, could drag Britain into an unnecessary war. Therefore, there was little room for an argument for colonial expeditions that was at odds with this criticism of the government's aggressive policy. As we have seen, some of the opposition, probably those affiliated with the Tories, were sympathetic to maritime war against Spain, but they were a minority.

Nevertheless, even in the ministerial press, which supported the active use of British naval power, the argument for colonial conquest was rare. One exception is a pamphlet entitled *An Historical Account of the Voyages and Adventures of Sir Walter Raleigh*, written by Daniel Defoe, who had been a tenacious supporter of colonial expeditions and was employed by the government at that time. In 1719, Defoe proposed to the South Sea Company a plan to establish a colony in Guiana, which was within the limit of the patent of the company, along with an account of a similar attempt made by Sir Walter Raleigh about one hundred year before.[52] But, apart from this, I could not find any other proposals to establish a settlement in Spanish America, either in the pamphlets or periodicals of this period that discussed the war with Spain.

Rather, interests in colonial conquest seem to have been greater among some colonists in the British American colonies who felt the threat from foreign colonies more directly than those in the mother country. For example, John Kelly, collector of Jamaica, mentioned a plan for taking the Bay of Campeche, which had been an important base for logwood cutting and was expected to provide a market for British manufactures and employment.[53] Likewise, in 1720, in a letter to James Craggs, Secretary of State for the South, Governor Woodes Rogers of the Bahamas implied that he had a plan for an attack on Mexico, which was based on information about discontent among the Native Americans at Spanish rule and the vulnerability of the city of Mexico, which came from one Dr Sinclair, an ex-captive of the Spaniards.[54] However, when Rogers wrote this letter, the war was already over and it was too late to carry out this plan.

52 Daniel Defoe, *An Historical Account of the Voyages and Adventures of Sir Walter Raleigh* (London, 1719), pp. 42–55.

53 TNA, CO 137/13, no. 36, fol. 165v, enclosure i, 'Extract of Letter from Mr Jn [John] Kelly', 30 April 1719.

54 TNA, CO 5/387, no. 16, fols 62–62v, Governor Woodes Rogers to Craggs, 21 December 1720, and enclosure ii, fols 65–66v, Deposition of Dr. George Sinclair [n.d.]. It seems that

What should be emphasised here is that, in spite of these proposals, there was no sign that the government contemplated any colonial expedition against Spanish America during the war. The records of the Board of Admiralty reveal scant evidence that the government was planning expeditions against Spanish America.[55] Instead, it seems that private individuals were more active in projects for colonial expeditions. For example, in July 1718, Hugh Thomas reported the existence of a secret plan for an expedition against the Spanish West Indies in which, he claimed, some Whigs and the emperor were involved.[56] According to Thomas, this plan was originally designed by some leading London merchants about 1713 when the treaty of Rastadt was still being negotiated, and it later obtained the emperor's support.[57] However, this project does not appear to have materialised in the end.[58]

The expedition against the Bahamas in 1718 by Woodes Rogers, who made his name with his privateering circumnavigation of 1708–11, might be regarded as a variant of the colonial expeditions.[59] Nevertheless, its aim was not to acquire a new territory but to recover the control of the colony, which had been temporarily

this plan was also inspired by a similar attempt on Mexico by the French, which Rogers reported to the Board of Trade in April 1720. TNA, CO 23/1, no. 23, fol. 122v, Rogers to Board of Trade, 20 April 1720.

[55] The sources that I checked for this purpose are TNA, ADM 1/4100, 1/4101, 1/4102 and ADM 3/32. There are some references to the Vigo expedition, which was conducted under the command of Admiral Mighell and Viscount Cobham in October 1719. However, there was no mention of West Indian expeditions.

[56] H.M.C. *Stuart*, VII, p. 65, H. Thomas to Mar, 8/19 July 1718. This was leaked by John Ker of Kersland, who was originally a Whig government spy among the Scottish Jacobites, but defected to them and made an approach to the Duke of Mar at that time. Later, in 1720, Ker himself proposed to the emperor a plan to establish a colony in the West Indies for the projected Ostend Company, though this plan was not realised. Gerald B. Hertz, 'England and the Ostend Company', *EHR* 22, no. 86 (1907), 258–9; Bryan Little, *Crusoe's Captain: Being the Life of Woodes Rogers, Seaman, Trader, Colonial Governor* (London, 1960), p. 176.

[57] H.M.C. *Stuart*, VII, pp. 523–4, H. Thomas to Mar, 30 October/10 November 1718. Thomas wrote as if Captain Woodes Rogers' expedition to the Bahamas in 1718 was connected with this plan. However, no evidence to support this has been found so far.

[58] Owing to the scarcity of information, it is difficult to know what this plan exactly was. It is, however, possible that this was an embryonic form of a plan for the Ostend Company, which was established in the Austrian Netherlands for the East India trade, but originally also included the West Indies within its scope, as we saw in Chapter 7. Soon after this report, in November, Thomas mentioned that the emperor's plan was to establish an East India Company at Antwerp by agreement with George I, into which some foreign merchants would be admitted, and he reported that Britain was planning to lend to the emperor sixteen men-of-war under the command of George Viscount Forbes. H.M.C. *Stuart*, VII, p. 623, H. Thomas to Mar, 31 November 1718. In fact, in 1719, at the request of George I, Viscount Forbes served the emperor to help him to build up the imperial navy, though this plan was frustrated by the tacit obstruction of the imperial ministers. H.M. Chichester, rev. Randolph Cock, 'Forbes, George, third Earl of Granard (1685–1765)', *ODNB*.

[59] For Rogers' expedition against the Bahamas, see Little, *Crusoe's Captain*, Chapters 13 and 14.

occupied by pirates. Moreover, though the government helped Rogers by giving him naval and military assistance and appointing him as a new governor of the colony, the expedition was mainly planned and funded privately by Rogers himself and his co-partners, including Sir Charles Wager. Another Spanish-American expedition was actually carried out in this period albeit by private individuals: the last British privateering voyage to the South Sea, made by George Shelvocke and John Clipperton, which set sail from Plymouth in February 1719. Although their voyage did not see a dramatic capture as Woodes Roger had about a decade before, they safely returned home, Clipperton in June and Shelvocke in August 1722, with modest profit.[60]

Thus, though there were several projects for expeditions during the War of the Quadruple Alliance, they were planned and carried out chiefly by private individuals, and the government's involvement in them was indirect. The main theatres of this war were the Mediterranean and the Baltic, and the involvement of the British navy in the conflict in the Americas was mainly of a defensive nature, such as the defence of the Bahamas against the Spanish invasion in February 1720, and the effort of Captain Edward Vernon's squadron cruising off Havana to prevent further attack on the Bahamas.[61]

Plans for Colonial Expeditions during the Anglo-Spanish Conflict of 1726–29

This relative indifference of the government to Spanish American expeditions continued despite a dramatic change in British politics: the fall of the Stanhope–Sunderland faction and the emergence of Walpole and Townshend as new Whig leaders. In the period of the Anglo-Spanish conflict of 1726–29, there were some references to plans for Spanish-American expeditions. Nevertheless, as during the War of the Quadruple Alliance, the government does not seem to have considered any of them seriously.

In the early stage of the Anglo-Spanish conflict of 1726–29, there was an expectation that, with British naval assistance, the Spanish colonists might rise up against the government in Spain, as at the beginning of the War of the Spanish Succession. It was hoped that this rebellion might lead to the independence of those colonies, on which Britain was expected to have more influence. In January 1726, Daniel Dering, brother-in-law of Viscount Percival, expressed an optimistic view about the prospect of maritime war against Spain, especially in the West Indies. It was believed that the Spanish colonists were tired of Spanish rule and were waiting for an opportunity to revolt.[62] In March, when Hosier's fleet was

60 On the voyage of Shelvocke and Clipperton, see Williams, *The Great South Sea: English Voyages and Encounters*, pp. 197–201; Bradley, *British Maritime Enterprise*, pp. 512–20. Their voyage had some connection with the above-mentioned plan by the London merchants and the emperor. Initially they obtained the emperor's commission to seize Spanish ships, but soon obtained a British commission after Britain declared war on Spain. Bradley, *British Maritime Enterprise*, p. 512.

61 Richmond, *Navy as an Instrument of Policy*, p. 389.

62 BL, Add MS 47031, fol. 78v, Daniel Dering to [Lord Percival], 17 January 1725/6.

ordered to sail for the West Indies, Dering mentioned again this possibility of an uprising in Spanish America with British naval assistance.[63] Percival himself also referred to this idea of independence for the Spanish-American colonies, from which Britain might be able to obtain commercial privileges in return for naval support, though he personally thought that Britain should not be an aggressor.[64]

Moreover, among the government, there were occasional talks of colonial expeditions, especially to the South Sea. In November 1726, Horatio Walpole, British envoy in France, mentioned a proposal to establish a settlement in the South Sea, presented by one Join, a French abbot, to William Stanhope, though he was worried that this expedition might 'give perhaps too much jealousy and umbrage to the French nation'.[65] Similarly, Sir Charles Wager, one of the lords of the Admiralty at that time, appears to have been interested in the South Sea expedition. In May 1726, he received a proposal from Shelvocke for capturing the island of Chiloé off Chile, which was conveniently located to control the trade of the western coast of Spanish America including Peru and Mexico, and might be taken by the French if Britain did not take it.[66] Likewise, probably about 1727, Woodes Rogers, now governor of the Bahamas, gave advice on the South Sea expedition, which referred to a possibility of taking some part of Chile in cooperation with the Native Americans there and British privateers.[67]

In March 1727, Wager himself proposed a plan for a South Sea expedition in a letter to Walpole. According to his plan, while a British squadron with four or five ships was to be sent into the Pacific, land forces from New York and other places were to sail to Porto Bello with the West Indian squadron to capture that place. Then the land forces were to march over to Panama, where they were to meet the squadron in the Pacific that was to carry them to Lima or other places on the western coast of South America.[68] However, it seems that Wager soon gave

[63] BL, Add MS 47031, fol. 124v, Dering to Lord Percival, 24 March 1725/6.

[64] BL, Add MS 47031, fols 121v–122, Lord Percival to Dering, 15 March 1725/6.

[65] BL, Add MS 32748, fol. 232, Horatio Walpole to Newcastle, 5 November 1726 (N.S.). He also reported on a memorial presented by some French merchants to the French government that claimed that, by sending a squadron to the West Indies, England aimed not only to prevent the return of the galleons, but also to make a settlement there. He guessed that this was caused by leakage of Join's plan and recommended that Join should not be employed, lest Britain alienate the Dutch as well as the French. BL, Add MS 32748, fols 268v–269, Horatio Walpole to Newcastle, 15 November 1726 (N.S.). Join was a French priest with strong commercial interests in the Spanish colonies and had been on French trading expeditions to Spanish America several times since the end of the seventeenth century. Malamud Rikles, *Cádiz y Saint Malo*, pp. 188–9.

[66] BL, Add MS 19034, fols 84–86v, 'Capt Shelvock's Proposal for making an Establishment in the South Sea', 26 May 1726.

[67] BL, Add MS 19034, fols 70–70v, 'Capt Roger's acct of the South Sea' [n.d., but 1727?].

[68] Ch (H) MSS, Correspondence 1, 1410, fols 2v–3, Wager to Sir Robert Walpole, 14 March 1726/7. Wager's plan for the South Sea expedition later materialised in the form of Captain George Anson's expedition to the Pacific of 1740–44. Rodger, *Command of the Ocean*, pp. 236, 238–9. For Anson's voyage, see also Williams, *Prize of all the Ocean*.

up this plan for a military expedition, and instead proposed to Walpole another plan for a trading voyage to the South Sea, which the French did in the War of the Spanish Succession and, he thought, would do again in this war.[69]

These occasional discussions of colonial expeditions ceased in 1728, probably because of the Spanish accession to the preliminaries by the Convention of the Pardo in March of the same year. However, in 1729, with little progress made in the Congress of Soissons, interest in colonial expeditions resurfaced. In May 1729, at the request of Viscount Townshend, Secretary of State for the North, John Hart, ex-governor of the Leeward Islands, submitted a plan for an expedition against Porto Rico, which was one of the bases of Guarda-Costas and was suitably located to harass the other Spanish colonies and navigation in America.[70] Yet, this plan does not seem to have materialised either.

As we have seen so far, between 1714 and 1729, although there were some proposals for a colonial expedition, no colonial expedition was actually undertaken, either under the Stanhope–Sunderland ministry or under the Walpole–Townshend ministry. What could account for this indifference of the government to the colonial expeditions? In the case of the War of the Quadruple Alliance, the brevity of the period of the war could be one reason. Also in the Anglo-Spanish conflict of 1726–29, as Black has pointed out, the fact that war was not formally declared suffocated several plans for colonial expeditions.[71]

However, there was another important factor: a change in the priorities of British commercial policy in Spanish America. As G.C. Gibbs stated, as far as the affairs of western and central Europe went, the main concern of British foreign policy during 1714–19 was a search for security at three levels: commercial, national and international. In terms of British commercial interests, the government sought the security of commerce by correcting errors and unclear points in the two Anglo-Spanish commercial treaties of the Utrecht settlement.[72]

This seems to have reflected a change in the political circumstances surrounding Spanish-American trade. As we saw in Chapter 2, in the War of the Spanish Succession, the possible union between France and Spain caused a serious concern that Britain might be excluded from the Spanish American markets by France. This made an expedition against Spanish America to establish a trading base there one of the possible options for naval operations, especially in the early stages of the war, though the difficulties entailed in its actual execution were not fully realised by its promoters. The British acquisition of the Asiento trade after the peace of Utrecht dramatically changed this situation. In addition to illicit trade via Jamaica, Britain now gained direct and legal access to the Spanish-

[69] Ch (H) MSS, Correspondence 1, 1422, fol. 2v, Wager to Sir Robert Walpole, 9 May 1727.

[70] BL, Add MS 32694, fols 37–38v, Governor John Hart to Townshend, 8 May 1729.

[71] Jeremy Black, 'Anglo-Spanish Naval Relations in the Eighteenth Century', *MM* 67, no. 3 (1991), 242.

[72] Gibbs, 'Parliament and the Treaty of Quadruple Alliance', p. 287.

American market, which, at least in theory, placed her in a far more advantageous position than her main rival France. As Malamud Rikles states, this competition with the English was one of the important reasons that obliged the French merchants to return to the indirect trade with the Spanish colonies via Cadiz by silver fleets.[73]

Under the circumstances, from the viewpoint of the British government, military expeditions to establish a settlement in Spanish America were an unnecessary and risky option, which could endanger diplomatic relations with Spain and Britain's allies, and ruin what Britain had obtained in the peace of Utrecht. If there was any problem in Spanish-American trade, it should be solved first by diplomatic negotiations, rather than colonial expeditions. Thus, after the peace of Utrecht, protection of the newly acquired privileges in the Spanish-American trade and removal of the obstacles to the execution of the Asiento trade became the priority of the government's commercial policy in Spanish America. This does not seem to have been much affected by the political change in 1722, as the basic conditions of the Spanish-American trade remained the same. It was probably this shift in the government's priority in the policy on Spanish America that contributed to the relative scarcity of the argument for colonial expeditions in the ministerial press and the government's indifference to such expeditions between 1714 and 1729.

The Navy as a Protector of Trade

As we have seen in the previous chapter, in the period of the Anglo-Spanish conflict of 1726–29, when naval mobilisation was required, the government writers employed the pro-maritime war argument to defend the use of naval power. However, the change in government policy on the Spanish American colonies obliged them to alter the argument; they had to defend the exertion of naval force without stressing the prospect of colonial gains by the navy. For this purpose, the ministerial writers in this period came to emphasise another economic advantage of naval power: the security of British trade. They claimed that Britain was a trading nation, and even when she had to resort to force, it was not for territorial expansion but for the protection of trade.

When the tension with Spain increased in 1727, in support of the government's further action against the Vienna Alliance in an approaching war, Defoe claimed, '*Great Britain* is a Trading Nation, and trading Nations never covet War.' However, if Britain or her allies were insulted or their commerce invaded, 'Their power is always exerted to protect their Trade.'[74] It was also argued that territorial expansion was not what Britain aimed at. In another pamphlet, Defoe wrote as follows:

> Trading Nations seek no Conquest, aim at no Encrease of Power, or Agrandising of Persons or Families. *Great Britain* is Rich, and Strong, and Opulent enough in her own Wealth, Power and Commerce. She seeks no more but a peaceable Possessing her just Rights, and preserving to her People the free Extending their

[73] Malamud Rikles, *Cádiz y Saint Malo*, p. 109.

[74] Defoe, *Evident Approach of a War*, p. 13.

> Commerce, that they may Trade in Peace with all the World, and all the World with them.[75]

He tried to present Britain as 'the World's Protector', and claimed that, in cooperation with the allies, the British king opposed the aggressors to prevent their design.[76]

After the peace negotiations with Spain started at the conclusion of the Convention of the Pardo in March 1728, the ministerial writers used a similar logic to defend the British government's naval policy against an attack from the opposition that criticised the government for its alleged timidity towards the Spaniards. In the defence of the government's instruction to Hosier, the *British Journal* of 11 January 1729 stressed that Hosier's squadron successfully achieved its end just by blockading, and that the more aggressive measures that the opposition demanded, such as capture of the silver fleet, were unnecessary. Then it claimed, 'we wanted not to take Towns, or ransack Provinces; popular as such Knight Errantry may be. We endeavoured to prevent a War, by making it unnecessary.'[77] Likewise, the author of a ministerial pamphlet entitled *Peace and Trade, War and Taxes* pointed out the futility of war in terms of its economic gains, and claimed, 'We are a *trading People*, and should value ourselves upon the happy *Success* of *Peace*, not upon the *Trophies* of *War*.'[78] The author went on to say,

> *England* seeks no *Conquest*, no *Acquisitions* of Dominions by a War: Though we are as well qualify'd for the War, and have as good Sprits to carry it on, as most *Nations*; yet 'tis *Peace*, not *Conquest*, that is our Business. We seek to *preserve* and *enrich* our own *Possessions* and want not to possess those of other Men.[79]

A similar argument was repeated in another ministerial pamphlet entitled *The Treaty of Seville, and the Measures that Have been Taken for the Four Last Years, Impartially Considered*, which was published in 1730. Its author praised the ministry's effort to avoid a war and pointed out the foolishness of fighting with Spain, by which Britain would inevitably lose more than her opponent because of the gap in the amount of trade between the two countries. He also cast doubt on the effectiveness of a West Indian expedition, referring to the loss of seamen and damage to ships owing to the inhospitable climate that was encountered during Hosier's recent operation. Moreover, even if Britain might succeed in the expedition, it would be more advantageous for her to leave the colonies in the hands of the Spaniards. The author went on to say, 'In short, we want no Conquests ourselves, nor are there any we can wish to be made by our Allies.'[80] Thus, in the

75 Defoe, *Evident Advantages*, p. 29.

76 *Ibid.*, p. 30.

77 *British Journal or The Censor*, no. 52, 11 January 1729.

78 Thomas Merchant, Esq., *Peace and Trade, War and Taxes: or, the Irreparable Damage of our Trade in Case of a War* (London, 1729), p. 5.

79 *Ibid.*, p. 9.

80 A.B., *Treaty of Seville*, pp. 16–17.

defence of the government's naval policy, the ministerial press in this period stressed not prospect of colonial gains but security of trade.[81]

On the other hand, in the writings of the opposition writers, proposals for a colonial expedition were occasionally found, though, in this period, it does not seem to have been as noticeable as in the late 1730s. For example, the author of *Great Britain's Speediest Sinking Fund is a Powerful Maritime War* maintained that, by cooperation between the navy and private adventurers, Britain might be able to make a settlement on the coast of Chile, from which they could launch a further attack on the other Spanish colonies on the Pacific coast.[82] Two trading companies, the East India Company and the South Sea Company, whose interests were threatened by the Ostend Company, were also expected to join in this attempt. In particular, the author warned, the South Sea Company would lose all its trade in case of war with Spain unless it made an effort to open trade with the Spanish colonies on the Pacific coast.[83] Likewise in 1729, the author of *Reasons for a War, in order to Establish the Tranquillity and Commerce of Europe* suggested taking Chile, which was 'the richest in Gold, the weakest in Strength, and capable of being improv'd, even to Prodigy, far beyond any of the other Dominions of the *Spaniards* in *America*'.[84]

Furthermore, the opponents of the South Sea Company, who did not have to care for the company's interests, had no scruples about supporting colonial conquests. In 1730, one pamphleteer, who severely criticised the South Sea Company and advocated free trade with the Spanish-American colonies, proposed establishing a settlement in the area between the River Meschacebe [Mississippi] and St Augustine. In his plan, this new settlement was to be a staple for the Spanish-American trade, together with Jamaica. Moreover, he suggested using a part of a new type of navy that he proposed creating by incorporating the army into the navy, in order to put pressure on the Spaniards if they refused to trade and to control the navigation of European powers that sailed to and from this region.[85]

Thus, the change in circumstances in the Spanish-American trade affected the government's pro-maritime war argument to defend its naval policy in Spanish America. Instead of stressing the prospect of colonial acquisitions by the naval

[81] There is one exception to this tendency. In *The Evident Advantages to Great Britain and its Allies from the Approaching War*, Defoe proposed establishing a settlement in the Bay of Honda on the north coast of Cuba as a base to interrupt Spanish-American commerce. He expected that this would eventually encourage the Spanish colonies to open illicit trade with Britain. Defoe, *Evident Advantages*, pp. 41, 43–4. Given that he had been a staunch supporter of Spanish-American expedition to obtain a trading base since the period of the War of the Spanish Succession, it is likely that this was an expression of his personal view, rather than an opinion as a government spokesman.

[82] *Great Britain's Speediest Sinking Fund is a Powerful Maritime War*, pp. 16–17.

[83] *Ibid.*, pp. 26–9.

[84] *Reasons for a War, in order to Establish the Tranquillity and Commerce of Europe*, pp. 28–9.

[85] *A Specimen towards a New and Compleat Plan for Regulating and Settling the Military Power of Great Britain, in Concert with Commerce by Incorporating the Land and Sea Forces and Vesting the American Trade in our Selves …* (London, 1730), pp. 33, 36–8.

force, in this period, ministerial writers tended to put more emphasis on the usefulness of naval power in defence of British trade, whereas the proposals to establish a new colony were occasionally seen in pamphlets by opposition writers or critics of the South Sea Company.[86]

As we have seen so far, from 1714 to 1729, British naval operations were mainly confined to those of a precautionary nature. The two means to deprive Spain of its financial power that were often proposed in the War of the Spanish Succession – seizure of the Spanish silver fleet and colonial expeditions to establish settlements – were not attempted during this period. It is true that consideration for the allies' interests, which also hampered the attempt at colonial expeditions during the War of the Spanish Succession, was again an important reason for the government's hesitation to take aggressive naval action in Spanish America. However, after the commencement of the Asiento trade by the South Sea Company, the company's commercial interests emerged as a new factor that affected British naval policy against the Spanish colonies. While the Asiento treaty gave Britain a right to direct trade with the Spanish colonies, it also provided Spain with a suitable hostage that could be held in case of a rupture with Britain.

Thus, as long as the South Sea Company continued the Asiento trade, the British government had to think twice about taking aggressive action against the Spanish American colonies, such as the seizure of the silver fleet and colonial conquests. This impact of the Asiento trade by the South Sea Company on British naval policy has not been fully appreciated, but consideration for the company's interests was one important factor that obliged the British government to modify its naval policy in Spanish America.

This change in policy also affected the pro-maritime war argument presented by the ministerial pamphleteers. In order to defend the government's naval policy, especially the blockade by Hosier, the ministerial writers had to downplay the

86 It is possible that the emphasis on protection of trade instead of colonial conquest in ministerial writers' argument also reflected the contemporary debate on the ideal form of empire that could make liberty and greatness compatible. David Armitage has described the development of an idea in early modern England (later, Britain), which regarded the country as a commercial and maritime empire, not an empire oriented to territorial expansion. In this conception, unlike the latter empire epitomised by France under Louis XIV, which was believed to be aiming at the universal monarchy and hence threatened the liberties of Europe, the former type of commercial and maritime empire represented by England was freed from the dangers supposedly inherent in the land-based empire, such as tyranny, large armies and over-extension. David Armitage, *The Ideological Origins of the British Empire* (Cambridge, 2000), Chapter 5. See also, John Robertson, 'Universal Monarchy and the Liberties of Europe: David Hume's Critique of an English Whig Doctrine', *Political Discourse in Early Modern Britain*, ed. Nicholas Phillipson and Quentin Skinner (Cambridge, 1993), pp. 349–73. It is possible that the emphasis on protection of trade instead of colonial conquest drew inspiration from this ideology. However, the direct content in which this emphasis appeared was the Anglo-Spanish conflict of 1726–29 and the change in the government's policy on the Spanish-American trade.

advantages of the aggressive naval policy demanded by the opposition, without denigrating the potential of the British naval power. For this purpose, they came to stress the protection of trade, instead of territorial expansion, as the economic advantage of exertion of naval forces. On the other hand, the opposition writers or opponents of the South Sea Company were not so hesitant about bringing up proposals for establishing a new colony in Spanish America. Thus, the shift in the government's Spanish-American policy had an impact not only on naval operations in the West Indies, but also on the content of the pro-maritime war argument and the political constellation of its supporters.

Conclusion

In the argument supporting war at sea during the War of the Spanish Succession, maritime war, especially war against Spanish America, was inseparably associated with two broad economic advantages. The first is an economic advantage intertwined with strategic considerations. Supporters of colonial maritime war claimed that maritime war in Spanish America was an economical or even profitable, means of warfare: it could subdue the enemy – Spain and France – quickly by cutting off their supposed source of the sinews of war – silver supply from Spanish America – while correspondingly bringing riches to England. They also often invoked glorious memory of war at sea during the Elizabethan period to support their argument.

In addition to these strategic and economic concerns combined with economic motives, colonial maritime war was often supported out of commercial considerations. This is the second economic advantage. Some of the supporters of colonial maritime war regarded colonial expeditions as a means to recover the Spanish colonial market, which was threatened by the increasing presence of French merchants in the Spanish-American trade, especially the South Sea trade. The supporters expected that by sending expeditions, Britain could put pressure on the Spanish colonists and open Spanish-American markets, or seize part of Spanish America, such as Havana, the Isthmus of Panama, Chile and the River Plate, to use it as a trading base. The supporters defended the conquest on the grounds of the sixth article of the Treaty of the Grand Alliance, which allowed England and the Netherlands to capture and hold enemy territory. However, exchanging the conquests for the right to free trade with Spanish colonies was also discussed, because it was feared that such conquests might cause discontent with England's allies. Thus, the maritime war in Spanish America was believed to have, first, strategic advantages combined with economic motives and, second, commercial advantages relating to the struggle over the Spanish-American trade.

The emphasis on these economic advantages was present in pro-maritime war arguments throughout various periods. However, the arguments were strongly influenced by the political and diplomatic situations of each period. During the War of the Spanish Succession, the struggle between emerging political parties, not least the Tories and Whigs, affected the pro-maritime war argument and diversified its contents and functions.

During the War of the Spanish Succession, there were three peak periods in which these politically charged pro-maritime war arguments appeared in the press: first, from about 1701 to 1702; second, from 1707 to 1708; and third, from 1711 to 1712. There were significant differences in content between the first pro-maritime war argument that appeared in 1701–2 and the second argument that became influential in 1711–12, such as the attitude towards continental land war, the armies and the allies. The political functions of the two arguments were also different: to dispose the nation towards the war; and to criticise the former ministry's policy on war and Spanish-American trade.

However, both arguments emphasised the supposed economic advantages of maritime war, which enabled the arguments to attract a wide array of support from politicians of various political stances. Prosecution of the war with little expense, or even at a profit, was an idea that most of the British politicians accepted without objection. Likewise, penetration into the Spanish-American market was a goal that politicians supported irrespective of their political loyalty. Thus, it was these supposed economic advantages that attracted politicians of different political stances to support the colonial maritime war.

During the War of the Spanish Succession, there were keen supporters of these arguments both inside and outside the government. Although some of them were not consistent in their backing supporters, the variety of their political positions was remarkably wide. They were not confined to the High Tories, such as Rochester and Buckingham; they also included the Junto Whigs, such as Halifax and Somers, and the Country Whigs, such as Onslow. The pro-maritime war argument was not monopolizsed by the opposition, either. There were supporters in the ministers, such as Vernon, Nottingham, Godolphin and Bolingbroke. These supporters tried to implement a pro-maritime war policy that included interception of Spanish silver fleets and colonial expeditions.

During the war, several attempts to promote colonial maritime war by legislation appeared in Parliament, which culminated in the enactment of the American Act of 1708. However, during the war, colonial expeditions or legislative attempts to promote colonial maritime war did not achieve the result supporters expected. The attempts were hampered by administrative and diplomatic difficulties and clashes of interests between groups concerned with the West Indian colonies and the Spanish-American trade. Thus, the pro-maritime war policy that politicians in the mother country supported was often based on over-optimistic assumptions, and it foundered on the complex reality and conflicting interests in the West Indian colonies and the Spanish-American trade.

In spite of these failures, support for colonial maritime war survived even after the war ended. This was partly related to the tendency to attribute the failures to a particular person, a corrupt government or simple problems that were easy for non-experts in naval operations to understand, such as the secrecy and timing of departures. This tendency often distracted supporters from mundane but important administrative difficulties, such as speedy transportation of forces and procurement of provisions. At the same time, it helped them to believe that if plans had not been disturbed by 'evil advisers', or if the above-mentioned simple problems were overcome, the expeditions would easily succeed. Thus, the very fact that the dream of easy and profitable colonial expeditions was not fulfilled allowed politicians endorsing a pro-maritime war policy, such as Bolingbroke, to maintain their beliefs.

Supporters of colonial maritime war were also found in the mercantile community, especially merchants with an interest in Spanish-American trade, such as Sir Gilbert Heathcote and Sir Bartholomew Gracedieu. Nevertheless, it should be emphasised that their motive for support was different from those politicians who favoured colonial maritime war out of strategic as well as commercial considerations. The ultimate goal of these merchants was to gain access to the Spanish-American market. For them, colonial expeditions were just one of the ways to regain Spanish colonial trade. Therefore, they did not persist in their support for the expeditions for acquiring trading bases or aggressive maritime war, as long as they could secure trading channel by other means. It might be possible to draw a parallel between such merchants' involvement in colonial expeditions and the business of privateering, in that they resorted to the measure as an alternative to trade only when normal trade was interrupted by war.

A conflict of interest also existed among the merchants interested in the Spanish-American market. This can be observed in an abortive plan by the South Sea Company to send an expedition to the Pacific coast of South America in 1712. Although most historians have dismissed this expedition as a mere political gesture, it was actually a serious plan by the directors of the South Sea Company to gain a trading base for the South Sea trade, the original aim of the company in its trading business. However, leading Whig West Indian merchants, such as Heathcote, were excluded from this project. This was partly because of the political struggle in the City between the supporters of the Harley ministry and supporters of the former ministry, including Heathcote. Moreover, for those Whig West Indian merchants who regained access to the Spanish-American market in 1704, the company's attempt to open a new South Sea trade was not only unnecessary, but even harmful. The South Sea expedition was an attempt by newcomers to the Spanish-American trade to infiltrate the Spanish-American market by a new channel through the Pacific rather than through the Caribbean. However, having failed to receive the naval support originally promised by the government, the company's directors gave up the plan for an expedition and the idea of South Sea trade. Instead, they had to content themselves with the Asiento trade and annual ship trade, a right for which the government procured for the company in the peace negotiations.

This was a turning point for British policy in Spanish America. Thereafter, and until the late 1730s, the government's priority for Spanish-American trade was security and improvement of the newly acquired Asiento trade as well as protection of illicit trade via the British West Indian colonies. In contrast, naval expeditions to secure new trading bases were temporarily laid aside as too risky an option because they could endanger commercial relations with Spain.

After the War of the Spanish Succession ended, and especially after 1728, a shift occurred in the supporters of the pro-maritime war argument. Although the Whig ministry initially employed the pro-maritime war argument to defend its policy against Spain, it gradually toned down the argument as peace negotiations with Spain progressed. Meanwhile, the opposition composed of both the Whigs and Tories, and associated with the interests of private merchants, endorsed the pro-maritime war argument in their criticism of what they saw as the government's timidity towards the Spaniards.

In the period after the War of the Spanish Succession, the British government was obliged to moderate its naval policy towards the Spanish-American colonies, and refrained from taking aggressive action or attempting at territorial conquests in conflicts with Spain. The direct and legal access to the Spanish-American market by the Asiento trade, as well as illicit trade via Jamaica, put Britain in a more advantageous position than her trading rivals – France and the Netherlands. This made naval expeditions to establish a settlement in Spanish America an unnecessary option that could endanger Britain's newly acquired privileges and the assets of the South Sea Company in Spanish America in case of war with Spain.

This was a great contrast with a situation in the period before the War of the Spanish Succession, when Britain's commercial interests were seriously threatened by the possible union between France and Spain, and the advancement of the French merchants in the Spanish-American market, which made colonial expeditions a more necessary and sensible option to recover Spanish-American trade. The change also affected the content of the ministerial writers' argument. In the late 1720s, in defence of the government's naval policy, they came to stress security of trade, instead of colonial gains, as an economic advantage of maritime war.

Thus, after 1714, the British government became hesitant to take aggressive measures against Spanish colonies owing to the interests of the South Sea Company. By contrast, the opposition, which advocated the interests of private merchants and was free from such considerations, increasingly demanded tougher measures against Spain to criticise the government's supposed timidity. This led to a propaganda campaign by the opposition, which was pressing for vigorous maritime war in Spanish America in the late 1730s as new war with Spain approached.

The War of Jenkins' Ear, which merged with the War of the Austrian Succession in 1740, started auspiciously for Britain with Vice-Admiral Edward Vernon's capture of Porto Bello in November 1739.[1] For the supporters of the pro-maritime war argument, especially those in the opposition, this was a proof of rightness of their claim. An attempt to support colonial maritime war by legislation also reappeared in Parliament. In 1740, at the instigation of William Pulteney, the fourteenth clause of the American Act of 1708 to encourage private expeditions against the enemy was revived, and together with some other clauses, incorporated into a new act that passed the same year despite protests from Walpole and the South Sea Company.[2]

After the initial victory, however, the navy was not able to repeat its success. Subsequent operations in 1741–42 against Cartagena, Santiago de Cuba, and

[1] For these wars, see Woodfine, *Britannia's Glories*; and Richard Harding, *The Emergence of Britain's Global Naval Supremacy: The War of 1739–1748* (Woodbridge, 2010).

[2] Pares, *War and Trade in the West Indies*, p. 67; 'An Act for the More Effectual Securing and Encouraging the Trade of his Majesty's British Subjects to *America*, and for the Encouragement of Seamen to Enter into his Majesty's Service', 23 George II C. 4, *Statutes at Large*, vol. 6, pp. 379–84.

Panama by Vernon and Brigadier Thomas Wentworth, and attacks in early 1743 on La Guiara and Caracas, and on Porto Cabello by Commodore Charles Knowles were all unsuccessful, though Commodore George Anson's return from his circumnavigation in 1744 with treasure from a Manila galleon that he captured during his voyage made up for these failures to a certain extent, and it demonstrated that operations against the Spanish empire could be profitable.

In spite of the unimpressive performances in the early years of the war, the navy's reputation was not severely damaged. As Harding has pointed out, the blame for the failure was often placed on Walpole, the administration and the army, and this helped to preserve the conviction of the usefulness of British naval power and the advantages of maritime war.[3]

The latter half of the war saw some successes in North America and the Caribbean, such as capture of Louisbourg in June 1745, Knowles' attack on Port Louis, Saint-Domingue, in March 1748, and his engagement with the Spanish fleet off Havana in October 1748. On the other hand, in home waters, the Western Squadron, created in 1745, increasingly gained control of the Western Approaches and disrupted French commerce by attacking her convoys, which led to victories in two battles of Finisterre in May and October 1747. All in all, at sea, Britain maintained naval superiority over her enemy in this war. Nevertheless, the acquisition of a new territory in Spanish America proposed by the supporters of the pro-maritime war argument did not materialise.

It was not until the Seven Years War that the navy met the expectations of supporters of the pro-maritime war argument, which included William Pitt the Elder, Secretary of State for the South, though he also recognised the importance of war in Germany.[4] Under the leadership of the competent and experienced First Lord of the Admiralty, Lord Anson, the naval administration functioned efficiently enough to help the navy conduct successful operations, including colonial expeditions, though it did not experience a fundamental reform.[5] In particular, a late stage of the war saw a series of successful colonial operations. While Britain conquered French Canada – which increasingly became a new focal point of colonial war – by 1760, it also launched naval expeditions against the Spanish and French colonies in the Caribbean. Those resulted in several successful captures: the capture of Guadeloupe by Commodore John Moore and Brigadier John Barrington in May 1759, the capture of Martinique by Rear Admiral George Rodney in March 1762, and the capture of Havana by Admiral Sir George Pocock and Lieutenant-General George Keppel (the third Earl of Albemarle) in August 1762.[6]

3 *Ibid.*, p. 338.

4 For recent literature on this war, see Daniel Baugh, *The Global Seven Years War 1754–1763: Britain and France in a Great Power Contest* (Harlow and New York, 2011).

5 For naval administration under Anson, see Richard Middleton, 'Naval Administration in the Age of Pitt and Anson, 1755–1763', *The British Navy and the Use of Naval Power in the Eighteenth Century*, ed. Jeremy Black and Philip Woodfine (Leicester, 1988), pp. 109–27.

6 In addition, we may be able to count the capture of Manila by Colonel William Draper and Rear Admiral Samuel Cornish in October 1762 as a successful attack on the Spanish colony, though it did not take place in the Caribbean. For details on this expedition, see

To seize a city or a colony is one thing, to hold it is another. Outbreaks of yellow fever and malaria often hit the British troops severely in the Caribbean. Newly arrived from Europe, the troops had no immunity to those diseases.[7] This not only hampered the operations themselves, but also made it burdensome and hazardous for the troops to hold the conquests in the Caribbean, as was seen after the capture of Havana.[8]

The conquests in the Caribbean were also given up for diplomatic considerations. To offset the loss of the allies' territory in Europe, Britain sometimes returned conquests in peace negotiations. In the case of Guadeloupe and Martinique, in order to smooth the path to peace with France, the Earl of Bute, political adviser of George III and the Prime Minister at that time, chose to return the islands while retaining Canada (and Grenada and the Neutrals Islands in the eastern Caribbean), a decision that the French government was more likely to accept.[9] Thus, while Britain acquired the ability and experience necessary for successful colonial expeditions by the time of the Seven Years War, the colonial conquests came to assume new importance for British politicians compared with the period of the early eighteenth century.

The idea of easy and economically advantageous colonial maritime war against Spanish America continued to survive. It was still seen in the Nootka Sound Crisis of 1790 with Spain. Yet, this event did not lead to an actual war. This was because Britain was, at that time, embroiled in intricate negotiations to end the war that had begun in 1787 between Austria and Russia on one side, and the Ottoman

Nicholas Tracy, *Manila Ransomed: The British Assault on Manila in the Seven Years War* (Exeter, 1995).

[7] For the impact of yellow fever and malaria on warfare in the Caribbean in the eighteenth century, see John R. McNeill, *Mosquito Empires: Ecology and War in the Greater Caribbean, 1620–1914* (Cambridge, 2010), Chapter 5; John R. McNeill, 'The Ecological Basis of Warfare in the Caribbean, 1700–1804', *Adapting to Conditions: War and Society in the Eighteenth Century*, ed. Marten Ultee (Tuscaloosa, AL, 1986), pp. 26–42. McNeil explained that, in battles in that region against expeditionary forces from Europe, especially Britain, the presence of yellow fever tended to work in favour of the defenders, the Spanish and French colonists, who were often immune to the disease. McNeill, 'The Ecological Basis of Warfare', pp. 37–8.

[8] The drain of manpower through disease was still a serious problem for the British expeditions against French West Indian colonies during the French Revolutionary Wars. For example, in 1796, it has been estimated that Britain lost about 14,000 soldiers, composed of British and foreign units, through disease in the Caribbean. This amounted to more than two-fifths of the expeditionary forces that had arrived there that year. Duffy, *Soldiers, Sugar, and Seapower*, pp. 254–7, 334–8.

[9] Pares, *War and Trade*, pp. 225–6. Although pressure from the West Indian planters has been often mentioned as a factor that influenced this decision, Pares points out that the opinions of the planters in the British West Indian colonies were not actually unanimous on this issue. There were some among the British planters, especially those of Barbados and the Leeward Islands, who supported acquisition of Guadeloupe and Martinique, which were notorious nests of French privateers, for the security of the British West Indian colonies. *Ibid.*, pp. 219–23.

Empire on the other, and was reluctant to get involved in a new conflict with Spain.[10] Likewise, the capture of Buenos Aires in 1806 and attacks on Montevideo and Buenos Aires in the following year by Britain were motivated by, and stimulated an expectation of, taking control of Spanish-American markets for Britain, which was an important feature of the argument supporting war against Spanish America.[11] In the end, apart from a settlement in Honduras (modern Belize) that served as a base for logwood cutting, and British Guiana (modern Guyana), Britain did not succeed in securing any new territory on the mainland of Central and South America.

Nevertheless, after the former Spanish and Portuguese colonies in Latin America became independent in the 1810s and 1820s, Britain increased its economic and cultural influence in those newly independent countries, especially Argentina and Brazil. Although her influence was still limited in the first half of the nineteenth century, as the century went on, Britain's penetration into the Latin American economy advanced, financially as well as commercially, with the assistance of the local 'collaborating elites'. British dominance in the Latin American economy continued until the turn of the twentieth century, when it was challenged by emerging industrial powers, such as Germany and the United States, and by Latin American nationalists.[12]

As we have seen, then, war at sea, especially maritime war against Spanish America, was expected to serve British economic interests in many ways. Although the claim was not necessarily based on sound calculations, the appeal of these alleged economic advantages helped the pro-maritime war argument win the support of a wide range of people, and influence British politics and naval policy, especially in conflicts with Spain. The idea of maritime war conducted out of economic motives, which had its origin in part in European medieval commercial and private warfare, found a new lease of life in the early modern Atlantic world, where the struggle over the wealth of the 'New World' often took the form of plundering as well as trade, and the pro-maritime war argument that reflected this idea survived well into the early nineteenth century.

10 Jeremy Black, 'Naval Power, Strategy and Foreign Policy, 1775–1791', *Parameters of British Naval Power 1650–1850*, ed. Michael Duffy (Exeter, 1992), pp. 111–13.

11 Rodger, *Command of the Ocean*, p. 548.

12 For British relations with Latin American countries after their independence, see Alan Knight, 'Britain and Latin America', *The Oxford History of the British Empire, Volume III: The Nineteenth Century*, ed. Andrew Porter (Oxford, 1999, repr. 2001), pp. 122–45.

BIBLIOGRAPHY

Manuscript Sources

Bodleian Library, Oxford

Manuscripts English History (MS Eng. Hist.)
d. 147–148

Boughton House, Northamptonshire

Shrewsbury Papers
[Microfilm at the Institute of Historical Research: *Letters from James Vernon to the Duke of Shrewsbury, 1696–1708, from the Shrewsbury Papers in Boughton House, Northamptonshire*, ed. Dennis Rubini (East Ardsley, 1980)]

British Library, London

Additional Manuscripts (Add. MSS)
12437: Proposal for Settling on the Isthmus of Darien
19034: Drafts and Copies of Papers relating to the Navy and to Admiral Sir Charles Wager's Service
19332: Original Instructions and Dispatches from the Government to Vice-Admiral Francis Hosier
22265: Papers relating to the Navy, Trade, etc.
25494–25495: South Sea Company, Court Minutes
25555, 25557: Official Copies of Home Letters and Memorials of the Court of Directors of the South Sea Company
25559–25560: South Sea Company, Memorial etc.
25562: Official Copies of the Most Material Letters Received by the South Sea Company
25567: Official Copies of Instructions to the several Commanders of Ships in the South Sea Companies' Service from the Court of Directors
28058: Official Papers relating to Military Operations in Spain
28140: Miscellaneous Papers, Chiefly Connected with the Navy
29587–29588, 29591, 29595: Hatton Finch Papers
31143, 32687: Wentworth Papers
32694, 32748, 32753, 32755, 32794: Newcastle Papers
33028: Papers relating to the Affairs of the American and West Indian Colonies
34348: Correspondence between James Vernon and William Blathwayt to William III
40775–40776: Vernon Papers

42840: Rose Papers
47031–47032: Egmont Papers
61126, 61196, 61500, 61515, 61581, 61583, 61585, 61643, 61644A: Blenheim Papers
69938, 69941: Coke Papers
70026–70027, 70028, 70044, 70049, 70163–70164, 70185, 70277, 70291, 70296, 70300, 70310–70311, 70332, 70338: Harley (Portland) Papers
Proclamations, James II to Anne

Cambridge University Library, Cambridge
Cholmondeley (Houghton) Manuscripts (Ch (H) MSS)
Political Papers 16: Navy Papers relating to Jamaica
Correspondence 1

Library of Congress, Washington, DC
The Vernon–Wager Manuscripts (Vernon–Wager MSS)
[Microfilm at the Institute of Historical Research: *The Vernon–Wager Manuscripts in the Library of Congress* (Washington, DC, 1977)]

Longleat House, Wiltshire
Portland Papers (PO)
[Microfilm at the Institute of Historical Research: *The Portland Papers* (East Ardsley, 1971)]
PO/VOL V

National Maritime Museum, Greenwich
Phillipps–Southwell Collection (SOU)
10: Admiralty Jurisdiction, including Papers about Prizes and Wrecks

Northamptonshire Record Office, Northampton
Finch Hatton Manuscripts (FH MSS)
275–277: Letters of Earl of Nottingham

Parliamentary Archives, London
Records of the House of Lords
Committee Office (HL/PO/CO)
1/7: Minutes of Committees
Journal Office (HL/PO/JO)
5/1/37–38: Minutes of Proceedings (Manuscript Minutes)
10/6: Main Papers, 1700–49

Society of Antiquaries of London, London
Manuscripts in the Society of Antiquaries of London [SAL/MS]
444/A

The National Archives, Kew

Records of the Admiralty (ADM)
1/230: Letters from Senior Officers, Jamaica
1/3810: Letters from Chartered Companies
1/4087–4088, 1/4090–4091, 1/4093–4094, 1/4096, 1/4100–1/4102, 1/4105–4106, 1/4107: Letters from Secretaries of State
2/365–366: Lord's Letters, Secretaries of State
2/400, 2/419: Secretary's Letters
3/16, 3/26, 3/32: Board's Minutes

Records of 'Colonial Office' [Colonial State Papers and records of the Old Board of Trade] (CO)
5/3–4: Dispatches and Miscellaneous
5/9: Expedition against Canada
5/387: South Carolina
7/1: Antigua
23/1: Bahamas
28/7, 28/10, 28/43, 29/8, 29/10, 31/6: Barbados
137/5–9, 137/12–13, 137/45–46, 137/51, 138/11–12: Jamaica
152/39, 152/42: Leeward Islands
194/2: Newfoundland
239/1: St. Christopher (St. Kitts), Nevis and Anguilla
318/3: West Indies, Military Dispatches
323/5–6: Colonies, General, Board of Trade
324/8–9: Entry Books, Commissions, Instructions, Board of Trade Correspondence, etc.
324/30: Grants and Warrants

State Papers (SP)
8/18: King William's Chest, Letters and Paper
42/6–7, 42/11, 42/67, 42/80: Naval
44/101–2: Entry Books, Secretary's Letter Books
44/206, 44/208–9: Entry Books, Naval
84/225: State Papers Foreign, Holland
104/79: State Papers Foreign, Entry Books, Holland
105/63: Correspondence and Papers of Sir George Stepney

Treasury Papers (T)
1/79: Treasury Board Papers and In-Letters

Seventeenth- and Eighteenth-Century Printed Works

I. Newspapers and periodicals

British Journal [between 1728 and 1729, *The British Journal or The Censor*]
British Merchant; Or, Commerce Preserv'd
Country Journal, or the Craftsman

Daily Courant
Daily Post
Evening Post
Examiner
Farley's Exeter Journal
Fog's Weekly Journal
London Gazette
London Journal
Mist's Weekly Journal
Observator
Political State of Great Britain
Post Boy
St. James's Evening Post
Weekly Journal or British Gazetteer
Weekly Journal or Saturday's Post
Whitehall Evening Post

II. Pamphlets

A.B., *The Treaty of Seville, and the Measures that Have been Taken for the Four Last Years, Impartially Considered. In a Letter to a Friend* (London, 1730).

Allen, Robert, *An Essay on the Nature and Methods of Carrying on a Trade to the South-Sea* … (London, 1712).

Addison, Joseph, *The Present State of the War, and the Necessity of an Augmentation, Consider'd* (London, 1708).

Amhurst, Nicholas, *Some Farther Remarks on a Late Pamphlet, Intitled, Observations on the Conduct of Great-Britain* … (London, 1729).

An Account of What Will Do; or An Equivalent for Thoulon … (London, 1707).

An Answer to a Calumny: with Some Remarks upon an Anonimous Pamphlet, Address'd to his Grace the Duke of Newcastle, Entitled, Some Observations on the Asseinto Trade…by the Factor to the South-Sea Company … (London, 1728).

An Argument against War: In Opposition to Some Late Pamphlets, Particularly; the First and Second Part of The Duke of Anjou's Succession … (London, 1701).

Bacon, Francis, *Certain miscellany works of the Right Honourable Francis Lord Verulam* (London, 1670).

Bolingbroke, Henry St. John, Viscount, *The Craftsman Extraordinary. Being Remarks on a Late Pamphlet, Intitled, Observations on the Conduct of Great Britain, &c* … (London, 1729).

Bolingbroke, Henry St John, Viscount, *The Craftsman Extraordinary; Containing an Answer to the Defence of the Enquiry into the Reasons of the Conduct of Great-Britain* … (London, 1729).

Bolingbroke, Henry St John, Viscount, *A Letter to the Examiner.* ([London], 1710).

Bolingbroke, Henry St John, Viscount, *Letters and Correspondence, Public and Private, of the Right Honourable Henry St. John, Lord Visc. Bolingbroke* … ed. Gilbert Parke (4 vols, London, 1798), vol. I,

Bolingbroke, Henry St John, Viscount, *One Word with the Craftsman Extraordi-*

nary (London, 1729).

Burchett, Josiah, *Mr. Burchett's Justification of His Naval-memoirs. In Answer to Reflections Made by Col. Lillingston …* ([London], 1704).

Clarendon, Edward Hyde, Earl of, *The History of the Rebellion and Civil Wars in England, Begun in the Year 1641…* (3 vols, Oxford, 1702), vol. I.

The Conduct of the Courts of Great-Britain and Spain, as to the Present Posture of Affairs, Briefly Set Forth and Consider'd … (London, 1718).

The Considerable Advantages of a South-Sea Trade to Our English Nation (London, [1711?]).

Coxe, William, *Memoirs of the Life and Administration of Sir Robert Walpole* (3 vols, London 1798, repr. London, 1800), vol. II.

The Dangers of Europe, from the Growing Power of France. With Some Free Thoughts on Remedies … By the Author of, The Duke of Anjou's Succession Considered (London, 1702).

Davenant, Charles, *Essays upon I. The Ballance of Power. II. The Right of Making War, Peace, and Alliances. III. Universal Monarchy* (London, 1701).

Davenant, Charles, *A Report to the Honourable the Commissioners for Putting in Execution the Act, Intitled, An Act, for the Taking, Examining, and Stating the Publick Accounts of the Kingdom* (London, 1712).

Davenant, Charles, *Sir Thomas Double at Court, and in High Preferments. In Two Dialogues, between Sir Thomas Double and Sir Richard Comover, alias Mr. Whiglove* ([London], 1710).

A Debate between Three Ministers of State on the Present Affairs of England. In Relation to the Disposition of the Nation at Home, Our Alliances … (London, 1702).

Defoe, Daniel, *Armageddon: or, The Necessity of Carrying on the War, If Such a Peace Cannot be Cbtained as May Render Europe Safe, and Trade Secure* (London, [1711]).

Defoe, Daniel, *An Essay on the South-Sea Trade. With an Inqury into the Ground and Reasons of the Present Dislike and Complaint against the Settlement of a South Sea Company…* (London, 1712 [1711]).

Defoe, Daniel, *The Evident Advantages to Great Britain and its Allies from the Approaching War: Especially in Matters of Trade. To which is Added Two Curious Plans, one of the Ports and Bay of Havana; the Other of Porto Bello …* (London, 1727).

Defoe, Daniel, *The Evident Approach of a War; and Something of the Necessity of It, in Order to Establish Peace, and Preserve Trade. To which is Added, an Exact Plan and Description of the Bay and the City of Gibraltar…* (London, 1727).

Defoe, Daniel, *An Historical Account of the Voyages and Adventures of Sir Walter Raleigh. Also a Particular Account of his Several Attempts for the Discovery of…* (London, 1719).

Defoe, Daniel, *Reasons against a War with France, or an Argument Shewing that the French King's Owning the Prince of Wales as King of England, Scotland and Ireland; is no Sufficient Ground of a War* (London, 1701).

Defoe, Daniel, *Reasons Why this Nation Ought to Put a Speedy End to this Expensive War…* 2nd edn ([London], 1711).

Defoe, Daniel, *The Two Great Questions Consider'd I. What the French King Will Do, with Respect to the Spanish Monarchy, II. What Measures the English Ought to Take* (London, 1700).

Dennis, John, *A Proposal for Putting a Speedy End to the War, by Ruining the Commerce of the French and Spaniards, and Securing Our Own, without Any Additional* ... (London, 1703).

Division our Destruction: or, a Short History of the French Faction in England (London, 1702).

The Duke of Anjou's Succession Considered, as to Its Legality and Consequences ... 2nd edn (Dublin, 1701).

The Duke of Anjou's Succession Further Consider'd, as to the Danger That May Arise from it to Europe in General; but More Particularly to England, ... (London, 1701).

Europa Libera: or, A Probable Expedient (the like Scarce Ever to be Hop'd for Again) to Restore and Secure the Publick Peace of Europe, for this ... (London, 1703).

Fletcher, Andrew, *A Discourse concerning Militia's and Standing Armies with relation to the Past and Present Governments of Europe and of England in Particular* (London, 1697).

Forman, Charles, *Mr. Forman's Letter to the Right Honourable William Pulteney, Esq; Shewing How Pernicious, the Imperial Company of Commerce and Navigation* ... (London, 1725).

A Full Answer to the Conduct of the Allies: To Which is Added, Some Observations on the Remarks on the Barrier Treaty ... (London, 1712).

Gibson, *Memoirs of Queen Anne: Being a Compleat Supplement to the History of her Reign* ... (London, 1729).

Gordon, Thomas, *The Character of an Independent Whig*, 2nd edn (London, 1719).

Great Britain's Speediest Sinking Fund is a Powerful Maritime War, Rightly Manag'd, and Especially in the West Indies (London, 1727).

Hoadly, Benjamin, *A Defence of the Enquiry into the Reasons of the Conduct of Great-Britain, &c.* ... (London, 1729).

Hoadly, Benjamin, *An Enquiry into the Reasons of the Conduct of Great Britain, with relation to the Present State of Affairs in Europe* (London, 1727).

The Humble Petition of the Mayor, Sheriffs, Justices, Aldermen and Common-Council of the City of Norwich; to His Majesty King George ([Norwich?], [1718?]).

The Importance of the Ostend-Company Consider'd (London, 1726).

An Inquiry into the Causes of Our Naval Miscarriages: with Some Thoughts on the Interest of This Nation as to a Naval War ... 2nd edn (London, 1707).

A Letter from a Merchant at Amsterdam, to His Correspondent in London ([London], [1718]).

A Letter from a Merchant in Amsterdam to a Friend in London, about the South Sea Trade (London, 1712).

A Letter from an Exchange Broker to a Country Gentleman, Concerning Peace and South-Sea Stock (London, 1711).

A Letter to a Friend at the Hague, concerning the Danger of Europe, and Particularly of Great-Britain ... (London, 1718).

A Letter to a Member of Parliament concerning Trade; and Particularly the Trade of the Spanish West-Indies (London, 1707).

A Letter to a Member of Parliament, on the Settling a Trade to the South-Sea of America ([London], [1711]).

A Letter to a Member of the October-Club: Shewing, that to Yield Spain to the Duke of Anjou by a Peace, Wou'd be the Ruin of Great Britain (London, 1711).

A Letter to Caleb D'Anvers, Esq; Occasioned by the Depredations Committed by the Spaniards in the West-Indies … (London, 1729).

A Letter to Sir William Robinson, in relation to a Proposal for a Trade to the Spanish West-Indies (London, 1707).

Le Wright, John, *Two Proposals Becoming England at This Juncture to Undertake One, for Securing a Collony in the West-Indies … And the Other, for Advancing Merchandize, and the Crown-Revenue to at least 40000l. p. an* ([London?], 1706).

Martyn, Richard, *A Modest Representation of the Past and Present State of Great Britain, Occasion'd by the Late Change in the Administration* (London, 1711).

Maynwaring, Arthur, *A Letter to a High-Churchman, in Answer to a Pamphlet, Intitled, Reasons Why This Nation Should Put a Speedy End to this Expensive War* (London, 1711).

Maynwaring, Arthur, *Remarks upon the Present Negotiations of Peace Begun between Britain and France* (London, 1711).

Merchant, Thomas, Esq., *Peace and Trade, War and Taxes: or, the Irreparable Damage of Our Trade in Case of a War* (London, 1729).

Moll, Herman, *A View of the Coasts, Countries and Islands within the Limits of the South-Sea-Company …* (London, 1711).

Observations and Remarks upon the Declaration of War against Spain, and upon the Manifesto Publish'd in the Name of the King of France … (London, 1719).

Observations on the Conduct of Great Britain, with regard to the Negociations and Other Transactions Abroad (Edinburgh, 1729).

The Observations on the Treaty of Seville Examined (London, 1730).

Oldmixon, John, *Remarks on a False, Scandalous, and Seditious Libel, Intituled, The Conduct of the Allies …* (London, 1711).

The Pacifick Fleet: a New Ballad (London, 1729).

The Present Condition of the English Navy Set Forth in a Dialogue betwixt Young Fudg of the Admiralty, and Capt. Steerwell, on Oliverian Commander (London, 1702).

Proposals for Carrying on an Effectual War in America, against the French and Spaniards (London, 1702).

Pullen, John, *Memoirs of the Maritime Affairs of Great Britain, Especially in relation to Our Concerns in the West-Indies …* (London, 1732).

Pulteney, William, Earl of Bath, *A Short View of the State of Affairs, with relation to Great Britain, for Four Years Past …* (London, 1730).

Reasons against a War. In a Letter to a Member of Parliament. By an Old Whig (London, 1727).

Reasons for a War, in order to Establish the Tranquillity and Commerce of Europe (London, 1729).

Reasons for a War with France and Spain, wherein Some Late Arguments against it are

Consider'd (London, 1702).

Reasons Shewing the Necessity of Reducing the Army, and, Proving that the Navy of England is her Only, and Natural Strength and Security (London, 1728).

Remarks upon a Late Pamphlet Intitul'd The Two Great Questions Consider'd I. What the French King will Do with Respect to the Spanish Monarchy, II. What Measures the English Ought to Take (London, 1700).

Remarks upon the Two Great Questions. Part II. Wherein the Grand Question of All is Considered, viz. What the Dutch Ought to Do at This Juncture? (London, 1701).

Some Observations upon a Late Pamphlet, Intitled, A Modest Representation of the Past and Present State of Great Britain, Occasion'd by the Late Change in the Admistration … (London, 1711).

Some Queries, which being Nicely Answered may Tend Very Much to the Encouragement of the South-Sea Company … ([n.p.], 1711).

Somers, John, *Jura Populi Anglicani: or, the subjects right of petitioning set forth. Occasioned by the case of the Kentish petitioners* (London, 1701).

South Sea Company, *Abstract of the Charter of the Governour and Company of Merchants of Great Britain, Trading to the South-Seas, and Other Parts of America, and* … ([London], [1711]).

A Specimen Towards a New and Compleat Plan for Regulating and Settling the Military Power of Great Britain, in Concert with Commerce by Incorporating the Land and Sea Forces and Vesting the American Trade in our Selves … (London, 1730).

The State of the Island of Jamaica. Chiefly in relation to its Commerce, and the Conduct of the Spaniards in the West-Indies … (London, 1726).

Stepney, George, *An Essay upon the Present Interest of England. To which are Added, the Proceedings of the House of Commons in 1677* … (London, 1701).

The Succession of Spain Discuss'd. With a Project of Reconciling all the Present Pretensions to that Crown … (London, 1701).

Swift, Jonathan, *The Conduct of the Allies, and of the Late Ministry, in Beginning and Carrying on the Present War*, 2nd edn, corrected (London, 1711).

The Tallies of War and Peace: or, What may be Expected from the Present Situation of Affairs in Europe (London, 1727).

Trenchard, John, *An Argument, Shewing that a Standing Army is Inconsistent with a Free Government and Absolutely Destructive to the Constitution of the English Monarchy* (London, 1697).

A True Account of the Design, and Advantages of the South-Sea Trade: with Answers to All the Objections Rais'd against it … (London, 1711).

A View of the Depredations and Ravages Committed by the Spaniards on the British Trade and Navigation (Dubln [i.e. Dublin], 1730).

Walpole, Robert, Earl of Orford. *Observations upon the Treaty between the Crowns of Great-Britain, France, and Spain, Concluded at Seville on the Ninth of November, 1729, N.S.* (London, 1729).

Williams, Reeve, *A Letter from a Merchant to a Member of Parliament, relating to the Danger Great Britain is in of Losing her Trade, by the Great Increase of the Naval Power of Spain*, the 2nd edn (London, 1718).

Modern Editions of Primary Sources

I. Official Publications

Acts of the Privy Council of England, Colonial Series, 1613–1783, ed. William Lawson Grant and James Munro (6 vols, London, 1908–12, repr. Nendeln, Leichtenstein, 1966), vol. III.

Cobbett, William, *Cobbett's Parliamentary History of England: From the Norman Conquest, in 1066, to the Year, 1803* (36 vols, London, 1806–20), vols, VI, VIII.

Journals of Assembly of Jamaica [microfilm] (14 vols, St Jago de la Vega, 1811–29, repr. Wilmington, DE, n.d.), vol. I.

Journal of the Commissioners for Trade and Plantations 1704–1782 (15 vols, London, 1920–38).

Journals of the House of Commons, vol. XIII–XVI.

Journals of the House of Lords, vol. XVII, XIX, XXIII.

The Statutes at Large, of England and of Great Britain: From Magna Carta to the Union of the Kingdoms of Great Britain and Ireland, ed. Thomas E. Tomlins (10 vols, London, 1811), vol. VI.

II. Historical Manuscripts Commission

Historical Manuscripts Commission, *Calendar of the Manuscripts of the Marquess of Bath, preserved at Longleat, Wiltshire* (5 vols, London, 1904–80), vol. I.

Historical Manuscripts Commission, *Calendar of the Stuart Papers belonging to His Majesty the King, preserved at Windsor Castle*, ed. F.H. Blackburne Daniell (7 vols, London, 1902–23), vols VI–VII.

Historical Manuscripts Commission, *Eighth Report of the Royal Commission on Historical Manuscripts, 3 parts* (London, 1881).

Historical Manuscripts Commission, *Manuscripts of the Earl of Carlisle, preserved at Castle Howard* (London, 1897).

Historical Manuscripts Commission, *The Manuscripts of the Earl Cowper* (3 vols, London, 1888–89), vol. II.

Historical Manuscripts Commission, *Manuscripts of the Earl of Egmont: Diary of the First Earl of Egmont (Viscount Percival)* (3 vols, London, 1920–23), vol. III.

Historical Manuscripts Commission, *Manuscripts of the House of Lords*, ed. C. Headlam and J.B. Hotham, new ser. (11 vols, London, 1900–62).

Historical Manuscripts Commission, *Report on the Manuscripts of the Duke of Portland, preserved at Welbeck Abbey* (8 vols, London, 1891–1931), vols IV–VII.

III. Selected Printed Primary Sources

Browning, Oscar, ed., *The Journal of Sir George Rooke, Admiral of the Fleet, 1700–1702* (Navy Records Society, vol. 9, 1897).

Burnet, Gilbert, *Bishop Burnet's History of his Own Time*, ed. M.J. Routh (6 vols, Oxford, 1833), vols IV–V.

Callender, Geoffrey, ed., *The Life of Sir John Leake: Rear-Admiral of Great Britain by Stephen Martin-Leake* (2 vols, London, 1920), vol. II.

Defoe, Daniel, *Defoe's Review: Reproduced from the Original Editions, with an Intro-*

duction and Bibliographical Notes by Arthur Wellesley Secord, Facsimile book 1–22 of vol. I–[IX]; Feb. 19, 1704–June 11, 1713 (New York, 1938).

De Beer, Esmond S., ed., *The Correspondence of John Locke* (8 vols, Oxford, 1976–89), vol. VII.

Ellis, Frank H., ed., *Poems on Affairs of State: Augustan Satirical Verse, 1660–1714* (New Haven and London, 1963–75), vol. VI.

Graham, G.S., ed., *The Walker Expedition to Quebec, 1711* (London, 1953).

Graham, Walter, ed., *The Letters of Joseph Addison* (Oxford, 1941).

Grimblot, Paul, ed., *Letters of William III and Louis XIV and Their Ministers (1697–1700)* (2 vols, London, 1848), vols I–II.

Hattendorf, John B., 'Benbow's Last Fight', *The Naval Miscellany, volume V*, ed. N.A.M. Rodger (Navy Records Society, vol. 125, 1984).

Legg, L.G. Wickham, 'Torcy's Account of Matthew Prior's Negotiations at Fontainebleau in July 1711', *EHR*, vol. 29, no. 115 (1914), 525–32.

Murray, Sir George, ed., *The Letters and Dispatches of John Churchill, first Duke of Marlborough* (5 vols, London, 1845), vols I, IV.

Newman, Aubrey, ed., *The Parliamentary Diary of Sir Edward Knatchbull, 1722–30* (London, 1963).

Rogers, Woodes, *A Cruising Voyage Round the World, with Introduction and Notes by G.E. Mainwaring* (London, 1928).

Singer, S.W., ed., *The Correspondence of Henry Hyde, Earl of Clarendon, and of his Brother Laurence Hyde, Earl of Rochester* (2 vols, London, 1828), vol. II.

Snyder, Henry L., ed., *The Marlborough–Godolphin Correspondence* (3 vols, Oxford, 1975), vols I–III.

Trevelyan G.M., ed., *Select Documents for Queen Anne's Reign: Down to the Union with Scotland, 1702–7* (Cambridge, 1929, repr. Wilmington, DE and London, 1973).

Van 'T Hoff, B., ed., *The Correspondence 1701–1711 of John Churchill, First Duke of Marlborough and Anthonie Heinsius, Grand Pensionary of Holland* (The Hague, 1951).

Vernon, James, *Letters Illustrative of the Reign of William III from 1696 to 1708 addressed to the Duke of Shrewsbury*, ed. G.P.R. James (3 vols, London, 1841), vol. III.

Williams, Harold, ed., *The Correspondence of Jonathan Swift* (5 vols, Oxford, 1963–65).

Published Secondary Sources

Adams, S.L., 'Foreign Policy and the Parliaments of 1621 and 1624', *Faction and Parliament: Essays on Early Stuart History*, ed. Kevin Sharpe (Oxford, 1978), pp. 139–71.

Adams, S.L., 'Spain or the Netherlands? The Dilemmas of Early Stuart Foreign Policy', *Before the English Civil War*, ed. Howard Tomlinson (London, 1983), pp. 79–101.

Ahn, Doohwan, 'The Anglo-French Treaty of Commerce of 1713: Tory Trade

Politics and the Question of Dutch Decline', *History of European Ideas* 36 (2010), 167–80.

Allen, Douglas W., 'The British Navy Rules: Monitoring and Incompatible Incentives in the Age of Fighting Sail', *Explorations in Economic History* 39 (2002), 204–31.

Allen, Robert J., 'William Oldisworth: the Author of the *Examiner*', *Philological Quarterly* 26, no. 4 (1947), 159–80.

Alsop, J.D., 'A Darien Epilogue: Robert Allen in Spanish America, 1698–1707', *Americas* 43, no. 2 (Oct. 1986), 197–201.

Andrews, Kenneth R., 'Beyond the Equinoctial: England and South America in the Sixteenth Century', *JICH* 10, no. 1 (1981), 4–24.

Andrews, Kenneth R., *Elizabethan Privateering: English Privateering during the Spanish War 1585–1603* (Cambridge, 1964).

Andrews, Kenneth R., *The Spanish Caribbean: The Trade and Plunder 1530–1630* (New Haven and London, 1978).

Andrews, Kenneth R., *Trade, Plunder and Settlement: Maritime Enterprise and the Genesis of the British Empire, 1480–1630* (Cambridge, 1984).

Appleby, John C., 'An Association for the West Indies? English Plans for a West India Company 1621–29', *JICH* 15, no. 3 (May 1987), 213–41.

Armitage, David, *The Ideological Origins of the British Empire* (Cambridge, 2000).

Barbour, James S., *A History of William Paterson and the Darien Company* (Edinburgh and London, 1907).

Barker, Hannah, *Newspapers, Politics and English Society, 1695–1855* (Themes in British Social History) (Harlow, 2000).

Bastian, Frank, *Defoe's Early Life* (London, 1981).

Battick, John F., 'A New Interpretation of Cromwell's Western Design', *Journal of the Barbados Museum and Historical Society* 34 (1972), 76–84.

Baugh, Daniel, *The Global Seven Years War 1754–1763: Britain and France in a Great Power Contest* (Harlow and New York, 2011).

Baugh, Daniel A., 'Great Britain's "Blue Water" Policy, 1689–1815', *International History Review* 10, no. 1 (1988), 33–58.

Baugh, Daniel A., 'Maritime Strength and Atlantic Commerce', *An Imperial State at War: Britain from 1689 to 1815*, ed. Lawrence Stone (London and New York, 1994), pp. 185–223.

Baugh, Daniel A., 'Sir Charles Wager, 1666–1743', *Precursors of Nelson: British Admirals of the Eighteenth Century*, ed. Peter le Fevre and Richard Harding (London and Mechanicsburg, PA, 2000), pp. 101–26.

Black, Jeremy, 'Anglo-Spanish Naval Relations in the Eighteenth Century', *MM* 77, no. 3 (1991), 235–58.

Black, Jeremy, *British Foreign Policy in the Age of Walpole* (Edinburgh, 1985).

Black, Jeremy, *The Collapse of the Anglo-French Alliance, 1727–1731* (Gloucester, 1987).

Black, Jeremy, *The English Press in the Eighteenth Century* (London and Sydney, 1987).

Black, Jeremy, 'Foreign Policy in the Age of Walpole', *Britain in the Age of Walpole*, ed. Jeremy Black (London, 1984), pp. 145–69.

Black, Jeremy, 'Naval Power, Strategy and Foreign Policy, 1775–1791', *Parameters of British Naval Power 1650–1850*, ed. Michael Duffy (Exeter, 1992), pp. 93–120.

Black, Jeremy, 'Parliament and the Political and Diplomatic Crisis of 1717–1718', *Parliamentary History* 3 (1984), 77–101.

Bourne, Ruth, *Queen Anne's Navy in the West Indies* (New Haven, 1939).

Bradley, Peter T., *British Maritime Enterprise in the New World: From the Late Fifteenth to the Mid-Eighteenth Century* (Lewiston, NY, 1999).

Bradley, Peter T., *The Lure of Peru: Maritime Intrusion into the South Sea, 1598–1701* (Basingstoke and London, 1989).

Brenner, Robert, *Merchants and Revolution: Commercial Change, Political Conflict, and London's Overseas Traders, 1550–1653* (Princeton, NJ, 1993, repr. London and New York, 2003).

Brewer, John, *The Sinews of Power: War Money and the English State, 1688–1783* (London, 1988, repr., Cambridge, MA, 1990).

Bromley, John S., 'The French Privateering War, 1702–13', *Corsairs and Navies, 1660–1760*, ed. John S. Bromley (London and Ronceverte, 1987), pp. 213–41.

Bromley, John S., 'Prize Office and Prize Agency at Portsmouth, 1689–1748', *Corsairs and Navies, 1660–1760*, ed. John S. Bromley(London and Ronceverte, 1987), pp. 463–93.

Buchet, Christian, 'The Royal Navy and the Caribbean, 1689–1763', *MM* 80 (1994), 30–44.

Carswell, John P., *The South Sea Bubble* (London, 1960, repr. Stroud, 1993).

Cherry, George L., 'The Development of the English Free-Trade Movement in Parliament, 1689–1702', *JMH* 35, no. 2 (June 1953), 103–19.

Clark, Dora Mae, 'The Impressment of Seamen in the American Colonies', *Essays in Colonial History: Presented to Charles McLean Andrews by his Students* (Free Port, New York, 1966), pp. 198–224.

Clark, George N., 'War Trade and Trade War, 1701–1713', *EcHR* 1 (1928), 262–80.

Cogswell, Thomas, *The Blessed Revolution: English Politics and the Coming of War, 1621–1624* (Cambridge, 1989).

Coombs, Douglas, *The Conduct of the Dutch: British Opinion and the Dutch Alliance during the War of the Spanish Succession* (The Hague, 1958).

Craven, W. Frank, 'The Earl of Warwick, a Speculator in Piracy', *Hispanic American Historical Review* 10, no. 4 (November 1930), pp. 457–47.

Crewe, Duncan G., *Yellow Jack and the Worm: British Naval Administration in the West Indies, 1739–1748* (Liverpool, 1993).

Crowhurst, Patrick, *The Defence of British Trade 1689–1815* (Folkestone, 1977).

De Krey, Gary S., *A Fractured Society: The Politics of London in the First Age of Party, 1688–1715* (Oxford, 1985).

Dickey, Laurence, 'Power, Commerce and Natural Law in Daniel Defoe's Political Writings, 1698–1707', *A Union for Empire: Political Thought and the British Union of 1707*, ed. John Robertson (Cambridge, 1995), pp. 63–96.

Dickinson, Harry T., *Bolingbroke* (London, 1970).
Dickinson, Harry T., 'Popular Politics in the Age of Walpole', *Britain in the Age of Walpole*, ed. Jeremy Black (London, 1984), pp. 45–68.
Dickson, P.G.M., *The Financial Revolution in England: A Study in the Development of Public Credit, 1688–1756* (London, 1967).
Donnan, Elizabeth, 'The Early Days of the South Sea Company, 1711–1718', *JEBH* 2 (1930), 419–50.
Downie, James A., 'The Commissioners of Public Accounts and the Formation of the Country Party', *EHR* 91, no. 358 (January 1976), 33–51.
Downie, James A., 'The Conduct of the Allies: The Question of Influence', *The Art of Jonathan Swift*, ed. Clive T. Probyn (London, 1978), pp. 108–28.
Downie, James A., *Robert Harley and the Press: Propaganda and Public Opinion in the Age of Swift and Defoe* (Cambridge, 1979).
Duffy, Michael, *Soldiers, Sugar, and Seapower: The British Expeditions to the West Indies and the War against Revolutionary War* (Oxford, 1987).
Dunmore, John, *French Explorers in the Pacific: I, The Eighteenth Century* (Oxford, 1965).
Dyer, Florence E., 'Captain John Strong, Privateers and Treasure Hunter', *MM* 13, no. 2 (1927), 145–58.
Earle, Peter, *The Pirate Wars* (London, 2003, repr. London, 2004).
Earle, Peter, *The Sack of Panama: Sir Henry Morgan's Adventures on the Spanish Main* (New York, 1981).
Ehrman, John, *The Navy in the War of William III, 1689–1697: Its State and Direction* (Cambridge, 1953).
Fernández Duro, Cesáreo, *Armada Española desde la Unión de los Reinos de Castilla y de Aragón* (9 vols, Madrid, 1895–1903), vol. VI.
Feiling, Keith, *British Foreign Policy, 1660–1672* (London, 1930).
Fewster, Joseph M., 'Prize-Money and the British Expedition to the West Indies of 1793–94', *JICH* 12, no. 1 (1984), 1–28.
Flinn, Michael W., 'Sir Ambrose Crowley and the South Sea Scheme of 1711', *Journal of Economic History* 20, no. 1 (March 1960), 51–66.
Francis, A.D., *The First Peninsular War, 1702–1713* (London and Tonbridge, 1975)
Francis, A.D., 'John Methuen and Anglo-Portuguese Treaties of 1703', *HJ* 3, no. 2 (1960), 103–24.
Francis, A.D., *The Methuens and Portugal, 1691–1708* (Cambridge, 1966).
Frostin, Charles, 'Les Ponchartrain et la Pénétration Commercial Française en Amérique Espagnole (1690–1715)', *Revue Historique* 498 (Avril–Juin 1971), 307–36.
Furbank, P.N., and W.R. Owens, *A Political Biography of Daniel Defoe* (Eighteenth-Century Political Biographies Series, 1) (London, 2006).
Gallup-Diaz, Ignacio, *The Door of the Seas and Key to the Universe: Indian Politics and Imperial Rivalry in the Darién, 1640–1750* (New York, 2004).
Gibbs, G.C., 'Britain and the Alliance of Hanover, April 1725 – February 1726', *EHR* 73 (1958), 404–30.
Gibbs, G.C., 'Parliament and the Treaty of Quadruple Alliance', *William III and*

Louis XIV: Essays 1680–1720 by and for Mark A. Thomson, ed. Ragnhild Hatton and J.S. Bromley (Liverpool, 1968), pp. 287–305.

Glass, Robert E., 'The Image of the Sea Officer in English Literature, 1660–1710', *Albion: A Quarterly Journal Concerned with British Studies* 26, no. 4 (Winter 1994), 583–9.

Goldgar, Bertrand A., *Walpole and the Wits: The Relation of Politics to Literature, 1722–42* (Lincoln, NE and London, 1976).

Goslinga, Cornelis Ch., *The Dutch in the Caribbean and in the Guianas, 1680–1791*, ed. Maria J.L. van Yperen (Assen, Netherlands and Dover, NH, 1985).

Guttridge, G.H., *The Colonial Policy of William III in America and the West Indies* (Cambridge, 1922).

Harding, Richard, *Amphibious Warfare in the Eighteenth Century: The British Expedition to the West Indies, 1740–1742* (Woodbridge, 1991).

Harding, Richard, 'British Maritime Strategy and Hanover 1714–1763', *The Hanoverian Dimension in British History, 1714–1837*, ed. Brendan Simms and Torsten Riotte (Cambridge, 2007), pp. 252–74.

Harding, Richard, *The Emergence of Britain's Global Naval Supremacy: The War of 1739–1748* (Woodbridge and Rochester, NY, 2010).

Harding, Richard, 'The Ideology and Organisation of Maritime War: An Expedition to Canada in 1746', XIV International Economic History Congress, Helsinki 2006, session 69.

Haring, Clarence H., *The Buccaneers in the West Indies in the XVII Century* (New York, 1910, repr. Hamden, CT, 1966).

Hattendorf, John B., *England in the War of the Spanish Succession: A Study of the English View and Conduct of Grand Strategy, 1702–1712* (New York and London, 1987).

Hatton, Ragnhild, 'John Drummond in the War of the Spanish Succession: Merchant Turned Diplomatic Agent', *Studies in Diplomatic History: Essays in Memory of David Bayne Horn*, ed. Ragnhild Hatton and M.S. Anderson (London, 1970), pp. 69–96.

Hayton, David, 'The "Country" Interest and the Party System, 1689–*c.*1720', *Party and Management in Parliament, 1660–1784*, ed. Clyve Jones (Leicester, 1984), pp. 37–85.

Hayton, David, Eveline Cruickshanks and Stuart Handley, *The House of Commons, 1690–1715* (History of Parliament) (5 vols, London, 2002), vols III–V.

Hertz, Gerald B., 'England and the Ostend Company', *EHR* 22, no. 86 (1907), 255–79.

Hill, B.W., 'Oxford, Bolingbroke, and the Peace of Utrecht', *HJ* 16, no. 2 (June 1973), 241–63.

Holmes, Geoffrey S., *British Politics in the Age of Anne* (London, 1967, repr. London and Ronceverte, 1987).

Holmes, Geoffrey S., *The Electorate and the National Will in the First Age of Party* (Lancaster, 1976).

Hoppit, Julian, 'The Myths of the South Sea Bubble', *TRHS*, 6th ser, 12 (2002), 141–65.

Horsley, Lee S., 'The Trial of John Tutchin, Author of the "Observator"', *Yearbook of English Studies* 3 (1973), 124–40.

Horwitz, Henry, *Parliament, Policy and Politics in the Reign of William III* (Manchester, 1977).

Hutchinson, Gillian, 'Herman Moll's View of the South Sea Company', *Journal for Maritime Research* 6, no. 1 (2004), 87–112.

Johnston, J.A., 'Parliament and the Protection of Trade, 1689–94', *MM* 57, no. 4 (November 1971), 399–413.

Jones, Donald, *Captain Woodes Roger's Voyage round the World, 1708–1711* (Bristol, 1992).

Jones, Dwyryd W., *War and Economy in the Age of William III and Marlborough* (Oxford, 1988).

Jones, J.R., *The Anglo-Dutch Wars of the Seventeenth Century* (London and New York, 1996).

Jubb, Michael, 'Economic Policy and Economic Development', *Britain in the Age of Walpole*, ed. Jeremy Black (London, 1984), pp. 121–44.

Kamen, Henry, 'The Destruction of the Spanish Silver Fleet at Vigo in 1702', *BIHR* 39 (1966), 165–73.

Kamen, Henry, *The War of Spanish Succession in Spain, 1700–15* (London, 1969).

Knight, Alan, 'Britain and Latin America', *The Oxford History of the British Empire, Volume III: The Nineteenth Century*, ed. Andrew Porter (Oxford, 1999, repr. Oxford, 2001), pp. 122–45.

Kramnick, Isaac, *Bolingbroke and his Circle: The Politics of Nostalgia in the Age of Walpole* (Cambridge, MA and London, 1968).

Kupperman, Karen O., 'Errand to the Indies: Puritan Colonization from Providence Island through the Western Design', *WMQ*, 3rd ser, 45, no. 1 (January 1988), 70–99.

Kupperman, Karen O., *Providence Island, 1630–1641: The Other Puritan Colony* (Cambridge, 1993, repr. Cambridge, 1995).

Lane, Kris E., *Pillaging the Empire: Piracy in the Americas 1500–1750* (Armonk, NY and London, 1998).

Lespagnol, Andreé, *Messieurs de Saint Malo: Une Élite Negociante au Temps de Louis XIV* (2 vols, Rennes, 1997).

Liss, Peggy K., *Atlantic Empires: The Network of Trade and Revolution, 1713–1826* (Baltimore, 1983).

Little, Bryan, *Crusoe's Captain: Being the Life of Woodes Rogers, Seaman, Trader, Colonial Governor* (London, 1960).

Lynch, John, *Bourbon Spain, 1700–1808* (Oxford, 1989).

MacLachlan, A.D., 'The Road to Peace, 1710–13', *Britain after the Glorious Revolution, 1689-1714*, ed. Geoffrey Holmes (London and New York, 1969), pp. 197–215.

Malamud Rikles, Carlos Daniel, *Cádiz y Saint Malo en el Comercio Colonial Peruano (1698– 1725)* (Cádiz, 1986).

Marichal, Carlos, 'Money, Taxes, and Finance', *The Cambridge Economic History of Latin America*, ed. Victor Bulmer-Thomas et al. (2 vols, Cambridge, 2006), vol.

I, pp. 423–60.

McLachlan, Jean O., *Trade and Peace with Old Spain 1667–1750: A Study of Commerce on Anglo-Spanish Diplomacy in the First Half of the Eighteenth Century* (Cambridge, 1940).

McNeill, John R., 'The Ecological Basis of Warfare in the Caribbean, 1700–1804', *Adapting to Conditions: War and Society in the Eighteenth Century*, ed. Marten Ultee (Tuscaloosa, AL, 1986), pp. 26–42.

McNeill, John R., *Mosquito Empires: Ecology and War in the Greater Caribbean, 1620–1914* (Cambridge, 2010).

Michael, Wolfgang, *England under George I, vol. 2: The Quadruple Alliance*, trans. and adapted from the German by Annemarie MacGregor and George E. MacGregor (London, 1939).

Middleton, Richard, 'Naval Administration in the Age of Pitt and Anson, 1755–1763', *The British Navy and the Use of Naval Power in the Eighteenth Century*, ed. Jeremy Black and Philip Woodfine (Leicester, 1988), pp. 109–27.

Moore, J.R., 'Daniel Defoe: King William's Pamphleteer and Intelligence Agent', *HLQ* 34, no. 3 (May 1971), 251–60.

Moore, J.R., 'Defoe and the South Sea Company', *Boston Public Library Quarterly* 5 (1953), 175–88.

Morgan, William T., 'The British West Indies during the King William's War (1689–97)', *JMH* 2 (1930), 378–409.

Morgan, William T., 'The Expedition of Baron de Pointis against Cartagena', *AHR* 37, no. 2 (January 1932), 237–54.

Morgan, William T., 'The Origins of the South Sea Company', *Political Science Quarterly* 44, no. 1 (1929), 16–38.

Morgan, William T., 'Some Attempts at Imperial Co-operation during the Reign of Queen Anne', *TRHS,* 4th ser, 10 (1927), 171–94.

Morgan, William T., 'The South Sea Company and the Canadian Expedition in the Reign of Queen Anne', *HAHR* 8 (1928), 143–66.

Morriss, Roger, *The Foundations of British Maritime Ascendancy: Resources, Logistics and the States, 1755–1815* (Cambridge, 2011).

Moses, Norton H., 'The British Navy and the Caribbean, 1689–1697', *MM* 52 (1966), 13–40.

Murphy, Anne L., *The Origins of English Financial Markets: Investment and Speculation before the South Sea Bubble* (Cambridge, 2009).

Murphy, Antoin E., *Richard Cantillon, Entrepreneur and Economist* (Oxford, 1986).

Murray, John J. *George I, the Baltic and the Whig Split of 1717: A Study in Diplomacy and Propaganda* (London and Chicago, 1969).

Nelson, George H., 'Contraband Trade under the Asiento, 1730–1739', *AHR* 51 (1945), 55–67.

Nettels, Curtis, 'England and Spanish-American Trade, 1680–1715', *JMH* 3 (1931), 1–32.

Newson, Linda A., 'The Demographic Impact of Colonization', *The Cambridge Economic History of Latin America*, ed. Victor Bulmer-Thomas et al. (2 vols, Cambridge, 2006), vol. I, pp. 143–84.

Newton, Arthur P., *The European Nations in the West Indies, 1493–1688* (London, 1933).

Onnekink, David, *The Anglo-Dutch Favourite: The Career of Hans Willem Bentinck, 1st Earl of Portland (1649–1709)* (Aldershot, 2007).

Owen, John H., *War at Sea under Queen Anne, 1702–1708* (Cambridge, 1938).

Oxford Dictionary of National Biography [Online version]

Pares, Richard, 'American versus Continental Warfare, 1739–63', *HER* 51, no. 203 (1936), 429–65.

Pares, Richard, 'The Manning of the Navy in the West Indies, 1702–63', *TRHS*, 4th ser, 20 (1937), 31–60.

Pares, Richard, *War and Trade in the West Indies, 1739–1763* (Oxford, 1936, repr. London, 1963).

Paul, Helen J., *The South Sea Bubble: An Economic History of its Origins and Consequences* (Abington and New York, 2011).

Pettigrew, William A., 'Free to Enslave: Politics and the Escalation of Britain's Transatlantic Slave Trade, 1688–1714', *William and Mary Quarterly*, 3rd ser, 64, no.1 (January 2007), 3–38.

Phillips, Carla R., *The Treasure of the San Jose: Death at Sea in the War of the Spanish Succession* (Baltimore, 2007).

Pincus, Steven, 'The English Debate over Universal Monarchy', *A Union for Empire: Political Thought and the British Union of 1707*, ed. John Robertson (Cambridge, 1995), pp. 37–62.

Pocock, J.G.A., *The Machiavellian Moment: Florentine Political Thought and the Atlantic Republican Tradition* (Princeton, NJ, 1975).

Prebble, John, *The Darien Disaster* (London, 1968).

Pritchard, James, *In Search of Empire: The French in the Americas* (Cambridge, 2004).

Quinn, David B., and A.N. Ryan, *England's Sea Empire, 1550–1642* (London, 1983).

Reinhartz, Dennis, *The Cartographer and the Literati: Herman Moll and His Intellectual Circle* (Lewiston, NY, 1997).

Richmond, Sir Herbert W., *The Navy as an Instrument of Policy, 1558–1727*, ed. E.A. Hughes (Cambridge, 1953).

Robertson, John, 'Universal Monarchy and the Liberties of Europe: David Hume's Critique of an English Whig Doctrine', *Political Discourse in Early Modern Britain*, ed. Nicholas Phillipson and Quentin Skinner (Cambridge, 1993), pp. 349–73.

Rodger, N.A.M., *The Command of the Ocean: A Naval History of Britain, 1649–1815* (London, 2004, repr. London, 2005).

Rodger, N.A.M., 'The New Atlantic: Naval Warfare in the Sixteenth Century', *War at Sea in the Middle Ages and the Renaissance*, ed. John B. Hattendorf and Richard W. Unger (Woodbridge, 2003), pp. 233–47.

Rodger, N.A.M., 'Queen Elizabeth and the Myth of Sea-Power in English History', *TRHS*, 6th ser, 14 (2004), 153–74.

Rodger, N.A.M., *The Safeguard of the Sea: A Naval History of Britain, 660–1649* (New York and London, 1998).

Rogers, B.M.H., 'Dampier's Voyage of 1703', *MM* 10, no. 4 (1924), 366–81.
Rogers, Nicholas, *The Press Gang: Naval Impressment and its Opponents in Georgian Britain* (London and New York, 2007).
Roscoe, Edward S., *A History of the English Prize Court* (London, 1924).
Rubini, Dennis, *Court and Country, 1688–1702* (London, 1967).
Sachse, William L., *Lord Somers: A Political Portrait* (Manchester, 1975).
Scammell, Geoffrey V., '"A Very Profitable and Advantageous Trade": British Smuggling in the Iberian Americas circa 1500–1750', *Itinerario* 24, issue 3–4 (2000), 135–72.
Scelle, Georges, 'The Slave-Trade in Spanish Colonies of America: The Assiento', *American Journal of International Law* 4 (1910), 612–61.
Schwoerer, Lois, G., *"No Standing Armies!": The Antiarmy Ideology in Seventeenth-Century England* (Baltimore and London, 1974).
Sheridan, Richard B., 'The Formation of Caribbean Plantation Society, 1689–1748', *The Oxford History of the British Empire, Volume II: The Eighteenth Century*, ed. Peter J. Marshall (Oxford, 1998), pp. 394–414.
Sheridan, Richard B., *Sugar and Slavery: An Economic History of the British West Indies, 1623–1775* (Baltimore, 1974).
Simms, Brendan, *Three Victories and a Defeat: The Rise and Fall of the First British Empire, 1714–1783* (London, 2007).
Snyder, Henry L., 'Queen Anne Versus the Junto: The Effort to Place Oxford at the Head of the Admiralty in 1709', *HLQ* 35, no. 4 (August 1972), 323–42.
Sperling, John G., *The South Sea Company: An Historical Essay and Bibliographical Finding List* (Boston, MA, 1962).
Speck, William A., *The Birth of Britain: A New Nation 1700–1710* (Oxford and Cambridge, MA, 1994).
Speck, William A., 'Political Propaganda in Augustan England', *TRHS*, 5th ser, 22 (1972), 17–32.
Speck, William A., 'The Whig Schism under George I', *HLQ* 40, no. 2 (1977), 171–9.
Spence, Richard, T. *The Privateering Earl: George Clifford, 3rd Earl of Cumberland, 1558–1605* (Stroud, 1995).
Stark, Francis R., *The Abolition of Privateering and the Declaration of Paris* (New York, 1897, repr. Honolulu, HI, 2002).
Starkey, David J., *British Privateering Enterprise in the Eighteenth Century* (Exeter, 1990).
Stein, Stanley J., and Barbara H. Stein, *Silver, Trade, and War: Spain and America in the Making of Early Modern Europe* (Baltimore and London, 2000).
Swanson, Carl E., *Predators and Prizes: American Privateering and Imperial Warfare, 1739–1748* (Columbia, SC, 1991).
Symcox, Geoffrey, *The Crisis of French Sea Power, 1688–1697: From the Guerre d'Escadre to the Guerre de Course* (The Hague, 1974).
Szechi, Daniel, *The Jacobites: Britain and Europe, 1688–1788* (Manchester and New York, 1994).
Taylor, S.A.G., *The Western Design: An Account of Cromwell's Expedition to the*

Caribbean (Kingston, Jamaica, 1965, repr. London, 1969).

Thomson, Mark A., 'Louis XIV and the Origins of the War of the Spanish Succession', *William III and Louis XIV: Essays 1680–1720 by and for Mark A. Thomson*, eds Ragnhild Hatton and J.S. Bromley (Liverpool, 1968), pp. 140–61.

Thornton, A.P., *West-India Policy under the Restoration* (Oxford, 1956).

Tracy, Nicholas J., *Manila Ransomed: the British Assault on Manila in the Seven Years War* (Exeter, 1995).

Venning, Timothy, *Cromwellian Foreign Policy* (New York, 1995).

Waddell, D., 'Charles Davenant (1656–1714) –A Biographical Sketch', *EcHR*, new ser, 11, no. 2 (1958), 279–88.

Waddell, David, 'The Writings of Charles Davenant (1656–1714)', *Library (1956) s5-XI(3)*, 206–12.

Walker, Geoffrey J., *Spanish Politics and Imperial Trade, 1700–1789* (Bloomington and London, 1979).

Watt, Douglas, *The Price of Scotland: Darien, Union and the Wealth of Nations* (Edinburgh, 2007).

Wernham, R.B., 'Elizabethan War Strategy', *Elizabethan Government and Society*, ed. S.T. Bindoff et al. (London, 1961), pp. 340–68.

Williams, Basil, *Stanhope: A Study in Eighteenth-Century War and Diplomacy* (Oxford, 1932, repr. Oxford, 1968).

Williams, Glyndwr, *The Great South Sea: English Voyages and Encounters, 1570–1750* (New Haven, CT and London, 1997).

Williams, Glyndwr, *The Prize of all the Ocean: The Triumph and Tragedy of Anson's Voyage Round the World* (London, 1999, repr. London, 2000).

Williams, Neville, *The Sea Dogs: Privateers, Plunder & Piracy in the Elizabethan Age* (London, 1975).

Willis, Sam, *The Admiral Benbow: The Life and Times of a Naval Legend* (London, 2010, repr. 2011).

Wilson, Arthur M., *French Foreign Policy during the Administration of Cardinal Fleury, 1726–1743* (Cambridge, MA and London, 1936).

Wilson, Kathleen, 'Empire, Trade and Popular Politics in Mid-Hanoverian Britain: The Case of Admiral Vernon', *Past and Present* 121 (1988), 74–109.

Woodfine, Philip, *Britannia's Glories: The Walpole Ministry and the 1739 War with Spain* (Woodbridge, 1998).

Woodfine, Philip, 'Ideas of Naval Power and the Conflict with Spain, 1737–1742', *The British Navy and the Use of Naval Power in the Eighteenth Century*, ed. Jeremy Black and Philip Woodfine (Leicester, 1988), pp. 71–90.

Zahedieh, Nuala, *The Capital and the Colonies: London and the Atlantic Economy, 1660–1700* (Cambridge, 2010).

Zahedieh, Nuala, 'The Merchants of Port Royal, Jamaica, and the Spanish Contraband Trade, 1655–1692', *WMQ*, 3rd ser, 43 (1986), 570–93.

Zahedieh, Nuala, 'Regulation, Rent-seeking, and the Glorious Revolution in the English Atlantic Economy', *EcHR* 63, no. 4 (2010), 877–86.

Unpublished Theses

Denman, Terence J., 'The Political Debate over War Strategy, 1689–1712' (unpublished Ph.D. thesis, Cambridge University, 1985).

Hanham, Andrew A., 'Whig Opposition to Sir Robert Walpole in the House of Commons, 1727–1734' (unpublished Ph.D. thesis, University of Leicester, 1992).

Johnston, J. A., 'Parliament and the Navy, 1688–1714' (unpublished Ph.D. thesis, University of Sheffield, 1968).

Mather, Ian R., 'The Role of the Royal Navy in the English Atlantic Empire, 1660–1720' (unpublished Ph.D. thesis, Oxford University, 1995).

McMains, Howard F., 'The Parliamentary Opposition to Sir Robert Walpole, 1727–1731' (unpublished Ph.D. thesis, Indiana University, 1970).

Sorsby, Victoria G., 'British Trade with Spanish America under the Asiento 1713–1740' (unpublished Ph.D. thesis, University of London, 1975).

INDEX

Printed and bound by CPI Group (UK) Ltd, Croydon, CR0 4YY

16/09/2026

14963172-0001